Correcting Fallacies About Educational and Psychological Testing

Correcting Fallacies About Educational and Psychological Testing

Edited by
Richard P. Phelps

American Psychological Association • Washington, DC

Published by
American Psychological Association
750 First Street, NE
Washington, DC 20002
www.apa.org

To order
APA Order Department
P.O. Box 92984
Washington, DC 20090-2984
Tel: (800) 374-2721; Direct: (202) 336-5510
Fax: (202) 336-5502; TDD/TTY: (202) 336-6123
Online: www.apa.org/books/
E-mail: order@apa.org

In the U.K., Europe, Africa, and the Middle East, copies may be ordered from
American Psychological Association
3 Henrietta Street
Covent Garden, London
WC2E 8LU England

Typeset in Goudy by Stephen McDougal, Mechanicsville, MD

Printer: Maple-Vail Book Manufacturing Group, York, PA
Cover Designer: Mercury Publishing Services, Rockville, MD
Technical/Production Editor: Harriet Kaplan

The opinions and statements published are the responsibility of the authors, and such opinions and statements do not necessarily represent the policies of the American Psychological Association.

Library of Congress Cataloging-in-Publication Data
Correcting fallacies about educational and psychological testing / edited by Richard P. Phelps.
   p. cm.
  Includes bibliographical references and index.
  ISBN-13: 978-1-4338-0392-5
  ISBN-10: 1-4338-0392-5
  1. Educational tests and measurements—Standards. 2. Psychological tests—Standards. 3. Employment tests—Standards. 4. Professional education—Standards. I. Phelps, Richard P.

  LB3051.C6386 2009
  371.26'2—dc22
                                                   2008026233

British Library Cataloguing-in-Publication Data
A CIP record is available from the British Library.

Printed in the United States of America
First Edition

CONTENTS

CONTRIBUTORS

Wayne J. Camara, College Board, New York, NY

Janet F. Carlson, University of Nebraska—Lincoln

Kurt F. Geisinger, University of Nebraska—Lincoln; Buros Center for Testing, Lincoln, NE

Linda S. Gottfredson, University of Delaware, Newark

Ronald K. Hambleton, University of Massachusetts at Amherst

Jacqueline P. Leighton, University of Alberta, Edmonton, Alberta, Canada

Michael A. McDaniel, Virginia Commonwealth University, Richmond

Thomas Oakland, University of Florida, Gainesville; International Foundation for Children's Education, Gainesville, FL

Ernest H. O'Boyle Jr., Virginia Commonwealth University, Richmond

Richard P. Phelps, ACT, Inc., Iowa City, IA

Stephen G. Sireci, University of Massachusetts at Amherst

FOREWORD

THOMAS OAKLAND

Test use is universal. In virtually every industrialized country, tests are used to measure innumerable aspects of one's physical, mental, emotional, and social development and health, from the Apgar test for newborn health to the broad array of tests for dementia and other conditions more common at older ages. Tests of intelligence, academic knowledge and skills, and occupational aptitudes are commonly used with students and job seekers.

Tests are used within the behavioral sciences to describe current behaviors and other qualities; estimate future behaviors; assist guidance and counseling services; evaluate progress; screen for special needs; diagnose disabling disorders; help prepare persons for jobs or programs; and assist in determining whether people should be credentialed, admitted or employed, retained, or promoted. Tests also are used widely in research and for various administrative and planning purposes.

The ever-increasing use of tests reflects their importance to decision making. This increase is seen in various ways, including the following examples. Within the past 15 years, every state has developed and now uses exit-level exams that help determine whether a student is eligible for a high school diploma. Teachers increasingly are using curriculum-based measures to help guide and evaluate instruction. Additionally, many psychologists in their 60s and older remember when they had three well-standardized tests of intelligence from which to choose: the Stanford–Binet, Wechsler Intelligence Scale for Children, and the Wechsler Adult Intelligence Scale. Psychologists now have a dozen or more from which to choose. Three psychologists formed the Psychological Corporation about 100 years ago because existing companies refused to publish tests. Now more than 2,400 tests are published and used in the United States (Maddox, 2003).

Tests provide an objective and generally reliable and valid assessment of important human qualities that help test takers and testing professionals to improve decision making. Unlike those who do informal evaluations, tests do not know one's age, gender, skin color, or social status; the part of town where one lives; one's religious affiliation; one's criminal record; or other qualities that tend to bias views and expectations.

Tests can reveal information that some may not want to believe. The assertion of Thomas Jefferson in 1776 as expressed in the Declaration of Independence, that all men are created equal, is not self-evident. For some individuals, signs of inequality appear early in life (e.g., autism, pervasive developmental disorders, reactive attachment, Rett's disorder). For others, the signs become apparent on entering school (e.g., learning disabilities, attention-deficit/hyperactivity disorder) or when attempting to obtain one's first important job (skill deficiencies, recreational drug residue in one's body fluids). Test data that reveal group differences on some important qualities (e.g., higher levels of intellectual giftedness among Asian students, lower levels of achievement among Black students) may seem socially insensitive. One may be tempted to question the accuracy of this information and instead believe that the messenger—the test—is at fault.

Tests are not always used well. As with other tools, when put in the hands of those who are not well trained, who take shortcuts when performing their work, and whose intentions are contrary to the personal and public good, tests are likely to miss their intended mark, which is to describe behavior accurately and to provide information that serves the individual and the public.

Test data can have consequences. Some test consequences are short term (e.g., failing a Friday afternoon third-grade spelling test) and thus have a low-stakes impact. Other tests' consequences are long term (e.g., not passing the exit test required for high school graduation or receiving a low score on the ACT or SAT and thus being denied admission to one's preferred university) and thus have a high-stakes impact. Higher stakes tests are more likely to be scrutinized in scientific laboratories, journalist newsrooms, and the courts and to be imbued with controversy.

You probably have heard or read one or more of the following arguments for not using tests:

- Test data do not improve decision making.
- Tests are so flawed that laws prohibit their use.
- People easily cheat on tests and fake their scores.
- Human behavior is too complex to assess accurately.
- Multiple-choice tests reduce creativity and deep thinking.
- Teachers' grades provide a more accurate evaluation of student performance.
- Achievement tests assess qualities unrelated to what children actually learn in school.
- Tests are developed by White middle-class men to help reinforce their control and power.

- Tests provide information that can be obtained from other, more reliable sources.
- Aptitude tests are biased against persons from lower class homes.
- Tests are unfair, culture bound, biased, and discriminatory.
- Complex decisions are made solely on the basis of test scores.
- Only institutions, not people, benefit from test use.
- We spend too much time and money on testing.
- Testing unnecessarily invades one's privacy.

The public and the professions that serve it want and need straight answers to these and other allegations. This requires the communication of viewpoints objectively formed following a review of a large body of reliable and valid evidence. Many who engage in test bashing display a disrespect for these qualities and instead often focus on isolated anecdotes and poorly conducted studies. Anecdotes and bad science do not provide sound evidence.

Some years ago, I began writing on issues pertaining to the assessment of minority children (e.g., Oakland, 1977), given my belief that a review of literature, including that from test critics, would reveal both strengths and flaws in our work. Criticism is good to the extent it is used constructively and leads to the development and refinement of technology and applications that better serve the public. I found that some criticisms offered constructive solutions, some were not founded on science or practice, and others seemed designed to disrupt the testing industry and professions that use tests.

I have taught graduate courses on testing throughout my career. I ask students whether they have heard of evidence that teachers become biased toward students after receiving test data about them. Many have heard this from other professors. Some recall the study by Rosenthal and Jacobson (1968), called by some the "late-blooming study," in which the authors provided fictitious test data to teachers at the beginning of the year and told them that some children were average and others were late bloomers and thus would achieve at higher levels by the end of the school year.

The authors later returned to see whether this occurred. Their results supported their beliefs. Students who were labeled average generally performed at this level, whereas those who were labeled late bloomers achieved at higher levels.

These results were featured immediately and prominently in newspapers and professional newsletters and spawned additional studies to examine further the belief that test data have a discernable impact on others' behaviors. Pundits asked, "If test results can promote high achievement, can they also promote low achievement?" Many principals began limiting teachers' access to test data out of a fear that teachers would form impressions that some students were incapable of learning after seeing their scores.

Reviews highly critical of this research (e.g., Elashoff & Snow, 1971) went largely unreported in newspapers and professional newsletters—sources that had highlighted the results of the original study. One reviewer suggested the credibility of this study was similar to a clock striking 13. None of the eight replication studies found comparable evidence. This information also went unreported. Reporters rarely pursue scientific evidence with the same fervor as do scientists. Thus, although I am not surprised when students mischaracterize this issue, I remain dismayed that even those who should be aware of the later findings are not. Myths associated with test development and use seem endemic to our society.

The professions associated with education and psychology also share some of the blame for not being more objective and forthright. For example, psychology's pervasive liberal zeitgeist has been described as decreasing the ecological validity of its work, thus adversely affecting contributions from its researchers, policy advocates, clinicians, and educators (Redding, 2001). The title of a recent book, *Destructive Trends in Mental Health: The Well-Intentioned Path to Harm*, written by two stalwarts in psychology, Rogers Wright and Nicholas Cummings (2005), underscores this zeitgeist. Political agendas within psychology and other behavioral sciences continue to color what is studied and reported, including views toward testing.

The American Psychological Association is to be commended for publishing *Correcting Fallacies About Educational and Psychological Testing*. Furthermore, editor Richard Phelps and contributors Wayne Camara, Janet Carlson, Kurt Geisinger, Linda Gottfredson, Ronald Hambleton, Jacqueline Leighton, Michael McDaniel, Ernest O'Boyle Jr., and Stephen Sireci are to be commended for summarizing evidence from scientific and other forms of scholarship that address many controversies associated with test development and use. The following chapters provide detailed evidence grounded in science that addresses many of the arguments listed earlier. I have been informed by their contents, and I believe other readers will be as well.

REFERENCES

Elashoff, J., & Snow, R. (1971). *Pygmalion reconsidered*. Worthington, OH: Charles A. Jones.

Maddox, T. (2003). *Tests: A comprehensive reference for assessment in psychology, education, and business* (5th ed.). Austin, TX: PRO-ED.

Oakland, T. (Ed.). (1977). *Psychological and educational assessment of minority children*. New York: Brunner/Mazel.

Redding, R. (2001). Sociopolitical diversity in psychology: The case for pluralism. *American Psychologist, 56*, 205–215.

Rosenthal, R., & Jacobson, L. (1968). *Pygmalion in the classroom*. New York: Holt, Rinehart & Winston.

Wright, R., & Cummings, N. (2005). *Destructive trends in mental health: The well-intentioned path to harm*. New York: Routledge.

Correcting Fallacies About Educational and Psychological Testing

INTRODUCTION

RICHARD P. PHELPS

Fallacies do not cease to be fallacies because they become fashions.
—G. K. Chesterton

Educators and psychologists are the most frequent developers and users of standardized tests. Educators measure academic achievement (i.e., mastery of knowledge or skills), diagnose learning problems or aptitudes, and select candidates for higher academic programs. Psychologists measure beliefs, attitudes, and preferences; diagnose psychological problems or strengths; and select candidates for employment (Phelps, 2007).

None of this measurement is, or can be, perfect, and no one claims that it is. Other measures in common use are imperfect as well, some of them notoriously so. These include some in medicine (e.g., certain tests for cancer), meteorology (e.g., tornado prediction), economics (e.g., service-sector productivity), and other fields in which hard evidence and measurement precision are highly valued but not always achievable.

The measures are used, despite their imperfections, because in most situations, in science as well as in life, some information for making decisions is better than none. Measurements can be useful when the benefits the information provides outweigh any cost and imprecision, and these positive net benefits exceed those of any practical alternative.

"Standardized tests have a bad reputation," wrote Stephen G. Sireci, "but it is an undeserved one" (Sireci, 2005, p. 113). He continued,

> People accuse standardized tests of being unfair, biased and discriminatory. Believe it or not, standardized tests are actually designed to promote test fairness. Standardized simply means that the test content is equivalent across administrations and that the conditions under which the test is administered are the same for all test takers. . . . I am not going to defend all standardized tests, for surely there are problems with some

of them . . . [but] just because a test is standardized does not mean that it is "bad," or "biased," or that it measures only "unimportant things." It merely means it is designed and administered using uniform procedures. Standardized tests are used to provide objective information. For example, employment tests are used to avoid unethical hiring practices (e.g., nepotism, ethnic discrimination, etc.). If an assessment system uses tests that are not standardized, the system is likely to be unfair to many candidates.

For understandable reasons, standardized tests tend to attract more scrutiny when they bear consequences, or *stakes*. Fail an occupational licensure examination, for example, and one may receive no license regardless of having completed a substantial amount of coursework. Fail a secondary school graduation test, and one may receive no diploma, despite having spent more than a decade in school. Exhibit 1 describes what standardized tests are.

The title of this volume incorporates the common, general meaning of the term *fallacy*, as in "a false idea or notion," as well as the more specific and technical definition of the term as it might be used by logicians. Indeed, David Hackett Fischer's (1970) excellent book *Historians' Fallacies: Toward a Logic of Historical Thought* might have served well as a model had the current volume been written by a single author. Throughout, Fischer organized *Historians' Fallacies* by fallacy rather than by historical topic. For better or worse, I chose to organize this volume by testing type and recruited some of North America's best-informed experts on those topics. I felt that expertise in the topic was more important for the purpose than expertise in the concepts and terms of logicians.

NORTH AMERICAN EXCEPTIONALISM

The authors of this volume write about standardized testing as we know it, and we know it primarily in its North American context. Although many aspects of testing are universal, some are not.

Standardized testing features that have been more common in North America than elsewhere include aptitude tests, machine scoring, multiple-choice formats, commercial test development firms operating in competitive markets, and standardized university admission tests. Typically, outside North America, consequential large-scale standardized educational achievement examinations have been developed essentially as extra-large versions of classroom tests, with open-ended questions written and scored by groups of classroom teachers; educational achievement tests have been developed, administered, and scored by governmental agencies; and universities have administered their own entrance examinations (Phelps, 2007, chap. 2).

Likewise, the politics of standardized testing differs between North America and the larger world. Much of North America's political rhetoric and media coverage remains existential: Are standardized tests good or bad?

EXHIBIT 1
What Are Standardized Tests?

A common misconception equates the term *standardized test* with multiple-choice test items and machine-readable (i.e., "bubble") answer sheets. On the contrary, if any aspect of a test—format, procedures, or administration—is standardized across test takers, it is a standardized test. Thus, tests with written, oral, or otherwise "constructed" instructions or responses can be standardized.

Physical tests, such as those conducted by engineers, can be standardized, of course, but in this volume, we focus on the measurement of latent (i.e., nonobservable) mental, and not physical, traits.

Both surveys and tests measure mental traits. However, surveys typically measure attitudes or opinions, whereas tests typically measure proficiencies or aptitudes. Like surveys, however, tests are composed of items (e.g., questions, prompts).

Well-constructed standardized tests are *reliable*—producing consistent results across time, conditions, and test takers—and *valid*—measuring those traits that they are intended to measure and not others (Sireci, 2005, pp. 116–118). When used for selection (e.g., university admission, employment hiring), an effective test has strong *predictive validity*—a high correlation between test scores and future performance (see chaps. 4 and 5, this volume).

Should we use standardized tests or not? For North American test developers weary of these old debating points, political discussions in other countries, where journalists and the general public alike accept tests as givens and discuss—often with considerable expertise—the quality or appropriateness of test content in some detail, might seem refreshing (Eckstein & Noah, 1993; Zeng, 1999).

WALKING THE TIGHTROPE

In any country, however, standardized testing bears the twin burdens of controversy and complexity and is difficult for many to understand either dispassionately or technically. Testing is both technical and political. In North America, where so much test development occurs outside direct governmental control, the response has been to regulate its use tightly.

In the United States, for example, state and federal judges have rendered many decisions affecting the content, administration, and use of standardized tests. These court decisions cover the full range of test types, with important cases concerning intelligence testing (e.g., *Larry P. v. Riles*), educational and psychological diagnosis (e.g., *Pennsylvania Assn. for Retarded Children v. Commonwealth of Pennsylvania*), educational achievement (e.g., *Debra P. v. Turlington*), university admissions (e.g., *Regents of the State of California v. Bakke*), employment (e.g., *Detroit Edison Co. v. National Labor Relations Board*), and occupational licensing (e.g., *Bartlett v. New York State Board of Law Examiners*).

Standardized tests are now developed through a demanding and time-consuming process according to detailed and rigorous technical standards that have, for many purposes, become legal requirements (see, e.g., Buckendahl & Hunt, 2005; chap. 5, this volume; Geisinger, 2005; Plake, 2005). Some critics of standardized testing seem unaware of both the extent of the technical safeguards related to test development and the imperative for test developers to follow them. Indeed, psychometricians long ago addressed many persistent criticisms, and their conclusions have been written into one or more sets of technical standards that test developers, in turn, have followed scrupulously for years. This is not to say that test developers do not sometimes make mistakes—we all do—or sometimes try to cut corners too sharply under budget pressure. However, as some of the accusations proffered by critics and accepted unreservedly by journalists become more outdated and farfetched, the potential demands on the test development process become more unreasonable.

Technical standards for test development and administration have been composed or endorsed by dozens of professional organizations (see Exhibit 2). The various standards documents continue to be revised and updated as needed. Putting all the standards documents together would produce a pile thousands of pages high. Exhibit 2 lists the citations for some of the documents produced by North American or international organizations. Governments and professional organizations outside North America have produced many more (see, e.g., Leach & Oakland, 2007).

ORGANIZATION AND OVERVIEW OF THIS BOOK

Correcting Fallacies About Educational and Psychological Testing is divided into chapters according to test type and use. The reader will find chapters on standardized testing used for diagnosis in education and in psychology; for selection by higher education institutions, professions, and employers; and to measure achievement (i.e., level of mastery) in education and for occupational credentialing.

The chapter order of this volume is roughly chronological, starting with the test types and uses that were developed earliest (in the late 19th century) and ending with those developed most recently. Certainly, one could argue with the validity of this order. For example, given that Chinese civil service examinations are often cited as the oldest known large-scale standardized tests, why have we chosen to place our credentialing chapter later in the book rather than opening with it? Any ordering would be imperfect. However, every chapter author of *Correcting Fallacies* is an accomplished scholar, steeped in the research literature of his or her topic. For us, the research literature—the scientific study of standardized testing—began in the 19th century, in the slipstream of advances in mathematics and statistics in the preceding centuries. The scientific standardized test was first developed at the fin de siècle through the experimentation with educational achievement

EXHIBIT 2
Professional Standards and Guidelines for Test Use: Selected Citations

American Counseling Association & Association for Assessment in Counseling. (2003). *Responsibilities of users of standardized tests* (3rd ed.). (RUST). Alexandria, VA: Authors.

American Educational Research Association, American Psychological Association, & National Council on Measurement in Education. (1999). *Standards for educational and psychological testing.* Washington, DC: Authors.

American Federation of Teachers, National Council on Measurement in Education, & National Education Association. (1990). *Standards for teacher competence in educational assessment of students.* Washington, DC: Authors.

American Psychological Association. (1992). *Ethical principles of psychologists and code of conduct.* Washington, DC: Author.

American Psychological Association, Practice and Science Directorates. (2000). *Report of the task force on test user qualifications.* Washington, DC: Author.

American Psychological Association. (2001, May). *Appropriate use of high-stakes testing in our nation's schools.* Washington, DC: Author.

Association for Assessment in Counseling and Education. (2002, November). *Standards for educational and psychological testing—What counselors need to know.* Alexandria, VA: Author.

Association for Assessment in Counseling. (2003). *Standards for multicultural assessment.* Alexandria, VA: Author.

Association of Test Publishers. (2002). *Guidelines for computer-based testing.* Washington, DC: Author.

International Personnel Management Association—Assessment Council. (2004, June). *Policies and procedures manual.* Alexandria, VA: Author.

International Test Commission. (2001). International guidelines for test use. *International Journal of Testing, 1,* 93–114.

International Test Commission. (2005). *International guidelines on computer-based and Internet-delivered testing.* Retrieved July 19, 2008, from http://www.intestcom.org/guidelins/index.html

Joint Advisory Committee. (1993). *Principles for fair assessment practices for education in Canada.* Edmonton, Alberta, Canada: Author.

Joint Committee on Standards for Educational Evaluation. (2007). *The personnel evaluation standards.* Thousand Oaks, CA: Sage.

Joint Committee on Standards for Educational Evaluation. (2007). *The program evaluation standards* (2nd ed.). Thousand Oaks, CA: Sage.

Joint Committee on Standards for Educational Evaluation. (2007). *The student evaluation standards.* Thousand Oaks, CA: Sage.

Joint Committee on Testing Practices. (2005). *Code of fair testing practices in education.* Washington, DC: Author.

National Association of College Admission Counselors. (1988). *Statement of principles of good practice.* Alexandria, VA: Author.

National Commission for Certifying Agencies. (2004). *Standards for the accreditation of certification programs.* Washington, DC: National Organization for Competency Assurance.

National Council on Measurement in Education Ad Hoc Committee on the Development of a Code of Ethics. (1995). *Code of professional responsibilities in educational measurement.* Washington, DC: Author.

Nester, M. A., Bruyere, S., & Wall, J. (2003). *Pre-employment testing and the ADA.* Alexandria, VA: Association for Assessment in Counseling and Education; Cornell, NY: American Rehabilitation Counseling Association.

Test Taker Rights and Responsibilities Working Group of the Joint Committee on Testing Practices. (1998, August). *Rights and responsibilities of test takers: Guidelines and expectations.* Rockville, MD: American Speech–Language–Hearing Association. Retrieved July 19, 2008, from http://www.asha.org/docs/html/RP2002-00198.html

Society of Industrial and Organizational Psychology. (2003). *Principles for the validation and use of personnel selection procedures* (4th ed.). Bowling Green, OH: Author.

U.S. Department of Labor & U.S. Department of Justice, Civil Service Commission, Equal Employment Opportunity Commission. (1978). Uniform guidelines on employee selection procedures. *Federal Register, 43*(166), 38290–39315.

testing by such pioneers as the (German-influenced) Americans Joseph Mayer Rice and E. L. Thorndike and the intelligence and aptitude tests of the French physiologists Alfred Binet and Théophile Simon (Phelps, 2007, chap. 2).

Chapter 1 thus begins this volume with the topic of intelligence and aptitude testing. Linda S. Gottfredson classifies the fallacies used to discredit them into three groups related to measurement (design, scoring, and validation) and two others related to cause and effect and test utility. For example, test scoring fallacies include arguments that intelligence is malleable, inseparable from environmental context, or of negligible variation because genetic variation among humans is slight. Causal network fallacies include phenotype equals genotype, biology equals genetics, social effect proves social cause, and environment is nongenetic.

Some of the early intelligence tests were used, appropriately or not, for individual psychological and educational diagnosis. However, psychologists in the early half of the 20th century began to develop a variety of other, targeted diagnostic tests for a variety of practical needs. In chapter 2 of this volume, Janet F. Carlson and Kurt F. Geisinger provide an overview of the current generation of diagnostic tests and the fallacious criticisms they attract.

Another evolutionary branch sprouted from early intelligence tests is educational aptitude testing, which in turn gave rise to norm-referenced educational achievement tests. Standards-based educational achievement testing, however, might more properly be traced to different origins in 19th-century quality control and education system monitoring programs (see Phelps, 2007). The distinction is lost on some when they criticize a test essentially for not being a type it was never intended to be. However, as I describe in chapter 3, most critics of educational achievement testing work inside education and understand these subtleties but oppose "external" evaluation of their productivity, which typically includes its measurement, in part, through standardized testing.

North American universities were responsible for the most prominent use of aptitude testing—standardized admission testing. In recent decades, however, the SAT (formerly the Scholastic Aptitude Test) has eschewed most of its aptitude features in favor of more achievement characteristics, even dropping the term *aptitude* from its name. Its rival, the ACT (formerly the American College Test) was from its origin more curriculum based. As Wayne J. Camara explains in chapter 4, however, this and other changes in focus do not seem to have satisfied critics of standardized admission tests, even when the change embodies an earlier recommendation made by the critics themselves.

In chapter 5, Ernest H. O'Boyle Jr. and Michael A. McDaniel survey the criticisms of employment testing, especially that used in employee selection. Arguably, in no other practical use of standardized tests have fallacious beliefs had more impact—through regulatory requirements that reduce the effectiveness of testing. Improvements to those regulations could bring them into closer alignment with professional psychometric standards and closer to agreement with scientific research findings.

In chapter 6, Stephen G. Sireci and Ronald K. Hambleton bring us up to date on the controversy affecting the field of occupational testing for licensure and certification. Much certification testing occurs away from the public eye; tests exist for hundreds of highly specialized occupational fields with content and standards that may be comprehensible to few outsiders. Nonetheless, certification testing is highly regulated and often the subject of lively legal discussions.

In chapter 7, a fitting capstone to this volume, Jacqueline P. Leighton reminds us that *psychometrics*—the scientific study of testing—remains a dynamic field of active study in persistent search of improved methods of mental measurement. In explaining the fallacious beliefs about large-scale cognitive diagnostic testing (LS–CDT), she introduces a practical use of testing that may be new and unfamiliar to many of us. Her introduction is worth studying well because the advantages of LS–CDT suggest a much greater popularity in its future.

In chapter 8, Linda S. Gottfredson and I integrate the themes of all the chapters by describing some of the common sources of opposition to most standardized testing.

The Glossary defines technical terms related to testing and psychometrics. Four appendixes can be found on the Web (see http://www.apa.org/books/resources/Phelps/). Appendix A contains extended examples of logical arguments against intelligence testing found in scientific and popular literature. Appendix B is a brief article that outlines conclusions regarded as mainstream among researchers of intelligence on the nature, origins, and practical considerations of individual and group differences in intelligence. Appendix C is an extended example of flaws in research that purported to expose high-stakes educational achievement testing as the main source of artificial score inflation. Appendix D is a case study that deconstructs a National Research Council Report that critiqued the use of the General Aptitude Test Battery for employee hiring decisions.

REFERENCES

Bartlett v. New York State Board of Law Examiners, 226 F.3d 69, 75 (2d Cir. 2000).

Buckendahl, C. W., & Hunt, R. (2005). Whose rules? The relation between the "rules" and "law" of testing. In R. P. Phelps (Ed.), *Defending standardized testing* (pp. 147–158). Mahwah, NJ: Erlbaum.

Debra P. v. Turlington, 644 F.2d 397, 6775 (5th Cir. 1981).

Detroit Edison Co. v. National Labor Relations Board, 440 U.S. 301 (1979).

Eckstein, M. A., & Noah, H. J. (1993). *Secondary school examinations: International perspectives on policies and practice.* New Haven, CT: Yale University Press.

Fischer, D. H. (1970). *Historians' fallacies: Toward a logic of historical thought*. New York: Harper & Row.

Geisinger, K. F. (2005). The testing industry, ethnic minorities, and individuals with disabilities. In R. P. Phelps (Ed.), *Defending standardized testing* (pp. 187–204). Mahwah, NJ: Erlbaum.

Larry P. v. Riles, 793 F.2d 969 (9th Cir. 1984).

Leach, M. M., & Oakland, T. (2007). Ethics standards impacting test development and use: A review of 31 ethics codes impacting practices in 35 countries. *International Journal of Testing, 7,* 71–88.

Pennsylvania Assn. for Retarded Children v. Commonwealth of Pennsylvania, 334 F. Supp. 1257 (E.D. PA 1972).

Phelps, R. P. (2007). *Standardized testing primer*. New York: Peter Lang.

Plake, B. S. (2005). Doesn't everybody know that 70% is passing? In R. P. Phelps (Ed.), *Defending standardized testing* (pp. 175–186). Mahwah, NJ: Erlbaum.

Regents of the State of California v. Bakke, 438 U.S. 265 (1978).

Sireci, S. G. (2005). The most frequently *unasked* questions about testing. In R. P. Phelps (Ed.), *Defending standardized testing* (pp. 111–122). Mahwah, NJ: Erlbaum.

Zeng, K. (1999). *Dragon gate: Competitive examinations and their consequences*. London: Cassell.

1

LOGICAL FALLACIES USED TO DISMISS THE EVIDENCE ON INTELLIGENCE TESTING

LINDA S. GOTTFREDSON

Human intelligence is one of the most important yet controversial topics in the whole field of the human sciences. It is not even agreed whether it can be measured or, if it can, whether it should be measured. The literature is enormous and much of it is highly partisan and, often, far from accurate. (Bartholomew, 2004, p. xi)

Intelligence testing may be psychology's greatest single achievement, but it is also among its most publicly reviled activities. Measurement technology is far more sophisticated than in decades past, but antitesting sentiment has not waned. The ever denser, proliferating network of interlocking evidence concerning intelligence is paralleled by ever thicker knots of confusion in public debate over it. Why these seeming contradictions?

Mental measurement, or *psychometrics*, is a highly technical mathematical field, but so are many others. Its instruments have severe limitations, but so do the tools of all scientific trades. Some of its practitioners have been wrongheaded and some of its products misused, but this does not distinguish mental measurement from any other expert endeavor. The problem with intelligence testing, one suspects, is that it succeeds too well at its intended job.

HUMAN VARIATION AND THE DEMOCRATIC DILEMMA

IQ tests, like all standardized tests, are structured, objective tools for doing what individuals and organizations otherwise tend to do haphazardly, informally, and less effectively: assess human variation in an important psychological trait—in this case, general proficiency at learning, reasoning, and abstract thinking. The intended aims of testing are both theoretical and practical, as is the case for most measurement technologies in the sciences. The first intelligence test was designed for practical ends—specifically, to identify children unlikely to prosper in a standard school curriculum, and indeed, school psychologists remain the major users of individually administered IQ test batteries today. Vocational counselors, neuropsychologists, and other service providers also use individually administered mental tests, including IQ tests, for diagnostic purposes.

Group-administered aptitude batteries (e.g., Armed Services Vocational Aptitude Battery [ASVAB], General Aptitude Test Battery [GATB], SAT) have long been used in applied research and practice by employers; the military; universities; and other mass institutions seeking more effective, efficient, and fair ways to screen, select, and place large numbers of individuals. Although not designed or labeled as "intelligence tests," these batteries often function as good surrogates for them. In fact, all widely used cognitive ability tests measure general intelligence (the general mental ability factor, g) to an important degree (Carroll, 1993; Jensen, 1998; Sattler, 2001).

Psychological testing is governed by detailed professional codes (e.g., American Educational Research Association, American Psychological Association, & National Council on Measurement in Education, 1999; Society of Industrial and Organizational Psychology, 2003). Developers and users of intelligence tests also have special legal incentives to adhere to published test standards because among mental tests, those that measure intelligence best (are most g loaded) generally have the greatest disparate impact on Blacks and Hispanics (Schmitt, Rogers, Chan, Sheppard, & Jennings, 1997). That is, such tests yield lower average scores for these populations than for Asians and Whites. In employment settings, differing average results by race or ethnicity constitute prima facie evidence of illegal discrimination against the lower scoring groups, a charge that the accused party must then disprove, partly by showing adherence to professional standards (see chap. 5, this volume).

Tests of intelligence are also widely used in basic research in diverse fields, from genetics to sociology. They are useful, in particular, for studying human variation in cognitive ability and the ramifying implications of that variation for societies and their individual members. Current intelligence tests gauge relative, not absolute, levels of mental ability (their severest limitation, as described later). Other socially important sociopsychological measures are likewise *norm-referenced indicators*, not *criterion-referenced indicators*. Oft-used examples include neuroticism, grade point average, and occupational prestige.

Many of the pressing questions in the social sciences and public policy are likewise norm referenced, that is, they concern how far the various members of a group fall above or below the group's average on some social indicator (e.g., academic achievement, health) or hierarchy (e.g., occupation, income), regardless of what the group average may be: Which person in the applicant pool is most qualified for the job to be filled? Which sorts of workers are likely to climb highest on the corporate ladder or earn the most and why? Which elementary school students will likely perform below grade level (a group average) in reading achievement, or which college applicants will fail to maintain a grade point average of at least C, if admitted?

Such questions about the relative competence and well-being of a society's members engage the core concern of democratic societies—social equality. Democratic nations insist that individuals should get ahead on their own merits, not through their social connections. Democracies also object to some individuals or groups getting too far ahead of or behind the pack. They favor not only equal opportunities for individuals to deploy their talents but also reasonably equal outcomes. Yet when individuals differ substantially in merit, however it is defined, societies cannot simultaneously and fully satisfy both of these goals. Mandating strictly meritocratic advancement will guarantee much inequality of outcomes, and, conversely, mandating equal outcomes will require that talent be restrained or its fruits redistributed (J. W. Gardner, 1984). This is the democratic dilemma, which is created by differences in human talent. In many applications, the chief source today of the democratic dilemma is the wide dispersion in human intelligence because higher intelligence has been well documented as providing individuals with more practical advantages in modern life than any other single attribute, including social class background (Ceci, 1996a; Herrnstein & Murray, 1994).

Democratic societies are reluctant, by their egalitarian nature, to acknowledge either the wide dispersion in intelligence or the conflicts among core values that this creates for them. Human societies have always had to negotiate such trade-offs, often institutionalizing their choices through legal, religious, and social norms (e.g., meat-sharing norms in hunter-gatherer societies).

One effect of research on intelligence tests has been to make such choices and their societal consequences clearer and more public. A sizeable literature now exists in personnel selection psychology, for example, that estimates the costs and benefits of sacrificing various levels of test validity to improve racial balance by varying degrees when selecting workers for different kinds of jobs (e.g., Schmitt et al., 1997). This literature also shows that the more accurately a test identifies who is most and least intellectually apt within a population, the more accurately it predicts which segments of society will gain or lose from social policies that attempt to capitalize on ability differences, to ignore them, or to compensate for them.

Such scientific knowledge about the distribution and functional importance of general mental ability can influence prevailing notions of what constitutes a just social order. Its potential influence on public policy and practice (e.g., require racial preferences? ban them?) is just what some applaud and others fear. It is no wonder that different stakeholders often disagree vehemently about whether test use is fair. Test use, misuse, and nonuse all provide decision makers tools for tilting trade-offs among conflicting goals in their preferred direction.

In short, the enduring, emotionally charged, public controversy over intelligence tests reflects mostly the enduring, politically charged, implicit struggle over how a society should accommodate its members' differences in intelligence. Continuing to dispute the scientific merits of well-validated tests and the integrity of persons who develop or use them is a substitute for, or a way to forestall, confronting the vexing realities that the tests expose.

That the testing controversy is today mostly a proxy battle over fundamental political goals explains why no amount of scientific evidence for the validity of intelligence tests will ever satisfy the tests' critics. Criticizing the yardstick rather than confronting the real differences it measures has sometimes led even testing experts to promulgate supposed technical improvements that actually reduce a test's validity but provide a seemingly scientific pretext for implementing a purely political preference, such as racial quotas (Blits & Gottfredson, 1990a, 1990b; Gottfredson, 1994, 1996). Tests may be legitimately criticized, but they deserve criticism for their defects, not for doing their job.

GULF BETWEEN SCIENTIFIC DEBATE AND PUBLIC PERCEPTIONS

Many test critics would reject the foregoing analysis and argue that evidence for the validity of the tests and their results is ambiguous, unsettled, shoddy, or dishonest. Although mistaken, this view may be the reigning public perception. Testing experts do not deny that tests have limits or can be misused. Nor do they claim, as critics sometimes assert (Fischer et al., 1996; Gould, 1996), that IQ is fixed, all important, the sum total of mental abilities, or a measure of human worth. Even the most cursory look at the professional literature shows how false such caricatures are.

In "Mainstream Science on Intelligence" (1994; Gottfredson, 1997), 52 experts summarized 25 of the most elementary and firmly established conclusions about intelligence and intelligence testing. In brief, professionally developed IQ tests are reliable, valid, unbiased measures of a general proficiency in learning, reasoning, and abstract thinking (the exception being verbal tests given to nonnative speakers). IQ differences among individuals are stable and highly heritable by adolescence, and they correlate genetically with many brain structures and processes. IQ level is the best single predictor of many important life outcomes, but its predictive validity varies from low to high depending on kind of outcome (e.g., .2 for law abidingness; .6 for years of education; and .2–.8 for job performance, the correlations rising with job complexity). Average racial–ethnic differences in IQ are the rule world-wide, typically reflect average differences in phenotypic intelligence, predict average differences in life outcomes, and are perhaps both genetic and nongenetic in origin. Received wisdom outside the field is often quite the opposite (Snyderman & Rothman, 1987, 1988), in large part because of the fallacies I describe here.

Table 1.1 illustrates how the scientific debates involving intelligence testing have advanced during the past half century. The list is hardly exhaustive and no doubt reflects the particular issues I have followed in my career, but it makes the point that public controversies over testing bear little relation to what experts in the field actually debate today. For example, researchers directly involved in intelligence-related research no longer debate whether IQ tests measure a "general intelligence," are biased against American Blacks, or predict anything more than academic performance.

Those questions were answered several decades ago (answers: yes, no, and yes; e.g., see Bartholomew, 2004; Brody, 1992; Carroll, 1993; Deary, 2000; Deary et al., 2004; Gottfredson, 1997b, 2004; Hartigan & Wigdor, 1989; Hunt, 1996; Jensen, 1980, 1998; "Mainstream Science on Intelligence," 1994; Murphy & Davidshofer, 2005; Neisser et al., 1996; Plomin, DeFries, McClearn, & McGuffin, 2001; Sackett, Schmitt, Ellingson, & Kabin, 2001; Schmidt & Hunter, 1998; Wigdor & Garner, 1982).

The new debates can be observed in special journal issues (e.g., Ceci, 1996b; Frisby, 1999; Gottfredson, 1986, 1997a; Lubinski, 2004; Williams, 2000), handbooks (e.g., Colangelo & Davis, 2003; Frisby & Reynolds, 2005), edited volumes (e.g., Detterman, 1994; Flanagan, Genshaft, & Harrison, 1997; Jencks & Phillips, 1998; Neisser, 1998; Plomin & McClearn, 1993; Sternberg & Grigorenko, 2001, 2002; Vernon, 1993), reports from the National Academy of Sciences (e.g., Hartigan & Wigdor, 1989; Wigdor & Garner, 1982; Wigdor & Green, 1991; see also Yerkes, 1921), and the pages of professional journals such as *American Psychologist*; *Exceptional Children*; *Intelligence*; *Journal of Applied Psychology*; *Journal of Psychoeducational Assessment*; *Journal of School Psychology*; *Personnel Psychology*; and *Psychology, Public Policy, and Law*.

Scientific inquiry on intelligence and its measurement has therefore moved to new questions. To take an example, yes, all IQ tests measure a highly general intelligence, albeit imperfectly (more specifically, they all measure a general intelligence factor, g), but do all yield exactly the same g continuum? Technically speaking, do they converge on the same g when factor analyzed? This illustrates how the questions debated today are more tightly focused, more technically demanding, and more theoretical than those of decades past.

In contrast, public controversy seems stuck in the scientific controversies of the 1960s and 1970s, as if those basic questions remained open or had not been answered to the critics' liking. The clearest recent example is the

TABLE 1.1
Examples Illustrating How Scientific Debate on Intelligence and IQ Tests Has Advanced Over the Past Half Century

Early debates	More recent debates
What fundamental distinctions (constructs) do intelligence tests measure, and how well?	
Do IQ tests measure a general intelligence or just a narrow academic ability?	Do different IQ test batteries yield the same general intelligence factor (converge on the same true g) when factor analyzed?
Which specific mental abilities add up to create overall intelligence?	To what extent does g constitute the common core of different specific mental abilities?
Do IQ tests yield statistically reliable (consistent) results?	Do different methods of factor analysis yield the same g factor?
Do test items and formats that more closely resemble the criterion (i.e., have higher face validity, or fidelity) have higher predictive validity? If so, do they simultaneously reduce disparate impact against Blacks and Hispanics?	Raw scores on IQ tests have risen over time (the *Flynn Effect*), so do IQ tests measure different things in different epochs, or has general intelligence (g) increased over time, or both?
Are people's IQ levels stable over the life course?	To what extent is stability (and change) in IQ/g relative to agemates traceable to genetic influences? To nongenetic ones?
Can early interventions raise low IQs?	Can the fade-out of IQ gains be prevented if early interventions are continued into adolescence?
Is IQ level heritable (do differences in IQ phenotype partly reflect differences in genotype)?	How does the heritability of IQ/g differ by chronological age, epoch, and social circumstance?
Can broad abilities (verbal, spatial ability, etc.) be measured independently of IQ?	What is the joint heritability (and environmentality) of g with the group factors measured by IQ tests (verbal ability, memory, etc.) and with outcomes such as academic achievement and occupational status?
Are IQ tests biased against (systematically mismeasuring) members of minority groups (i.e., is there measurement bias)?	Does a given IQ test battery measure exactly the same construct(s) in different races, sexes, and age groups?
Do IQ tests predict important life outcomes, and how well (including relative to other predictors)?	
Do IQ levels above some low threshold (e.g., not mentally retarded) predict differences in job or school performance?	Do IQ levels above some high threshold (e.g., giftedness) predict differences in job or school performance?
Does a whole battery of different ability tests (verbal, spatial, etc.) predict outcomes (e.g., educational or occupational) substantially better than just an overall IQ score?	Which classes of cognitive and noncognitive tests provide incremental validity, when used with g, in predicting performance on different classes of tasks (instrumental, socioemotional)?

Do IQ tests predict performance of nonacademic tasks in everyday life?	Why does IQ predict performance to some extent in most domains of daily life, but better in some than others?
Do IQ tests predict job performance equally well for all races (i.e., is there prediction bias)?	Do IQ scores predict adult outcomes (e.g., job level, health, law abidingness) better than does socioeconomic background?

Proper test use and test utility

Should schools stop using IQ scores for placing students into special education, gifted education, or ability groups?	Should schools stop using IQ tests (i.e., IQ-achievement gaps) to help diagnose learning disabilities?
How can clinicians make best use of subtest profiles?	When evaluating individual students, should school psychologists stop analyzing a child's profile of subtest scores (factor discrepancies) and focus just on the (more reliable) overall IQ and composite scores?
Should IQ tests be used to identify students who are intellectually gifted?	Should *giftedness* include noncognitive talents, and should selection into gifted programs rely on teacher, parent, and self ratings?
Should employers give less weight to technical expertise and more to organizational citizenship when hiring employees in order to improve racial balance?	Should colleges give less weight to cognitive abilities and more to noncognitive strengths when admitting students in order to improve racial balance?
Should the federal government race-norm its employment tests in order to equalize, by race, the scores it reports to potential employers?	Should courts allow colleges to use different SAT and ACT requirements for different races?
Which noncognitive tests should employers use instead of cognitive tests when selecting employees?	Which noncognitive tests should employers use in addition to cognitive tests when selecting employees?
Should IQ testing be banned in deciding whether an underperforming Black student is eligible for special education?	Should IQ testing be required in deciding whether a convicted killer is ineligible for the death penalty?

cacophony of public denunciation that greeted publication of *The Bell Curve* in 1994 (Herrnstein & Murray, 1994). Many journalists, social scientists, and public intellectuals derided the book's six foundational premises about intelligence as long-discredited pseudoscience when, in fact, they represent some of the most elemental scientific conclusions about intelligence and tests. Briefly, Herrnstein and Murray (1994) stated that six conclusions are "by now beyond serious technical dispute": individuals differ in general intelligence level (i.e., intelligence exists), IQ tests measure those differences well, IQ level matches what people generally mean when they refer to some individuals as being more intelligent or smarter than others, individuals' IQ scores (i.e., rank within age group) are relatively stable throughout their lives, properly administered IQ tests are not demonstrably culturally biased, and individual differences in intelligence are substantially heritable. The cautious John B. Carroll (1997) detailed how all these conclusions are "reasonably well supported" (p. 25).

Statements by the American Psychological Association (Neisser et al., 1996) and the previously mentioned group of experts (see Gottfredson, 1997a; "Mainstream Science on Intelligence," 1994), both of whom were attempting to set the scientific record straight in both public and scientific venues, did little if anything to stem the tide of misrepresentation. Reactions to *The Bell Curve*'s analyses illustrate not just that today's received wisdom seems impervious to scientific evidence but also that the guardians of this wisdom may only be inflamed further by additional evidence contradicting it.

Mere ignorance of the facts cannot explain why accepted opinion tends to be opposite the experts' judgments (Snyderman & Rothman, 1987, 1988). Such opinion reflects systematic misinformation, not lack of information. The puzzle, then, is to understand how the empirical truths about testing are made to seem false, and false criticisms made to seem true. In the millennia-old field of *rhetoric* (verbal persuasion), this question falls under the broad rubric of *sophistry*.

SOPHISTRIES ABOUT THE NATURE AND MEASUREMENT OF INTELLIGENCE

In this chapter, I describe major logical confusions and fallacies that in popular discourse seem to discredit intelligence testing on scientific grounds but actually do not. My aim here is not to review the evidence on intelligence testing or the many misstatements about it but to focus on particularly seductive forms of illogic. As noted earlier, many aptitude and achievement tests are de facto measures of *g* and reveal the same democratic dilemma as do IQ tests, so they are beset by the same fallacies. I am therefore referring to all highly *g*-loaded tests when I speak here of intelligence testing.

Public opinion is always riddled with error, of course, no matter what the issue. However, fallacies are not simply mistaken claims or intentional lies, which could be answered effectively with facts contradicting them. Instead, fallacies tend to corrupt public understanding systematically. They not only present falsehoods as truths but also reason falsely about the facts, thus making those persons they persuade largely insensible to correction. Effectively rebutting a fallacy's false conclusion therefore requires exposing how its reasoning turns the truth on its head. For example, a fallacy might start with an obviously true premise about Topic A (within-individual growth in mental ability), then switch attention to Topic B (between-individuals differences in mental ability) but obscure the switch by using the same words to describe both ("change in"), and then use the uncontested fact about A (change) to seem to disprove well-established but unwelcome facts about B (lack of change). Contesting the fallacy's conclusion by simply reasserting the proper conclusion leaves untouched the false reasoning's power to persuade—in this case, its surreptitious substitution of the phenomenon being explained.

The individual antitesting fallacies that I describe in this chapter rest on diverse sorts of illogic and misleading argument, including non sequiturs, false premises, conflation of unlikes, and appeals to emotion. Collectively they provide a grab bag of complaints for critics to throw at intelligence testing and allied research. The broader the barrage, the more it appears to discredit anything and everyone associated with intelligence testing.

The targets of fallacious reasoning are likewise diverse. Figure 1.1 helps to distinguish the usual targets by grouping them into three arenas of research and debate: Can intelligence be measured, and if so, how? What are the causes and consequences of human variation in intelligence? Finally, what are the social aims and effects of using intelligence tests—or not using them—as tools in making decisions about individuals and organizations? These are labeled in Figure 1.1, respectively, as the measurement model, the causal network, and the politics of test use. Key phenomena (actually, fields of inquiry) within each arena are distinguished by numbered entries to illustrate more easily which fact or field each fallacy works to discredit. The arrows ($\rightarrow$) represent the relations among the phenomena at issue, such as the causal impact of genetic differences on brain structure (Entry 1 $\rightarrow$ Entry 4 in Figure 1.1), or the temporal ordering of advances in mental measurement (Entries 8 $\rightarrow$ 9 $\rightarrow$ 10 $\rightarrow$ 11 in Figure 1.1). As we shall see, some fallacies work by conflating different phenomena (e.g., Entry 1 with 4, 2 with 3, 8 with 11 in Figure 1.1), others by confusing a causal relation between two phenomena (e.g., 1 $\rightarrow$ 5) with individual differences in one of them (5), yet others by confusing the social criteria (6 and 7) for evaluating test *utility* (the costs and benefits of using a valid test) with the scientific criteria for evaluating its validity for measuring what is claimed (11), and so on.

MEASUREMENT MODEL

Psychological tests and inventories aim to measure enduring, underlying personal traits, such as extraversion, conscientiousness, or intelligence. The term *trait* refers to notable and relatively stable differences among individuals in how they tend to respond to the same circumstances and opportunities: For example, Jane is sociable, and Janet is shy among strangers. A psychological trait cannot be seen directly, as can height or hair color, but is inferred from striking regularities in behavior across a wide variety of situations—as if different individuals follow different internal compasses as they engage the world around them. Because they are inferred, traits are called *theoretical constructs*. They therefore represent causal hypotheses about why

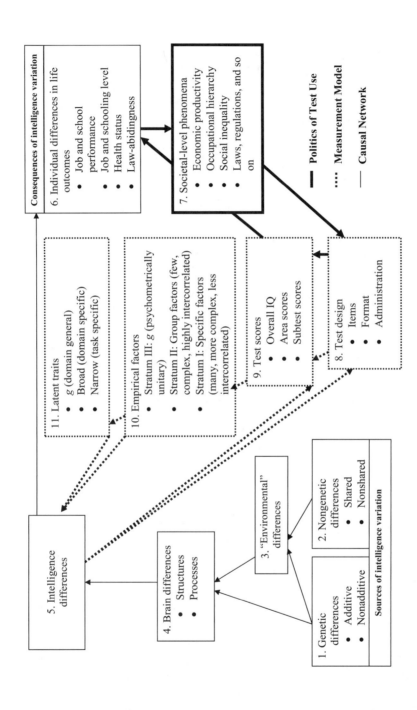

Figure 1.1. Three foci of fallacious reasoning: Measurement of intelligence, causes and consequences of intelligence differences, and the politics of test use.

individuals differ in patterned ways. Many other disciplines also posit influences that are not visible to the naked eye (e.g., gravity, electrons, black holes, genes, natural selection, self-esteem) and that must be detected through their effects on something that is observable. Intelligence tests consist of a set of tasks that reliably instigates performances requiring mental aptness and of procedures to record quality of task performance.

The measurement process thus begins with a hypothesized causal force and ideas about how it manifests itself in observable behavior. This nascent theory provides clues to what sort of task might activate it. Designing those stimuli and ways to collect responses to them in a consistent manner is the first step in creating a test. It is but the first step, however, in a long forensic process in which many parties collect evidence to determine whether the test does indeed measure the intended construct and whether initial hypotheses about the construct might have been mistaken. Conceptions of the phenomenon in question and how best to capture it in action evolve during this collective, iterative process of evaluating and revising tests. General intelligence is by far the most studied psychological trait, so its measurement technology is the most developed and thoroughly scrutinized of all psychological assessments.

As techniques in the measurement of intelligence have advanced, so, too, have the fallacies about it multiplied and mutated. Figure 1.1 delineates the broad stages (Entries 8 through 11 in Figure 1.1) in this coevolution of intelligence measurement and the fallacies related to it. In this section, I describe the basic logic guiding the design, the scoring, and the validation of intelligence tests and then, for each in turn, several fallacies associated with them. Later sections describe fallacies associated with the causal network for intelligence and with the politics of test use. Table 1.2 lists several examples of each fallacy. The examples illustrate that many important opinion makers use these fallacies, some use them frequently, and even rigorous scholars (Examples xx, xxi, and xxix) may inadvertently promulgate them. Each example is quoted at length and dissected more fully in Appendix A (see http://www.apa.org/books/resources/Phelps/).

Test-Design Fallacies

There were no intelligence tests in 1900 but only the perception that individuals consistently differ in mental prowess and that such differences have practical importance. Binet and Simon (1916), who produced the progenitor of today's IQ tests, hypothesized that such differences might forecast which students have extreme difficulty with schoolwork. So they set out to invent a measuring device (Entry 8 in Figure 1.1) to reveal and quantify differences among schoolchildren in that hypothetical trait (Entry 5 in Figure 1.1), as Binet's observations had led him to conceive it. The French Ministry of Education had asked Binet to develop an objective way to identify

TABLE 1.2
Thirteen Especially Influential Logical Fallacies About Intelligence Testing and Where to Find Examples of Each

Example no.	Reference	Context
	Test-design fallacy 1. Yardstick mirrors construct: Portrays the superficial appearance of a test as if it mimicked the inner essence of the phenomenon it measures.	
i	Fischer et al. (1996, pp. 42–43, 56–59)	The authors argued that the Armed Forces Qualification Test (AFQT) does not measure IQ or "intelligence broadly understood" but only learning in school.
ii	Flynn (2007, p. 55)	The author proposed a skills-based definition of intelligence that is "narrow enough to offer good advice to those who want to make intelligence measurable and specific."
iii	Sternberg, Wagner, Williams, and Horvath (1995, p. 913)	The authors argued that different item formats ("academic" vs. "practical") necessarily call forth different intelligences. They claimed that IQ tests use only the former and thus can measure only an "academic intelligence" (g).
	Test-design fallacy 2. Intelligence is marble collection: Portrays general intelligence (g) as if it were just an aggregation of many separate specific abilities or skills, not a singular phenomenon in itself, because IQ batteries calculate IQs by adding up scores on different subtests.	
iv	Flynn (2007, p. 55), from example ii above	The author proposed a skills-based definition of intelligence that is "narrow enough to offer good advice to those who want to make intelligence measurable and specific."
v	Flynn (2007, pp. 4, 9–10, 18)	The author explained how secular increases in IQ test scores might represent a rise in overall intelligence but not in g, the issue at hand being that scores on some highly g-loaded IQ subtests (e.g., Similarities) have risen a lot but others (e.g., Vocabulary) hardly all—"or, how can IQ gains be so contemptuous of g loadings?"
vi	Howe (1997, pp. 161–162)	The author listed what he viewed as "Twelve Well-Known 'Facts' about Intelligence Which Are Not True."

Test-score-differences fallacy 1. Nonfixedness proves malleability: Uses evidence of any fluctuation or growth in the mental functioning of individuals as if it were proof that their rates of growth can be changed intentionally.

vii	Blakemore (1994)	This ABC newscast contested *The Bell Curve's* claim that intelligence is a stable, measurable trait.
viii	Howe (1997, p. 138)	The author discussed what he considered better alternatives to "traditional intelligence theory."

Test-score-differences fallacy 2. Improvability proves equalizability: Uses evidence that intellectual skills and achievements can be improved within a population as if it were proof that they can be equalized in that population.

ix	Howe (1997, pp. 62–63)	The author argued for interventions to raise the IQs of individuals in disadvantaged groups.
x	The White House (2001)	The Executive Summary of the No Child Left Behind Act of 2001, which appeared on the White House Web site, highlighted the Act's intent to close achievement gaps by bringing all students up to the same high level of achievement.
xi	Dionne (1994, p. A17)	This *Washington Post* columnist argued that *The Bell Curve* "is not a 'scientific' book at all but a political argument offered by skilled polemicists aimed at defeating egalitarians."

Test-score-differences fallacy 3. Interactionism (gene–environment codependence) nullifies heritability: Portrays the gene–environment partnership in creating a phenotype as if conjoint action within the individual precluded teasing apart the roots of phenotypic differences among individuals.

xii	Sternberg (1997, p. 48)	The author distinguished what he described as the "conventional IQ-based view" of intelligence from his proposed notion of "successful intelligence."
xiii	Andrews and Nelkin (1996, p. 13)	This letter to *Science* disputed key conclusions in *The Bell Curve.*

continues

TABLE 1.2
Continued

Example no.	Reference	Context
	Test-score-differences fallacy 4.	99.9% similarity negates differences: Portrays the study of human genetic variation as irrelevant or wrong-headed because humans are 99.9% (or 99.5%) alike genetically, on average.
xiv	Park (2002, pp. 395–398)	This anthropology textbook discussed "why [in its author's view] there are no biological races within the human species."
xv	Holt (1994, p. A23)	This *New York Times* opinion–editorial piece disputed the idea that racial differences in intelligence could have any genetic basis.
xvi	Marks (1995, pp. 273–275)	The author summed up his argument by saying that genetic differences by race are minor but are exaggerated in order to justify and perpetuate social inequality.
	Test-validation fallacy 1.	Contending definitions negate evidence: Portrays lack of consensus in verbal definitions of intelligence as if this negated evidence for the construct validity of IQ tests.
xvii	Singham (1995, pp. 272, 278)	The author advised educators that *The Bell Curve* is, in his view, unscientific and ideological.
xviii	"The 'Bell Curve' agenda" (1994, p. A16)	This *New York Times* editorial argued that "what is new about [*The Bell Curve* book]—the fixation on genes as destiny—is surely unproved and almost surely wrong" and that therefore IQ level actually is manipulable.
	Causal-network fallacy 1: *Phenotype* equals *genotype*:	Portrays phenotypic differences in intelligence as if they were necessarily genotypic.
xix	Duster (1995, p. 1)	The author argued that "there has always been a tendency to link existing social orders with so-called innate physical, intellectual and spiritual qualities."
xx	Bartholomew (2004, pp. 122–123)	The author described the difficulty of determining whether the Black–White IQ difference originates in whole or part in the genes or whether it can be wholly accounted for by environmental factors.

Causal-network fallacy 2. *Biological* equals *genetic:* Portrays biological differences (such as brain phenotypes) as if they were necessarily genetic.

xxi Bartholomew (2004, p. 138) The author discussed possible sources of the "Flynn effect" (the secular rise in IQ).

xxii "Race and Intelligence" (2007) National Public Radio's *News & Notes* program followed up an interview with J. P. Rushton, who reported correlations between race, brain size, and intelligence, by interviewing a critic of intelligence research.

Causal-network fallacy 3. *Environmental* equals *nongenetic:* Portrays external environments as if they were necessarily nongenetic, that is, unaffected by and unrelated to the genotypes of individuals in them.

xxiii Monastersky (2008, ¶ 1) This news article reported research on "how poverty alters the brain."

xxiv Fischer et al. (1996, p. 68) The authors argued that the AFQT measures differences in opportunity to learn, not "raw intelligence."

Standards-of-evidence fallacy 1. Imperfect measurement pretext: Maintains that valid, unbiased intelligence tests should not be used for making decisions about individuals until the tests are made error free.

xxv FairTest (2007, ¶¶ 12, 14, and 17) One of FairTest's University Testing Fact Sheets on its Web site argues that the ACT, SAT, and SAT Subject Tests are not accurate enough to be used in evaluating applicants for college admissions and scholarships.

xxvi Miller (2001, p. A14) This news article in *Chronicle of Higher Education* reported complaints in the education profession about large-scale testing.

xxvii Hartigan and Wigdor (1989, pp. 7–8) The authors of this National Academy of Sciences report explained why they recommended that the U.S. Employment Service continue to race-norm job applicants' employment test scores.

continues

TABLE 1.2
Continued

Example no.	Reference	Context
	Standards-of-evidence fallacy 2. Dangerous-thoughts trigger: Maintains that scientific conclusions purported to be divisive or dangerous should not be entertained until proved beyond all possible doubt.	
xxviii	C. Kiesler (January 17, 1980, personal communication to A. R. Jensen)	The editor of the *American Psychologist* explained why he rejected Arthur Jensen's manuscript, "The Nature of the Average Difference between Whites and Blacks on Psychometric Tests: Spearman's Hypothesis" (which was later published in another journal as a target article; see Jensen, 1985).
xxix	Hunt and Carlson (2007, p. 210)	The authors proposed standards for conducting and evaluating research on group differences in intelligence.
	Standards-of-evidence fallacy 3. Happy-thoughts leniency: Maintains that mere theoretical possibility elevates the scientific credibility of a politically popular idea above that of an empirically plausible but unpopular conclusion.	
xxx	Diamond (1999, pp. 16, 19)	The author argued that "biological differences" cannot account for "why . . . human development proceed[ed] at such different rates on different continents" over human history, despite seemingly compelling arguments that they do.
xxxi	"The 'Bell Curve' agenda" (1994, p. A16)	This *New York Times* editorial argued that "what is new about [*The Bell Curve* book]—the fixation on genes as destiny—is surely unproved and almost surely wrong" and that therefore IQ level actually is manipulable.

Note. See Appendix A (on the following Web site: http://www.apa.org/books/resources/Phelps/) for extensive, annotated excerpts from the cited sources.

students who would not succeed academically without special attention. He began with the observation that students who had great difficulty with their schoolwork also had difficulty doing many other things that children their age usually can do. Intellectually, they were more like the average child a year or two younger—hence the term *retarded* development. According to Binet and Simon (1916), the construct to be measured is manifested most clearly in quality of reasoning and judgment in the course of daily life:

> It seems to us that in intelligence there is a fundamental faculty, the alteration or lack of which is of the utmost importance for practical life. This faculty is judgment, otherwise called good sense, practical sense, initiative, the faculty of adapting one's self to circumstances. To judge well, to reason well, these are the essential activities of intelligence. A person may be a moron or an imbecile if he is lacking in judgment: but with good judgment he can never be either. Indeed the rest of the intellectual faculties seem of little importance in comparison with judgment. (pp. 42–43)

This conception provided a good starting point for designing tasks that might effectively activate intelligence and cause it to leave its footprints in observable behavior. Binet and Simon's (1916) strategy was to develop a series of short, objective questions that sampled specific mental skills and bits of knowledge that the average child accrues in everyday life by certain ages, such as asking the child to point to nose, eyes, and mouth (age 3); count 13 pennies (age 6); note omissions from pictures of familiar objects (age 8); arrange five blocks in order of weight (age 10); and discover the sense of a disarranged sentence (age 12). In light of having postulated a highly general mental ability or broad set of intellectual skills, it made sense to assess performance on a wide variety of mental tasks children are routinely exposed to outside of schools and are expected to master in the normal course of development. For the same reason, it was essential not to focus on any specific domain of knowledge or expertise, as would a test of knowledge in a particular job or school subject.

The logic is that mastering fewer such everyday tasks than is typical for one's age signals a lag in the child's overall mental development; that a short series of items that are strategically selected, carefully administered, and appropriately scored (a *standardized test*) can make this lag manifest; and that poorer performance on such a test will forecast greater difficulty in mastering the regular school curriculum (i.e., the increasingly difficult series of cognitive tasks that schools pose for pupils at successively higher grade levels). For a test to succeed, its items must range sufficiently in difficulty at each age in order to capture the range of variation at that age. Otherwise, it would be like having a weight scale that can register nothing below 50 pounds or above 100 pounds.

Most modern intelligence tests still follow the same basic principle—test items should sample a wide variety of cognitive performances at different difficulty levels. Over time, individually administered intelligence test batteries have grown to include a dozen or more separate subtests (e.g., Wechsler Intelligence Scale for Children, 4th ed. [WISC–IV; Wechsler, 2003] subtests such as Vocabulary, Block Design, Digit Span, Symbol Search, Similarities) that systematically sample a range of cognitive processes. Subtests are usually aggregated into broader content categories (e.g., the WISC–IV's four index scores: Verbal Comprehension, Perceptual Reasoning, Working Memory, and Processing Speed). The result is to provide at least three tiers of scores (see Entry 9 in Figure 1.1): individual subtests, clusters of subtests (area scores, indexes, composites, etc.), and overall IQ. The overall IQs from different IQ test batteries generally correlate at least at .8 among themselves (which is not far below the maximum possible in view of their reliabilities of .9 or more), so they are capturing the same phenomenon. Mere similarity of results among IQ tests is necessary, of course, but not sufficient to confirm that the tests measure the intended construct.

Today, item content, test format, and administration procedure (Entry 8 in Figure 1.1) are all tightly controlled to maximize accuracy in targeting the intended ability and to minimize contamination of scores by random error (e.g., too few items to get consistent measurement) or irrelevant factors (e.g., motivation, differential experience, or unequal testing circumstances). Test items therefore ideally include content that is either novel to all test takers or to which all test takers have been exposed previously. Reliable scoring is facilitated (measurement error is reduced) by using more numerous test items and by using questions with clearly right and wrong answers.

The major intelligence tests, such as the Stanford–Binet and the Wechsler series for preschoolers (Wechsler Preschool and Primary Scale of Intelligence; Wechsler, 2002), school-aged children (WISC; Wechsler, 2003), and adults (Wechsler Adult Intelligence Scale [WAIS; Wechsler, 1997]) are administered orally to test takers one on one, item by item for 1 hour or more, by highly trained professionals who follow written scripts governing what they must and must not say to the individual to ensure standard conditions for all test takers (Sattler, 2001). Within those constraints, test administrators seek to gain rapport and otherwise establish conditions to elicit maximal performance.

The foregoing test-design strategies increase the likelihood of creating a test that is reliable and valid—one that consistently measures the intended construct and nothing else. Such strategies cannot guarantee this happy result, of course. This is why tests and the results from all individual test items are required to jump various statistical hurdles after tryout and before publication and why, after publication, tests are subjected to continuing research and periodic revision. These guidelines for good measurement result, however, in tests with superficial appearances that make them highly vulnerable to fallacious reasoning of the following sorts.

Test-Design Fallacy 1: Yardstick Mirrors Construct

This fallacy involves portraying the superficial appearance of a test (Entry 8 in Figure 1.1) as if it mimicked the inner essence of the phenomenon it measures (Entry 5 in Figure 1.1). For example, it would be nonsensical to claim that a thermometer's outward appearance provides insight into the nature of heat or that differently constructed thermometers obviously measure different kinds of heat. Yet some critiques of intelligence testing rest precisely on such reasoning. For example, Fischer et al. (1996; see also Appendix A, Example i, and Table 1.2, this volume) decided on face value that the Armed Forces Qualification Test (AFQT) measures "mastery of school curricula" and nothing deeper, and Flynn (2007; Appendix A, Example ii) asserted that various WISC subtests measure "what they say." Sternberg, Wagner, Williams, and Horvath (1995; see also Appendix A, Example iii) argued that IQ tests measure only "academic" intelligence because they pose tasks that appear to their eye only academic: well-defined tasks with narrow, esoteric, or academic content of little practical value that always have right and wrong answers and do not give credit for experience.

All three examples reinforce the fallacy they deploy: that one can know what a test measures by just peering at its items. Like reading tea leaves, critics list various superficialities of test content and format to assert, variously, that IQ tests measure only an aptness with paper-and-pencil tasks, a narrow academic ability, familiarity with the tester's culture, facility with well-defined tasks with unambiguous answers, and so on. Not only are these inferences unwarranted, but their premises about content and format are often wrong. In actuality, most items on individually administered batteries require neither paper nor pencil, most are not timed, many do not use numbers or words or other academic-seeming content, and many require knowledge of only the most elementary concepts (up–down, large–small, etc.). Neither the mechanics nor superficial content of IQ tests reveals the essence of the construct they capture. Manifest item content—*content validity*—is critical for certain other types of tests, specifically, ones meant to gauge knowledge or achievement in some particular content domain, such as algebra, typing, or jet engine repair.

Figuring out what construct(s) a particular test actually measures requires extensive validation research, which involves collecting and analyzing test results in many circumstances and populations (American Educational Research Association, American Psychological Association, & National Council on Measurement in Education, 1999). As described later in this chapter, such research shows that ostensibly different tests can be used to measure the same latent ability. Spearman (1927) characterized this as the "indifference to the indicator" (pp. 197–198). The yardstick–mirrors–construct fallacy, by contending that a test measures only what it "looks like," allows critics to assert, a priori, that IQ tests cannot possibly measure a highly general mental capability. It thereby precludes, on seemingly scientific grounds, the very success that tests have already demonstrated.

Test-Design Fallacy 2: Intelligence Is Marble Collection

This fallacy involves portraying general intelligence (*g*) as if it were just an aggregation of many separate specific abilities, not a singular phenomenon in itself (Entry 10 in Figure 1.1) because of the way IQ scores are typically calculated, which essentially is to add up a person's scores on the various subtests in a battery (Entry 9 in Figure 1.1). This fallacy is similar to the previous one in that it presumes that the manner of calculating scores from IQ tests (the *measure*) mirrors how general intelligence itself (the hypothetical entity or *construct*) is constituted. That is, the marble-collection fallacy holds that intelligence is made up of separable components, the sum total of which we label *intelligence*. It is not itself an identifiable entity but, like marbles in a bag, just a conglomeration or aggregate of many separate things we choose to add to the collection.

Flynn (2007) conceptualized intelligence in this manner to cast doubt on the psychological reality of *g*. He viewed IQ subtests as isolating various "components" of "intelligence broad" (p. 55; see Appendix A, Example iv). "Understanding intelligence is like understanding the atom." Its parts can be "split apart," "assert their functional autonomy," and "swim freely of *g*" (pp. 4, 10, 18; see Appendix A, Example v). For Howe (1997), the IQ is no more than a "range of mental tasks" (p. 162; see Appendix A, Example vi).

This conglomeration view holds IQ tests hostage to complaints that they cannot possibly measure intelligence because they do not include the complainant's preferred type or number of marbles. Williams (1996), for example, suggested that "a broader perspective on intelligence may enable us to assess . . . previously unmeasured aspects of intelligence" (pp. 529–530). She favored an expansive conception of intelligence that includes a "more ecologically relevant set of abilities" (p. 350), including motivation, Sternberg's proposed practical and creative intelligences, and Gardner's postulated seven-plus multiple intelligences.

The conglomeration conception may have been a viable hypothesis in Binet's time, but it has now been decisively disproved. As discussed later in the chapter, *g* (Entry 10 in Figure 1.1) is not the sum of separate, independent cognitive skills or abilities but is the common core of them all. In this sense, general intelligence is psychometrically unitary. Whether *g* is unitary at the physiological level is an altogether different question (Jensen, 1998, 2006), but most researchers think that is unlikely.

Test-Score-Differences Fallacies

Answers to items on a test must be scored in a way that allows for meaningful interpretation of test results. The number of items answered correctly, or *raw score*, has no intrinsic meaning. Nor does percentage correct, because the *denominator* (total number of test items) also has no substantive meaning. Percentage correct can be boosted simply by adding easier items to the test, and it can be decreased by using more difficult ones. Scores become interpretable only when placed within some meaningful frame of reference. For example, an individual's score may be *criterion referenced*, that is, compared with some absolute performance standard ("90% accuracy in multiplying two-digit numbers") or it may be *norm referenced*, that is, lined up against others in some carefully specified normative population ("60th percentile in arithmetic among American fourth graders taking the test last year"). The first intelligence tests allowed neither sort of interpretation, but virtually all psychological tests are norm referenced today.

Binet and Simon (1916) attempted to provide interpretable intelligence test results by assigning a *mental age* (MA; the age at which the average child answers a given item correctly) to each item on their test. Because mental capacity increases over childhood, a higher MA score can be interpreted as a sign of more advanced cognitive development. To illustrate, if 8-year-olds answer an average of 20 items correctly, then a raw score of 20 on that test can be said to represent a mental age of 8; if 12-year-olds correctly answer an average of 30 items, then a raw score of 30 represents MA = 12. Thus, if John scores at the average for children aged 10 years, 6 months, he has a mental age of 10.5. How his mental age is interpreted depends, of course, on how old John is. If he is 8 years old, then his MA of 10.5 indicates that he is brighter than the average 8 year old (whose MA = 8.0, by definition). If he is age 12, his mental development lags behind that of other 12-year-olds (whose MA = 12.0).

In today's terms, Binet and Simon (1916) derived an *age equivalent*, analogous to the *grade equivalent* (GE) that is frequently used in reporting academic achievement in elementary school: "Susie's GE score on the school district's math test is 4.3"; that is, she scored at the average for children in the 3rd month of Grade 4.

The 1916 version of the Stanford–Binet Intelligence Scale began factoring the child's actual age into the child's score by calculating an *intelligence quotient* (IQ), specifically by dividing mental age by chronological age (CA) and multiplying by 100, to eliminate decimals. By this new method, if John were aged 10 (or 8, or 12), his MA of 10.5 would give him an IQ of 105 (or 131, or 88). IQ thus came to represent relative standing within one's own age group (MA/CA), not among children of all ages (MA). One problem with this innovation was that because mental age usually begins leveling off in adolescence but chronological age continues to increase, the MA/CA quotient yields nonsensical scores beyond adolescence.

The 1972 version of the Stanford–Binet inaugurated the *deviation IQ*, which has become standard practice. It indexes how far above or below the average, in standard deviation units, a person scores relative to others of the same age (by month for children, and by year for adults). Distance from an age group's average is quantified by normalizing test scores, that is, transforming raw scores into locations along the normal curve (z scores, which have a mean of 0 and standard deviation of 1). This transformation preserves the rank ordering of the raw scores. For convenience, the Stanford–Binet transformed the z scores to have a mean of 100 and a standard deviation of 16 (the Wechsler and many other IQ tests today set SD = 15). Fitting test scores onto the normal curve in this way means that 95% of each age group get scores within 2 standard deviations of the mean, that is, between IQs 68 and 132 (when SD is set to 16) or between IQs 70 and 130 (when SD is set to 15). Translating z scores into IQ points is similar to changing temperatures from Fahrenheit into centigrade. The resulting deviation IQs are more interpretable than the MA/CA IQ, especially in adulthood, and normalized scores are far more statistically tractable. The deviation IQ is not a quotient, but the acronym *IQ* was retained—not unreasonably because the two forms of scores remain highly correlated in children.

With deviation IQs, intelligence became fully norm referenced. Norm-referenced scores are extremely useful for many purposes, but they, too, have serious limitations. To see why, look at the example of temperature. Consider the centigrade scale: Zero degrees is assigned to the freezing point for water and 100 degrees to its boiling point (at sea level). This gives substantive meaning to thermometer readings. IQ scores have never been anchored in this way to any concrete daily reality that would give them additional meaning. Norm-referenced scores such as the IQ are valuable when the aim is to predict differences in performance within a given population, but they allow us to rank individuals only relative to each other and not against anything external to the test. One searches in vain, for instance, for a good accounting of the capabilities that 10-year-olds, 15-year-olds, or adults of IQ 110 usually possess but similarly aged individuals of IQ 90 do not, or which particular intellectual skills a Verbal score of 600 on the SAT usually reflects. Such accountings are possible but require special research. Lack of detailed criterion-related interpretation is also teachers' chief complaint about many standardized achievement tests: "I know Sarah ranked higher than Sammie in reading, but what exactly can either of them do, and on which sorts of reading tasks do they each need help?"

IQ tests are not intended to isolate and measure highly specific skills and knowledge. This is the job of suitably designed achievement tests. However, the fact that the IQ scale is not tethered at any point to anything concrete that people can recognize understandably invites suspicion and misrepresentation. It makes IQ tests black boxes into which people can project all sorts of unwarranted hopes and fears. Psychometricians speaking in statistical tongues may be perceived as psychomagicians practicing dark arts.

Thermometers illustrate another limitation of IQ tests. We cannot be sure that IQ tests provide interval-level measurement rather than just ordinal-level (i.e., rank-order) measurement. Fahrenheit degrees are 1.8 times larger than centigrade degrees, but both scales count off from zero and in equal units (degrees). So the 40-degree difference between 80 degrees and 40 degrees measures off the same difference in heat as does the 40-degree difference between 40 degrees and zero, or zero and –40. Not so with IQ points. Treating IQ as an interval-level scale has been a reasonable and workable assumption for many purposes, but we really do not know whether a 10-point difference measures the same intellectual difference at all ranges of IQ.

There is a more serious technical limitation, shared by both IQ tests and thermometers, which criterion-referencing cannot eliminate—lack of ratio measurement. Ratio scales measure absolute amounts of something because they begin measuring, in equal-sized units, from zero (total absence of the phenomenon). Consider a pediatrician's scales for height and weight, both of which start at zero and have intervals of equal size (inches or pounds). In contrast, zero degrees centigrade does not represent total lack of heat (absolute zero), nor is 80 degrees twice the amount of heat as 40 degrees, in absolute terms. Likewise, IQ 120 does not represent twice as much intelligence as IQ 60. We can meaningfully say that Sally weighs 10% more today than she did 4 years ago, she grew taller at a rate of 1 inch per year, or she runs 1 mile per hour faster than her sister. We can also chart absolute changes in all three rates. We can do none of this with IQ test scores because they measure relative standing only, not absolute mental power. They can rank but not weigh.

This limitation is shared by all measures of ability, personality, attitude, social class, and probably most other scales in the social sciences. We cannot say, for example, that Bob's social class increased by 25% last year, that Mary is 15% more extroverted than her sister, or that Nathan's self-esteem has doubled since he learned to play baseball. Although lack of ratio measurement might seem an abstruse matter, it constitutes the biggest measurement challenge facing intelligence researchers today (Jensen, 2006). Imagine trying to study physical growth if scales set the average height at 4 feet for all ages and variability in height to be the same for 4-year-olds as for 40-year-olds. Norm-referenced height measures like these would greatly limit our ability to study normal patterns of growth and deviations around it. Yet better this "deviation height" scoring than assigning ages to height scores and dividing that "height age" by chronological age to get "height quotient" because a height quotient would seem to show adults getting shorter and shorter with age! Such has been the challenge in measuring and understanding general intelligence.

Lack of ratio measurement does not invalidate psychological tests by any means, but it does limit what can be learned from them. It also nourishes certain fallacies about intelligence testing because without the absolute results to contradict them, critics can falsely represent differences in IQ scores (relative standing in ability) as if they gauged absolute differences in ability to ridicule and discredit the test results. The following four measurement fallacies are not used to dispute the construct validity of intelligence tests, as did the two test-design fallacies. Rather, they target well-established facts about intelligence that would, if accepted, require acknowledging social trade-offs that democratic societies would rather not ponder. All four work by confusing different components of variation: (a) how individuals typically grow or change over time versus differences among them in growth or change, (b) changes in a group's mean versus changes in the spread of scores within the group, (c) the basic inputs required for any individual to develop (hence, not concerning variation at all) versus differences in how individuals develop, and (d) differences within a species versus differences between species.

Test-Score-Differences Fallacy 1: Nonfixedness Proves Malleability

This fallacy uses evidence of any fluctuation or growth in the mental functioning of individuals as if it were proof that their rates of growth can be changed intentionally. IQ level is not made malleable by any means yet devised (Brody, 1996), but many a critic has sought to dismiss this fact by pointing to the obvious but irrelevant fact that individuals grow and learn. The nonfixedness-proves-malleability fallacy succeeds by using the word change for two entirely different phenomena as if they were the same phenomenon. It first points to developmental "change" within individuals to suggest, wrongly, that IQ levels (relative differences between age mates) can be readily "changed." Asserting that IQ is stable (unchanging) despite this obvious growth (change) therefore makes one appear foolish or doggedly ideological.

Consider, for instance, the November 22, 1994, "American Agenda" segment of *World News Tonight With Peter Jennings* (Blakemore, 1994), which was devoted to debunking several of *The Bell Curve*'s six foundational premises (Appendix A, Example vii). It reported that intelligence is "almost impossible to measure" and cannot be "largely genetic and fixed by age 16 or 17" because the brain is constantly changing owing to "hydration, nutrition, and stimulation"; "learning"; and "everything it experiences, from its first formation in utero." Howe (1997; Appendix A, Example viii) provided a more subtle but more typical example when he criticized "intelligence theory" for "ignor[ing] the fact human intelligence develops rather than being static" (p. 138). By thus confusing within-individual growth with the stability of between-individual differences, he can accuse the field of denying that development occurs simply because it focuses on a different question.

Figure 1.2 distinguishes the two phenomena being confused: absolute growth versus growth relative to age mates. The three curves represent in stylized form the typical course of cognitive growth and decline for individuals at three levels of relative ability: IQs 70, 100, and 130. All three sets of individuals develop along similar lines, their mental capabilities rising in childhood (in absolute terms), leveling off in adulthood, and then falling somewhat in old age. The mental growth trajectories for brighter individuals are steeper, so they level off at a higher point. This typical pattern has been ascertained from various specialized tests whose results are not age normed. As noted earlier, current tests cannot gauge absolute level of intelligence ("raw mental power" in Figure 1.2), so the shape of the curves cannot be verified. Evidence is unambiguous, however, that they differ greatly across individuals.

Current IQ tests cannot chronicle amount of growth and decline over a lifetime because they are not ratio measures. They compare individuals only with others of the same age, say, other 20-year-olds. If an individual scores at the average for his age group every year, then that person's IQ score will always be 100. In technical terms, the IQ will be *stable* (i.e., rank in age group remains the same). IQ level is, in fact, fairly stable in this sense from the elementary grades to old age. The stability of IQ rank at different ages dovetails with the disappointing results of efforts to raise low IQ levels, that is, to accelerate the cognitive growth of less able children and thereby move them up in IQ rank relative to some control group.

Ratio measurement would make the nonfixedness fallacy as transparent for intelligence as it would be for height: Children change and grow, so their differences in height must be malleable. Absent this constraint, it is easy for critics to use the inevitability of within-person change to deny the observed stability of between-person differences. One is invited to conclude that cognitive inequality need not exist. The next fallacy builds on the current one to suggest that the means for eradicating it are already at hand and only ill will blocks their use.

Test-Score-Differences Fallacy 2: Improvability Proves Equalizability

This fallacy portrays evidence that intellectual skills and achievements can be improved within a population as if it were proof that they can be equalized in that population. Stated more statistically, this fallacy asserts that if social interventions succeed in raising mean levels of skill, they must necessarily be effective for eradicating its members' differences in skill level. This flouts the fact that interventions that raise a group's mean usually *increase* (not decrease) its standard deviation (cf. Ceci & Papierno, 2005), a phenomenon so regular that Jensen christened it the "second law of individual differences" (Sarich & Miele, 2004, p. 258). Howe (1997) appealed to the improvability-proves-equalizability fallacy when he argued that

> in a prosperous society, only a self-fulfilling prophecy resulting from widespread acceptance of the false visions expounded by those who refuse to see that intelligence is changeable would enable perpetuation of a permanent caste of people who are prevented from acquiring the capabilities evident in successful men and women and their rewards. (pp. 62–63; see Appendix A, Example ix)

The equalizability fallacy is a virtual article of faith in educational circles. Public education was meant to be the great equalizer by giving all children a chance to rise in society regardless of their social origins, and thus nowhere has the democratic dilemma been more hotly denied yet more conspicuous than in the schools. Spurning the constraints of human cognitive diversity, the schooling-related professions generally hold that schools can simultaneously achieve equality and excellence—hence the catchphrase "EQuality" or "E-Quality"—and that beliefs to the contrary threaten both goals (Smith & Lusthaus, 1995). They contend, further, that schools could achieve both simultaneously if only educators were provided sufficient resources. Perhaps ironically, policymakers now use highly g-loaded tests of achievement to hold schools accountable for achieving the EQuality educationists have said is within their power to produce. Most dramatically, the federal No Child Left Behind Act of 2001 (The White House, 2001) requires public schools not only to close the long-standing demographic gaps in student achievement but to do so by raising all groups of students to the same high level of academic proficiency by 2014: "Schools must be accountable for ensuring that all students, including disadvantaged students, meet high academic standards" (The White House, 2001; see Appendix A, Example x). Schools that fail to level up performance on schedule face escalating sanctions, including state takeover.

The converse of the equalizability fallacy is equally common but far more pernicious—namely, the fallacy that nonequalizability implies nonimprovability. Thus did *Washington Post* columnist Dionne (1994) speak of the "deep pessimism about the possibility of social reform" owing to "the revival of interest in genetic explanations for human inequality" (see Appendix A, Example xi):

> If genes are so important to [inequality of] intelligence and intelligence is so important to [differences in] success, then many of the efforts made over the past several decades to improve people's life chances were mostly a waste of time. (p. A17)

This is utterly false. One can improve lives without equalizing them.

Test-Score-Differences Fallacy 3: Interactionism (Gene-Environment Codependence) Nullifies Heritability

This fallacy portrays the gene–environment partnership in creating a phenotype as if conjoint action within the individual precluded teasing apart the roots of phenotypic differences among individuals. Although the nonfixedness and equalizability fallacies seem to discredit a phenotypic finding (stability of IQ rank within one's age group), the fallacy of so-called "interactionism" provides a scientific-sounding excuse to denigrate as self-evidently absurd all evidence for a genetic influence (Entry 1 in Figure 1.1) on intelligence (Entry 5 in Figure 1.1).

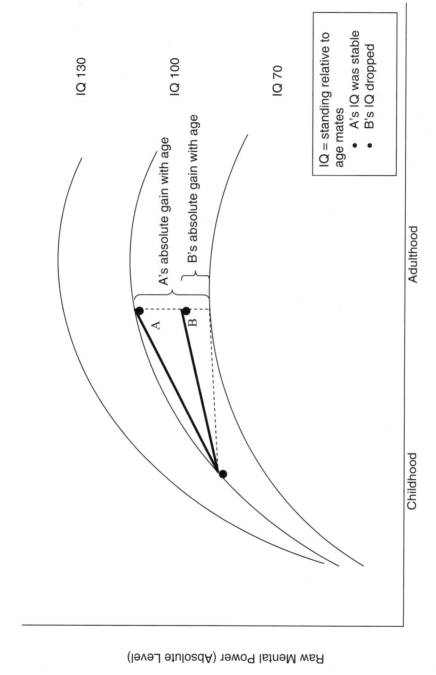

Figure 1.2. An oft-muddled distinction: Changes in relative versus absolute levels of intelligence.

To avoid confusion, I should clarify two concepts. First, *heritability* refers to the origins of observed—*phenotypic*—variation among individuals in a particular population. For example, if the heritability of height differences among White Canadian adult males were estimated to be 80%, this would mean that 80% of these men's differences in height are owing to their differences in genotype and 20% to their differences in environmental (nongenetic) circumstances and error of measurement. Second, the technical term *gene–environment interaction* refers to something altogether different than does the appeal to "interactionism." In behavior genetics, *gene-environment interaction* refers to a particular kind of nonadditive genetic effect in which environmental (nongenetic) effects are conditional on genotype, for example, when possessing a particular version (allele) of a gene renders the individual unusually susceptible to a particular pathogen.

The interactionism fallacy states an irrelevant truth to reach an irrelevant conclusion in order to dismiss peremptorily all estimates of heritability while appropriating a legitimate scientific term to connote scientific backing. The irrelevant truth is that an organism's development requires genes and environments to act in concert. The two forces are inextricable, mutually dependent, and constantly interacting. Development is their mutual product, like the dance of two partners. The irrelevant conclusion is that it is therefore impossible to apportion credit for the pair's joint product to each partner separately—say, 40% of the pair's steps to the man and 60% to the woman. The inappropriate generalization is that behavior geneticists cannot possibly do what they claim—namely, to decompose phenotypic variation among individuals within a particular population into its genetic and nongenetic sources of variation. This is analogous to saying that it would be impossible to estimate whether differences in quality of tango performances among American couples is owing more to skill variation among the male partners than to skill variation among the female partners (i.e., genetic vs. nongenetic variation)—or to what extent differences among couples in their quality of performance depend on the chemistry between two partners (i.e., gene–environment interaction).

To illustrate, Sternberg (1997) spoke of how it is "extremely difficult" to separate the genetic and nongenetic sources of variation in intelligence "because they interact in many different ways" (p. 48; see also Appendix A, Example xii). A letter to *Science* (Andrews & Nelkin, 1996) invoked the authority of geneticists and ethicists to dispute the claim that individual differences in intelligence are highly heritable "given the complex interplay between genes and environments" (p. 13; see also Appendix A, Example xiii). Both examples confuse the essentials for development (genes and environments must both be present and work together) with how the two requisites might differ from one person to another and thus head them down somewhat different developmental paths. Sternberg (1997; see also Appendix A, Example xii) implied that estimating heritabilities is absurd by further confusing the issue—specifically, when he likened calculating a heritability (the ratio of genetic variance to phenotypic variance in a trait) to calculating the average temperature in Minnesota (a simple mean, but all means obscure variability, just as average quality of dancing has no bearing on why some couples dance better than others).

The interactionism fallacy creates its illusion by focusing attention on the preconditions for behavior (the dance requires two partners), as if that were equivalent to examining variation in the behavior itself (some couples dance better than others, perhaps mostly because the men differ in competence at leading). It confuses two important but quite different scientific questions (Jensen, 1981, p. 112): What is the typical course of human development versus to what extent can variations in development be traced to genetic variation in the population?

The field of behavior genetics seeks to explain not the common human theme but variations on it. It does so by measuring phenotypes for pairs of individuals who differ systematically in genetic and environmental relatedness. Such data allow decomposition of phenotypic variation in behavior within a population into its nongenetic (Entry 2 in Figure 1.1) and genetic (Entry 1 in Figure 1.1) sources. The field has actually gone far beyond estimating the heritabilities of traits such as intelligence. For instance, it can determine to what extent the phenotypic covariation between two outcomes, say, intelligence and occupational level in Sweden, represents a genetic correlation between them in that population (Plomin et al., 2001; Plomin & Petrill, 1997; Rowe, Vesterdal, & Rodgers, 1998).

Critics often activate the interactionism fallacy simply by caricaturing the unwanted evidence about heritability. When researchers speak of IQ's heritability, they are referring to the percentage of variation in IQ, the phenotype, which has been traced to genetic variation within a particular population. However, critics transmogrify this into the obviously false claim that an individual's intelligence is "predetermined" or "fixed at birth," as if it were preformed and emerged automatically according to some detailed blueprint, impervious to influence of any sort. No serious scientist believes that today. One's genome is fixed at birth, but its actions and effects on the phenotype are not fixed, predetermined, or predestined. The genome is less like a blueprint than a playbook for responding to contingencies, with some parts of the genome regulating the actions or expression of others depending on cellular conditions, themselves influenced by location in the body, age, temperature, nutrients available, and the like. Organisms would not survive without the ability to adapt to different circumstances. The behavior genetic question is, rather, whether different versions of the same genes (alleles) cause individuals to respond differently in the very same circumstances.

Test-Score-Differences Fallacy 4: Similarity of 99.9% Negates Differences

This fallacy portrays the study of human genetic variation as irrelevant or wrongheaded because humans are 99.9% (or 99.5%) alike genetically, on average. Of recent vintage, the 99.9% fallacy impugns even investigating human genetic variation by implying, falsely, that a 0.1% average difference in genetic profiles (3 million base pairs) is trivial. (Comparably estimated, the human and chimpanzee genomes differ by about 1.3%.) The fallacy is frequently used to reinforce the claim, as one anthropology textbook explained (Park, 2002; see also Appendix A, Example xiv), that "there are no races" (p. 395). Its author reasoned that if most of that 0.1% genetic variation is among individuals of the same race, then "all the phenotypic variation that we try to assort into race is the result of a virtual handful of alleles" (pp. 397–398). Reasoning in like manner, Holt (1994) editorialized in the *New York Times* that "genetic diversity among the races is miniscule," a mere "residue" of human variation (p. A23; see also Appendix A, Example xv). The implication is that research into racial differences, even at the phenotypic level, is both scientifically and morally suspect. As spelled out by another anthropology text (Marks, 1995), "Providing explanations for social inequalities as being rooted in nature is a classic pseudoscientific occupation" (p. 273; see also Appendix A, Example xvi).

More recent estimates point to greater genetic variation among humans (only 99.5% alike; Hayden, 2007), but any big number will do. The fallacy works by having us look at human variation against the backdrop of evolutionary time and the vast array of species. By this reasoning, human genetic variation is inconsequential in human affairs because we humans are more similar to one another than to dogs, worms, and microbes. The fallacy focuses our attention on the 99.9% genetic similarity that makes us all human, *Homo sapiens*, to distract us from the 0.1% that makes us individuals. Moreover, as illustrated in diverse life arenas, "it is often the case that small differences in the input result in large differences in the final outcome" (Hart, 2007, p. 112).

The identical parts of the genome are called the *nonsegregating genes*, which are termed evolutionarily *fixed* in the species because they do not vary among its individual members. The remaining genes, for which humans possess different versions (alleles), are called *segregating genes* because they segregate (*reassort*) during the production of eggs and sperm. Only the segregating genes are technically termed *heritable* because only they create genetic differences that may be transmitted from parent to offspring generations. Intelligence tests are designed to capture individual differences in developed mental competence, so it is among the small percentage of segregating genes that scientists search for the genetic roots of those phenotypic differences. The 99.9% fallacy would put this search off limits.

Test-Validation Fallacies

Validating a test refers to determining which sorts of inferences may properly be drawn from the test's scores, most commonly whether it measures the intended construct (such as conscientiousness) or content domain (jet engine repair, matrix algebra) or whether it allows more accurate predictions about individuals when decisions are required (college admissions, hiring). A test may be valid for some uses but not others, and no single study can establish a test's validity for any particular purpose. For instance, Arthur may have successfully predicted which films would win an Oscar this year, but that gives us no reason to believe he can also predict who will win the World Series, the Kentucky Derby, or a Nobel Prize. Further, we certainly should hesitate to put our money behind his Oscar picks next year unless he has demonstrated a good track record in picking winners.

IQ tests are designed to measure a highly general intelligence, and they have been successful in predicting individual differences in just the sorts of academic, occupational, and other performances that a general intelligence theory would lead one to expect (Entry 6 in Figure 1.1). The tests also tend to predict these outcomes better than does any other single predictor, including family background (Ceci, 1996a; Herrnstein & Murray, 1994). This evidence makes it plausible that IQ tests measure differences in a very general intelligence, but it is not sufficient to prove that they do so or that intelligence actually causes those differences in life outcomes.

Test validation, like science in general, works by pitting alternative claims against one another to see which one best fits the totality of available evidence: Do IQ tests measure the same types of intelligence in different racial–ethnic groups? Do they measure intelligence at all, or just social privilege or familiarity with the culture? Advances in measurement have provided new ways to adjudicate such claims. Entries 10 and 11 in Figure 1.1 represent two advances in identifying, isolating, and contrasting the constructs that cognitive tests may be measuring—respectively, factor analysis and latent trait modeling. Both provide tools for scrutinizing tests and test items in action (Entry 9 in Figure 1.1) and asking whether they behave in accordance with one's claims about what is being measured. If not in accord, then the test, the theory it embodies, or both need to be revised and then reexamined. Successive rounds of such psychometric scrutiny reveal a great deal—not only about tests but also about the phenomena they poke and prod into expressing themselves.

Psychometricians have spent decades trying to sort out the phenomena that tests reveal. More precisely, they have been charting the structure, or relatedness, of cognitive abilities as assayed by tests purporting to measure intelligence or components of it. From the first days of mental testing, it was observed that people who do well on one mental test tend to perform well on all others, regardless of item type, test format, or mode of administration. All mental ability tests correlate positively with all others, suggesting that they all tap into the same underlying abilities.

Intelligence researchers developed the method of factor analysis to extract those common factors (Entry 10 in Figure 1.1) from any large, diverse set of mental tests administered to representative samples of individuals. With this tool, the researchers can ask the following questions: How many common factors are there? Are those factors the same from battery to battery, population to population, age to age, and so on? What kinds of abilities do they seem to represent? Do tests with the same name measure the same construct? Do tests with different names measure different abilities? Intent is no guarantee.

These are not esoteric technical matters. They get to the heart of important questions such as whether there is a single broadly useful general ability versus many independent coequal ones specialized for different tasks and whether IQ batteries measure the same abilities equally well in all demographic groups (answers thus far: only one, and yes). For present purposes, the three most important findings from the decades of factor analytic research (Carroll, 1993) are that (a) the common factors running through mental ability tests differ primarily in level of generality, or breadth of content (from very narrow to widely applicable) for which that factor enhances performance; (b) only one factor, g, consistently emerges at the most general level (which Carroll [1993] labeled "Stratum III," the highest level in his model); and (c) the group factors in Carroll's Stratum II, such as verbal or spatial ability, correlate moderately highly with each other because all reflect mostly g—explaining why Carroll (1993) referred to them as different "flavors" of the same g.

Carroll (1993, p. 641) noted that some of the Stratum II abilities in his model probably coincide with four of H. Gardner's (1983) seven intelligences: linguistic, logical–mathematical, visuospatial, and musical. The remaining three appear to fall mostly outside the cognitive domain: bodily–kinesthetic, intrapersonal, and interpersonal. Carroll (1993, p. 639) also noted that although the Horn–Cattell model (Horn, 1988) claims there are two gs, fluid and crystallized, evidence usually locates both at the Stratum II level or finds fluid g isomorphic with g itself. In like manner, Sternberg's (1997) claim to have found three intelligences also rests, like Horn and Cattell's claim for two gs, on stopping the factoring process just below the most general level (Brody, 2003), thus precluding its discovery.

In short, there are many cognitive abilities, but all turn out to be suffused with or built around g. Their most important feature, overall, is how broadly applicable they are for performing different tasks, ranging from the all-purpose (g) to the narrow and specific (e.g., associative memory, reading decoding, pitch discrimination). The hierarchical structure of mental abilities discovered through factor analysis, represented in Carroll's three-stratum model, has integrated the welter of tested abilities into a theoretically unified whole. This unified system, in turn, allows one to predict the magnitude of correlations among tests and the size of group differences that will be found in new samples.

The g factor is highly correlated with the IQ (usually .8 or more), but the distinction between g (Entry 10 in Figure 1.1) and IQ (Entry 9 in Figure

1.1) cannot be overstated (Jensen, 1998). The IQ is nothing but a test score, albeit one with social portent and, for some purposes, considerable practical value. However, g, is a discovery—a replicable empirical phenomenon, not a definition. It is not yet fully understood, but it can be described and reliably measured. It is not a thing, but a highly regular pattern of individual differences in cognitive functioning across many content domains. Various scientific disciplines are tracing the phenomenon from its origins in nature and nurture (Entries 1 and 2 in Figure 1.1; Plomin et al., 2001) through the brain (Entry 4 in Figure 1.1; Deary, 2000; Jung & Haier, 2007), and into the currents of social life (Entries 6 and 7 in Figure 1.1; Ceci, 1996a; Gottfredson, 1997a; Herrnstein & Murray, 1994; Lubinski, 2004; Williams, 2000). It exists independently of all definitions and any particular kind of measurement.

The g factor has been found to correlate with a wide range of biological and social phenomena outside the realm of cognitive testing (Deary, 2000; Jensen, 1998; Jensen & Sinha, 1993), so it is not a statistical chimera. Its nature is not constructed or corralled by how one chooses to define it but is inferred from its patterns of influence, which wax and wane under different circumstances and from its co-occurrence with certain attributes (e.g., reasoning) but not others (e.g., sociability). It is reasonable to refer to g as general intelligence because the g factor captures empirically the general proficiency at learning, reasoning, problem solving, and abstract thinking—the construct—that researchers and laypersons alike usually associate with the term *intelligence* (Snyderman & Rothman, 1987, 1988). Because the word *intelligence* is used in so many ways and comes with so much political baggage, researchers usually prefer to stick with the more precise empirical referent, g.

Discovery of the g factor has revolutionized research on both intelligence (the construct) and intelligence testing (the measure) by allowing researchers to separate the two—the phenomenon being measured, g, from the devices used to measure it. Its discovery shows that the underlying phenomenon that IQ tests measure (Entry 10 in Figure 1.1) has nothing to do with the manifest content or format of the test (Entry 8 in Figure 1.1): It is not restricted to paper-and-pencil tests, timed tests, ones with numbers or words, or academic content, or any particular format. The active ingredient in intelligence tests is something deeper and less obvious—namely, the cognitive complexity of the various tasks to be performed (Gottfredson, 1997b). The same is true for tests of adult functional literacy—it is complexity and not content or readability per se that accounts for differences in item difficulty (Kirsch & Mosenthal, 1990).

This separation of phenomenon from measure also affords the possibility of examining how well different tests and tasks measure g or, stated another way, how heavily each draws on or taxes g (how g loaded each is). To illustrate, the WAIS Vocabulary subtest is far more g loaded than the Digit Span subtest (.83 vs. .57; Sattler, 2001, p. 389). The more g loaded a test or task, the greater the edge in performance it gives individuals of higher g. Just as individuals can be characterized by g level, tests and tasks can be characterized by their g loadings and thereby show us which task attributes ratchet up their cognitive complexity (amount of distracting information, number of elements to integrate, inferences required, etc.). Such analyses would allow more criterion-related interpretations of intelligence test scores as well as provide practical guidance for how to reduce unnecessary complexity in school, work, home, and health, especially for lower g individuals. We may find that tasks are more malleable than people, g loadings more manipulable than g level.

All mental tests, not just IQ test batteries, can be examined for how well each measures not just g but something in addition to g. Using hierarchical factor analysis, psychometricians can strip the lower order factors and tests of their g components to reveal what each measures uniquely and independently of all other tests. This helps to isolate the contributions of narrower abilities to overall test performance because they tend to be swamped by g-related variance, which is usually greater than it is for all the other factors combined. Hierarchical factor analysis can also reveal which specialized ability tests are actually functioning mostly as surrogates for IQ tests and to what degree. Most tests intended to measure abilities other than g (verbal ability, spatial perception, mathematical reasoning, and even seemingly noncognitive abilities such as pitch discrimination) actually measure mostly g, not the specialized abilities that their names suggest. This is important because people often wrongly assume that if there are many kinds of tests, each intended to measure a different ability, then there must actually be many independent abilities—like different marbles. This is not true.

All the factor analyses mentioned thus far use *exploratory factor analysis*, which extracts a parsimonious set of factors to explain the commonalities running through tests and causes them to intercorrelate. It posits no constructs but waits to see which dimensions emerge from the process (Entry 10 in Figure 1.1). It is a data reduction technique, which means that it provides fewer factors than tests to organize test results in a simpler, clearer, more elegant manner. The method has been invaluable for pointing to the existence of a general factor, although without guaranteeing one.

Another measurement advance has been to specify theoretical constructs (ability dimensions) before conducting a factor analysis and then determine how well the hypothesized constructs reproduce the observed correlations among tests. This is the task of *confirmatory factor analysis*. It has become the method of choice for ascertaining which constructs a particular IQ test battery taps (Entry 11 in Figure 1.1), that is, its construct validity. Variations of the method provide a new, more exacting means of vetting tests for cultural bias (lack of construct invariance).

The following test-validation fallacy would seem to indicate, however, that nothing important has been learned about intelligence tests since Binet's time to sweep aside a century of construct validation. It ignores the discovery of *g* and promotes outdated ideas to dispute the possibility that IQ tests could possibly measure such a general intelligence.

Test-Validation Fallacy: Contending Definitions Negate Evidence

This fallacy portrays lack of consensus in verbal definitions of intelligence as if this negated evidence for the construct validity of IQ tests. Critics of intelligence testing frequently suggest that IQ tests cannot be presumed to measure intelligence because scholars cannot agree on a verbal definition or description of it. By this reasoning, one could just as easily dispute that gravity, health, or stress can be measured. Scale construction always needs to be guided by some conception of what one intends to measure, but careful definition hardly guarantees that the scale will do so, as noted earlier. Likewise, competing verbal definitions do not negate either the existence of a suspected phenomenon or the possibility of measuring it. What matters most is not unanimity among proposed definitions or descriptions but construct validation or "dialogue with the data" (Bartholomew, 2004, p. 52).

Insisting on a consensus definition is an excuse to ignore what has already been learned, especially about *g*. To wit,

> Intelligence is an elusive concept. While each person has his or her own intuitive methods for gauging the intelligence of others, there is no a prior definition of intelligence that we can use to design a device to measure it. (Singham, 1995, p. 272; see also Appendix A, Example xvii)

Thus Singham (1995) suggested that everyone recognizes the phenomenon but that it will nonetheless defy measurement until we all agree on how to do so—which is never. Expanding on its critique of *The Bell Curve,* the editorial page of the *New York Times* ("The 'Bell Curve' agenda," 1994) stated, "Further, there is wide disagreement about what intelligence consists of and how— or even if—it can be measured in the abstract" (p. A16; see also Appendix A, Example xviii). The editorial had just remarked on the wide agreement among intelligence researchers that mental acuity—the supposedly unmeasurable—is influenced by both genes and environments.

Critics often appeal to the intelligence-is-marbles fallacy to propose new, "broadened conceptions" of intelligence, as if pointing to additional human competencies nullified the demonstrated construct validity of IQ tests for measuring a highly general mental ability, or *g*. Some such calls for expanding test batteries to capture more "aspects" or "components" of intelligence, more broadly defined, make their case by confusing the construct validity of a test (does it measure a general intelligence?) with its utility for predicting some social or educational outcome (how well does it predict job performance?). Much else besides *g* matters, of course, in predicting success in training, on the job, and any other life arena, which is why personnel selection professionals (e.g., Campbell & Knapp, 2001) routinely advise that selection batteries include a variety of cognitive and noncognitive measures (e.g., conscientiousness). General intelligence is hardly the only useful human talent, nor need everything good be labeled intelligence to be taken seriously.

Yet critics implicitly insist that it be so when they cite the limited predictive validity of *g*-loaded tests to argue for "broadened conceptions of intelligence" before we can take tests seriously. One such critic, Rosenblum (1996), said this change would "enable us to assess previously unmeasured aspects of intelligence" (p. 622) as if, absent the relabeling, those other aspects of human competence are not or cannot be measured. He then chided researchers who, in "sharp contrast . . . stress validities of the traditional intelligence tests" (that is, stress what *g*-loaded tests do moderately well) and for "oppos[ing] public policies or laws" that would thwart their use in selection when tests do not provide, in essence, the be-all-and-end-all in prediction (see also the imperfect-prediction fallacy later in this chapter).

CAUSAL NETWORKS

Entries 1 through 7 in Figure 1.1 represent the core concepts required in any explanation of the causes of intelligence differences in a population (*vertical* processes, Entries 1–5 in Figure 1.1; Jensen, 1998) and the effects they produce on it collectively and its members individually (*horizontal* processes, Entries 5–7 in Figure 1.1). This schema is obviously a highly simplified rendition of the empirical literature (e.g., by omitting feedback processes and other personal traits that influence life outcomes), but its simplicity helps to illustrate how fundamental are the confusions perpetuated by the following three causal network fallacies.

Causal-Network Fallacies

Causal-Network Fallacy 1: Phenotype *Equals* Genotype

This fallacy portrays phenotypic differences in intelligence (Entry 5, Figure 1.1) as if they were necessarily genotypic (Entry 1, Figure 1.1). Intelligence tests measure only observed or *phenotypic* differences in intelligence. In this regard, IQ tests are like the pediatrician's scale for measuring height and weight (phenotypes). They allow physicians to chart a child's development, but such scales, by themselves, reveal nothing about why some children have grown larger than others. Differences in intelligence can likewise be real without necessarily being genetically caused, in whole or part. Only genetically informative research designs can trace the roles of nature and nurture in making some children larger or smarter than others. Such designs might include identical twins reared apart (same genes, different environments), adopted children reared together (different genes, same environment), and other combinations of genetic and environmental similarity in order to determine whether similarity in outcomes within the pairs follows similarity of their genes more closely than it does their similarity in environments. Nonexperimental studies including only one child per family tell us nothing about the genetic or nongenetic roots of human variation.

The default assumption in all the social sciences, including intelligence testing research, is therefore that one is speaking only of phenotypes when describing developed differences among individuals and groups—unless one explicitly states otherwise. The phenotype–genotype distinction, which often goes without saying in scholarly circles, is not obvious to the public, however. Indeed, the average person may perceive the distinction as mere hairsplitting, because scientific research and common intuition both point to various human differences being heavily influenced by one's fate in the genetic lottery. In fact, it is now well established that individual differences in adult height and IQ—within the particular races, places, and eras studied so far—can be traced mostly to those individuals' differences in genetic inheritance (Plomin et al., 2001).

News of genetic causation of phenotypic variation in these peoples, places, and times primes the public to accept the fallacy that all reports of real differences are ipso facto claims for genetic ones. The *phenotype-equals-genotype* fallacy thus exposes scholars to false allegations that they are actually asserting genetic differences whenever they fail to repudiate them pointedly. For example, critics often insinuate that scientists who report racial gaps in measured intelligence (Entry 5 in Figure 1.1) are thereby asserting "innate" (genetic) differences (Entry 1 in Figure 1.1) between the races.

Duster (1995; see also Appendix A, Example xix) provided a fairly subtle example. In the context of discussing "those making the claims about the genetic component of an array of behavior and conditions (crime, mental illness, alcoholism, gender relations, intelligence)," he referred to "a sociologist, Robert Gordon (1987), who argues that race differences in delinquency are best explained by IQ differences between the races" (Duster, 1995, p. 1). Gordon's article, however, discussed only phenotypes, specifically, whether socioeconomic status or IQ is the better predictor of Black–White differences in crime and delinquency.

Some scholars have tried to preempt such false attributions by taking pains to point out that they are not claiming genetic causation for the phenotypic differences they observe, race related or not. Testing companies routinely evade the attribution by going further (Camara & Schmidt, 1999, p. 13). They align themselves with strictly nongenetic explanations by routinely blaming lower tested abilities and achievements on social disadvantages such as poverty and poor schooling, even when facts say otherwise for the population in question—for example, despite the evidence, for Whites in general, that shared family effects on the IQ and achievement of siblings mostly fade away by adolescence and that there are sizeable genetic correlations among IQ, education, and social class in adulthood (Plomin & Petrill, 1997; Rowe, 1997; Rowe et al., 1998).

The *phenotype-equals-genotype* fallacy is reinforced by the confusion, noted earlier, between two empirical questions: (a) Do IQ differences represent real differences in ability, or, instead, do IQ tests mismeasure intelligence? For example, are they biased against certain races? (b) If the measured differences are real differences in intelligence, what causes them? For example, does poverty depress intelligence? The first question concerns a test's construct validity for measuring real differences; the second question concerns the role of nature and nurture in creating them. Even highly rigorous scholars can be read as confusing the two questions:

> A test is biased if it gives an advantage to one group rather than the other. In other words, we cannot be sure whether the score difference is due to ability to do the test or to environmental factors which affect the groups differently" (Bartholomew, 2004, pp. 122–123; see also Appendix A, Example xx)

This fallacy was also greatly reinforced by public commentary following publication of *The Bell Curve*. Although the book analyzed strictly phenotypic data, both its friends and detractors used its results on the relative predictive power of IQ versus social class to debate the relative contributions to social inequality of genes versus environments. They did this when they used IQ differences as a stand-in for genetic differences and social class as a stand-in for nongenetic influences. For example, one economist argued that Herrnstein and Murray "grossly underestimate the relative effect of environment versus intelligence in accounting for individual differences in various dimensions of achievement" (Loury, 1995, p. 19).

Causal-Network Fallacy 2: Biological *Equals* Genetic

This fallacy portrays biological differences (such as brain phenotypes, Entry 4 in Figure 1.1) as if they were necessarily genetic (Entry 1 in Figure 1.1). This is a corollary of the *phenotype-equals-genotype* fallacy, because an organism's observed form and physiology are part of its total phenotype. Like height and weight, many aspects of brain structure and physiology (Entry 4 in Figure 1.1) are under considerable genetic control (Entry 1 in Figure 1.1), but nongenetic differences, say, in nutrition or disease (Entry 2 in Figure 1.1) can also produce variation in these physical traits. When authors use the terms *biological* and *genetic* interchangeably (Bartholomew, 2004; see also Appendix A, Example xxi), they confuse phenotype with genotype.

Research in behavior genetics does, in fact, confirm a large genetic contribution to phenotypic differences in IQ, brain biology, and correlations between the two (Deary, 2000; Jensen, 1998). The genetic correlations between IQ and various brain attributes suggest potential mechanisms by which genes could influence speed and accuracy of cognitive processing, yielding a higher intelligence. However, they do not rule out nongenetic effects. Instead, they tilt plausibility toward certain nongenetic mechanisms (micronutrients, etc.) and away from others (teacher expectations, etc.).

So far, however, this growing network of psychometric and biological evidence exists only for Whites. Extant evidence confirms mean racial differences in phenotypic intelligence and a few brain attributes, such as head size, but since the 1970s no scientific discipline has been willing to conduct genetic or brain research on non-White populations that could be tied to intelligence. The evidence for genetic influence on differences within the White population enhances the plausibility of a part-genetic-component rather than a no-genetic-component explanation for the average White–Black difference in phenotypic intelligence. Scholars legitimately differ in how skewed the evidence must be before they provisionally accept one hypothesis over another or declare a scientific contest settled. Nonetheless, until scientists are willing to conduct the requisite research, it remains fallacious to suggest that average racial differences in intelligence and brain physiology are necessarily owing to genetic differences between the races.

When scientists seem to overstate the evidence for a "controversial" conclusion, or are falsely depicted as doing so, their seeming overstatement is used to damage the credibility not only of that conclusion but also of all similar-sounding ones, no matter how well validated scientifically the latter may be and even when they have nothing to do with race—for example, the conclusion that IQ differences among Whites are substantially heritable.

The *biological*-equals-*genetic* corollary will become more common as knowledge of the physiological correlates of intelligence spreads. Protagonists in the nature–nurture debate have long conceptualized environmental influences as educational and cultural: Favorable social environments deliver more bits of skill and knowledge or they enhance the mind's learning and reasoning software. Judging by my own students' reactions, all mental behaviors that do not have any immediately obvious cultural origin (e.g., choice reaction time) tend to be perceived as necessarily genetic, as is everything physiological (e.g., brain metabolism). Treating the terms *biological* and *genetic* as synonyms reflects an implicit hypothesis, plausible but unproved. This implicit hypothesis may explain the strident efforts to deny any link between brain size and intelligence (e.g., Gould, 1981), as well as the just plain silly ones (Race and Intelligence, 2007; see also, Appendix A, Example xxii)—for example, that we should have "serious doubts" about such research because Albert Einstein "had a brain slightly below average for his size" (Race and Intelligence, 2007).

Causal-Network Fallacy 3: Environmental *Equals* Nongenetic

This fallacy portrays environments (Entry 3 in Figure 1.1) as if they were necessarily nongenetic (Entry 2 in Figure 1.1)—that is, unaffected by and unrelated to the genotypes of individuals in them. It is the environmentalist counterpart to the hereditarian *biological*-equals-*genetic* fallacy. Environments are physically external to individuals, but, contrary to common belief, this does not make them independent of genes. Individuals differ widely in interests and abilities, partly for genetic reasons; individuals select, create, and reshape their personal environments according to their interests and abilities; therefore, as behavior genetic research has confirmed, differences in personal circumstances (e.g., degree of social support, income) are likewise somewhat genetically shaped (Entry 1 in Figure 1.1). Both childhood and adult environments (Entries 3 and 6 in Figure 1.1) are therefore influenced by the genetic proclivities of self and genetic kin. People's personal environments are their extended phenotypes (Dawkins, 1999).

Near-universal deference in the social sciences to the *environmental*-equals-*nongenetic* fallacy has fostered mostly causally uninterpretable research (on socialization theory, see Scarr, 1997; on family effects theory and passive learning theory, see Rowe, 1997). It has also freed testing critics to misrepresent the phenotypic correlations between social status and test performance as prima facie evidence that poorer environments, per se, cause lower intelligence. In falsely portraying external environments as strictly nongenetic, critics inappropriately commandeer all IQ–environment correlations as evidence for pervasive and powerful nongenetic causation.

Describing strictly phenotypic studies in this vein, *The Chronicle of Higher Education* (Monastersky, 2008) reported that "the new results from neuroscience indicate that experience, especially being raised in poverty, has a strong effect on the way the brain works" (¶ 1; see also Appendix A, Example xxiii). The article quoted one of the researchers as saying, "It's not a case of bad genes." It is likely, however, that the study participants who lived in better circumstances performed better because they had genetically brighter parents. Brighter parents tend to have better jobs and incomes and also to bequeath their offspring more favorable genes for intelligence. Parental genes can also enhance offspring performance more directly if they induce parents to create more cognitively effective child-rearing environments. In none of the studies had the investigators ruled out such genetic contributions to the child's rearing "environment." Adherence to the *environmental*-equals-*nongenetic* fallacy remains the rule, not the exception, in social science research.

Fischer et al. (1996) illustrated this fallacy when they argued that scores on the military's AFQT reflect differences not in intellectual ability but in the environments to which individuals have been exposed: "Another way to understand what we have shown is that test takers' AFQT scores are good summaries of a host of prior experiences (mostly instruction) that enable someone to do well in adult life" (Fischer et al., 1996, p. 68; see also Appendix A, Example xxiv).

Helms (2006) used the *environmental*-equals-*nongenetic* fallacy to argue a different point. Whereas Fischer et al. (1996) used it to claim that *g*-loaded tests measure exposure to knowledge that we ought to impart equally to all, Helms used it to argue that the Black–White IQ gap reflects culturally caused differences in performance that have nothing to do with intellectual competence. In particular, racial differences in test scores must be presumed, "unless research proves otherwise, to represent construct irrelevant variance," that is, "systematic variance, attributable to the test taker's psychological characteristics, developed in response to socialization practices or environmental conditions" (p. 847). To make this claim, Helms must treat individuals as passive receivers of whatever influence happens by.

When combined, the three causal network fallacies can produce more convoluted ones. As noted earlier, protagonists in *The Bell Curve* debate often conjoined the phenotype-is-genotype fallacy with the *environmental-equals-nongenetic* fallacy when they used strictly phenotypic data to debate whether genes or environments create more social inequality.

POLITICS OF TEST USE

The previous sections on the measurement and correlates of cognitive ability have been directed to answering one question: What do intelligence tests measure? That is a scientific question with an empirical answer. However, the question of whether a cognitive test should be used to gather information for decision-making purposes is an administrative or political choice.

Standards-of-Evidence Fallacies

The decision to administer a test for operational purposes should rest on good science—principally, evidence that the test is valid for one's intended purpose. For example, does the proposed licensing exam accurately screen out practitioners who would endanger their clients, or would an IQ test battery help diagnose why failing students are failing? Validity is not sufficient reason for testing, however. The utility of tests in applied settings depends on practical considerations as well, including feasibility and cost of administration, difficulties in maintaining test security and operational validity, vulnerability to litigation or misuse, and acceptability to test takers (Murphy & Davidshofer, 2005). Valid tests may not be worth using if they add little to existing procedures, and they can be rendered unusable by high costs, chronic legal challenge, adverse publicity, and unintended consequences.

When used for operational purposes, testing is an intervention. Whether it be the aim of testing or just its consequence, test scores (Entry 9 in Figure 1.1) can influence the tested individuals' life chances (Entry 6 in Figure 1.1). This is why good practice dictates that test scores (or any other single indicator) be supplemented by other sorts of information when making decisions about individuals, especially decisions that are irreversible and have serious consequences. Large-scale testing for organizational purposes can also have societal-level consequences (Entry 7 in Figure 1.1). For example, although personnel selection tests can improve workforce productivity, their use changes who has access to the best jobs.

Nor is the choice not to test a neutral act. If testing would provide additional valid, relevant, cost-effective information for the operational purpose at hand, then opting not to test constitutes a political decision to not consider certain sorts of information and the decisions they would encourage. Like other social practices, testing—or not testing—tends to serve some social interests and goals over others. This is why testing comes under legal and political scrutiny and why all sides seek to rally public opinion to their side to influence test use. Therefore, just as testing can produce a chain of social effects (Entry 9 → Entry 6 → Entry 7 in Figure 1.1), public reactions to those effects can feed back to influence how tests are structured and used, if at all (Entry 7 → Entry 8 → Entry 9 in Figure 1.1).

The measurement and causal-network fallacies described earlier are rhetorical devices that discourage test use by seeming to discredit scientifically the validity of intelligence tests. They fracture logic to make the true seem false and the false seem true in order to denigrate one or more of the three facts on which the democratic dilemma rests—the phenotypic reality, limited malleability, and practical importance of g. However, they otherwise observe the rules of science: Ideas must compete, and evidence matters.

The following standards-of-evidence fallacies violate these rules in the guise of honoring them. They accomplish this by invoking criteria for assessing the practical utility of tests as if they were criteria for assessing the scientific validity of the information they provide. This then allows critics to ignore the rule for adjudicating competing scientific claims—the preponderance of evidence, or which claim best accounts for the totality of relevant evidence to date. In this manner, critics can shelter favored ideas from open scientific contest while demanding that tests and test results meet impossibly rigorous scientific standards before their use can be condoned.

Scientific double standards are commonly triggered, for example, by insinuating that certain scientific conclusions pose special risks to the body politic. In other words, the standards-of-evidence fallacies invoke a criterion for test utility (alleged social risk) to justify their demand that particular tests or ideas be presumed scientifically inferior to—less valid than—all competitors until they meet insurmountable quality standards. Social risks must be weighed, of course, but for what they are—as elements in a political decision—and not as indicators of technical quality.

Standards-of-Evidence Fallacy 1: The Imperfect Measurement Pretext

This fallacy maintains that valid, unbiased intelligence tests should not be used for making decisions about individuals until the tests are made error free. It labels highly *g*-loaded tests as flawed because they are not error free (reliability <1.0, or predictive validity <1.0). Nothing in human affairs is without error, of course, but the implication is that such tests allow socially unacceptable errors, even when they reduce error overall. The implied flaw is usually that tests rule out some candidates who would actually have performed well if hired or admitted (*false negatives*). Concern usually focuses on minority false negatives, in particular, even though valid tests tend to reduce such decision errors. The insinuation, however, is that valid, unbiased tests are biased, which allows opponents to call for suspending their use until they are cleansed of such "flaws."

FairTest (2007) argued just that: "[ACT] test scores should be optional in college admissions" because "ACT scores are imprecise" and the "ACT's flaws have serious consequences" (¶¶ 12, 14, 17; see also Appendix A, Example xxv). In like manner, an article in *The Chronicle of Higher Education* (Miller, 2001) reported that "educational researchers have begun describing testing's dark side": "Standardized tests, they say, are too limited, too imprecise, and too easily misunderstood to form the basis of crucial decisions about students. . . . [A] reliability of .9 ain't all it's cracked up to be" (p. A14; see also Appendix A, Example xxvi). Such critics express no concern over the precision or reliability of testing's alternatives, such as holistic admissions, which also have serious consequences but rest on subjective judgments framed as "individualized reviews" or assessments of the "whole person." As described by Jaschik (2007) in the journal *Inside Higher Ed*,

> In holistic admissions, colleges evaluating applicants replace grids of grades and test scores with more individualized reviews of would-be students. The practice is most commonly associated with liberal arts colleges or with public universities at which affirmative action has been banned. (¶ 1)

Although the imperfection pretext is most often used to justify eliminating valid tests, it is sometimes offered as a seemingly scientific rationale to increase a test's measurement error for the purpose of social leveling. For example, imperfect reliability of measurement is the rationale given for test score *banding*, which groups broad swaths of unequally qualified job applicants together as equally qualified (Cascio, Outtz, Zedeck, & Goldstein, 1991). Its purpose is to reduce disparate impact, and it does so by throwing away valid information, thereby reducing a test's reliability and validity. In like manner, the National Research Council of the National Academy of Sciences cited imperfect predictive validity to justify its 1989 recommendation that valid, unbiased employment tests be race normed (Hartigan & Wigdor, 1989; see also Appendix A, Example xxvii). Race norming reduces disparate impact by introducing systematic error designed to favor lower scoring races and disfavor higher scoring ones.

The demand for technical improvement is clearly pretextual. Testing is hardly the only useful source of information about students and employees, but few are as reliable, construct valid, and predictive in education and employment settings as are *g*-loaded tests. Using a *g*-loaded test generally results in fewer false negatives (and fewer false positives) than not using one because the alternatives to testing tend to be less valid. Increasing a *g*-loaded test's validity would reduce the rate of false negatives (and false positives) in all groups, to be sure, but would thereby more accurately distinguish between less and more able individuals. As noted earlier, increasing the accuracy of a *g*-loaded test generally increases, not decreases, its disparate impact. This is why the fallacy demands perfect measurement—superior measurement is precisely what must be avoided.

This is not to say that all kinds of error are equal in affecting test utility, as illustrated by the trade-offs in medical diagnostics between *test specificity* (proportion of true negatives detected; e.g., true absence of HIV) and *test sensitivity* (proportion of true positives detected; e.g., actual presence of HIV). Balancing different kinds of error is a political, monetary, or ethical decision, however, not a technical one. The imperfection fallacy provides a pretext for imposing a political choice among social goods in the guise of insisting on greater scientific accuracy.

Standards-of-Evidence Fallacy 2: The Dangerous-Thoughts Trigger

This fallacy maintains that scientific conclusions purported to be divisive or dangerous should not be entertained until proved beyond all possible doubt. It sets as selective and insurmountable an evidentiary standard for unwelcome scientific conclusions as does the imperfection standard for *g*-loaded tests. Under this fallacy, opponents insinuate that an idea is fraught with danger to press their case for one-sided scientific rigor. The putative danger is rarely explained but connoted by allusions to physical harm (dangerous sports, risky human experimentation, genocide, etc.). Labeling a well-validated scientific conclusion dangerous allows any fear, any manufactured doubt, to trump the preponderance of the evidence for it, no matter how lopsided the evidence may be. The implicit premise seems to be that unsettling truths do no good and comforting lies no harm.

The dangerous-thoughts standard has appeared in various forms over the years. When rules governing research with human subjects were first formulated in the 1970s, there was an effort to bar research posing questions or suggesting answers that might offend minority groups. Many journal editors and manuscript reviewers act on the same impulse, and occasionally an editor will reject a submission explicitly on the grounds that "divisive" research should not be published unless it meets the most exacting technical standards. In the guise of heightened scientific rigor, the dangerous-thoughts fallacy shelters comforting ideas from competition. It is applied most aggressively today to stifle reportage and discussion of racial gaps on intelligence tests, especially their possible genetic component (Gottfredson, 2007).

In rejecting a manuscript testing the hypothesis that Black–White IQ differences represent differences in *g*, the editor of *American Psychologist* (C. Kiesler, 1980, personal communication to A. R. Jensen, January 17, 1980; see Appendix A, Example xxviii) explained to the author that because "this area is so controversial and important to our society, I should not accept any manuscript that is less than absolutely impeccable." Given the "hanging implication" of a genetic difference, one has to "assure one's self [*sic*] that other possibilities are not possible or plausible." More than 2 decades later, Hunt and Carlson (2007) used the same rationale for recommending special treatment of research on group differences: "We do not see any need for [Jensen's] potentially divisive 'default hypothesis' . . . in the absence of convincing evidence that rules out other hypotheses" (p. 210; see also Appendix A, Example xxix). In both cases, the author was expected to prove his hypothesis beyond all conceivable doubt before it would be allowed even to compete in the scientific arena. Simply insinuating harm is usually sufficient to trigger impossible scientific standards.

Authors are sometimes asked to pull the dangerous-thoughts trigger on themselves, ostensibly in the name of scientific balance. For example, when I recently submitted a manuscript analyzing the systematic public misrepresentation of current intelligence research, one reviewer asked that I also discuss the "sordid history of intelligence testing." Acceding to such requests does not enhance scientific balance but selectively burdens the research at hand by morally tainting it through guilt by association. The reviewer offered no examples, perhaps assuming them to be obvious.

Critics usually draw on two kinds of examples: either accusations that leading intelligence researchers have been scientifically dishonest or that their science has abetted mass oppression or murder. However, none of these lurid accusations have withstood scrutiny. In fact, my reading of the historical accounts (e.g., Anderson, 1997; Carroll, 1995; Lohman, 1997; Snyderman & Herrnstein, 1983; White, 2000; Wigdor & Green, 1991, chap. 1) and the archives of psychology (e.g., Terman, 1928, and other articles in the same volume) is that much of the field's supposedly sordid history has been, and continues to be, manufactured by the field's detractors. For instance, the claim that Cyril Burt committed scientific fraud now seems fraudulent itself (Fletcher, 1991; Joynson, 1989; Rushton, 2002; Samelson, 1992), and the only ideologically motivated mismeasurements of human skulls that Gould (1981, 1996) demonstrated were his own (Michael, 1988; Rushton, 1997; Samelson, 1982).

The reviewer mentioned earlier eventually suggested that I discuss eugenics as one example. Because eugenics has been associated in the public mind with genocide, I was, in essence, being asked to reinforce a falsehood that would morally taint my own scientific analysis. The falsehood is that claiming there is scientific evidence for genetic differences in valued human traits encourages mean-spiritedness and inhumane public policy, whereas environmentalism promotes justice and compassion. This notion has gained false credibility (hence the request) partly because critics deploy historical examples selectively to taint as immoral the scientific evidence that they would override. For instance, they fail to acknowledge that environmentalist ideologies, not just hereditarian ones, have been used to justify genocide: Stalin's Communist Union of Soviet Socialist Republics and Pol Pot's Communist Cambodia, not just Hitler's Fascist Germany, perpetrated unspeakable atrocities to reshape their citizenries.

Standards-of-Evidence Fallacy 3: Happy-Thoughts Leniency

This fallacy maintains that mere theoretical possibility elevates the scientific credibility of a politically popular idea above that of an empirically plausible but unpopular conclusion. It is the obverse of the dangerous-thoughts fallacy: If some scientific conclusions must not be entertained until proved beyond all possible doubt, then their competitors may be accepted if they simply offer hypothetical situations that seem to contradict the evidence they would have us ignore. In the dangerous-thoughts examples, we saw arguments that genetic differences between races may not be entertained until conclusively proved, no matter the preponderance of evidence. Diamond (1999) illustrated happy-thoughts leniency by beginning with the "seemingly compelling" evidence that Australian Aborigines are observed to have lower intelligence than White immigrants to the continent because they have less favorable genes (p. 19; see also Appendix A, Example xxx). He then invoked the dangerous-thoughts fallacy to dismiss that evidence when he stated, "The objection to such racist explanations is not just that they are loathsome, but also that they are wrong" (p. 19). Finally, he introduced the happy alternative to which he invited us to ascribe greater credibility: "In fact . . . modern 'Stone Age' peoples are on the average probably more intelligent, not less intelligent, than industrialized peoples" (p. 19).

The most famous example of hypothesizing an implausible alternative reality is Lewontin's (1976) thought experiment about growing two handfuls of seed corn, one under excellent conditions and the other being deprived of essential nutrients. He used his thought experiment to argue that because it is possible experimentally to induce a 100% heritability for height differences within both groups but a 0% heritability for resulting height differences between them, we must dismiss the high within-race heritabilities of IQ as having no bearing on questions of racial differences or the malleability of intelligence. By Lewontin's reasoning, what is theoretically possible but empirically implausible for humans—namely, no genetic differences among races and no constraints on the malleability of intelligence—ought to be considered the most plausible scientific stance, until proved otherwise. In explaining why we can ignore the failures of compensatory education, Lewontin argued, "It is empirically wrong to argue that, if the richest environmental experience we can conceive does not raise IQ substantially, that we have exhausted the environmental possibilities " (p. 91).

Lewontin's (1976) happy possibility is commonly invoked for the same purposes. Consider an editorial in the *New York Times* ("The 'Bell Curve' Agenda," 1994) that sought to discredit *The Bell Curve*'s conclusion that intelligence has limited malleability:

> An example proves the point. Plants grown together under ideal conditions will achieve different heights based solely on individual genetic makeup. But lock half the plants in a dark closet and the difference in average height of the two groups will be due entirely to environment. (p. A16; see also Appendix A, Example xxxi)

Unlike Lewontin's hypothetical plants, humans are not randomly assigned to environments but to some extent select and shape their personal circumstances. His thought experiment thus works partly by inviting us to commit the *environmental*-equals-*nongenetic* fallacy.

The happy-thoughts fallacy also works by appealing to a false presumption rarely questioned—namely, that genetic influences limit human freedom and equality, whereas environmental influences do not. In my undergraduate courses on intelligence, I assign a paper in which I ask students to imagine changing any single fact about intelligence they wish. The charge is to describe what their new world will look like. Many choose to make intelligence differences entirely environmental. Yet instead of discovering their expected utopia, many find the opposite. In their new world, there is no genetically conditioned resilience to poor environments and no rising out of poverty, there is more assortative mating by wealth, and there are even laws holding parents accountable for children's "failure to learn." The students realize that genetic differences between parents and children guarantee some social mobility, but environmental causation does not. So just as supposedly dangerous thoughts about intelligence seem less fearsome when looked in the eye, so, too, do happy thoughts look less appealing.

Experts themselves sometimes seem to accept the three standards-of-evidence fallacies. They seem at once seduced by the appeal to scientific rigor and intimidated by the presumption that their ideas do social harm. Instead of rejecting the double standards, they seem defensive about not meeting them. In not questioning or probing the premise that democratic citizenries must be protected from certain ideas, they acquiesce to it.

CONCLUSION

All human groups exhibit large, enduring variations in intelligence that they must somehow accommodate for collective benefit. Mechanisms for accommodation evolve, as they must, when small populations grow and formerly distinct ones mix and jostle. The fallacies about intelligence testing all work to deny the need for accommodation by focusing hostility on the testing enterprise, as if it were responsible for human inequality. This explains why its critics prefer to focus on intelligence testing's technical flaws, even though it has fewer than the alternatives they favor. This also explains why critics often respond to mounting scientific support for its construct validity, predictive value, and lack of bias with yet more strident critiques of the tests, test results, and persons giving them credence.

The 13 fallacies I have described seem to hold special power in the public media, academic journals, college textbooks, and the professions. I have also observed them frequently in conversations with journalists, college students, practitioners, and scholars in diverse fields. My aim in dissecting them has been to show how they work to persuade. Fallacies are tricks of illogic to protect the false from refutation. This is why they are more persuasive and more corrosive than outright falsehoods. Experts usually sense that fallacious arguments are specious but do not engage them for precisely that reason. Researchers would rather parse the evidence, not faulty reasoning about it. However, illogic does not yield to their showings of empirical evidence. Sophistry is best dealt with by recognizing it for what it is: arguments whose power to persuade resides in their logical flaws.

What can be done? First, fallacies must be anticipated. Not only is everyone susceptible to them, but antitesting fallacies are avidly pressed on the public. As teachers know, students do not come to academic subjects as blank slates but often with basic misconceptions that create barriers to learning unless the teacher takes them into account. When the topic is intelligence testing, we must assume that one or more of the foregoing fallacies will impede understanding unless neutralized.

Second, fallacies must be confronted to be neutralized. Their impact can be greatly reduced if everyone contributes to the effort. Small preventive acts by many people can add up to a big difference. Preventive actions include taking care not to repeat or acquiesce unthinkingly to fallacious claims, communicating in a manner that clarifies oft-conflated distinctions, openly questioning the false premises and illogic of common fallacies and objecting to their persistent use, and calling major perpetrators to account.

Antitesting fallacies are rhetorical gambits that serve political ends. They hobble good science, impede the proper use of tests, and distort understandings of human diversity. They probably also interfere with democratic peoples negotiating more constructive accommodations of their differences.

REFERENCES

American Educational Research Association, American Psychological Association, & National Council on Measurement in Education. (1999). *Standards for educational and psychological testing*. Washington, DC: American Educational Research Association.

Anderson, L. W. (Ed.). (1997). Educational testing and assessment: Lessons from the past, directions for the future [Special issue]. *International Journal of Educational Research, 27*, 357–399.

Andrews, L. B., & Nelkin, D. (1996, January 5). *The Bell Curve:* A statement [Letter to the editor]. *Science, 271*, 13–14.

Bartholomew, D. J. (2004). *Measuring intelligence: Facts and fallacies*. Cambridge, England: Cambridge University Press.

The "Bell Curve" agenda. (1994, October 24). *New York Times*, p. A16.

Binet, A., & Simon, T. (1916). *The development of intelligence in children* (E. S. Kit, Trans.). Baltimore: Williams & Wilkins.

Blakemore, B. (Executive Producer). (1994, November 22). The American agenda [Television news broadcast]. On *World news tonight with Peter Jennings* (Transcript #4232). New York: ABC News.

Blits, J. H., & Gottfredson, L. S. (1990a, Winter). Employment testing and job performance. *The Public Interest, 98*, 18–25.

Blits, J. H., & Gottfredson, L. S. (1990b). Equality or lasting inequality? *Society, 27*(3), 4–11.

Brody, N. (1992). *Intelligence* (2nd ed.). San Diego, CA: Academic Press.

Brody, N. (1996). Intelligence and public policy. *Psychology, Public Policy, and Law, 2*, 473–485.

Brody, N. (2003). Construct validation of the Sternberg Triarchic Abilities Test (STAT): Comment and reanalysis. *Intelligence, 31*, 319–329.

Camara, W. J., & Schmidt, A. E. (1999). *Group differences in standardized testing and social stratification*. New York: College Examination Board.

Campbell, J. P., & Knapp, D. J. (Eds.). (2001). *Exploring the limits of personnel selection and classification*. Mahwah, NJ: Erlbaum.

Carroll, J. B. (1993). *Human cognitive abilities: A survey of factor-analytic studies*. New York: Cambridge University Press.

Carroll, J. B. (1995). Reflections on Stephen Jay Gould's The Mismeasure of Man (1981): A retrospective review. *Intelligence, 21*, 121–134.

Carroll, J. B. (1997). Psychometrics, intelligence, and public perception. *Intelligence, 24*, 25–52.

Cascio, W. F., Outtz, J., Zedeck, S., & Goldstein, I. L. (1991). Statistical implications of six methods of test score use in personnel selection. *Human Performance, 4*, 233–264.

Ceci, S. J. (1996a). General intelligence and life success: An introduction to the special theme. *Psychology, Public Policy, and Law, 2*, 403–417.

Ceci, S. J. (Ed.). (1996b). Special theme: IQ in society. *Psychology, Public Policy, and Law, 2*, 403–645.

Ceci, S. J., & Papierno, P. B. (2005). The rhetoric and reality of gap closing—when the "have-nots" gain but the "haves" gain even more. *American Psychologist, 60*, 149–160.

Colangelo, N., & Davis, G. A. (Eds.). (2003). *Handbook of gifted education* (3rd ed.). Boston: Allyn & Bacon.

Dawkins, R. (1999). *The extended phenotype: The long reach of the gene*. Oxford, England: Oxford University Press.

Deary, I. J. (2000). *Looking down on human intelligence: From psychometrics to the brain*. Oxford, England: Oxford University Press.

Deary, I. J., Whiteman, M. C., Starr, J. M., Whalley, L. J., & Fox, H. C. (2004). The impact of childhood intelligence on later life: Following up the Scottish Mental Surveys of 1932 and 1947. *Journal of Personality and Social Psychology, 86*, 130–147.

Detterman, D. K. (Ed.). (1994). *Current topics in human intelligence: Vol. 4. Theories of intelligence*. Norwood, NJ: Ablex.

Diamond, J. (1999). *Guns, germs, and steel: The fate of human societies*. New York: Norton.

Dionne, E. J., Jr. (1994, October 18). "Race and IQ: Stale notions." *Washington Post*, p. A7.

Duster, T. (1995). What's new in the IQ debate. *The Black Scholar, 25*(1), 25–31.

FairTest (2007, August 20). *The ACT: Biased, inaccurate, and misused* [FairTest University testing fact sheet]. Retrieved March 17, 2008, from http://www.fairtest.org/act-biased-inaccurate-and-misused

Fischer, C. S., Hout, M., Jankowski, M. S., Lucas, S. R., Swidler, A., & Voss, K. (1996). *Inequality by design: Cracking the bell curve myth*. Princeton, NJ: Princeton University Press.

Flanagan, D. P., Genshaft, J. L., & Harrison, P. L. (Eds.). (1997). *Contemporary intellectual assessment: Theories, tests, and issues*. New York: Guilford Press.

Fletcher, R. (1991). *Science, ideology and the media: The Cyril Burt scandal*. New Brunswick, NJ: Transaction Press.

Flynn, J. R. (2007). *What is intelligence?: Beyond the Flynn effect*. New York: Cambridge University Press.

Frisby, C. L. (Ed.). (1999). Straight talk about cognitive assessment and diversity [Special issue]. *School Psychology Quarterly, 14*(3).

Frisby, C. L., & Reynolds, C. R. (Eds.). (2005). *Comprehensive handbook of multicultural school psychology*. New York: Wiley.

Gardner, H. (1983). *Frames of mind: The theory of multiple intelligences*. New York: Basic Books.

Gardner, J. W. (1984). *Excellence: Can we be equal and excellent too?* (rev. ed.). New York: Norton.

Gordon, R. A. (1987). SES vs. IQ in the Race-IQ Delinquency Model. *International Journal of Sociology and Social Policy, 7*, 30–96.

Gottfredson, L. S. (Ed.). (1986). The *g* factor in employment [Special issue]. *Journal of Vocational Behavior, 29*(3).

Gottfredson, L. S. (1994). The science and politics of race-norming. *American Psychologist, 49*, 955–963

Gottfredson, L. S. (1996). Racially gerrymandering the content of police tests to satisfy the U.S. Justice Department: A case study. *Psychology, Public Policy, and Law, 2*, 418–446.

Gottfredson, L. S. (Ed.). (1997a). Intelligence and social policy [Special issue]. *Intelligence, 24*(1).

Gottfredson, L. S. (1997b). Mainstream science on intelligence: An editorial with 52 signatories, history, and bibliography. *Intelligence, 24*, 13–23.

Gottfredson, L. S. (2004). Intelligence: Is it the epidemiologists' elusive "fundamental cause" of social class inequalities in health? *Journal of Personality and Social Psychology, 86*, 174–199.

Gottfredson, L. S. (2007). Applying double standards to "divisive" ideas: Commentary on Hunt and Carlson (2007). *Perspectives on Psychological Science, 2*, 216–220.

Gould, S. J. (1981). *The mismeasure of man.* New York: Norton.

Gould, S. J. (1996). *The mismeasure of man* (Rev. ed.) New York: Norton.

Hart, M. H. (2007). *Understanding human history: An analysis including the effects of geography and differential evolution.* Augusta, GA: Washington Summit Publishers.

Hartigan, J. A., & Wigdor, A. K. (Eds.). (1989). *Fairness in employment testing: Validity generalization, minority issues, and the General Aptitude Test Battery.* Washington, DC: National Academy Press.

Hayden, E. C. (2007, October 17). So similar, yet so different. *Nature*, 762–763.

Helms, J. E. (2006). Fairness is not validity or cultural bias in racial-group assessment: A quantitative perspective. *American Psychologist, 61*, 845–859.

Herrnstein, R. J., & Murray, C. (1994). *The bell curve: Intelligence and class structure in American life.* New York: Free Press.

Holt, J. (1994, October 19). Anti-social science? *New York Times*, p. A23.

Horn, J. L. (1988). Thinking about human abilities. In J. R. Nesselroade & R. B. Cattell (Eds.), *Handbook of multivariate experimental psychology* (2nd ed., pp. 645–685). New York: Plenum Press.

Howe, M. J. A. (1997). *IQ in question: The truth about intelligence.* London: Sage.

Hunt, E. (1996). When should we shoot the messenger? Issues involving cognitive testing, public policy, and the law. *Psychology, Public Policy, and Law, 2*, 486–505.

Hunt, E., & Carlson, J. (2007). Considerations relating to the study of group differences in intelligence. *Perspectives on Psychological Science, 2*, 194–213.

Jaschik, S. (2007, March 2). Making holistic admissions work. *Inside Higher Ed.* Retrieved March 2, 2008, from http://www.insidehighered.com/news/2007/03/02/holistic

Jencks, C., & Phillips, M. (Eds.). (1998). *The Black–White test score gap.* Washington, DC: Brookings Institution Press.

Jensen, A. R. (1980). *Bias in mental testing.* New York: Free Press.

Jensen, A. R. (1981). *Straight talk about mental testing*. New York: Free Press.

Jensen, A. R. (1985). The nature of the Black–White difference on various psycho-metric tests: Spearman's hypothesis. *Behavioral and Brain Sciences, 8*(2), 193–263.

Jensen, A. R. (1998). *The g factor: The science of mental ability*. Westport, CT: Praeger.

Jensen, A. R. (2006). *Clocking the mind: Mental chronometry and individual differences*. New York: Elsevier.

Jensen, A. R., & Sinha, S. N. (1993). Physical correlates of human intelligence. In P. A. Vernon (Ed.), *Biological approaches to the study of human intelligence* (pp. 139–242). Norwood, NJ: Ablex.

Joynson, R. B. (1989). *The Burt affair*. London: Routledge.

Jung, R. E., & Haier R. J. (2007). The parieto-frontal integration theory (P-FIT) of intelligence: Converging neuroimaging evidence. *Behavior and Brain Sciences, 30*, 135–187.

Kirsch, I. S., & Mosenthal, P. B. (1990). Exploring document literacy: Variables underlying the performance of young adults. *Reading Research Quarterly, 25*, 5–30.

Lewontin, R. C. (1976). Race and intelligence. In N. J. Block & G. Dworkin (Eds.), *The IQ controversy* (pp. 78–92). New York: Pantheon Books.

Lohman, D. F. (1997). Lessons from the history of intelligence testing. *International Journal of Educational Research, 27*, 359–377.

Loury, L. D. (1995, August). An exchange. IQ, race, and heredity: Charles Murray and his critics. *Commentary*, 18–19.

Lubinski, D. (Ed.). (2004). Introduction to the special section on cognitive abilities: 100 years after Spearman's (1904) "General Intelligence, Objectively Determined and Measured." *Journal of Personality and Social Psychology, 86*, 96–111.

Mainstream science on intelligence. (1994, December 13). *Wall Street Journal*, p. A18.

Marks, J. (1995). *Human biodiversity: Genes, race, and history*. New York: Aldine de Gruyter.

Michael, J. S. (1988). A new look at Morton's craniological research. *Current Anthropology, 29*, 349–354.

Miller, D. W. (2001, March 2). Scholars say high-stakes tests deserve a failing grade. Studies suggest students an educator are judged by faulty yardsticks. *The Chronicle of Higher Education*, p. A14.

Monastersky, R. (2008, February 18). Researchers gain understanding of how poverty alters the brain. *The Chronicle of Higher Education*. Available at http://chronicle.com/daily/2008/02/1705n.htm

Murphy, K. R., & Davidshofer, C. O. (2005). *Psychological testing: Principles and applications* (6th ed.). Upper Saddle River, NJ: Pearson Prentice Hall.

Neisser, U. (Ed.). (1998). *The rising curve: Long-term gains in IQ and related measures*. Washington, DC: American Psychological Association.

Neisser, U., Boodoo, G., Bouchard, T. J., Jr., Boykin, A. W., Brody, N., Ceci, S. J., et al. (1996). Intelligence: Knowns and unknowns. *American Psychologist, 51*, 77–101.

Park, M. A. (2002). *Biological anthropology* (3rd ed.). Boston: McGraw-Hill.

Plomin, R., DeFries, J. C., McClearn, G. E., & McGuffin, P. (2001). *Behavioral genetics* (4th ed.). New York: Worth.

Plomin, R., & McClearn, G. E. (Eds.). (1993). *Nature, nurture, and psychology.* Washington, DC: American Psychological Association.

Plomin, R., & Petrill, S. A. (1997). Genetics and intelligence: What's new? *Intelligence, 24*, 53–77.

Race and intelligence: Politicizing the findings [Interview by F. Chideya with Bill Tucker, author of *The intelligence controversy*]. (2007, October 23). *News & Notes* [Radio program]. Audio retrieved June 27, 2008, from http://www.npr.org/templates/story/story.php?storyId=15560405

Rosenblum, V. G. (1996). On law's responsiveness to social scientists' findings: An intelligible nexus? *Psychology, Public Policy, and Law, 2*, 620–634.

Rowe, D. C. (1997). A place at the policy table? Behavior genetics and estimates of family environmental effects on IQ. *Intelligence, 24*, 53–77.

Rowe, D. C., Vesterdal, W. J., & Rodgers, J. L. (1998). Herrnstein's syllogism: Genetic and shared environmental influences on IQ, education, and income. *Intelligence, 26*, 405–423.

Rushton, J. P. (1997). Race, intelligence, and the brain: The errors and omissions of the "revised" edition of S. J. Gould's *The Mismeasure of Man* (1996) [Book review]. *Personality and Individual Differences, 23*, 169–180.

Rushton, J. P. (2002). New evidence on Sir Cyril Burt: His 1964 speech to the Association of Educational Psychologists. *Intelligence, 30*, 555–567.

Sackett, P. R., Schmitt, N., Ellingson, J. E., & Kabin, M. B. (2001). High-stakes testing in employment, credentialing, and higher education: Prospects in a post-affirmative-action world. *American Psychologist, 56*, 302–318.

Samelson, F. (1982, February 5). Intelligence and some of its testers [Review of the book *The mismeasure of man*]. *Science, 215*, 656–657.

Samelson, F. (1992). Rescuing the reputation of Sir Cyril [Burt] [Review of the books *The Burt affair* and *Science, ideology, and the media: The Cyril Burt scandal*]. *Journal of the History of the Behavioral Sciences, 28*, 221–233.

Sarich, V., & Miele, F. (2004). *Race: The reality of human differences.* Boulder, CO: Westview.

Sattler, J. M. (2001). *Assessment of children: Cognitive applications* (4th ed.) San Diego, CA: Sattler.

Scarr, S. (1997). Behavior-genetic and socialization theories of intelligence: Truce and reconciliation. In R. J. Sternberg & E. L. Grigorenko (Eds.), *Intelligence, heredity, and environment* (pp. 3–41). Cambridge, England: Cambridge University Press.

Schmidt, F. L., & Hunter, J. E. (1998). The validity and utility of selection methods in personnel psychology: Practical and theoretical implication of 85 years of research findings. *Psychological Bulletin, 124,* 262–274.

Schmitt, N., Rogers, W., Chan, D., Sheppard, L., & Jennings, D. (1997). Adverse impact and predictive efficiency of various predictor combinations. *Journal of Applied Psychology, 82,* 719–730.

Singham, M. (1995). Race and intelligence: What are the issues? *Phi Delta Kappan,* December, 271–278.

Smith, W. J., & Lusthaus, C. (1995). The nexus of equality and quality in education: A framework for debate. *Canadian Journal of Education, 20,* 378–391.

Snyderman, M., & Herrnstein, R. J. (1983). Intelligence tests and the immigration act of 1924. *American Psychologist, 38,* 986–995.

Snyderman, M., & Rothman, S. (1987). Survey of expert opinion on intelligence and aptitude testing. *American Psychologist, 42,* 137–144.

Snyderman, M., & Rothman, S. (1988). *The IQ controversy: The media and public policy.* New Brunswick, NJ: Transaction.

Society of Industrial and Organizational Psychology. (2003). *Principles for the validation and use of personnel selection procedures* (4th ed.). Bowling Green, OH: Author.

Spearman, C. (1927). *The abilities of man: Their nature and measurement.* New York: McMillan.

Sternberg, R. J. (1997). *Successful intelligence: How practical and creative intelligence determine success in life.* New York: Plume.

Sternberg, R. J., & Grigorenko, E. L. (Eds.). (2001). *Environmental effects on cognitive abilities.* Mahwah, NJ: Erlbaum.

Sternberg, R. L., & Grigorenko, E. L. (Eds.). (2002). *The general intelligence factor: How general is it?* Mahwah, NJ: Erlbaum.

Sternberg, R. J., Wagner, R. K., Williams, W. M., & Horvath, J. A. (1995). Testing common sense. *American Psychologist, 50,* 912–927.

Terman, L. M. (1928). The influence of nature and nurture upon intelligence scores: An evaluation of the evidence in Part 1 of the 1928 Yearbook of the National Society for the Study of Education. *Journal of Educational Psychology, 19,* 362–373.

Vernon, P. A. (Ed.). (1993). *Biological approaches to the study of human intelligence.* Norwood, NJ: Ablex.

Wagner, R. K., & Sternberg, R. J. (1985). Practical intelligence in real-world pursuits: The role of tacit knowledge. *Journal of Personality and Social Psychology, 49,* 436–458.

Wechsler, D. (1997). *Wechsler Adult Intelligence Scale—Third edition (WAIS–III) and Wechsler Memory Scale—Third edition (WMS–III) technical manual.* San Antonio, TX: Psychological Corporation.

Wechsler, D. (2002). *Wechsler Preschool and Primary Scale of Intelligence—Third edition (WPPSI–III) technical and interpretive manual.* San Antonio, TX: Psychological Corporation.

Wechsler, D. (2003). *Wechsler Intelligence Scale for Children—Fourth edition (WISC–IV) technical and interpretive manual*. San Antonio, TX: Psychological Corporation.

White, S. H. (2000). Conceptual foundations of IQ testing. *Psychology, Public Policy, and Law, 6*, 33–43.

The White House. (2001). *Foreword by President George W. Bush* [No Child Left Behind Act of 2001]. Retrieved June 27, 2008, from http://www.whitehouse.gov/news/reports/no-child-left-behind.html

Wigdor, A. K., & Garner, W. R. (Eds.). (1982). *Ability testing: Uses, consequences, and controversies: Part I. Report of the committee. Part II. Documentation section.* Washington, DC: National Academy Press.

Wigdor, A. K., & Green, B. F. (Eds.). (1991). *Performance assessment for the workplace* (Vol. 1). Washington, DC: National Academy Press.

Williams, W. M. (1996). Consequences of how we define and assess intelligence. *Psychology, Public Policy, and Law, 2*, 506–535.

Williams, W. M. (Ed.). (2000). Special themes: Ranking ourselves: Perspectives on intelligence testing, affirmative action, and educational policy. *Psychology, Public Policy, and Law, 6*, 1–252.

Yerkes, R. M. (Ed.). (1921). *Psychological examining in the United States Army.* Washington, DC: National Academy of Sciences.

2

PSYCHOLOGICAL DIAGNOSTIC TESTING: ADDRESSING CHALLENGES IN CLINICAL APPLICATIONS OF TESTING

JANET F. CARLSON AND KURT F. GEISINGER

Psychologists have long been recognized as experts in developing, standardizing, and validating tests on which a variety of assessments rest. Individual achievement, ability, knowledge, personality, skills, and intelligence are only some of the dimensions that psychologists have worked to operationalize and measure reliably and accurately. Indeed, "psychological assessment has been a defining practice of professional psychology since the field's inception" (Camara, Nathan, & Puente, 2000, p. 141).

Although *tests* and *assessments* are not the same thing, a substantial portion of assessment activities depend on the use and interpretation of results obtained from individual tests. Assessment refers to the integration of information collected from a large number of sources, some of which likely include formal test data (American Educational Research Association, American Psychological Association, & National Council on Measurement in Education [AERA, APA, & NCME], 1999). Tests often provide information that is essential to a comprehensive assessment. Good tests, used properly, demonstrate that they are dependable and valid, a claim that cannot be made by less rigorously developed assessment processes, such as some observational and interview techniques.

Discussion within this chapter is limited to psychological diagnostic (or clinical) testing. For our purposes, we view this form of testing as comprising a major component of assessment processes that are applied within clinical contexts. Most of the contexts we consider involve treatment-based practices, such as mental health establishments and forensic facilities. For the most part, tests used in these settings would not be regarded as high stakes, although there may be exceptions on a case-by-case basis. Numerous assessment practices in educational contexts, with their attendant myths and fallacies, are addressed in the following chapters. Tests commonly associated with educational classification and eligibility determinations, such as placement tests or those used primarily to determine educational needs (e.g., to determine eligibility to receive special educational services) are not part of the discussion that follows. Our discussion centers on tests that are best described as clinical, personality, or psychodiagnostic in nature. Although we have not intentionally addressed either high-stakes educational testing or intelligence testing, some of the points we make may have relevance in educational and clinical neuropsychological arenas as well. Correspondingly, some points enumerated in the final chapter concerning large-scale cognitive diagnostic testing may resonate with portions of our discussion.

The kinds of measures we have envisioned while articulating our points are those that are administered as part of an assessment battery, given to an individual. The goals of such an assessment are to specify a diagnostic category or impression of some kind that will be used to formulate a treatment or intervention aimed at helping the test taker achieve a more satisfying level of functioning. Because prognosis is routinely considered a part of diagnostic efforts, prediction is important to our discussion. Of course, predictions often are influenced by many factors besides diagnoses. For example, the number of months a soon-to-be-discharged patient remains in the community may be affected directly by funding cuts to social programs, regardless of his or her diagnostic test results and regardless of his or her diagnosis at the time of discharge.

On an individual basis, psychological diagnostic testing involves a customized process in which several psychological measures are administered to individuals who are considered by themselves or by others to be in need of assistance or treatment for mental health issues. Measures may include a variety of techniques that produce useful and informative data—everything from interviews to objective tests that use optically scanned formats. As noted by Regier et al. (1998), "No assessment of clinical status is independent of the reliability and validity of the methods used to determine the presence of a diagnosis—be it by an unstructured clinical interview, a structured clinical assessment, or a highly structured instrument" (p. 114). To ensure that conclusions suggested by the data are the result of a multivariate assessment paradigm, test users are obligated to use multiple data sources, which often include a clinical interview together with a number of tests selected on the basis of the test taker's presenting problems, characteristics, and needs (Garb, 2005; Yates & Taub, 2003). Unfortunately, although standards for testing require multivariate assessment (i.e., a "test battery"), "there is no empirical measure of the validity of a battery of tests . . . [in fact,] there is no uniform definition of the validity of a battery of tests" (Cates, 1999, p. 636).

Until recently, clinicians largely felt free to choose whichever tests they believed would serve their assessment purposes. Many practitioners who received training on specific measures during their graduate educations tended to use these same measures with their patients or clients (Cates, 1999). As a result, test batteries often were static, and some may have included tests that had little to do with a particular diagnostic quandary. Alternatively, some test batteries may have failed to include tests that would have been of considerable assistance in reaching a differential diagnosis. Evidence has accumulated since about the mid-1990s to indicate that assessment batteries have become less a force of habit. Today clinicians are exhorted to base test selection on the reason for the assessment and are more likely to use tests that address specific referral questions (Cates, 1999; Fong, 1995; Griffith, 1997; Meyer et al., 2001; Yates & Taub, 2003). This positive shift appears to be attributable in part to the constraints of managed care and third-party payers who require sound justifications for expenses submitted for reimbursement or prior approval.

Immediate goals of psychological diagnostic testing may include one or more of the following:

- to address more fully or accurately individuals' mental health needs,
- to improve treatment effectiveness,
- to guide interventions,
- to track treatment progress,
- to satisfy insurance requirements, and
- to satisfy managed care restrictions.

We believe that test results may be used effectively to achieve these aims. Psychodiagnostic tests can be used to promote accurate conceptualizations (diagnoses) of individuals who may be experiencing emotional discomfort or mental disturbance, whose ability to manage important aspects of living has deteriorated, whose ability to function in social or occupational spheres is impaired, or who may be demonstrating abnormal or bizarre behaviors or behaviors that are deeply disturbing or disruptive to others. Furthermore, we believe that psychological diagnostic testing may be used to help illuminate appropriate interventions for such individuals.

HISTORY OF CONTROVERSIAL ISSUES

Controversies surrounding clinical assessment have been around for many decades. One of the earliest, most influential, and well-reasoned set of observations was made by Meehl in 1954. Meehl's seminal work compared the accuracy of clinical and statistical approaches to prediction that together with other works in a similar vein (Ben-Porath, 1997; Grove & Meehl, 1996; Meehl, 1986) have cast doubt on the value of clinical judgment and expertise, particularly in light of equal or superior outcomes that could be produced using mechanical or actuarial approaches. Meehl, however, claimed that he did not intend to bring about the demise of clinical practitioners. In the preface to his reprinted work (Meehl, 1954/1996) and elsewhere (Meehl, 1986), he expressed what appears to be surprise and, perhaps, frustration with the various interpretations and simplifications of his original treatise, in which he went to considerable effort to present balanced evidence of merit on both "sides" of the argument. Meehl (1954/1996) stated that he "developed a certain Buddhist detachment" (p. xi) about the debate and seemed to take umbrage at suggestions that he was "grinding one axe or another" (p. x). Since the genesis of the clinical versus statistical debate, many writers—including Meehl (1986, 1954/1996)—have urged psychologists to abandon what developed into something of a red herring, but many elements of the debate linger and continue to manifest in various forms (Grove, Zald, Lebow, Snitz, & Nelson, 2000; Holt, 1986; Kleinmuntz, 1990; Meehl, 1986; Westen & Weinberger, 2004).

Intentional or not, the challenge posed by Meehl's early assertions helped to create an atmosphere that fostered closer scrutiny of clinical training, especially concerning diagnostic and assessment practices and judgments emanating from them (e.g., Cates, 1999; Garb, 1989). Nearly 40 years after the publication of Meehl's original work, Masling (1992, p. 53) observed that

> the ability to use psychological assessment methods is a unique and valuable skill in clinical psychology. Beyond that there is considerable controversy. It is something psychologists are uniquely qualified to do, but what it is intended to do and how well we do it remain unspecified.

Assessments involve integration of information from many sources: clinical interviews, behavioral observations, clinical histories, and, of course, psychological tests. Most clinicians depend on tests as an integral component of their assessment practices, although much evidence has accrued that substantiates a marked decline in test usage beginning near the latter part of the 20th century (Ben-Porath, 1997; Eisman et al., 2000; Meyer et al., 2001) and a corresponding decline in training in testing and assessment within graduate programs (Aiken, West, Sechrest, & Reno, 1990; Hayes, Nelson, & Jarrett, 1987). In response to a recent survey concerning test usage (Camara et al., 2000), clinical psychologists reported that they most frequently tested for personality or diagnostic reasons (i.e., determination of presence or type of psychopathology). These findings are consistent with an earlier survey, cited by Camara et al. (2000), indicating that psychologists "primarily used assessments for diagnostic purposes, and 53% also used testing as an indicator of what type of therapy would be most effective" (O'Roark & Exner, 1989, as quoted in Camara et al., 2000, p. 142).

Few tests of personality or psychopathology rise to the level of being truly diagnostic instruments, such that a particular test result can be used to pinpoint a specific Axis I or Axis II disorder within the taxonomy of the *Diagnostic and Statistical Manual of Mental Disorders* (*DSM*; American Psychiatric Association, 2000). Rather, many measures serve primarily as screening measures for particular symptoms or groups of symptoms that comprise essential features of certain mental disorders. Measures do not exist for all psychological diagnoses, of course, nor for every symptom or symptom cluster that may be indicative of the presence of particular disorders. It is unlikely that additional tests will be developed to such an extent that all—or nearly all—diagnoses are addressed, given the extensiveness of the current and recent *DSM* nosology. In addition, numerous codes and qualifiers exist within the *DSM* to indicate an unclear or incomplete symptom picture. For example, disorders may be designated as "atypical," "NOS" (not otherwise specified), or "unspecified mental disorder." When available information is not sufficient to render a differential diagnosis, the notation "diagnosis deferred" is made. Alternatively, the notation of "provisional diagnosis" is made when the clinician expects the individual will meet the specified criteria but does not do so currently, either because a full symptom picture cannot be provided by the client or because the duration of one or more symptoms falls short of that required by *DSM* criteria (and, with time, that requirement is expected to be met). Obviously, measures of any kind will be of little or no help in codifying these poorly differentiated, atypical cases. Likewise, conditions that may be the focus of treatment but that are not considered mental disorders (e.g., various relational problems, problems related to abuse or neglect) are coded as "V-codes" per *DSM* procedures. Such situations are not now, nor will they likely ever be, amenable to psychodiagnostic testing per se.

Measures used to screen for or identify particular *DSM* disorders often comprise items that closely mirror *DSM* criteria. Content validity of such tests generally rests on the extent to which the test scores and resultant interpretations align with essential diagnostic features. For example, the Beck Depression Inventory—II (BDI–II; Beck, Steer, & Brown, 1996), a screening measure for depressive symptomatology, represents a modification of an earlier version of this instrument. In the latter version, test directions and item content were revamped specifically to make them more consistent with diagnostic elements of the *DSM*.

It follows from the foregoing discussion that as diagnostic criteria undergo revisions, measures that had been developed to reflect those criteria may not perform at the same level. By extension, truly diagnostic tests become less valid for diagnostic use as a function of revisions to diagnostic criteria. Changes in diagnostic criteria may lead to dramatic differences in reported prevalence rates (Regier et al., 1998) that have little to do with genuine epidemiological changes. Nevertheless, differential rates of diagnosis may lead to more or less research funding for particular disorders and assessment. Also, public attention may follow apparent upsurges in the incidence of particular psychological disorders. The legitimacy of classification systems has been questioned many times and has stirred up much controversy over the years. These issues call into question the value and probity of diagnoses as well as the precise definitions of mental illness and mental health. Although these issues are beyond the scope of this chapter, they comprise the backdrop against which the discussion occurs and also create ongoing pressure for revisions to the current taxonomy of mental disorders. Psychological diagnostic tests will need to keep apace with revisions prompted by this discourse.

The remainder of this chapter addresses specific myths and fallacies associated with psychological diagnostic testing, disregarding as much as possible the controversies surrounding clinical diagnosis. When controversies have relevance to a particular point of discussion, we draw on the controversy to enrich and frame our position rather than try to resolve long-standing debates, many of which have no actual answers. We have imagined that the controversies, myths, and fallacies described could be proffered by a variety of individuals or groups, at least some of whom may use tests or may be considering using them.

CURRENT CONTROVERSIES, MYTHS, AND FALLACIES

Several challenges have emerged since the 1990s concerning clinical assessment and psychodiagnostic testing. A number of these issues can be traced to the expanding influence of managed mental health care and third-party payers. These ubiquitous enterprises operate from a business framework, with emphasis placed on cost containment, cost–benefit analyses, and accountability. Clearly, third-party reimbursement and the stipulations of managed care affect the use of psychological tests for the purpose of clarifying, rendering, or differentiating clinical diagnoses. It is understandable that third parties are disinclined to pay for services solely on the basis of treating psychologists' requests. Clinicians must propose and justify to payers interventions that follow logically from the particulars of the case under treatment. Insurers have treated requests by practitioners for reimbursement of services involved in the administration of diagnostic tests in the same way as more traditional therapeutic interventions. As far as practitioners are (or should be) concerned, a number of researchers have demonstrated the therapeutic value of clinical tests and have encouraged the use of such tests as interventions in and of themselves (Ben-Porath, 1997; Finn & Tonsager, 1997; Hayes et al., 1987).

Substantial evidence supports the treatment utility of assessments, making the "notable decrease in the clinical use of psychological testing" (Finn & Martin, 1997, p. 374) observed by several authors (e.g., Camara et al., 2000; Finn & Martin, 1997; Griffith, 1997; Kubiszyn et al., 2000) perplexing and difficult to explain. Some writers have suggested that the lack of effective public relations within the helping professions is partly to blame; for example, Finn and Martin (1997) suggested that a "confusing message [has been sent] to non-psychologists about the value of psychological assessment" (p. 374).

Among the fallacious beliefs and misconceptions about psychological diagnostic tests are the ideas that (a) tests are too costly to justify their use, (b) tests are not valid, (c) tests cannot be used effectively in multicultural contexts, (d) test content is peculiar and irrelevant, and (e) tests are easily manipulated by respondents who wish to engineer a particular outcome. Each of these myths is addressed in the following discussion.

Psychodiagnostic Tests Are Too Expensive

Costs of psychodiagnostic testing can be substantial for several reasons, many related to test development issues. Test development is a costly endeavor, especially if one adheres faithfully to existing standards. Many reputable test publishers do attend carefully to these standards, and it is not surprising that costs associated with doing so are largely passed along to the consumer, as with other products on the market. The standards for testing (AERA, APA, & NCME, 1999) establish policies to guide the development of tests in ways that ensure their relevance, dependability of scores, and validity of their use for specific purposes.

A well-developed test depends on input from numerous experts, such as content or measurement specialists, some who write items for possible inclusion on the test under development and others who review items for potential bias and the extent to which the content domain has been sampled adequately. After a pool of items has been developed, item tryouts are conducted, and some items are culled because of their poor empirical performance. Other items are revised or edited in some way. For norm-referenced tests, the next step involves obtaining a group of individuals on whom test norms are developed. This group must be similar to the group for whom the test is intended for use. Often this involves a national (or international) sample, with demographic characteristics that correspond with appropriate U.S. Census Bureau data. Tests that are well grounded psychometrically achieve this status by amassing evidence that supports their reliability and validity. Most often, this evidence derives from empirical studies that examine features such as test–retest and interscorer reliability, internal consistency estimates, and construct and other forms of validity, such as the test's ability to classify correctly a recognized clinical group. For instance, the BDI–II, described earlier, would be evaluated for its ability to correctly differentiate depressed from nondepressed individuals. Many psychodiagnostic measures contain subscales that represent components of the larger construct. For example, as a measure of personality, the Minnesota Multiphasic Personality Inventory—2 (MMPI–2; Butcher, Dahlstrom, Graham, Tellegen, & Kaemmer, 1989) consists of 10 basic clinical scales that represent specific personality aspects, each of which may be developed to greater or lesser extents within a particular individual. The structure of such scales is verified using sophisticated factor-analytic techniques.

The foregoing description is offered to provide an overview of the processes involved in the development of measures, such as those developed for psychodiagnostic purposes. It represents a thumbnail sketch of the major steps that a relatively straightforward diagnostic test would undergo as it is being shaped into a psychometrically sound and marketable measure of personality or some aspect of personality. Essentially, we agree that well-developed tests are expensive, but we do not necessarily believe that the costs are excessive in light of all that goes into their development, not to mention the prospective value of information gleaned from the test results. Ultimately, the use of such measures may reduce costs because they quickly and efficiently gather information, thereby expediting treatment that is targeted appropriately for the problem.

Some readers may believe that clinicians decide to "run some tests" more as a way to pad their bills than to obtain essential information about a client with whom they are working. Not only would such behavior constitute a serious abrogation of ethical principles of practice (American Psychological Association, 2002), it would also be fiscally unsound as well. Results from a survey conducted by Camara et al. (2000) indicate that experienced clinical psychologists take more than 3.5 hours to administer, score, and interpret a full psychological battery. Assessment services are not always reimbursable by insurance. When these services are reimbursed, survey respondents indicated that reimbursement limits of less than 2 hours are most typical, leaving an average of 1.5 hours of assessment services not reimbursed for each individual for whom a full assessment battery is completed.

During the late 1980s and early 1990s, computer-based test administration, scoring, interpretation, and report-generation software burgeoned and prompted some writers to opine that more clinicians would avail themselves of these options to counteract diminishing insurance reimbursements. However, data from Camara et al. (2000) reveal that most clinicians continue to administer, score, and interpret tests themselves. Few respondents reported turning over administration or scoring responsibilities to someone with less training, despite some earlier concerns that this practice would become commonplace. Similarly, few reported that they invoked computer-based interpretation or report-generation programs.

At least in terms of time needed to conduct a comprehensive assessment versus time compensated, the balance does not favor those who administer tests. The decline in the use of tests may be related to a fiscal reality concerning a less than favorable ratio of time spent to hours reimbursed (e.g., Camara et al., 2000; Garb, 2003). Griffith (1997) examined this issue by interviewing several of the major third-party payers with regard to their practices and offered guidance for ways in which psychologists should justify interventions, including assessment activities. She stressed the need to speak the language of the payers by relating costs to benefits. In a similar vein, other authors have noted that it is essential to emphasize the effectiveness of assessment and to present the rationale in objective, financial terms that demonstrate the utility of assessments in improving treatment (Yates & Taub, 2003).

It is important to recognize that asking questions of an individual test taker represents a form of data collection for which a number of standardized instruments exist. Data from structured, semistructured, or unstructured interviews are frequently part of the assessment process. Many questions are posed directly to the individual being assessed, and his or her responses comprise an important component of many assessment batteries. Some may question the value of tests, above and beyond information that could be gleaned as easily by direct inquiry of the test taker. This question also revolves around the issue of validity, but not in the same vein as has been discussed thus far. Those who challenge the "value added" by data derived from a standardized test do not necessarily challenge whether the test achieves its intended purpose. Rather, they take issue with whether there is a large enough gain to be made beyond what is readily available from sources other than tests, especially in light of cost considerations. Arguments of this kind hinge on a cost–benefit analysis and have been used to impugn the incremental validity of tests (Finn & Martin, 1997; Garb, 2003; Hunsley & Meyer, 2003; Yates & Taub, 2003).

Garb (2003) discussed incremental validity with respect to the assessment of psychopathology using a variety of data collection procedures, including interviews, personality inventories, projective techniques, and brief self- and clinician-rated measures. He found that diagnostic efforts were aided by the use of self-report inventories in addition to conducting clinical interviews. Garb noted as well that projective techniques such as the Rorschach were helpful in more circumscribed areas, such as evaluating the presence of a thought disorder. In terms of personality and psychopathology, incremental gains were evident when a variety of assessment information was collected, including information from interview data, personality inventories, projective techniques, and self- and clinician-rated measures. Using a multifaceted assessment approach provides the most complete understanding of the clinical symptom picture. Whether critics choose to be influenced by statistical findings of significance in this regard amounts to an idiosyncratic decision. Although treatment outcomes should be maximally and positively affected by assessments undertaken to establish a favorable cost–benefit ratio, many clinical outcomes are not monetary per se and "cannot be transformed into monetary units" (Yates & Taub, 2003, p. 480). Yates and Taub (2003) urged the inclusion of such nonmonetary factors in considering costs and benefits in stating that "the desired outcomes of many assessments are . . . reliable and valid descriptions of the status of psychological, biological, and social variables that are of potential use in delivering clinical services" (p. 480).

In assessing incremental validity, several authors have argued (or implied) that it is important to bear in mind the real world within which clinicians operate. Specifically, Garb (1989) described some ways in which studies of clinical versus mechanical prediction typically do not mirror clinicians' everyday experiences. In the studies reviewed by Garb, "judges were given a set of protocols and instructed to perform a specific task. In actual clinical practice, however, no one tells clinicians what judgments need to be made or what information they should obtain" (p. 392). In further discussion, the author noted that diagnostic accuracy was substantially higher for experts than for nonexperts when certainty of one's judgment was considered. This finding brings up a realistic issue—diagnostic certainty—that may be reflected in clinical practice to a much greater extent than can be captured in studies such as those reviewed by Garb. In practice, clinicians denote diagnostic uncertainty in several ways. For example, they may indicate that one or more other diagnoses need to be considered and ruled out before the differential diagnosis can be made. Alternatively, they may note that diagnosis is "deferred." Both differential and deferred diagnoses are coded (that is, made part of the clinical record) and remain in force, often pending receipt of additional information that may involve a physical examination, comprehensive medical history, consultation with family to corroborate certain facts, and so forth. Furthermore, clinicians in practice should not render diagnoses until the data are sufficiently clear. In research such as that described by Garb (1989), clinicians offered diagnoses on the basis of test protocols and instructions handed to them and could not seek out information they would need "in real life" to make a diagnosis.

Psychodiagnostic Tests Are Not Valid

The notion of validity of course requires a system of prediction and of understanding those predictions in the context of a model. At least four fallacious criticisms of personality tests emerge under the general theme of validity. The first of these relates primarily to the sheer number of personality measures and theories. The second relates to the match between personality theories and measures. The third relates to a general lack of consensus about the criteria against which to evaluate personality tests and whether personality test data should be combined using clinical or statistical means. A fourth is discussed more fully in the section following this one: the apparent generalizability of personality approaches and tests across languages and cultures. Each of the other three is addressed briefly here.

The plethora of different models of personality and of personality assessment have led to a sense in the profession that when there are so many models, none can be truly valid or representative of the human person. In fact, all have some semblances of truth.

In his classic book on personality measurement, Wiggins (1973) concluded,

> An important but as yet unanswered question concerns the extent to which personality theories may facilitate the prediction of human behavior in applied settings. . . . In order for a personality theory to facilitate prediction, it must be relevant to the particular criterion situation, must be explicit enough to suggest the selection of specific testing instruments, must have definite implications for criterion performance, and must be capable of being evaluated. . . . [A personality test] can be justified only if it can be shown to produce incremental validity and a greater generality of application than does the use of procedures not guided by theoretical considerations. (p. 513)

Wiggins (1973) continued by describing a continuum of approaches to personality assessment and prediction. He identified the analytic approach as the one that places the greatest reliance on the theories of personality that undergird the assessments and their results. At the opposite extreme is the empirical approach, sometimes called *dustbowl empiricism*. This approach places the least weight on a theoretical approach to personality and focuses simply on the identification of different criterion groups or leads to the successful predictions of important criteria. Some criticisms of psychological tests have occurred from either end of the spectrum. Those holding dear the analytic approach find the empirical approaches lacking in explanation or theory; those embracing the empirical model simply seem not to understand the need for theory when their methods appear to work so much better. In an era when construct validity is preeminent, both theory (explanation) and predictions are required (Geisinger, 1992).

Regardless of the model, science requires both predicting and understanding the relationships among variables or constructs. As Wiggins (1973) concluded,

> The decision to rely on explicit theoretical considerations at various stages of the basic prediction paradigm does not commit the assessment psychologist to any particular theoretical model of personality. Nevertheless, despite predilections of any one psychologist for one type of theorizing over others, the personality models that are likely to be of greatest value to him [sic] are those whose principal constructs are most directly translatable into concrete testing procedures. (p. 514)

It is true that there is not a consensus about the criteria against which to evaluate personality tests. There are several reasons for this lack. One is that personality measures have been used in making a wide range of predictions, from psychodiagnosis to hiring firefighters and police officers, from making decisions regarding the nature of one's incarceration to evaluating one's likelihood of succeeding in college. Needless to say, each of these purposes requires a different kind of criterion. Even within single instances of use—say, in helping to decide whether to accept a college applicant (e.g., Sedlacek, 2004; Willingham, 1985)—success can be measured in numerous ways, from the traditional grade-point average, to completion of the college degree, to one's level of participation in nonacademic activities while in college. This fallacy needs to be understood rather as the perception that the tests have been seen as so robust that they have the potential for a wide range of predictions. Indeed, they have been found lacking in some settings. Even valid and appropriate medical tests cannot be used indiscriminately for a wide range of diseases. Using Wiggins's caution cited earlier, however, individuals should only use personality tests when theory suggests that the constructs are influential in leading to success.

Meehl's (1954/1996) work has been cited extensively to indicate that clinicians likely are not able to predict certain outcomes as well as a regression equation when clinicians and computers are provided the same information. An analogy to this finding is that even professional racetrack drivers cannot determine the velocity of a speeding car as well as radar. However, the driver is able to sense danger, whether the car is approaching its maximum performance and limits, and so on. Meehl did not suggest that clinicians should not make such predictions, only that they rely on statistical procedures and evidence whenever possible:

> Nobody disputes that it is possible to improve clinicians' practices by informing them of their track records actuarially. Nobody has ever disputed that the actuary would be well advised to listen to clinicians in setting up the set of variables. (Meehl, 1986, p. 372)

Thus Meehl certainly affirmed the use of personality measures in psychodiagnostic assessment. In fact, he ratified it and saw an important role for assessment psychologists as well. Moreover, he strongly affirmed the importance of clinicians engaging in therapy rather than making rare kinds of predictions (e.g., predictions to a parole board regarding the likelihood of recidivism).

Psychodiagnostic Tests Lack Cultural Generalizability

One myth of personality tests relates to the extent to which the results from such measures are culturally bound. One position holds that all measures are limited culturally to the country or culture in which they were built, validated, and used extensively. Indeed, the translation, or better, adaptation of measures has been a topic of great interest in recent years as evidenced by a conference held at Georgetown University in 1999; a book edited by Hambleton, Spielberger, and Merenda (2005) based primarily on the papers presented at that conference; the biannual conferences of the International Test Commission; and the guidelines that that commission has developed guiding the translation and adaptation of psychological and educational measures (see Coyne, 2001). The term *adaptation* is preferred to *translation* because changing a test from one language, one country, and one culture to another involves more than a linguistic translation of the measure. It typically also involves extensive knowledge of the culture, the characteristics being assessed and how they are manifested in both cultures, and subtleties of their interaction.

The guidelines are organized into several sections, relating to context (2 guidelines), test development and test adaptation (10 guidelines), test administration (6 guidelines), and documentation and test score interpretations (4 guidelines). The guidelines caution users against blindly translating and using tests from one language and culture to another. For instance, one must take into account cultural and semantic differences in the measures. Two test development and adaptation guidelines state, for example, "Test developers/publishers should provide evidence that the language use[d] in the directions, rubrics, and items themselves as well as in the handbook are appropriate for all cultural and language populations for whom the instrument is intended" (Coyne, 2001, ¶ D.2), and "Test developers/publishers should provide statistical evidence of the equivalence of questions for all intended populations" (Coyne, 2001, ¶ D.9). Similarly, a documentation and score interpretation guideline suggests that "when a test is adapted for use in another population, documentation of the changes should be provided, along with evidence of the equivalence" (Coyne, 2001, ¶ I.1). Thus these guidelines suggest that one must provide evidence that scales can be taken from one culture and used in another. Such efforts typically involve the translation of the test but also involve cultural adaptation. For ease of explanation, an example from an intelligence test for children is provided. Imagine an item from such a scale that asks a child to explain a proverb such as, "A stitch in time saves nine." Merely changing the language from the original or source language to a target language would not make the item equivalent to the original, and as part of such a translation, its level of difficulty and underlying meaning would be radically changed. Evidence is needed that the results of testing are equally meaningful in the new language and culture. Such evidence is far more comprehensive than simply validating a test. Rather, one must show that the measure is valid (e.g., in a predictive sense) in the new language and culture and also that the scores are similarly or equivalently meaningful in the new language. In other words, one must show that the validity of the use of the inventory or test in the new culture generalizes to or parallels that of the original culture. More complete descriptions of some of the issues involved in adapting tests across languages and cultures and in interpreting the results of such test use may be found in Geisinger (1994, 1998).

Because of the desire for efficiency among test publishers and researchers, evidence supportive of the use of some measures in different languages and cultures is currently emerging. Butcher, Cabiya, Lucio, and Garrido (2007; see also Butcher, 2004) have provided substantial evidence that the MMPI–2, one of the most frequently used measures in psychological settings in the United States (Camara et al., 2000), has highly similar validity and uses for Americans in the United States who come from Latin cultures. This evidence is based on research with such adaptations among Spanish-speaking clients in both the United States and Latin America. Moreover, such evidence is not limited to a single Spanish translation but to a series of them, often specific to different countries in Latin America. Discussions that psychopathology may be less culture specific than many have believed can be found in Butcher, Coelho Mosch, Tsai, and Nezami (2006) and Good and Kleinman (1985); these researchers reported that psychiatric diagnoses are likely not culture specific but that there may be differing manifestations in symptomatology between cultures.

Although literally hundreds of personality measures have been developed in the past century, personality theorists appear to have come to considerable consensus that a five-factor theory of personality subsumes most theories (e.g., Goldberg, 1990, 1993). The primary proponents of this model, McCrae and Costa (1999), although not contending that the five factors (Extraversion, Agreeableness, Conscientiousness, Neuroticism, and Openness to Experience) are the only aspects of personality, have fostered research to demonstrate that it appears these factors have generalizability across cultures (e.g., McCrae, 2000, 2001; Yang et al., 1999). The emergence of the five-factor theory has driven much research on personality assessment at least since the 1990s, with many measures—even some that were developed using very different conceptualizations of personality—having shown a degree of correspondence with this model.[1]

In summary, it appears that at least some psychological and personal constructs do appear relevant across cultures. Moreover, measures developed in one culture and country can be adapted to other cultures. We know that at least some of these measures are able to be used with success cross-culturally. One does still need, however, to follow the guidelines of the International Test Commission (see Coyne, 2001). In so doing, one must translate into the target language while keeping the measure sensitive to the target culture

---

[1]Some Eastern cultures have found a sixth factor in addition to these five. This sixth factor, which has been found in Chinese adaptations of personality instruments and has been seen in other Asian populations as well, has been identified as Interpersonal Relatedness (Cheung et al., 2001).

associated with that language and carefully document any changes made. Evidence demonstrating the equivalence of the instrument in the new culture is required. For some successful measures, however, it appears highly likely they are able to be used in a good number of cultures. Merely demonstrating that a measure is useful in several cross-cultural settings does not prove that it can be used in all cultures, but it does provide a hypothesis that it may be worth the effort to adapt.

Psychodiagnostic Test Content Is Peculiar and Irrelevant

Most of the discussion so far has focused on tests as likely elements of a larger assessment quandary pertaining to an individual. Evidence collected from standardized testing may be used to corroborate evidence collected from other sources. Attempting to evaluate the relevance of test content by removing the test from the context within which it is normally embedded may distort and underestimate its value. Test results must be integrated to form a coherent diagnostic picture. This point was made artfully by Cates (1999), who stated,

> The accumulation of data is not an assessment. The integration of data and subsequent interpretations comprise the assessment. The alphabetically arranged list of words, "and," "go," "I," "let," "then," "us," and "you" mean little. Arranged as "Let us go then, you and I . . . " they form the introductory line to one of the most famous poems of our century. (p. 638)

An analogous situation for our purposes might be seen if one were to assess treatment progress for an individual with an anxiety disorder purely on the basis of a score on a single measure of anxiety that indicates the presence or absence of anxiety-related symptoms. To understand fully the degree of improvement or decline for a specific patient, one would need to compare current levels of anxiety with both previous levels and other outcome measures, such as symptom duration and the extent to which symptoms interfere with other aspects of the client's life, such as the ability to reenter the workforce and maintain employment. However, because psychometric procedures are not available for multiple tests taken together, the psychometric soundness of individual tests continues to be evaluated on a test-by-test basis (and for specific populations and subpopulations) rather than as one component of the larger assessment process. Thus, in the anxiety example, it is highly likely that treatment progress will be gauged solely in terms of the presence or absence of anxiety-related symptoms, such as may be measured by a single inventory. The *Standards for Educational and Psychological Testing* (AERA, APA, & NCME, 1999) require a multivariate approach to assessment, but it is the individual tests that must each pass muster rather than the group of measures that actually might be used in a given assessment battery.

A related problem may occur when a test taker (or parents of a test taker, in the case of school-aged children) single out an item or subtest and question its inclusion. Frequently, such individuals inquire about the relevance of particular items or subtests for the characteristic being assessed. In essence, queries that arise in this way challenge a test's face validity but do so in a somewhat unorthodox—and possibly biased—way. It is likely that the questions recalled in these instances are the ones that stand out in the individual's recollection, because they were perceived to be unusual or unexpected in light of the test taker's understanding of the test's purpose. Typically, test takers do not recall and question items that appear to belong on the test—that is, are *face valid*. Face validity offers weak support for a measure, so much so that it is probably inappropriate to discuss it as a psychometric property. Face validity may do little to enhance the technical features of a given test, although higher levels of face validity may promote greater effort on the part of test takers if their belief in the test motivates them or makes them try harder. A substantial concern arises when items are viewed in isolation from the test itself. The functioning of individual items is important during test development, but the value of individual items is greatly diminished after the entire test has been built and validated. A comparable situation could occur when a physician records a person's height and that patient questions the relevance of his or her height as far as the determination of health status. Of course, when height is considered together with weight (and age and sex), a more complete assessment is achieved, which can serve as an important determinant of physical health status that also may affect estimates of risk for developing various medical conditions. A published test is not intended to be used in fragmented bits and pieces, and findings obtained from any sort of nonstandardized administration cannot rightly be considered accurate (Geisinger & Carlson, 2002). Test takers who question the content of tests should be advised of the reality that the entire test forms the basis for conclusions about his or her personality or psychological state of being.

Specialized scales developed for or from published tests (such as the myriad supplemental scales of the MMPI that assess for dominance, addiction potential, hostility, social responsibility, marital distress, and many other aspects of personality) are another matter entirely. Often these scales were developed in applied clinical settings, with the intention that they would have direct clinical relevance for patients and clients in those or highly similar settings. Many of these scales have undergone rigorous test development and psychometric scrutiny comparable to the originally published test. For example, Keane, Malloy, and Fairbank (1984) developed the Posttraumatic-Stress Disorder (PK) scale to assess for the presence of posttraumatic stress disorder (PTSD) using MMPI item responses of 60 male Vietnam combat veterans previously diagnosed with PTSD. Their responses were contrasted with a similar group of veterans who were diagnosed with disorders other than PTSD. The two groups answered 49 items differently, and these items formed the basis of the PK scale, which subsequently was evaluated for its ability to correctly classify veterans with and without PTSD and for its psychometric properties of reliability and validity.

Psychodiagnostic Tests May Be (Easily) Faked

Questions about test accuracy extend beyond questions about tests themselves to include the test setting and the test taker. The possibility that test takers may respond in less than truthful ways undercuts the confidence some people may have in test results and interventions derived from these results. In situations in which test takers have little to gain by practicing deception while responding to test items, face-valid tests may enhance rapport and motivation on the part of the test taker. The straightforward nature of such test items may encourage honest responding. For example, a patient who complains at intake about a sullen or dysphoric mood, sleep disturbances, and a sense of foreboding about the future may feel that a psychologist who administers a depression inventory understands the symptom picture and is attempting to gain more information that will be helpful in formulating effective interventions. Under these circumstances, the patient is likely to respond in accordance with his or her perceptions.

Under other circumstances, however, test takers indeed may be motivated to present themselves in a particular manner that does not accurately reflect their personality or clinical condition. Some tests comprise items that lend themselves to easy manipulation by test takers, because the items make obvious the purpose of the test and the likely manner in which results will be used. Prior and subsequent to test administration, psychologists must consider whether there is a discernible reason for test takers to be less than forthright in their responses and whether that reason might constitute a motive for faking. If so, the test giver must choose tests and interpret test findings with these possibilities in mind. In child custody debates, for example, one or both parents may be assessed for parental fitness. Either or both of them may attempt to present themselves in a too-favorable light. In an extreme case, either may attempt to exaggerate his or her stability in an effort to win custody. In such cases, using a test that is patently obvious in its intent would be inadvisable, because the motivation to "fake good" is apparent. Situations that may prompt test takers to "fake bad" are imagined easily within the context of the legal system or within forensic settings. An individual accused of a heinous crime may prefer to be regarded as "insane" instead of "guilty" and could attempt to distort his or her test responses accordingly. Malingering detection in such cases is crucial to protect the rights of all parties involved—victims and victims' families, as well as individuals who truly suffer from mental disorders such that they are unable to appreciate the wrongfulness of their acts or are unable to conform their behavior to legal standards.

Many self-report inventories have addressed the issue of faking by employing deception detection methods, which may take the form of validity scales embedded within the tests themselves. The first test to use this approach was the original MMPI (Hathaway & McKinley, 1943). Hathaway and McKinley added 4 validity scales to the 10 clinical scales to ensure that various test-taking attitudes (such as the tendency to present oneself in an overly positive manner) were understood and could be brought to bear in the interpretive process. It is interesting that the test authors built the MMPI using an empirical keying method of test construction, which greatly reduces the likelihood that such distortion will occur. This method let the data speak for themselves by using statistical analyses to determine scales to which an item contributes rather than using clinical judgment. Thus it is difficult for test takers to know what the test items are assessing. Even so, some authors have urged caution, especially when subsets of items from larger inventories are administered separately rather than by being culled from an administration of the entire inventory. The PK supplementary scale of the MMPI cited earlier, for example, may be susceptible to faking by veterans who wish to receive benefits or compensation (Fairbank, McCaffrey, & Keane, 1985). Since the publication of the original MMPI, many other personality measures have included validity scales to detect—and even correct for—response tendencies demonstrated by test takers.

CONCLUSION

As noted in this chapter, standardized assessment batteries are virtually nonexistent, even though the use of multiple assessment methods is routine and highly recommended by the *Standards* for testing (AERA, APA, & NCME, 1999). "The new challenges to this field will be to standardize assessment methods and to specify the scope of clinically significant disorders that are in need of treatment" (Regier et al., 1998, p. 110). It seems that much would be gained by the development of psychometrically sound assessment batteries. Certainly, diagnostic accuracy would be improved by greater standardization of assessment methods used for psychodiagnostic purposes.

> If some greater degree of standardizing assessment methods can . . . be accomplished, psychiatric epidemiological and services research will be positioned for another leap forward in both improving the understanding of the cause(s) of mental disorder and helping to focus limited resources in the most cost-effective manner. (Regier et al., 1998, p. 115)

Issues emanating from managed care, the age of accountability, and cost containment (Ben-Porath, 1997; Griffith, 1997; Meyer et al., 2001; Yates & Taub, 2003) are likely to be with us out into the foreseeable future. In this regard, treatment utility emerges as a key consideration because it provides the kind of model that is responsive to the accountability and cost–benefit demands embodied by managed mental health care (Ben-Porath, 1997; Finn & Tonsager, 1997; Griffith, 1997). This model casts assessment itself as a therapeutic intervention. In 1997, Finn and Tonsager observed that "treatment utility of assessment is weaker than many of us might want" (p. 375). Since then, evidence has continued to surface that suggests that clear gains have been made in establishing the effectiveness of this approach (Nelson-Gray, 2003).

Assessment is a human endeavor and carries with it the promises and pitfalls of being so. Practitioners have been unwilling, or at least slow, to embrace mechanical prediction models, which themselves have been slow to materialize (e.g., Kleinmuntz, 1990). Although the idea of highly accurate (mechanical) predictions is alluring in some respects, it may also be disturbing to some who may find it difficult to imagine making clinical decisions by a purely formulaic "crunching of numbers."

Much of the foregoing material that has focused on points of contention with regard to clinical diagnostic testing has also served to advance the field and to illuminate future directions for clinical research and practice related to psychodiagnosis. Informed assessment practices that use the best available measures in combination with one another, that build on a collaborative assessment process inclusive of the patient or client and are mindful of his or her culture, that identify the most effective interventions for that individual, and that practitioners are reasonably compensated for is an ideal toward which to strive.

REFERENCES

Aiken, L. S., West, S. G., Sechrest, L., & Reno, R. R. (1990). Graduate training in statistics, methodology and measurement in psychology: A survey of PhD programs in North America. *American Psychologist, 45*, 721–734.

American Educational Research Association, American Psychological Association, & National Council on Measurement in Education. (1999). *Standards for educational and psychological testing* (3rd ed.). Washington, DC: Author.

American Psychiatric Association. (2000). *Diagnostic and statistical manual of mental disorders* (4th ed., text revision). Washington, DC: Author.

American Psychological Association. (2002). Ethical principles of psychologists and code of conduct. *American Psychologist, 57*, 1060–1073.

Beck, A. T., Steer, R. A., & Brown, G. K. (1996). *Beck Depression Inventory manual* (2nd ed.). San Antonio, TX: Psychological Corporation.

Ben-Porath, Y. S. (1997). Use of personality instruments in empirically guided treatment planning. *Psychological Assessment, 9*, 361–367.

Butcher, J. N. (2004). Personality assessment without borders: Adaptation of the MMPI–2 across cultures. *Journal of Personality Assessment, 83*, 90–104.

Butcher, J. N., Cabiya, J., Lucio, E., & Garrido, M. (2007). *Assessing Hispanic clients using the MMPI–2 and MMPI–A.* Washington, DC: American Psychological Association.

Butcher, J. N., Coelho Mosch, S., Tsai, J., & Nezami, E. (2006). Cross-cultural applications of the MMPI–2. In J. N. Butcher (Ed.), *MMPI–2: A practitioner's guide* (pp. 505–537). Washington, DC: American Psychological Association.

Butcher, J. N., Dahlstrom, W. G., Graham, J. R., Tellegen, A., & Kaemmer, B. (1989). *Manual for administration and scoring: Minnesota Multiphasic Personality Inventory—2 (MMPI–2).* Minneapolis: University of Minnesota Press.

Camara, W. J., Nathan, J. S., & Puente, A. E. (2000). Psychological test usage: Implications in professional psychology. *Professional Psychology: Research and Practice, 31,* 141–154.

Cates, J. A. (1999). The art of assessment in psychology: Ethics, expertise, and validity. *Journal of Clinical Psychology, 55,* 631–641.

Cheung, F. M., Leung, K., Zhang, H. Z., Sun, F. A., Gan, Y. Q., Song, W. Z., & Zie, D. (2001). Indigenous Chinese personality constructs: Is the five-factor model complete? *Journal of Cross-Cultural Psychology, 32,* 407–433.

Coyne, I. (2001, April 21). *ITC test adaptation guidelines.* Retrieved July 1, 2008, from http://www.intestcom.org/test_adaptation.htm

Eisman, E. J. Dies, R., Finn, S. E., Eyde, L. D., Kay, G. G., Kubiszyn, T. W., et al. (2000). Problems and limitations in the use of psychological assessment in contemporary health care delivery. *Professional Psychology: Research and Practice, 31,* 131–140.

Fairbank, J., McCaffrey, R., & Keane, T. (1985). Psychometric detection of fabricated symptoms of post-traumatic stress disorder. *American Journal of Psychiatry, 142,* 501–503.

Finn, S. E., & Martin, H. (1997). Therapeutic assessment with the MMPI–2 in managed health care. In J. N. Butcher (Ed.), *Objective personality assessment in managed health care: A practitioner's guide* (pp. 131–152). New York: Oxford University Press.

Finn, S. E., & Tonsager, M. E. (1997). Information-gathering and therapeutic models of assessment: Complementary paradigms. *Psychological Assessment, 9,* 374–385.

Fong, M. L. (1995). Assessment and *DSM–IV* diagnosis of personality disorders: A primer for counselors. *Journal of Counseling & Development, 73,* 635–639.

Garb, H. N. (1989). Clinical judgment, clinical training, and professional experience. *Psychological Bulletin, 105,* 387–396.

Garb, H. N. (2003). Incremental validity and the assessment of psychopathology in adults. *Psychological Assessment, 15,* 508–520.

Garb, H. N. (2005). Clinical judgment and decision making. *Annual Review of Clinical Psychology, 1,* 67–89.

Geisinger, K. F. (1992). The metamorphosis in test validation. *Educational Psychologist, 27,* 197–222.

Geisinger, K. F. (1994). Cross-cultural normative assessment: Translation and adaptation issues influencing the normative interpretation of assessment instruments. *Psychological Assessment, 6*, 304–312.

Geisinger, K. F. (1998). Psychometric issues in test interpretation. In J. Sandoval, C. L. Frisby, K. F. Geisinger, J. D. Scheuneman, & J. R. Grenier (Eds.), *Test interpretation and diversity: Achieving equity in assessment* (pp. 17–30). Washington, DC: American Psychological Association.

Geisinger, K. F., & Carlson, J. F. (2002). Standards and standardization. In J. N. Butcher (Ed.), *Practical considerations in clinical personality assessment* (2nd ed., pp. 243–256). New York: Oxford University Press.

Goldberg, L. R. (1990). An alternative "description of personality": The Big-Five factor structure. *Journal of Personality and Social Psychology, 59*, 1216–1229.

Goldberg, L. R. (1993). The structure of phenotypic personality traits. *American Psychologist, 48*, 26–34.

Good, B., & Kleinman, A. (1985). Epilogue: Culture and depression. In A. Kleinman & B. Good (Eds.), *Culture and depression* (pp. 491–506). Berkeley: University of California Press.

Griffith, L. (1997). Surviving no-frills mental health care: The future of psychological assessment. *Journal of Practical Psychiatry and Behavioral Health, 3*, 255–258.

Grove, W. M., & Meehl, P. E. (1996). Comparative efficiency of informal (subjective, impressionistic) and formal (mechanical, algorithmic) prediction procedures: The clinical-statistical controversy. *Psychology, Public Policy, and Law, 2*, 293–323.

Grove, W. M., Zald, D. H., Lebow, B. S., Snitz, B. E., & Nelson, C. (2000). Clinical versus mechanical prediction: A meta-analysis. *Psychological Assessment, 12*, 19–30.

Hambleton, R. K., Spielberger, C. D., & Merenda, P. F. (2005). *Adapting educational and psychological tests for cross-cultural assessment.* Hillsdale, NJ: Erlbaum.

Hathaway, S. R., & McKinley, J. C. (1943). *The Minnesota Multiphasic Personality Inventory.* Minneapolis: University of Minnesota Press.

Hayes, S. N., Nelson, R. O., & Jarrett, R. B. (1987). The treatment utility of assessment: A functional approach to evaluating assessment quality. *American Psychologist, 42*, 963–974.

Holt, R. R. (1986). Clinical and statistical prediction: A retrospective and would-be integrative perspective. *Journal of Personality Assessment, 50*, 376–386.

Hunsley, J., & Meyer, G. J. (2003). The incremental validity of psychological testing and assessment: Conceptual, methodological, and statistical issues. *Psychological Assessment, 15*, 446–455.

Keane, T. M., Malloy, P. F., & Fairbank, J. A. (1984). Empirical development of an MMPI subscale for the assessment of combat-related post-traumatic stress disorder. *Journal of Consulting and Clinical Psychology, 52*, 888–891.

Kleinmuntz, B. (1990). Why we still use our heads instead of formulas: Toward an integrative approach. *Psychological Bulletin, 107*, 296–310.

Kubiszyn, T. W., Meyer, G. J., Finn, S. E., Eyde, L. D., Kay, G. G., Moreland, K. L., et al. (2000). Empirical support for psychological assessment in clinical health care settings. *Professional Psychology: Research and Practice*, *31*, 119–130.

Masling, J. M. (1992). Assessment and the therapeutic narrative. *Journal of Training and Practice in Professional Psychology*, *6*, 53–58.

McCrae, R. R. (2000). Beginning again on personality and culture [Review of the book *Personality and person perception across cultures*]. *Contemporary Psychology*, *45*, 38–40.

McCrae, R. R. (2001). Trait psychology and culture: Exploring intercultural comparisons. *Journal of Personality*, *69*, 819–846.

McCrae, R. R., & Costa, P. T., Jr. (1999). A five-factor theory of personality. In L. A. Pervin & O. P. John (Eds.), *Handbook of personality psychology* (pp. 139–155). New York: Guilford Press.

Meehl, P. E. (1986). Causes and effects of my disturbing little book. *Journal of Personality Assessment*, *50*, 370–375.

Meehl, P. E. (1996). *Clinical versus statistical prediction: A theoretical analysis and a review of the evidence*. Northvale, NJ: Jason Aronson. (Original work published 1954)

Meyer, G. J., Finn, S. E., Eyde, L., Kay, G. G., Moreland, K. L., Dies, R. R., et al. (2001). Psychological testing and psychological assessment: A review of evidence and issues. *American Psychologist*, *56*, 128–165.

Nelson-Gray, R. O. (2003). Treatment utility of psychological assessment. *Psychological Assessment*, *15*, 521–531.

O'Roark, A. M., & Exner, J. E. (Eds.). (1989). *History and directory: Society for personality assessment fiftieth anniversary*. Hillsdale, NJ: Erlbaum.

Regier, D. A., Kaelber, C. T., Rae, D. S., Farmer, M. E., Knauper, B., Kessler, R. C., & Norquist, G. S. (1998). Limitations of diagnostic criteria and assessment instruments for mental disorders. *Archives of General Psychiatry*, *55*, 109–115.

Sedlacek, W. E. (2004). *Beyond the big test: Noncognitive assessment in higher education*. San Francisco: Jossey-Bass.

Westen, D., & Weinberger, J. (2004). When clinical description becomes statistical prediction. *American Psychologist*, *59*, 595–613.

Wiggins, J. S. (1973). *Personality and prediction: Principles of personality assessment*. Reading, MA: Addison-Wesley.

Willingham, W. W. (1985). *Success in college: The role of personal qualities and academic ability*. New York: College Board.

Yang J., McCrae, R. R., Costa, P. T., Jr., Dai X., Yao S., Cai, T., & Gao, B. (1999). Cross-cultural personality assessment in psychiatric populations: The NEO-PI-R in the People's Republic of China. *Psychological Assessment*, *11*, 359–368.

Yates, B. T., & Taub, J. (2003). Assessing the costs, benefits, cost-effectiveness, and cost-benefit of psychological assessment: We should, we can, and here's how. *Psychological Assessment*, *15*, 478–495.

3

EDUCATIONAL ACHIEVEMENT TESTING: CRITIQUES AND REBUTTALS

RICHARD P. PHELPS

Fallacies in critiques of educational achievement testing are so numerous that an entire book could be written about them alone. Indeed, an entire book already has been written about them: *Defending Standardized Testing* (Phelps, 2005a). It includes separate chapters from four of the current volume's contributors—Kurt Geisinger, Ron Hambleton, Stephen Sireci, and me—as well as other testing experts. *Defending* is an excellent resource, and there is no cause to replicate it here. Instead, in this chapter, I focus on several fallacies that were not included in the earlier text. For interested readers, Table 3.1 lists many of the educational achievement testing fallacies dissected in *Defending Standardized Testing* and elsewhere, along with citations to expert rebuttals to those fallacies. Still more point–counterpoint can be found in chapter 2 of another book, *Kill the Messenger: The War on Standardized Testing* (Phelps, 2003). Citations to some of the many sources of the fallacies are included in these other two books.

The views expressed here are the author's own and not necessarily those of ACT, Inc.

TABLE 3.1

Selected Testing Opponent Fallacies and Rebuttal Sources

Fallacy	Rebuttal source
Teacher grading and testing is more valid and more reliable than standardized testing.	Brookhart, 1993; McMillan, 2001; Stiggins and Conklin, 1992
Tests are developed secretively and obscurely.	Sireci, 2005
The public opposes the use of high-stakes tests.	Phelps, 1998, 2005b
Tests promote improper test preparation and teaching to the test.	Phelps, 2003; Crocker, 2005; Roediger and Karpicke, 2006a, 2006b
The best way to prepare students for tests is to substitute focused test preparation for regular subject matter instruction.	Camara (chap. 4, this volume); Crocker, 2005; Moore, 1991; Palmer, 2002; Tuckman, 1994; Tuckman and Trimble, 1997
One can perform well on multiple-choice tests without knowing the subject matter simply by learning tricks.	Becker, 1990; Briggs, 2001; Powers and Rock, 1999
Multiple-choice penalizes deep thought and creativity.	Powers and Kaufman, 2002; Roediger and Marsh, 2005
Constructed-response test items are superior to multiple-choice test items.	Bridgeman, 1991; Feinberg, 1990; Rudman, 1992; Traub, 1993
Standardized tests reduce educational achievement.	Phelps, 2005c
Tests inevitably narrow the curriculum.	Crocker, 2005; Phelps, 2003; Roediger and Marsh, 2005
Tests are too costly in money, time, and lost opportunity.	Goodman and Hambleton, 2005; Phelps, 1994, 2000a, 2003;
Standardized tests do not measure what is important.	Camara (chap. 4, this volume); Goodman and Hambleton, 2005; Phelps, 2003
A test can only validly be used for a single purpose.	Eckstein and Noah, 1993
There is more testing in the United States than in their countries.	Phelps, 1996, 1997, 2000b
Large-scale assessments are full of biased test items.	Camara (chap. 4, this volume); Goodman and Hambleton, 2005; Phelps, 2007b
Too much emphasis is placed on a single test score.	Camara (chap. 4, this volume); Goodman and Hambleton, 2005; Phelps, 2007b
Passing scores are set arbitrarily.	Plake, 2005; Sireci, 2005
Passing scores are set too high.	Goodman and Hambleton, 2005; Plake, 2005
School score trends are too "volatile" to be useful.	Bourque, 2005; Rogosa, 2005
Education accountability systems rely solely on tests.	Goodman and Hambleton, 2005; Phelps, 2003
Ability and achievement are completely unrelated.	Gottfredson (chap. 1, this volume); Lohman, 2006
Standardized tests are unfair to women and minorities.	Cole and Willingham, 1997; Farkus, Johnson, Immerwahr, and McHugh, 1998; Sandham, 1998
Standardized tests are unfair to students with disabilities.	Geisinger, 2005

In this chapter, I focus on fallacies that have less to do with the character of educational achievement testing and more to do with the dissemination (or lack thereof) of information about such testing. I describe several fallacies that are the direct result of either wholesale censorship and information suppression or naive beliefs about how information, particularly education research, is disseminated in the United States. I also briefly describe the policy implications of widespread belief in each of the fallacies. Public policies based on fallacies are not likely to be optimal. First, however, I introduce some terminology.

Educational achievement (or *proficiency*) *tests* are designed to measure what has been learned. In program evaluation terminology, achievement tests are generally *summative*, particularly when they have *stakes* (i.e., consequences). When achievement tests are used, instead, to monitor progress, or set benchmarks, they can be identified as *formative*.

Achievement tests are meant to measure the level of knowledge or skill attained within a *content domain*, or subject matter area. *Standards-based* (or *criterion-referenced*) achievement tests are designed to cover a predetermined, and sometimes legally mandated, body of subject matter content, usually identified by *content standards*. *Norm-referenced* achievement tests are designed to measure a student's level of knowledge and skill relative to a norm group—typically a representative sample of students from a large population of interest (e.g., all U.S. fourth-graders)—and cover a content domain that is determined by the test developer and not through a state or local political process.

By definition, most teacher-made classroom tests are achievement tests. This chapter, however, focuses on large-scale, systemwide, standardized achievement tests and some of the attendant fallacies proffered by their critics.

This chapter is organized according to popular fallacies about education achievement testing pertaining to its cost, to score "inflation," to the research literature on the effects of testing on achievement, and to the cause of widespread misunderstanding about such testing. However, it could just as validly have been organized around a single overarching fallacy: You can't stop progress. Many believe the other fallacies simply because they are all they ever hear and, in some quarters, all they are allowed to hear. Counterpoints are censored, suppressed, or obfuscated, and those who dare to speak them may be demonized, ostracized, threatened, or otherwise silenced. A century's worth of research on educational achievement testing has been so successfully removed from the collective working memory that it was not even considered by policymakers in the design of the most far-reaching federal testing mandate in our country's history. Instead, the research was declared nonexistent. Critics of educational achievement testing have not only stopped research progress, they seem to be well along the way to reversing it.

Those outside the field may assume that education research is like any other type of research, to wit: The most prominent research has been fully vetted and so can be trusted; the most celebrated researchers are most likely the best; a wide range of evidence and points of view are fairly considered; and there is progress. Unfortunately, none of this validly characterizes contemporary research on educational achievement testing. In reality, educational achievement testing represents a threat to the status quo (because it monitors its productivity) and is treated as such.

Within the overarching fallacy, this chapter is organized by four other fallacies, each of which is illustrated by case studies:

- Fallacy 1: Tests cost too much.
- Fallacy 2: High stakes induce artificial test score increases.
- Fallacy 3: There is little evidence of the effects of testing and no evidence of its benefits.
- Fallacy 4: Testing is mischaracterized because it is difficult to understand.

Placed at the end of the chapter is a longer section on the policy implications of the overarching fallacy. The proved ability of vested interests to stop (and reverse) research progress on educational achievement testing portends the elimination of much of the past century's accumulated wisdom on the topic—an extinction vortex.

OVERARCHING FALLACY: YOU CAN'T STOP PROGRESS

A key component of our faith in progress is the corollary belief that our knowledge base continually expands—that is, we know what we already know, and we are always learning more. The continual expansion of knowledge requires both that the historical accumulation of knowledge be preserved and that new knowledge be welcomed. Moreover, modern society is so free and open, and the means of communication are now so varied, effortless, and cheap, that information suppression might be considered impossible. Ironically, the widespread belief that a continuous expansion of knowledge is inevitable and unstoppable helps to make its contraction possible because people do not consider the powerful constraints on research dissemination. To be sure, opponents of educational achievement testing neither burn books nor attempt to ban them—but then, they do not need to. Other, more subtle methods work well enough.

The simplest means of suppressing unwanted information is to ignore it—to pretend or even to declare that it does not exist. Most of the efforts to suppress thousands of scholarly studies of the effects of testing conducted over the past century have been of this type. There are several advantages to this method. First, it seems benign and not antagonistic because it is nonconfrontational (by contrast, asserting that someone has declared an extant research literature nonexistent can seem personal and antagonistic).

Second, if claimants are caught erroneously affirming the nonexistence of information, they can simply fall back on the excuse of innocent ignorance (i.e., there is plausible deniability). Third, declaring information nonexistent discourages efforts to look for it, thus helping to make such declarations self-fulfilling prophecies. Fourth, declaring nonexistent any research that competes with one's own helps to eliminate competition in the marketing of one's work.

Regression of research supports both the dominant ideologies in education, in which testing is considered bad for a variety of reasons, and the self-interest of the dominant groups. For with no valid, reliable, externally administered measure of their performance, these groups are free to do as they please.

High-Stakes Summative Testing: An Example of Poor Information Dissemination

The Association for Supervision and Curriculum Development (ASCD) is a professional organization with more than 160,000 members who

> span the entire profession of educators—superintendents, supervisors, principals, teachers, professors of education, and school board members. ASCD was initially envisioned to represent curriculum and supervision issues. Over the years, its focus has changed, and it now addresses all aspects of effective teaching and learning, such as professional development, educational leadership, and capacity building. (ASCD, 2005)

Because the ASCD is so large and offers its publications as part of membership, its books on testing (i.e., on authentic assessment or portfolios) can often be found at the top of best-selling rankings in the testing, assessment, standards, or accountability categories. It represents a powerful voice on these topics.

Each day I receive the ASCD's *SmartBrief*, an e-mail newsletter that contains a list of hyperlinked news stories that the organization considers interesting or important as well as job and sponsor advertisements and announcements of ASCD's own services and publications (ASCD, 2008). Also included are daily reminders of the positive value and importance of "authentic," formative, and performance-based testing, along with references and links to relevant books, professional development workshops, Internet instructional guides, and more. For any member interested in knowing more about authentic assessment, formative assessment, or performance testing, the ASCD offers a cornucopia of information and instruction.

However, what of the ASCD member interested in knowing more about the far more prevalent and consequential summative, selected-response standardized test? I have received ASCD *SmartBriefs* for more than a year and have yet to witness anything but an occasional blanket condemnation of such testing. For ASCD members curious to know more about the accountability testing that represents such a central part of their working lives—and how to cope with that testing—the ASCD offers no help whatsoever. In view of its failure to report research on tests with selected-response formats, one could conclude that ASCD advocates authentic assessment and promotes it as the only legitimate form of assessment.

Like many professional educator associations these days, the ASCD is an advocacy organization run by "soft despotism" or a "tyranny of the majority"(de Tocqueville, 1835 and 1840/2003). The leadership apparently has decided that authentic assessment is better than testing with selected-response formats, so it promotes only authentic assessment. Indeed, it acknowledges only authentic assessment as legitimate.

Consider one day's *SmartBrief* (ASCD, 2008). One link takes the reader to a local newspaper's editorial titled "Florida Needs to Move Beyond Testing." A link to an article in another ASCD publication is introduced thusly: "It's old news that high-stakes, summative assessment practices don't help students learn, although word hasn't yet trickled up to politicians."

During the 2000 presidential campaign, the ASCD commissioned two public opinion polls on standardized testing, which was at the time a prominent campaign issue. The unpublished results showed the public strongly supportive of high-stakes standards-based testing. The ASCD then shelved one of the two polls and, with the other, added the percentage of neutral responses (e.g., "don't know," "no opinion") to that of the negative responses. This creative arithmetic spawned statements such as, "Approximately half [of the poll respondents] disagree or are undecided about whether these tests should determine graduation." The actual results for that poll item were as follows: "agree," 51%; "disagree," 38%; and "neither," 11% (Phelps, 2005b, pp. 18–20).

The ASCD is not exceptional in practicing a soft form of censorship and information suppression. During the 2000 presidential campaign, I visited the Web sites of dozens of national organizations of professional educators and observed a propensity to present to their members evidence and points of view from only one side of the debate—the antitesting side. I wrote each of them with suggestions for links to Web sites (e.g., Mass Insight, the Southern Regional Education Board, Educational Testing Service) that offered alternative perspectives. None of the organizations added any of the suggested references.

Research Progress: 1895 to 1985

The other day, I was reading C. C. Ross's (1941) authoritative text *Measurement in Today's Schools* and was struck by its policy relevance. Ross summarized the findings of hundreds of research studies across more than 4 decades of scholarly effort and included one long chapter on the motivational effects of testing and other chapters on the optimal design of testing programs. Although relevant and informative, one sees scant reference to Ross's work these days. Moreover, to my knowledge, neither his insights nor those of any of the many research psychologists he cited have been considered in any of the recent testing program or accountability system design discussions among national policymakers or their advisors. Here are just some of the research findings included in *Measurement in Today's Schools* that could have helped policy planners recently—for example, in the design of the federal No Child Left Behind (NCLB) Act:

- Standardized tests with consequences influence teachers' degree of effort as well as their allocation of time and emphasis toward topics known or assumed to be covered on the tests (pp. 333–334).
- When past examination content is assumed to predict future examination content, or future examination content is otherwise known in advance, schools can become cramming schools, defeating the purpose of examinations (p. 334).
- Students learn more when there are known consequences to that learning.[1]
- Tests with consequences influence students' allocation of study time toward topics known or assumed to be covered on the tests; tests without consequences do not (pp. 360–361).
- The act of testing alone, irrespective of other factors, tends to improve achievement (p. 342).

Some other research findings covered in Ross's work relevant to contemporary testing policy discussions include the following:

- Using a single threshold, or cut score, for passing a test tends to motivate most those students whose academic performance would place them just below that threshold, but not the students whose academic performance places them comfortably above the threshold or some substantial distance below (pp. 334–335).
- Students learn more when they are made aware of the quality of their academic performance and allowed an opportunity to adjust (p. 336).
- Frequent testing helps low-achieving students more than it helps high-achieving students (pp. 340, 342–343, 362).
- Examination strengthens memory and the sooner an exam is given after exposure to the information the stronger will be the memory of that information (p. 341).

---

[1]Note that the NCLB Act applied consequences for performance to schools but not to students.

- Testing with review or feedback improves achievement even more (pp. 336, 342–343).
- The simple awareness that there will be an examination later on substantially improves achievement (if the examination has consequences)—both on expected subject matter and even on unexpected subject matter (pp. 343–346).

Indeed, Ross in his 1941 book summarized research topics that some current researchers have claimed to be the first to study. If Ross (who unfortunately passed away years ago) could have been involved in the crafting of the NCLB Act, its design and execution might have been better informed.

As one would expect, however, research on the effects of testing and the optimal design of testing and accountability programs did not stop in 1941. Instead, the large body of research that had accumulated to that point stimulated additional work that was more detailed, more sophisticated, and more varied. Research pertinent to testing and accountability policy blossomed over the next half century, with thousands of studies conducted by research psychologists, educational practitioners, and program evaluators.

Research on the effects of testing has been conducted in many fields (and subfields), of inquiry, including education research (language learning, mastery learning, remedial–developmental, gifted and talented, assessment, promotion and retention, selection, higher education assessment, admission, diagnosis, motivation, certification and licensure, school effectiveness, adult education), psychology (memory and cognition, industrial–organizational, selection, diagnosis and counseling, clinical, personnel, educational psychology, allocation, motivation), program evaluation, and sociology. Furthermore, research on the effects of testing has been sponsored by many types of organizations, such as educational institutions (at all levels), governments (at all levels), international organizations, the military, and most of the world's developed countries. Of all these categories, I have thus far conducted a thorough search through the literature of only the first: education research. There I found more than 1,000 studies on the effects of testing and test-based accountability. Some of the major concentrations of evidence surround particular research themes, such as those listed in Exhibit 3.1.

The research literature is deep and wide, painstakingly constructed over the course of a century by hundreds of hardworking, earnest scholars, including some of the giants in the history of psychology. Recent claims of a barren research literature and "first-ever" studies on the aforementioned topics should be placed for comparison alongside this mountain of knowledge and experience, then judged accordingly.

Research Regress: 1985 to Present

Research progress on educational achievement testing began to stall in the 1980s when the U.S. federal government started funding specialized research centers run by regressive groups, and these, in turn, co-opted other well-funded federal institutions—most notably the Board on Testing and Assessment at the National Research Council (NRC).

A *regressive* research group is one that denies or dismisses information and evidence, such as that embodied in a research literature. Typically, the dismissed research is replaced in their words and publications with their own and that of those who share their point of view. To be sure, more than one group in the field has denied or dismissed information and evidence related to educational achievement testing. However, the Center for Research on Evaluation, Standards, and Student Testing (CRESST) in particular has been the most successful at it. First funded by the federal government in the 1980s— the era of A *Nation at Risk* (National Commission on Excellence in Education, 1983)—as the Center for the Study of Evaluation, CRESST's direct funding from U.S. taxpayers for the period 1996–2006 alone totaled more than $35 million. Headquartered in the education schools at University of California, Los Angeles (UCLA) and the University of Colorado, CRESST has joined with various partners over the decades, most notably the Rand Corporation and the University of Pittsburgh.

CRESST's primary advantages in selling its ideas (and suppressing others) are money and the aura of intellectual authority. It has vastly greater financial resources at its disposal than do any of the individual scholars who might wish to contest its claims. Moreover, it has leveraged those resources productively to expand its reach even further. For example, CRESST can easily make deals (i.e., partnerships) with other researchers and research centers because it can offer pay, in-kind services, publicity, dissemination of publications, and more. CRESST appears authoritative for the simple reason that it has been the only federally funded research center uniquely devoted to the topics of standards and testing. It is the logical place for journalists to call for expertise about educational achievement testing. As I mentioned previously, CRESST is not nor has it ever been the only organization promoting regression in research on educational achievement testing; however, I argue that it has been the most successful and the most important. The following case studies illustrate how and why.

FALLACY 1: TESTS COST TOO MUCH

To people outside the field of education, the cost of standardized student testing would likely seem a rather straightforward topic. Within the field, however, it is an anxiety-producing subject that spawns tense arguments. These arguments tend to turn on the worth or intrinsic educational value of the tests themselves, the amount of time taken up by test taking and test preparation, and the assignment or lack thereof of particular cost components as attributable to standardized testing.

EXHIBIT 3.1
Selected Listing of Effects-of-Testing Research and Researchers

The mastery learning and mastery testing experiments conducted from the 1960s until the present vary incentives, frequency of tests, types of tests, and many other factors to determine the optimal structure of testing programs. Researchers have included such notables as L. W. Anderson, J. H. Block, B. Bloom, R. B. Burns, J. B. Carroll, K. P. Cross, S. L. Gates, T. R. Guskey, G. M. Hymel, E. H. Jones, F. Keller, J. Kulik, C.-L. Kulik, J. R. Okey, M. Tierney, and T. L. Wentling.

Psychologists' experimental work on memory retention and loss dates back more than a century and studies the optimal frequency of testing and other factors, again to determine the optimal structure of testing programs. Researchers have included H. A. Greene, E. H. Jones, A. N. Jorgensen, and C. C. Ross, who have been mentioned in the text of this chapter, as well as L. W. Anderson, R. L. Bangert-Drowns, G. Hanna, L. K. Henry, N. Keys, A. Khalaf, J. E. Kirkpatrick, J. Kulik, C.-L. Kulik, and B. F. Skinner.

Language acquisition researchers attempt to optimize the use of testing in language instruction and so are keen students of the "washback" (or backwash) effect of testing. Researchers have included J. C. Alderson, K. M. Bailey, J. B. Carroll, A. Hughes, and D. Wall.

Developmental (i.e., remedial) education researchers have conducted many studies to determine what works best to keep students from failing in their "courses of last resort," after which there are no alternatives. Researchers have included L. Bliss, B. Bonham, H. Boylan, D. Chang, S. Chen, C. Claxton, R. Kirk, J. Kulik, C.-L. Kulik, R. McCabe, J. Roueche, C. Schonecker, and C. Wheeler.

The vast literature on effective schools dates back a half century and arrives at remarkably uniform conclusions about what works to make schools effective—goal setting, high standards, and frequent testing. Researchers have included D. A. Astuto, C. R. Clark, K. Cotton, T. L. Good, D. A. Grouws, R. Kiemig, M. Jones, D. U. Levine, L. W. Lezotte, L. S. Lotto, S. C. Purkey, M. Rutter, M. S. Smith, A. Taylor, B. Valentine, and B. M. Wildemuth.

The many studies of district and state minimum competency or diploma testing programs popular from the 1960s through the 1980s found positive effects for students just below the cut score and mixed effects for students far below and anywhere above it. Researchers have included A. L. Abrams, J. L. Anderson, D. J. Bateson, B. Battiste, K. Bembry, D. Blackmore, H. Boylan, S. M. Brookhart, T. B. Corcoran, C. Fincher, W. D. Hawley, M. L. Herrick, F. H. Hultgren, M. Jackson, J. Jacobsen, S. Mazzoni, R. L. Mendro, W. Muir, T. Orsack, W. T. Rogers, D. P. Saxon, W. D. Schafer, C. C. Seubert, D. E. Tanner, W. J. Webster, D. Weerasinghe, and M. A. Zigarelli.

Many researchers have studied the role of testing in motivation. They have included R. Bootzin, S. M. Brown, C. Chen, M. V. Covington, T. J. Crooks, R. Drabman, A. Kazdin, K. D. O'Leary, J. W. Olmsted, S. L. Pressey, L. B. Resnick, D. P. Resnick, A. Staats, H. W. Stevenson, R. W. Tyler, H. J. Walberg, and R. G. Wood.

Others have considered the role of tests in incentive programs. These researchers have included R. Bootzin, J. Cameron, T. B. Corcoran, A. P. Csanyi, R. Drabman, M. A. Gonzales, L. Homme, A. Kaszdin, J. McMillan, K. D. O'Leary, W. D. Pierce, M. R. Rechs, A. Staats, and B. L. Wilson.

International organizations, such as the World Bank or the Asian Development Bank, have studied the effects of testing on education programs they sponsor. Researchers have included N. Brooke, U. Bude, D. W. Chapman, S. P. Heynemann, J. Oxenham, B. Pronaratna, G. Psacharopoulis, A. Ransom, A. Somerset, C. W. Snyder, and E. Velez.

Another major area of inquiry dating back many decades has been the effect of goal setting, standards, and alignment on teachers, instruction, and student learning. The researchers involved have included M. Csikszentmihalyi, J. Fontana, F. B. Knight,

M. A. Lowther, I. Panlasigui, C. Pine, M. Pomplun, L. B. Resnick, B. H. Robinson, K. M. Shaw, J. S. Stark, T. D. Thomas, and R. W. Tyler.

Finally, there has been considerable research on the learning effect of test taking, conducted by F. N. Dempster, S. M. Luipersbeck, H. L. Roediger, and T. C. Toppino, among others.

Note. For more detailed information, see Phelps (2005c).

If one chooses to believe, for example, that standardized test-taking and test-preparation time have no intrinsic instructional value and, further, that standardized tests are separate from and contribute nothing to the instructional plan of a school, then one might well consider standardized tests to be costly because they take up time that might otherwise be devoted to instruction. To such critics, the problematic costs associated with standardized tests are not represented by the purchase price paid to the commercial vendors but, rather, by the lost opportunity for learning that could have taken place in the time devoted to standardized tests.

Case Study: The Texas Teacher Test

Local son and corporate leader H. Ross Perot headed a blue ribbon commission in the early 1980s that studied the Texas school system, long considered one of the country's poorest performers. Two findings of the commission were that some Texas teachers were illiterate and that there were no high-stakes requirements for new teachers. The commission recommended the development of a basic literacy test, the Texas Examination of Current Administrators and Teachers (TECAT) and a requirement that all teachers pass it. By all accounts, the test was extremely easy, but nonetheless some teachers failed it—some after multiple attempts.

CRESST conducted a cost–benefit analysis of the test and declared its net benefits to be negative—by about $70 million (Shepard, Kreitzer, & Grau, 1987). Indeed, CRESST was extremely critical of every aspect of the test. CRESST recommended that the test not be high stakes and that if the test were used at all, failure should at most mean a teacher would be required to take a literacy course. CRESST's calculations, and my recalculations, can be found elsewhere (Phelps, 2003, pp. 105–115); I only summarize them here. CRESST attained its negative net-benefit figure through the following items:

- arbitrary exclusions of benefits (e.g., salary savings for more than half the teachers dismissed for failing the test—those in vocational education, industrial arts, special education, business education, and kindergarten—did not "count" in Shepard et al.'s [1987] benefit calculations because, the authors argued, literacy is not important in their work);
- arbitrary inclusions of costs (e.g., teacher time spent taking the test during one of their prescribed-topic in-service days is

counted as a pure cost, implying that tests are not acceptable vehicles for teaching subject matter; by contrast, passive listening to a lecture on literacy instead would not have been considered a cost);

- miscalculations of the value of time (they valued teachers' after hours at their full salary rate and ignored the future [discounted] value of recurring benefits); and
- counting certain costs as gross that should have been counted as net (i.e., to include the value of countervailing benefits).

Correcting only for the more obvious of Shepard et al.'s (1987) mistakes and using their own base assumptions and estimates pushes the TECAT program's net benefits into the black—and by a wide margin—to $330 million. Other fixes to their calculations, methods, and assumptions push the net-benefit figure still higher.

Policy Implications

CRESST's preference was to preserve the status quo, eschew accountability requirements, and continue citizens' sole reliance on input measures and trust in the schools' own quality control to provide the teachers who taught their children at their expense. Shepard et al. (1987) also criticized the TECAT as simplistic, too narrow in format, and too general in content, but they did not advocate a "better" testing program. They favored eliminating teacher tests altogether.

Shepard et al. (1987) repeatedly attacked the test for its alleged low-level nature. Yet ultimately that is beside the point, because the authors were opposed to any type of teacher test. It is beside the point, too, because it is clear that the citizens of Texas wanted some accountability in their teacher certification system and would not have been content with the minor modifications of the status quo—consisting of more input requirements—that the authors recommended. Even the authors admitted that half the teachers interviewed thought the test accomplished its purpose: "to weed out incompetent teachers and reassure the public" (p. iv).

An alternative that CRESST did not consider was to move the TECAT to an earlier point in the teacher training process, say, at the end of, or even at the beginning of, graduate school. This would have met the concerns of the citizens of Texas; it would have achieved all the same benefits. However, most of the costs that Shepard et al. (1987) enumerated would have evaporated. There would have been no loss of teacher time. The responsibility for preparing the teachers for the test would have been placed on the teacher training schools or, better, on the potential education students themselves. Best of all, the time of unqualified would-be teachers (and their students) would not have been wasted. A reasonable alternative to the authors' complaints about the alleged simplistic nature of the TECAT would have been to initiate a required "higher level" exam for teachers, in addition to the TECAT.

As it turns out, the citizens of Texas did not follow CRESST's advice. Rather, they followed the path just drawn, making the basic literacy exam an entrance exam for education school and requiring new teachers to pass another, newly created exam that focused on each teacher's content area and on pedagogy and professional development. They increased the benefits and reduced the costs, even according to CRESST's creative cost–benefit accounting criteria. Finally, they ended up with more tests, not fewer.

Case Study: The General Accounting Office Report on the Extent and Cost of Testing

In the early 1990s, the U.S. Congress asked its research agency, known then as the General Accounting Office (GAO), to estimate the extent and cost of systemwide standardized testing in the country and the potential overlap of President George H. W. Bush's proposed American Achievement Tests on that amount and cost. To complete its study, the U.S. GAO (1993) developed and administered surveys of local district and state testing directors and achieved a high rate of response from a nationally representative population. A who's who of notables in the evaluation, statistical, and psychometric worlds reviewed various aspects of the study. Nothing like it in quality or scale had ever been done.

During each of the next 3 years, CRESST invited papers and hosted panel discussions on the cost of testing at its annual conferences. The panels were populated by authors of other, competing studies of testing costs, including one sponsored by CRESST. The GAO report was lambasted as simplistic and poorly done. The primary accusation was that it did not consider personnel costs (e.g., the cost of teacher time spent proctoring exams). In fact it had, with personnel costs accounting for more than half of its cost estimates.

Having been involved in the GAO study as project director, I protested to the CRESST directors for the misrepresentation and for their refusal to allow me to join any of the panels. A vague promise of a correction in some future CRESST newsletter was hinted at but never fulfilled. Protests made to the researchers directly responsible for the false accusations were similarly ignored.

The characterization of the GAO report as "flawed" spread unimpeded. In its place, other reports were promoted and published purporting to show that standardized tests are enormously costly and overwhelm school schedules in their volume. The studies were based on (a) a single field trial in a few schools, (b) three telephone calls, and (c) one state (the CRESST report on testing costs was limited to Kentucky), or (d) the facts were just made up. The studies that used some data for evidence heaped all sorts of nontest activities into the basket and called them costs of tests. In the case of CRESST's Kentucky report, some teacher-respondents counted their entire school year as "test preparation time," and that time was then multiplied by classroom teachers' wage rates and counted as a cost of testing (Picus & Tralli, 1998).

It was only after several years and after the original directors of CRESST relinquished some of their directorial duties that anything was done about their continuing misrepresentation of the GAO report. A new director consented to correct one paragraph in CRESST's Kentucky report that had contained the most blatant mischaracterization.

Policy Implications

The GAO study produced the most reliable and complete estimates ever of the costs of testing. Moreover, it generated the most reliable and detailed database of state and school district testing programs developed to date. Yet to my knowledge, no scholar other than myself has ever used that database, which was meticulously built at taxpayer expense. The GAO study was extraordinarily well done and produced uniquely useful and trustworthy information; unfortunately, it was hounded into obscurity.

FALLACY 2: HIGH STAKES INDUCE ARTIFICIAL TEST SCORE INCREASES (TEST SCORE INFLATION)

In 1987, a West Virginia physician, John Jacob Cannell, published the results of a study in *Nationally Normed Elementary Achievement Testing in America's Public Schools*. He had been surprised that West Virginia students kept scoring "above the national average" on a national norm-referenced standardized test (NRT), given the state's low relative standing on other measures of academic performance. He surveyed the situation in other states and with other NRTs and discovered that the students in every state in the nation were "above the national average." The phenomenon was dubbed the "Lake Wobegon effect," in tribute to the mythical community of Lake Wobegon, where "all the children are above average." The Cannell report implied that half the school superintendents in the country were lying about their schools' academic achievement. It further implied that with poorer results, the other half might lie, too.

School districts could purchase NRTs off the shelf from commercial test publishers and administer them on their own. With no external proctors watching, school and district administrators were free to manipulate any and all aspects of the tests. They could look at the test items beforehand and let their teachers look at them as well. They could give the students as much time to finish as they desired. They could keep using the same form of the test year after year. They could even score the tests themselves. The results from these internally administered tests primed many a press release (see Cannell, 1989, chap. 3).

Cannell followed up with a second report (1989), *How Public Educators Cheat on Standardized Achievement Tests*, in which he added similar state-by-state information for the secondary grades. He also provided detailed results of a survey of test security practices in the 50 states (Cannell, 1989, pp. 50–102) and printed some of the feedback he received from teachers in response to an advertisement his organization had placed in *Education Week* in spring 1989 (Cannell, 1989, chap. 3).

Case Study: The Lake Wobegon Effect

The Cannell (1987, 1989) reports attracted a flurry of research papers (and no group took to the task more vigorously than CRESST). Most researchers concurred that the Lake Wobegon effect was real—across most states, many districts, and most grade levels, more aggregate average test scores were above average than would have been expected by chance, many more.

The CRESST researchers, however, asserted that deliberate educator cheating had nothing to do with the Lake Wobegon effect. Theirs are among the most widely cited and celebrated articles in the education policy research literature. For 2 decades, CRESST members have asserted that high stakes caused the "artificial" test score gains reported by Cannell (1987, 1989) and found elsewhere. They identified "teaching to the test" (i.e., test preparation or coaching) as the direct mechanism that produces this "test score inflation."

The empirical evidence cited by CRESST researchers to support their high-stakes-cause-test-score-inflation claim is less than abundant, however, and consists of the following:

- the Lake Wobegon reports of John Jacob Cannell (1987, 1989), as they interpret them;
- certain patterns in the pre- and posttest scores from the 1st decade or so of the Title I Evaluation and Reporting System (Linn, 2000, pp. 5, 6); and
- the "preliminary findings" from an unreplicable experiment that CRESST conducted in the early 1990s in an unidentified school district, with two unidentified tests, one of which was "perceived to be high stakes" (Koretz, Linn, Dunbar, & Shepard, 1991).

Furthermore, some strikingly subjective (nonempirical) observational studies have sometimes been cited as evidence as well (see, e.g., McNeil, 2000; McNeil & Valenzuela, 2000; Smith 1991a, 1991b, 1991c; Smith & Rottenberg, 1991). How good is this evidence?

Many educators and testing opponents consider the Cannell (1987, 1989) reports alone ample proof of the "score-inflationary" effects of high-stakes testing and propose banning such testing entirely, arguing that results from accountability tests cannot be trusted. Indeed, Cannell's data provide convincing evidence of artificial test score inflation. However, with the exception of one Texas test, none of those that Cannell analyzed had any stakes. Rather, all but one of his Lake Wobegon tests were used for system monitoring and diagnosis and carried no consequences for students or teachers.

Cannell's (1987, 1989) reports provide brief mentions of some state standards-based tests that had high stakes. Cannell contrasted their tight test security with the lax test security typical for the no-stakes NRTs he analyzed. He did not analyze the scores or trend in scores on the high-stakes standards-based tests. The Lake Wobegon tests—the tests with scores that were inflated artificially over time—were the no-stakes tests (Phelps, 2005d).

Being mostly or entirely under the control of education administrators, the NRTs could be manipulated and their resulting scores published, making the administrators look good. Cannell's (1987, 1989) data show that generally low-performing states were more prone to NRT score inflation, perhaps because administrators felt embarrassed by their states' showing on other measures and strove to compensate (Phelps, 2005d).

Because the score-inflated tests themselves had no stakes, how could states have inflated their scores? This would be possible only if the stakes attached to other tests somehow affected the administration of the NRTs. The states of Mississippi, North Carolina, and Arkansas, for example, exhibited strong score inflation with their NRTs in Cannell's (1987, 1989) data, and all three states had other testing programs with high stakes (with high levels of test security for those programs). However, Cannell's own state of West Virginia also had terribly inflated NRT scores and no high-stakes testing program. The same was true for the neighboring state of Kentucky (Phelps, 2005d).

Nonetheless, I decided to look further into the CRESST hypothesis. I surmised that if high stakes cause test score inflation, one should find the following:

- direct evidence that test coaching (i.e., teaching to the test), when isolated from other factors, increases test scores and
- grade levels that are closer to a high-stakes event (e.g., a high school graduation test) showing more test score inflation than grade levels that are further away.

This research is described in Appendix A (see http://www.apa.org/books/resources/Phelps/). In summary, the appendix indicates that the high-stakes-cause-test-score-inflation hypothesis is not supported by empirical evidence.

Why Low Stakes Are Associated With Test Score Inflation

Given current law and practice, the typical high-stakes test is virtually certain to be accompanied by item rotation, sealed packets, monitoring by external proctors, and the other test security measures itemized as necessary by Cannell (1987, 1989) in his late-1980s appeal to clean up the rampant corruption in educational testing and reporting.

Two decades ago, Cannell (1987, 1989) suspected a combination of educator dishonesty and lax test security to be causing test score inflation. However, educators are human, and educator dishonesty (in at least some proportion of the educator population) is not going away any time soon. So if Cannell's suspicions were correct, the only sure way to prevent test score inflation would be with tight test security. In Cannell's review of 50 states and even more tests, testing programs with tight security had no apparent problems with test score inflation. High stakes are associated with reliable test results, then, because high-stakes tests are administered under conditions of tight test security. That security may not always be as tight as it could be and should be, but it is virtually certain to be much tighter than the test security that accompanies low- or no-stakes tests (i.e., when the low- or no-stakes tests impose any test security at all).

In addition to current law and professional practice, other factors that can enhance test security and that also tend to accompany high-stakes tests are high public profile, media attention, and voluntary insider (be it student, parent, or educator) surveillance and reporting of cheating. Do a Web search for stories of test cheating, and you will find that in many cases, cheating teachers were turned in by colleagues, students, or parents (see, e.g., the link to "Cheating in the News" at http://www.caveon.com).

Public attention does not induce otherwise honest educators to cheat, as CRESST claims. The public attention enables otherwise successful cheaters to be caught. In contrast to CRESST's assertions, under current law and practice, it is typically high-stakes tests that are public, transparent, and explicit in their test attributes and public objectives, and it is typically low-stakes tests that are not.

The most certain cure for test-score inflation is tight test security and ample item rotation, which are common with externally administered, high-stakes testing. An agency external to the local school district must be responsible for administering the tests under standardized, monitored, secure conditions, just as is done in hundreds of other countries (see, e.g., American Federation of Teachers, 1995; Britton, Hawkins, & Gandal, 1996; Eckstein & Noah, 1993; Phelps, 1996, 2000b, 2001). If the tests have stakes, then students, parents, teachers, and policymakers alike tend to take them seriously, and adequate resources are more likely to be invested toward ensuring test quality and security.

Any test can be made a Lake Wobegon test. All that is needed is an absence of test security and item rotation and the slightest temptation for (some) education administrators to cheat. How a test is administered determines whether it becomes a Lake Wobegon test—one with artificial score gains over time. Ultimately, the other characteristics of the test—the name, the purpose, the content, the format—are irrelevant.

In addition to good test security and ample item rotation, both of which are more common with high-stakes tests, a second, quite different type of test administration can prevent artificial test score gains (i.e., score inflation). This type produces scores that are untraceable to schools or districts. Some system-monitoring and diagnostic tests bear this characteristic. Any test producing scores that are traceable to particular schools, districts, or states can also be used to make the administrators of those institutions look good. Cannell's (1987, 1989) studies demonstrate that little incentive is required to tempt at least some education administrators to cheat on standardized tests. Successful cheating, however, requires means, motive, and opportunity. When external agencies administer a test under tight security (with ample item rotation), motivated school administrators are denied the means and opportunity to cheat, and there is no test score inflation. There were no stakes for anyone, including teachers, with (all but one of) Cannell's Lake Wobegon tests—no external evaluation or oversight. Researchers who insisted after the fact that stakes were involved simply fabricated this excuse. Education administrators cheated, or set things up so that teachers could not help but passively cheat (e.g., by giving them the same test form to use year after year), reported the fake results, and then boasted. They did so because they wanted to and, more important, because they could. The motivation was not pressure but self-aggrandizement. Indeed, the cheating was made possible by an absence of pressure.

Policy Implications

For its part, CRESST took the clear evidence of widespread educator cheating and misrepresentation of test results and managed to convince most interested parties that those educators were not responsible for their actions. Rather, the pressure of high-stakes testing was to blame, regardless of the fact that the tests in question had no stakes.

Cannell's (1987, 1989) studies showed that artificial test score gains were the result of educators' opportunistic exploitation of lax security, which happens to be more common with no-stakes testing. A reasonable policy solution would have been to legislate high levels of security for all systemwide testing programs, regardless of the stakes. CRESST suggested in the 1980s, and continues to recommend to this day, a policy solution that is the opposite of what the evidence suggests is needed. Claiming that "teaching to the test" and high-stakes testing cause score inflation, CRESST labeled these bad practice. Yet in standards-based systems, teaching to the test is exactly what teachers are supposed to do.

Further, CRESST's questionable method of verifying the validity of test score trends—comparing score trends on a no-stakes test that is not based on a particular state's curriculum to those on a high-stakes test that is—was incorporated into the NCLB Act in early 2002. The National Assessment of Education Progress (NAEP) was to be used to shadow state standards-based tests, regardless of the fact that state standards varied widely, including in their degree of similarity to NAEP content.

FALLACY 3: THERE IS LITTLE EVIDENCE REGARDING THE EFFECTS OF TESTING AND NONE REGARDING ITS BENEFITS

The following passage from Greene and Jorgensen's (1929) authoritative handbook *The Use and Interpretation of Education Tests* struck me as representative for our times:

> Within the past score of years tests and measuring devices in nearly all subject matter fields have been developed. What the future of this movement will be no one can predict. In many ways the rapid development has been unfortunate for it has resulted in confusion on the part of the classroom teacher, the one who should profit most from the program. (p. 334)

Being thorough scholars, Greene and Jorgensen provided "a representative list" of 18 test distributors and publishers (their Appendix A), along with a 16-page "list of [several hundred] educational tests" that "is in no sense a complete catalogue of standard tests" (p. 337).

E. H. Jones (1923–1924) offered a masterful review of the research, "The Effects of Examination on the Permanence of Learning." Jones reviewed much of the experimental research literature on the optimal timing, spacing, and duration of testing for memory (i.e., permanent learning) that was available at the time. He sketched "frequency surfaces," illustrating memory "decay functions" under varying experimental conditions. Experiments included in Jones's review were conducted by many top research psychologists, including A. I. Gates, C. H. Kent, A. J. Rosanoff, Lanfan Lee Ang, and B. R. Simpson.

Harry Greene, Albert Jorgensen, and E. H. Jones are but a few of the thousands of scholars who some of today's most celebrated education researchers effectively claim never existed. Likewise for the experimental studies they cited—they simply never happened, according to some contemporary researchers. These researchers might well be offended by this casual dismissal of their life's work, but we will hear complaints from none of them—they have long since passed on.

Case Study: The National Research Council Study of Test Utility

The NRC appointed a Committee on the General Aptitude Test Battery, which wrote *Fairness in Employment Testing* (Hartigan & Wigdor, 1989), a report extraordinary in several aspects, including (a) the odd composition of the committee; (b) the repeated insistence of the committee that there was only meager evidence for the benefits of testing, in the face of thousands of studies in personnel psychology research demonstrating those benefits; (c) the theory of the zero-sum labor market; and (d) the logical contradiction in the report's primary assertions that all jobs are unique, so general ability tests will be invalid for each, but there is no benefit from selection because any worker's abilities will be equally useful anywhere they work, no matter what their training and no matter what the field of work. This research is described in Appendix D (see http://www.apa.org/books/resources/Phelps/).

Policy Implications

It would appear that those at the NRC responsible for the evaluation of testing issues were biased and, further, that the NRC Board on Testing and Assessment had been "captured" by education interests opposed to the use of high-stakes testing. Moreover, those interests extended their control of information outside of their own field of education and over a scholarly domain of psychologists, in this case personnel (i.e., industrial–organizational) psychologists.

As for the well-validated General Aptitude Test Battery (GATB), the U.S. Department of Labor heeded the NRC's advice and chose not to allow its use in employment centers throughout the United States. In the aftermath of the NRC report, the Canadian government weighed the evidence, perceived an opportunity, and purchased the GATB for use in its employment centers nationwide—to good effect, apparently, because the GATB is used in Canada to this day for the purpose for which it was originally intended in the United States.

Case Study: The National Research Council on High-Stakes Testing

In the late 1990s, an NRC study of high-stakes testing provided a similar example of antitesting bias: *High Stakes: Testing for Tracking, Promotion, and Graduation* (Heubert & Hauser, 1999). The most revealing aspect of the NRC's 1999 report is its choice of source material. Sources that buttressed the views of the Board on Testing and Assessment were included, and hundreds of sources that did not were ignored. The majority of citations went to CRESST research and researchers.

With large resources at its disposal (a budget of more than $1 million), the NRC board minimized its research effort. On issue after issue, it threw its lot in with a single researcher or a single group of researchers. For example, the chapter on tracking is really about the work of just one person. The counterevidence and counterarguments on that issue are kept completely hidden from the reader. The early childhood, readiness testing, and promotion and retention sections of the report also feature only one person's point of view. Chapter 10 cites only three sources. Chapter 11 essentially cites only two sources, George Madaus and Walt Haney, whose work is discussed later in the current chapter. In sum, two thirds of the citations in the report refer to fewer than a dozen research sources.

For a book on a psychometric topic, the NRC report strangely ignores psychology research. Only 10 citations of 400 come from psychology journals, and these pertain only to a discussion of assessment standards and theoretical concepts of validity. The report avoids the huge mass of accumulated empirical evidence on high-stakes selection from psychology journals. The report refers exclusively to research in education journals and reports and, even then, only to the work of a small group.

The opinions of the general public are dismissed just as effortlessly. The report acknowledges the high level of public support for high-stakes testing but discounts it thusly:

> Despite some evidence that the public would accept some of the potential tradeoffs, it seems reasonable to assume that most people are unaware of the full range of negative consequences related to . . . high-stakes test use. Moreover, it seems certain that few people are aware of limits on the information that tests provide. No survey questions, for example, have asked how much measurement error is acceptable when tests are used to make high-stakes decisions about individual students. The support for testing expressed in polls might decline if the public understood these things. (Heubert & Hauser, 1999, pp. 44–45)

Then again, it might not. Almost all adults are experienced former students. It so happens that they know something about school.

Policy Implications

High Stakes includes more than 40 recommendations. With some exceptions, any one of them taken alone seems reasonable. Taken together, they would impose a burden on the states that none could feasibly meet. The report even floats a proposal to require that tests be pretested before they can be used for high-stakes purposes, using a new, general standard of predictive validity. Because testing proponents argue that high-stakes tests promote more learning or better employment, the NRC board argued that we should hold off certifying the use of any high-stakes test until it can be proved that over time (e.g., once a student reaches college), the test increases learning and improves employment outcomes. It would take years to conduct such an experiment, even if the experiment were feasible. Of course, it is not. One cannot test the effects of high-stakes tests when the stakes are not high as, presumably, they would not be during the life of the experiment.

The NRC's (Heubert & Hauser, 1999) *High Stakes* report was released at a propitious time: just before the debate over and design of the NCLB Act. For those who regarded the NRC's work to be objective and trustworthy, it would serve as a caution and nothing more. A century's worth of program evaluations and experimental research on the optimal design of high-stakes test-based accountability systems was ignored, relegated to an information abyss. When the nation needed the information most and was most ready to use it, the NRC suppressed it.

Case Study: The October Surprise of the 2000 Presidential Campaign

In 2000, a small group of CRESST researchers working at its affiliate, the Rand Corporation, decided to conduct an analysis of the Texas testing program (Klein, Hamilton, McCaffrey, & Stecher, 2000). They said it was pure coincidence that their report was released only a few weeks before the presidential election. They also said it was only coincidence that they chose to study Texas, the home state of one of the presidential candidates, rather than any number of other states with testing programs similar to the one in Texas. As Rand's James A. Thomson (2000), chief executive officer of the "scrupulously nonpartisan institution" said in a press release, "Texas was studied because the state exemplifies a national trend toward using statewide exams as a basis for high-stakes educational decisions."

The Rand report condemned the Texas Assessment of Academic Skills (TAAS) program, asserting there was no evidence of the improvements in student academic achievement the program administrators had claimed and that in fact there was considerable evidence of harm. Moreover, Rand recommended that plans for similar testing programs should be postponed until more research could be done. Rand's claims were made against the following background: Of the states that had participated in the state-level NAEP math and reading assessments in the 1990s, only one other state, North Carolina, had improved its scores more than Texas. North Carolina tested its students even more often, and for higher stakes, than Texas did.

If one simply adds up the scale-score gains (or losses) over time from the various NAEP administrations for each state, one finds the following results: North Carolina increased by 33 scale points overall, Texas by 27 points, and Connecticut by 25 points. These top three states all tested their students a lot. In the case of Connecticut, high stakes were not attached to test performance for the students, but the state education department used the test information to evaluate schools and districts in a rigorous manner (Connecticut's education department was as intrusive in local affairs as many European national education departments, its quality monitoring being as thorough and intensive). After these top three states, the cumulative scale score gains dropped to 19 in Kentucky (another state with a lot of testing) and further down to −10 in the District of Columbia, which had no testing at the time.

The Rand report's criticism of the Texas testing program rested on the following claims:

- Although there was improvement in fourth-grade NAEP mathematics scores in Texas over time, there was no improvement in eighth-grade math scores or fourth-grade reading scores.
- What improvements there were in math and reading did not last past fourth grade. Between the fourth and eighth grades, the gain in scores over time was no greater than the average for the nation.
- Because TAAS scores improved by a greater proportion than Texas' NAEP scores, the TAAS scores must have been "inflated" and not reflective of "real" gains in achievement.

Texas' net cumulative score gains on the NAEP were more than twice the national average. The Rand researchers claimed the state's gains were no different from the rest of the nation's by separating the big picture (all the grade levels tested and compared across the entire time period) into several smaller pictures (each grade level tested separately and compared only with the nearest time period) and then relying on statistical-testing artifacts within each. This was methodologically invalid, because they reported a conclusion about the big picture without actually conducting a statistical test on it. Most researchers try to increase the size of their data sets and thus the power of their statistical tests; Rand did just the opposite. Instead, it looked at a segment of gains in fourth-grade math, a segment of gains in eighth-grade math, and so on. With each segment, the researchers conducted a statistical test that relied on arguably standard, but still arbitrary, cutoff thresholds to determine "statistically significant" differences. For each separate case in isolation, there is nothing wrong with this. The Rand researchers probably noticed, however, that for the segments in which the Texas gains did not reach the cutoff points, they just barely did not make it. The Texas gains in the case of every segment were large by normal standards of "large," just not large enough in each and every segment to make the cutoff point for the statistical test Rand chose to use in each case.

If one combines the various segments (in statistical jargon, this is called *pooling*), however, one can both increase the statistical power of the test (by increasing the sample size) and conduct the correct test—for the NAEP performance of Texas as a whole rather than for separate, discrete bits. Combining separate tests, or subtests, at the same level of difficulty, even on different subject matter, is often done when identical scales are used. Witness the many studies that use SAT combined (verbal + math) scores in their analyses.

The Rand researchers also argued that because the score gains on the TAAS exceeded those on the NAEP, they could not be "real" and must have been inflated. They used the same logic they had used in the CRESST Lake Wobegon study discussed earlier. Again, scores on two tests cannot be perfectly correlated without their being the exact same test. The TAAS and the NAEP were not the same, nor were they supposed to be, so their scores could not be perfectly correlated. The fact that the score increases in the TAAS over time were greater than Texas students' score gains on the NAEP was to be expected; any other result would have suggested a serious problem. The TAAS contained subject matter that matched the curriculum standards of the state of Texas. The NAEP did not. Teachers were supposed to teach the subject matter covered by the TAAS, not that covered by the NAEP.

Policy Implications

When accurate information was most needed, we got this instead. In late 2001, midway between the election of George W. Bush and the U.S. Congress' passage of the NCLB Act, I read the following statements in an education journal:

> Nearly 20 years later, the debate surrounding [minimum competency tests] remains much the same, consisting primarily of opinion and specu-lation. . . . A lack of solid empirical research has allowed the controversy to continue unchecked by evidence or experience. . . . The lack of em-pirical research on the achievement effects of mandatory graduation ex-ams is striking, particularly in light of their growing popularity across the nation. . . . The evidence on graduation exams and achievement is lim-ited and mixed. (Jacob, 2001, p. 334)

I assumed that an opponent of President Bush's policies and of the NCLB Act had written it. I wrote to the author, then employed as an instructor at one of my alma maters, and pointed out that there was, in fact, a great deal of empirical research on minimum competency testing and on the achieve-ment effects of mandatory graduation exams and that the empirical evidence on graduation exams and achievement was neither limited nor mixed. The author defended his statements by asserting that he had checked them with our country's foremost researchers on the effects of standardized educational achievement testing, naming four CRESST researchers, including three of the authors of the October surprise report. The joke was on the Republican Party, however. This fellow, whose carelessness undermined GOP education policy, became a trusted policy advisor.

Case Study: Co-Optation of the National Council on Measurement in Education

The National Council on Measurement in Education (NCME) had long served as a bulwark of psychometric respectability against the more re-gressive elements within education research that dominate the much larger American Educational Research Association (AERA). However, most NCME members are also AERA members; indeed, the two organizations hold their annual meetings at the same time and the same place. Moreover, most NCME members work in the education business, as professors in education schools or for firms that serve the education market. NCME is not impervious to regressive influences

The psychometrician William Mehrens (1998) delivered his presidential address to the NCME in the mid-1990s on the topic of the effects of standardized testing. He talked as if he had looked at the sum total of what is known about these effects. The picture he saw did not look pretty: Standardized testing, particularly when it had high stakes, seemed to do more harm than good. Unfortunately, Mehrens had apparently conducted no literature search whatsoever. Rather, he relied on his own instincts and assumed that what he happened to read over the years comprised a representative sample of the existing literature.

Among more than 60 citations in Mehrens's (1998) speech, one can find none from psychologists, program evaluators, sociologists, economists, or researchers outside the United States and only one dated earlier than 1984. Most of his attention (and more than one third of his citations), in fact, focused on the work of a single organization, CRESST. Half of the rest of the sources were outspoken, self-acknowledged opponents of high-stakes testing. Sadly, in the decade since Mehrens' address, testing opponents have eagerly and liberally cited his presidential address as authoritative evidence that the research literature on the effects of testing is meager at best.

As if to place a capstone atop the monument to CRESST's success in information suppression, researchers Dan Koretz and Laura Hamilton (2007) penned a chapter for the most current version of the "bible of testing research," the NCME-sponsored reference book, *Educational Measurement*. Their chapter, "Testing for Accountability in K–12," is more remarkable for what is left out than for what is included. Little of the abundant counterevidence to their work is mentioned and, when offered at all, is the weakest available. Among the 253 references are 82 (32%) to works by themselves and their CRESST colleagues. Another 10% are official works—legislation, government reports, statistical compendia, and the like. This still leaves a good bit of room for references to a century's worth of research on the effects of testing. Instead, one finds other sources that claim a research dearth and the plaint that much more research will be needed before we can dare to use tests responsibly.

In an appendix to *Defending Standardized Testing* (Phelps, 2005a), I listed more than 300 studies of the effects of testing, the vast majority of which provide empirical evidence of beneficial effects. Eighty of the listed studies are meta-analyses or reviews of multiple separate studies. I compared this list with the references in the Koretz and Hamilton (2007) chapter, which purports to summarize all of the available research. I found but three sources in common.

Policy Implications

Those who claim a paucity of research on the effects and benefits of testing or on the structure of test-based accountability systems either have not looked very hard or have not wished to find what is available in the literature. If the topic of the effects of standardized testing can be persistently exposed to the glare of journalists' floodlights yet successfully censored and suppressed, then any topic can be. Is the increasing concentration of education-research dissemination in fewer and fewer hands likely to improve education? It may not matter how one answers the question, for the forces working to dissolve and disintegrate the hard-won accumulation of education knowledge seem only to be growing stronger. The chief problem is that accurate and useful ideas and information in education—indeed, perhaps most accurate and useful ideas and information—are suppressed and ignored in policy discussions.

Case Study: Co-Optation of the Republican Policy Advisors

The following statements come from CRESST researchers:

- Despite the long history of assessment-based accountability, hard evidence about its effects is surprisingly sparse, and the little evidence that is available is not encouraging. (Koretz, 1996)
- Although much has been written on achievement motivation per se, there has been surprisingly little empirical research on the effects of different motivation conditions on test performance. (Kiplinger & Linn, 1993, p. 3)

Several years ago, I spent some time conducting computer searches and strolling library aisles for signs of the research literature on test-based accountability and the relationship between motivation and test performance that CRESST researchers have repeatedly declared either nonexistent or scarce. Lo and behold, I discovered a few hundred studies. My search was tedious, but it was not difficult. Given the height of the pile of books, articles, and bibliographies I have yet to comb through, it would appear that I will discover a few hundred more.

Studies measuring the effects of standardized testing in education date back to the early 1900s and range across virtually all relevant types of research methodologies—meta-analyses, controlled experiments, quasi-experiments, program evaluations, case studies and structured interviews, interrupted time series with shadow measures, pre–post designs, polls and surveys, cost–benefit analyses, multivariate regressions, multilevel structural equation models, and data analyses of administrative records (Phelps, 2005c).

CRESST researchers have probably been the most persistent in their paucity- and absence-of-research claims, but they have hardly been alone.

This assertion is widely advertised (see, e.g., Barth, 2006; Mitchell, 2006; Olson, 2002). Moreover, the belief now seems to transcend political and ideological boundaries. Both opponents and supporters of high-stakes standardized testing assert the claim (see, e.g., Cizek, 2001; Hanushek & Raymond, 2002, 2003; Jacob, 2001, 2002, 2003; Loveless, as cited in New Report Confirms, 2003; Roderick, Jacob, & Bryk, 2002). As the belief in the research literature's nonexistence has become more pervasive and deeply held, efforts to reference it have become less frequent, less thorough, or casually dismissed.

One might have reasonably assumed, given the thrust of U.S. education policy in the early 2000s, that this research literature would have been exposed, made widely familiar, and meticulously analyzed. Yet just the opposite happened—the bulk of an available research literature that could have helped to guide our society in the implementation of its primary, and controversial, education policy was declared nonexistent.

For example, consider the following characterizations of the research literature on the effects of test-based accountability. "Most of the evidence is unpublished at this point" (Olson, 2002, p. 13). "There is little empirical evidence on test-based accountability (also referred to as high-stakes testing)" (Jacob, 2002, p. 2). It is "a young and highly selective body of work" (Hanushek & Raymond, 2002, p. 1). "It is important to keep in mind the limited body of data on the subject. We are just getting started in terms of solid research on standards, testing and accountability" (Loveless, as cited in New Report Confirms, 2003, p. 1). "The evidence on this outcome is just beginning to come in" and "the evidence on positive and negative consequences is necessarily skimpy" (Cizek, 2001, p. 7). These quotes come from the period during which the NCLB Act was being considered or designed. All come from Republican policy advisors.

The presidential election campaign of 2000 was the first in U.S. history in which standardized testing was a central campaign issue; testing opponents were prominent and vocal throughout. What did the Republican policy advisors have to say? They declared there to be no evidence that high-stakes standardized testing did any good and that on balance, it seemed to be harmful. More research was needed on the topic (and these advisors were willing to do it). NCLB opponents could not have written the script any better themselves.

Policy Implications

With the election of George W. Bush, GOP policy advisors faced a historic opportunity, with enormous implications, to benefit U.S. education. They had the resources to blast open the seal of censorship covering a huge research literature on standardized testing's achievement effects. Instead, whether by mistake or design, they chose to reinforce the seal, despite the critical need of their Republican politician clients for exactly the opposite behavior.

After seconding testing opponents' claim that little to no research existed on the effects of standardized testing, some of the Republican think tankers declared themselves to be pioneers in conducting such research. Apparently, one assertion used to persuade Republican policymakers of the paucity-of-research hypothesis was that all education research was poorly done, so any research they (mostly economists) conducted would be the first high-quality research on the topic (see, e.g., Hanushek, 2006).

Think of the assumptions necessary for economists to adopt this line of thinking. Educational standards and standardized tests have existed for millennia. Psychologists first developed the "scientific" standardized test more than a century ago, and they, along with program evaluators and education practitioners, have conducted hundreds of thousands of studies with or about them since that time. Nonetheless, since the mid-1990s, a number of economists have proposed that none among these scores of psychologists and practitioners ever thought to study the various effects of educational testing (and that these professionals could not even conduct such studies responsibly). In their book chapter titled "Economics Wins, Psychology Loses, and Society Pays," Bazerman and Malhotra (2006) described several miserably failed public policies, crafted by economists, on topics for which psychologists had long developed expertise—expertise ignored by the economists in policy positions. With federal standardized testing programs in the first decade of the 21st century, economists may have added yet another such policy.

Being the first to conduct research on a topic can of course enhance one's career prospects fabulously, whereas citing and summarizing work already done by others can make one look like a slacker. To my knowledge, none of the cases cited earlier with erroneous "firstness" claims ultimately attracted any negative consequence toward the claimant. The act of dismissing a research literature, no matter how large, appears to be risk free. What consequence might that lack of consequence portend for the preservation of the education research literature?

Besides, who's going to complain about the regression? Most of the scientists and evaluators responsible for the past century's worth of research on the effects of testing are deceased. Many of those still alive work in the field of psychology and, even if they were to become aware of others' grandiose claims to pioneering the field, they have no standing in the other professions (e.g., economics) from which to lodge a complaint. Those working within education who might object have long since been professionally marginalized by the regressors. That leaves few to carry on as advocates for the preservation of an increasingly endangered research literature.

I have personally challenged some of the research regressors directly on their firstness and paucity-of-research claims. The typical reply insinuates something like, "You're just jealous because your work is not getting attention." Incidentally, I hear this retort whether my own work represents less than 1% of the relevant dismissed research literature or none of it.

One slightly more thoughtful reply suggests that declaring a century-old research literature nonexistent is of no practical consequence because people are conducting these studies now and surely will discover whatever previous researchers discovered anyway. Perhaps, but it might take them another hundred years and another thousand studies to accumulate as much knowledge. Besides, the knowledge was needed during the period 2000–2002, while the NCLB Act was being debated and designed. The few economists' studies conducted after 2003 were too late to be useful.

The co-optation of Republican policy advisors was hugely important. Not only did testing critics, including CRESST researchers, gain policy leverage, they were appointed to influential executive branch committees, commissions, and projects. Not bad for folk who tried to sabotage the Bush campaign just 3 weeks before the 2000 presidential election. Moreover, with the Republican think tankers on board, the most influential potential advocates for educational achievement testing programs were neutralized. The enormous resources of the federal government, business groups, and foundations that could have been organized to halt the research regression instead supported it. Finally, because most education journalists grant the small cadre of Republican think tankers an effective monopoly to represent the "other side" of most education issues, Republican acquiescence in snuffing a vibrant research literature represented for journalists unanimous confirmation of a fact: The research literature did not exist.

FALLACY 4: TESTING IS MISCHARACTERIZED BECAUSE IT IS DIFFICULT TO UNDERSTAND

Testing and measurement experts—*psychometricians*—tend to be smart people. Most have doctorates, which they earned after completing a dozen or more courses on abstruse topics in statistics, computer programming, scaling, equating, item response theory, and other technical exotica.

Some have assumed that the recondite nature of the subject matter is to blame both for the animosity felt by many education advocates toward testing (i.e., one fears what one does not understand) as well as the misrepresentation of the topic (i.e., it is simply too technical a topic for the average educator, or education journalist, to understand). I believe that fear of the unknown may well fuel the animosity, but I do not believe that the pervasive misrepresentation of the topic among education advocates can be explained by misunderstanding. By ideology, perhaps. By professional self-interest, perhaps. But not by ignorance.

The purpose of this section is to demonstrate how easy it is for advocates to repress the simplest, most easily verified facts and convince the public of falsehoods. This ease is illustrated with arguably the easiest to understand bit of information in the testing and measurement field.

Of the many testing controversies, counting the number of tests given may be the most trivial. Yet that is the point. Of all the claims about educational achievement testing, this is the easiest to verify, and the argument over this issue should be the easiest to settle. Instead, most citizens and policymakers remain misinformed on this presumably simple topic.

Case Study: Facts Unprecedented, Unparalleled, Indisputable

In an *Education Week* editorial titled "Standardized Testing and Its Victims," Alfie Kohn (2000) wrote:

> Standardized testing has swelled and mutated, like a creature in one of those old horror movies, to the point that it now threatens to swallow our schools whole. But let's put aside metaphors and even opinions for a moment so that we can review some indisputable facts on the subject.
>
> Fact 1: Our children are tested to an extent that is unprecedented in our history and unparalleled anywhere else in the world. . . . Few countries use standardized tests for children below high school age—or multiple-choice tests for students of any age.
>
> Fact 2: Our children are tested to an extent that is unprecedented in our history and unparalleled anywhere else in the world. (p. 60)

Similarly, in a September 2001 *Frontline* interview on the Public Broadcasting System, National Public Radio journalist John Merrow interviewed the U.S. Secretary of Education, Rod Paige (Interview: Rod Paige, 2001). In reference to the new NCLB program, he asked, "It raises the question of too much testing. American kids are already tested more often than kids in any other industrialized country. Are we testing our kids too much?" (¶ 22).

The original source of the "indisputable fact" that U.S. schools test more than do other countries' schools was a contractor report for the now-defunct U.S. Office of Technology Assessment (OTA) written by education professors George Madaus and Thomas Kellaghan (1991). Their report became a chapter in a longer OTA report (OTA, 1992, pp. 135–164) and later an article in a professional journal (Feuer & Fulton, 1994). Their claims have permeated the media and the education research literature (e.g., Kellaghan & Madaus, 1995; Kellaghan, Madaus, & Raczek, 1996; Madaus, 1991a, 1991b; Medina & Neill, 1990; National Commission on Testing and Public Policy, 1990; Neill, 1992; Rothman, 1995; Sacks, 1999; Viadero, 1994).

The aforementioned authors claimed all of the following:

- "American students are already the most heavily tested in the world." (Madaus, 1991a, 2)
- The trend in other developed countries was toward less standardized testing. (OTA, 1992, p. 144)

- The trend in other developed countries encompassed all levels of education "even at the postsecondary level." (OTA, 1992, p. 143)
- The trend in other developed countries was unidirectional—large-scale, external tests were being "abolished" (OTA, 1992, p. 143).
- External examinations in other developed countries were "no longer used to make decisions about students' educational paths during the period of compulsory education" (Kellaghan et al., 1996, p. 59).
- "Standardized national examinations before age 16 have all but disappeared from Europe and Asia" (OTA, 1992, pp. 135, 144).
- "The United States is unique in the extensive use of standardized tests for young children" (OTA, 1992, p. 135).
- "None of the countries studied by OTA has a single, centrally prescribed examination that is used for all purposes—classroom diagnosis, selection, and school accountability. Most examinations overseas are . . . not used for school or system accountability" (OTA, 1992, p. 135).

All these claims were false and unsupported by empirical data, but they nonetheless infused policy debates surrounding three presidential testing proposals from the early 1990s to the early 2000s—George H. W. Bush's American Achievement Tests, Bill Clinton's Voluntary National Tests, and George W. Bush's NCLB Act. The report's persuasive force relied on a single, plausible rationale: The authors argued that other countries were dropping large-scale external tests because they no longer needed them as selection devices. European and Asian countries had expanded the number of places available in secondary schools, polytechnics, and universities, so access had been made available to all, or at least most, who desired it. This proposed rationale for other countries' allegedly dropping educational selection tests served to distract from the weakness of the study's claims. One of the coauthors would go on to manage more than a decade's worth of research on standardized testing at the NRC; another would end up conducting research on standardized testing for the World Bank.

Around the same period of time, four other, more rigorous test-counting studies were conducted that went far beyond rationale and anecdote and were generally ignored. First, the Organisation for Economic Co-operation and Development (OECD) conducted a survey of its member countries in 1990–1991 addressing the number and duration of their systemwide tests. This survey revealed that U.S. students faced fewer hours and fewer numbers of high-stakes standardized tests than their counterparts in every one of the 13 other countries studied. Further, U.S. students underwent fewer hours of mandated tests than their counterparts in 12 of the 13 other countries (Phelps, 1996, p. 25).

Second, Eckstein and Noah's (1993, pp. 149, 167) classic eight-country set of case studies ranked the United States lowest both in "examination burden" and "examination difficulty." The authors concluded,

> In addition to certification and selection, other countries use their end-of-secondary-school examinations for a variety of other functions: for example, to define what knowledge and skills are of most worth, to set performance expectations of students, teachers, and schools, and to provide yardsticks against which individual schools and the school system as a whole can be assessed.
>
> The United States . . . lacks any systematic and general way of certifying completion of a specified course of secondary school study and, unlike other countries, has no consistent national criteria or means for selection beyond that stage, whether for employment or for particular types of postsecondary education or training. (pp. 238–239)

Third, in a seven-country survey of secondary school math and science examinations, Britton, Hawkins, and Gandal (1996) asserted,

> While only 6.6 percent of US students take Advanced Placement (AP) examinations, roughly a quarter to a half of all students in other nations take and pass advanced subject-specific examinations.
>
> In each country except the United States, college-bound students seeking to study in a university must pass demanding, subject-specific examinations. In France, Germany, and Israel, even many students who do not go on to college take these examinations because they are a prestigious credential in their societies. (pp. 202–203)

Finally, in a review of widely available documentary source material, I found that over the period 1974–1999 in 31 countries and provinces, 59 large-scale external testing programs were added, and only 5 were dropped. The OTA (1992) had implied that large-scale tests were used only for selection to or exclusion from the next level of education. During 1974–1999, however, other countries and states added 22 monitoring exams, 6 subject-area end-of-course testing programs, 2 primary-to-secondary-level achievement tests, and 2 diagnostic exams. Thirty tests with medium or high stakes were added, and only four were dropped (Phelps, 2000b, pp. 17, 18).

All the countries mentioned in the anecdotal Madaus–Kellaghan–Feuer study (i.e., Feuer & Fulton, 1994; Madaus & Kellaghan, 1991; OTA, 1992) were covered by these four more rigorous studies that presented empirical and case study evidence that U.S. students faced fewer and easier tests than did their counterparts in other nations. None of the latter studies received much attention in the education media or research literature, however, whereas the Madaus–Kellaghan–Feuer study received a lot.

Policy Implications

Why did a study void of evidence receive more attention than studies that incorporated data and first-person case studies? In my judgment, it is because education advocates can promote studies that reach conclusions they like and suppress studies reaching conclusions they do not like, and this can be based on ideology or self-interest.

In such an atmosphere of information dissemination, any topic needs only one study to promote a favored conclusion, and that one study only needs some trappings of legitimacy. Whether the study was done well or the conclusions were warranted may be irrelevant. In the case of the Madaus–Kellaghan–Feuer study, the OTA imprimatur was sufficient. The four other studies reaching contrary conclusions were simply ignored and disappeared from view.

In this manner, public policies "based on research" can amount to nothing more than a powerful interest group's preferences—the factual basis being that which the interest group wishes to be fact. Public policies formed this way will always serve the needs of the vested interests.

For their part, education journalists had plenty of opportunity to study the issue and apply a standard amount of journalistic skepticism to the more extravagant claims about the amount of testing in the United States alone or in comparison with other countries. However, I have yet to witness a journalist referring to the grandiose test-counting claims as anything but reliable and objective fact (see, e.g., Chandler, 1999; Merrow, 2002; Sacks, 1999; Strauss, 2006; Teel, 2001; Wolk, 2002). More on education journalists' profound lack of skepticism regarding claims made by testing opponents can be found in another source (see Phelps, 2003, chap. 6).

Case Study: The Amount of Testing Is Unknowable, and It Is a Huge Number

Madaus would serve as coauthor in another set of claims about the amount of testing that occurs, this time for the United States alone (Haney, Madaus, & Lyons, 1993):

> We contacted the College Board and ACT directly and were informed that 1,980,000 SATs and 1,000,000 ACTs were given in 1986–87. We thus have relatively firm figures on the number of such college admissions tests given. But there are several ways of counting the number of separately scorable subtests in these testing programs. The SAT has two subtests, the SAT—Verbal and the SAT—Math. Moreover, two subscores are reported for the SAT—Verbal, namely reading and vocabulary. Also, almost all students who take the SAT take the Test of Standard Written English. . . . Similarly, the ACT assessment has four subtests, but since a composite score is also calculated, we have used 4 and 5 as bases for high and low estimates. The results . . . indicate that

between nearly 4 million and 10 million SAT subtests and 4 million to 5 million ACT subtests are administered annually. . . . Altogether then we estimate that in 1986–87, 13 million to 22 million college admissions "tests" were administered. (pp. 65–66)

The passage continues to sum the total of all U.S. standardized student tests—and not just college entrance exams, but the quotation marks around the word "tests" disappears, *et voilà*, all parts of tests become whole tests.

In sum then . . . we estimate that between 143 million and 395 million tests are administered annually to the nation's population of roughly 44 million elementary and secondary school students, equivalent to between 3 and 9 standardized tests for each student enrolled in elementary and secondary schools. (Haney et al., 1993, p. 66)

At the beginning of the passage, a test is called a *test*. In the middle, the reader is told that tests have parts. Those separate parts are counted up, and in the next paragraph, the parts are called *tests*. After this semantic magic is complete, the authors assert that there are from 3 to 9 times as many standardized student tests administered annually as there actually are.

Another oddity of the passage is its use of the word *estimates*. Two telephone calls to the SAT and ACT offices provided exact counts of the numbers of their tests administered. Further, at the beginning of the passage, an ACT test is referred to in the singular and the total annual number of ACTs administered is declared to be 1 million. After the authors do their parts-as-wholes counting, they end up with an "estimate" for the annual number of ACTs of from 4 to 5 million. Four million is their "lower bound estimate" for a number of tests they had just claimed for a fact to be only 1 million.

One education professor finessed the issue this way:

No one knows for certain how many students are tested in a given year or how many tests the typical student takes because comprehensive and unambiguous data are not available. Richard Phelps (1997) estimates that 36 million district-wide and statewide tests are given each year in the United States. Peter Sacks (1999) cites estimates of 127 million standardized tests of all types being given in a year. Walter Haney, George Madaus, and Robert Lyons (1993) provide low and high estimates. . . . On the low end, they estimate that slightly more than 143 million students a year were tested and that the average child took 2.7 tests per year. On the high end, they estimate that just over 395 million students a year were tested and that the average child took 5.4 tests per year. (Snowman, 2002, p. 490)

The 36 million mentioned in the foregoing passage was an accurate estimate of the number of systemwide tests administered in U.S. public schools in the mid-1990s. This translates to less than 1 test and less than half a day of testing per year per student. All the other numbers mentioned in the passage were derived from the work of Haney, Madaus, and Lyons (1993), count subtests rather than tests, and double count some tests (Phelps, 1997).

Counting the number of tests, or even the number of test items, administered in any given year in the United States may be tedious, but it is easy. It is almost as easy to count the amount of time devoted to test administration (Phelps, 1997). Even if one chooses to count tests by more than one method—for example, by the number of test forms or the number of subtests—it is a remarkably easy task. Verification of the numbers requires no complex theory or special analytical skills, just some persistence and a mastery of simple arithmetic.

These days, most educational achievement tests are administered either nationwide or statewide. Those administered nationwide include the NAEP, the ACT, and the SAT. Their annual numbers of individual test (and subtest) administrations, as well as their durations and the fees paid, can be found in the respective organizations' publications or by telephoning them. Likewise with each of the 50 states, tests may be developed by private firms, but they are sponsored and typically administered by state education agencies.

Policy Implications

If even this, the most resolvable of standardized testing disputes, cannot be resolved or, rather, clarified with accurate information, how can any of the other, more complex issues be resolved? If even these, the most easily obtained facts about standardized testing, can be so effortlessly muddled and manipulated, how can any facts about educational testing be clearly communicated to and understood by the public?

Perhaps they simply cannot be. The fog of ambiguity and misinformation does not dissipate as one climbs the ladder of topical complexity. Other controversial issues, both simple and complex, are just as muddled, and the debate just as one sided. In the case of at least several issues, the factual information commonly accepted by most educators and journalists is not only erroneous but demonstrably the opposite of reality.

OVERARCHING POLICY IMPLICATIONS

To my observation, there is a clear quality difference between research conducted on educational achievement testing policy-related topics before the mid-1980s and the more prominent such work conducted after the mid-1980s. Most of the earlier work can be found in the scholarly psychology literature, although a good number of studies were conducted in the field by technically trained educational practitioners as well. Generally, the work is typical of open-minded scientific inquiry. All sides of issues and most previous relevant work seems to have been considered. Over the years, more knowledge accumulated and was built on top of what had previously been learned. There was progress in humanity's understanding of educational achievement testing.

Objective, open-minded, scholarly study of policy-related educational achievement testing topics continued beyond the mid-1980s but has largely been marginalized from public discussion. The work that seems to get the attention of both policymakers and the press is that conducted by prominent education professors, researchers in federally funded research centers, and several think tank–based economists or political scientists. They seldom have acknowledged the earlier work on educational achievement testing or any contemporary work conducted outside their own small circles of colleagues. Often they have claimed that there has been no study of particular effects of achievement testing before the start of their own work.

Some widely cited educational achievement testing studies have been rigged so that only negative results were possible; for example, see the survey instruments used by West and Viator for the National Science Foundation (Phelps, 2005b, pp. 19–20), the survey result interpretations of the ASCD (Phelps, 2005b, pp. 18–19), or the range of sources cited by the aforementioned Mehrens (1998) and NRC (Heubert & Hauser, 1999) studies. Still other widely cited studies produced results revealing positive effects from the use of educational achievement tests that were nonetheless presented by their authors as negative results (e.g., see Corbett & Wilson, 1991; B. D. Jones & Egley, 2003; B. D. Jones & Johnston, 2002; Kellaghan, Madaus, & Airasian, 1982). These efforts at information suppression, irrespective of their motivation, have been largely successful. Prominent education researchers have managed to delete large segments of the education research literature from the collective working memory and hide large amounts of information that could have informed U.S. education policy (Phelps, 2007a).

As if the suppression of information within the field of education were not detrimental enough, some of the same researchers have managed to expand their information removal activities into other fields, such as personnel psychology.

ONE HUNDRED YEARS OF RESEARCH AND
EXPERIENCE LEFT BEHIND

Imagine this scenario. After a new executive administration is elected and installed in Washington, a deadly epidemic spreads across the country. The administration's policy advisors declare that medications and supplies that could save lives do not exist, but, for a fee, they will build up a new stock. None of the policy advisors are epidemiologists, however; rather, they are cardiologists and orthopedic surgeons. The medical crisis runs its course, and many die because the new stock of supplies only becomes available after the crisis has passed. Much later, it is revealed that there had been a large stock of medical supplies available at the time of the outbreak, but the policy advisors had simply accepted someone else's word that it did not exist and had not looked for it.

An overly dramatic story, perhaps, but subtract the dead bodies, and it is essentially what happened during the period 2000–2002 while the NCLB Act was being designed and debated. A century's worth of useful experience and research was declared nonexistent and not even considered by the Bush administration's policy advisors. Instead, they offered to start a research literature from scratch, and their offer was accepted.

Few economists and political scientists had demonstrated an interest in educational achievement testing during the 20th century; the standardized test is the psychologist's invention. Yet virtually all the Bush administration's education policy advisors are economists and political scientists. Their small collection of research studies on the effects of testing has dribbled out since 2002, with some of those responsible declaring themselves research pioneers (see, e.g., Hanushek, 2006).

The jurist Richard A. Posner (2001) warned of the societal dangers of celebrity researchers, whom he labeled "public intellectuals," making claims outside their field where those with the requisite expertise can hold them accountable. Unfortunately, when the Bush administration's education policy advisors and think tank consultants have published naive research in economics journals, they have not been reviewed by scholars familiar with the relevant literature. Their work might never have passed muster with psychology and measurement journals. Examples of such naiveté include beliefs and assumptions that all tests are pretty much the same and validly comparable whether they have stakes, are administered securely, apply stakes to the teachers or the students, or are norm referenced or standards based.

Ironically, these faux pioneers were paid out of taxpayer funds—first, to replicate studies for which taxpayers had already paid, and second, to declare the earlier public investments nonexistent. The NCLB Act could have been informed by a cornucopia of research and experience. Instead, it was informed by virtually none. Prior research and experience would have told policymakers that most of the motivational benefits of standardized tests required consequences for the students, not just for the schools. Those stakes need not be high to be effective, but there must be some. Because NCLB imposes stakes on schools but not on students, who knows whether the students even try to perform well.

Prior research and experience would have informed policymakers that educators are intelligent people who respond to incentives and who will game a system if they are given an opportunity to do so (see, e.g., Cannell, 1987, 1989). The NCLB Act left many aspects of the test administration process that profoundly affect scores (e.g., incentives and motivation, cut scores, degree of curricular alignment) up for grabs and open to manipulation by local and state officials.

Prior research and experience would have informed policymakers that different tests get different results, and one should not expect average scores from different tests to rise and fall in unison over time (as some interpreters of the NCLB Act seem to expect with the NAEP benchmark). Prior research and experience would have informed policymakers that the public was not in favor of punishing poorly performing schools (as NCLB does), but was in favor of applying consequences to poorly performing students and teachers (which NCLB does not; see, e.g., Phelps 2005b).

What is the effect of test-based accountability? Appendix 3.1 lists a small sample of useful, insightful, relevant, well-done studies that effectively answer this question, could have informed the design of NCLB, and have been declared by prominent researchers not to exist.

One could not find these studies mentioned in the "what the research says" education policy advice pages of major, policy-influential organizations (e.g., Education Commission of the States, *Education Week*, the Education Writers Association, the National School Board Association's Center for Public Education) in the early 2000s while the NCLB Act was being considered and then implemented. In their place, one found mention of a paltry number of works from contemporary "Influentials" (to borrow a term popular with *Education Week*). Had the policymakers and planners involved in designing the NCLB Act simply read the freely available research literature instead of funding expensive new studies and waiting for their few results, they would have received more value for their dollars as well as more and better information, and they would have had this information earlier, when they actually needed it.

One person directly involved in research regression activities told me that there had been no research before the early 2000s that had been conducted under the exact conditions specified by the NCLB Act. However, I am unaware of research studies that focused exclusively on the effects of minimum-competency tests on left-handed students, on Tuesdays, in the month of February, and on rainy days. Does this mean, then, that we cannot make any assumptions about the effects of any tests if they are minimum-competency tests, if left-handed students are involved, and if the tests are administered on rainy February Tuesdays? To the contrary, we can, because we know which factors matter and which do not, and all of the factors that matter have been studied many times.

With the single exception of the federal mandate, there was no aspect of the NCLB accountability initiative that had not been tried and studied before. Every one of the NCLB Act's failings was perfectly predictable on the basis of decades of prior experience and research. Moreover, there were better alternatives for every characteristic of the program that had also been tried and studied thoroughly by researchers in psychology, education, and program evaluation. Yet policymakers were made aware of none of then.

CONCLUSION

Understanding of educational achievement testing may be shrinking among the public at large. The technical psychometric research literature would seem to be safe from the censorship and suppression of vested interests, but the research literature related to testing policy (i.e., its administration, program structure, use, extent, effects, cost, benefits, public opinion, and research dissemination) is diminishing. There are simply too few who cite the research literature in any substantial depth or breadth and too many who are eager to declare it barren. At the same time, there seems to be little hesitation on the part of many researchers to skip lightly past the annoying obligation of a search of the literature yet nonetheless to claim a mastery of it. A thorough literature review requires a great deal of time and patience, virtues often lacking among the most ambitious and narcissistic. In one effort of mine—accumulating studies on the impact of standardized testing—I started out thinking that there were probably a dozen or so such studies. A few years ago, I was aware that there were hundreds. Now I know that their number exceeds a thousand, and, despite the rhetoric of some critics, only a tiny proportion of them were conducted after the year 2000.

In the end, however, it will not matter for society's sake if we find 10,000 studies. There will remain other education researchers, prominent and with abundant resources at their disposal—researchers whose work is frequently covered by education journalists—who will continue to insist that no such studies ever existed. It is education research's dirty secret: Unpopular research and research that generates unpopular results can be successfully—and easily—censored and suppressed (see, e.g., Phelps, 1999, 2000a, 2003 [preface, chap. 7], 2005c [chap. 3]).

A biological species cannot survive when mating individuals cannot find each other. When numbers decline to such an extent that predators (or hunters) can more easily find members of a species than can potential mates, the species crosses a demographic threshold and heads toward its inevitable extinction. Those who work with endangered species call this the *extinction vortex*.

Similarly, the censorship and suppression of the research literature on the effects of educational achievement testing have become so successful that it has become difficult to find the literature's progenitors. For example, I may have spent more time than anyone else on Earth combing the research literature. Nonetheless, I was a few years into my effort before I discovered the work of Frank Dempster (1991, 1997), one of the world's foremost authorities, or that of Jim Haynie (e.g., 1994, 2007) in career and technical education. Why did it take me so long to find their work? It is not popular among the vested interests in education—they find the benefits of testing to be strong and persistent—and thus it is not widely advertised. Indeed, work like theirs is far more often declared nonexistent than recognized. Few miners persist in tunneling deep shafts for unfashionable gems. Likewise, few researchers pursue unfashionable topics in the face of persistent discouragement and very real professional disincentives (see, e.g., Phelps, n.d.).

U.S. education's single greatest need may be for an independent education press. Unfortunately, what we have now is anything but independent. Vested interest organizations are guaranteed seats on the board of the Education Writers Association, the only large professional organization of education journalists (Lieberman, 2007, chap. 11). The Goliath of education news publications, *Education Week*, is arguably the least independent of any education organization inside the (Washington, DC) Beltway. *Education Week* advertises its willingness to partner with other organizations on research and news projects. Its partners must bring resources to the table, however, and only those with power and money can do that. (Imagine the *New York Times* or the *Washington Post* entering into working research, news, and dissemination partnerships with think tanks, federally funded research centers, and professional advocacy groups.) *Education Week* editors serve on the boards of partisan organizations for which they provide headlines, thus freely participating in education's "interlocking directorates" of vested interests (see Domhoff, 2006).

Not surprisingly, *Education Week*'s pages often read like a wintry mix of PR Newswire and *Variety*, more focused on celebrity and influence than substance and accuracy. It spends ample resources ranking public intellectuals in its periodic popularity contest of the "Influentials" while it ignores an abundance of important information and evidence that could be provided by the many it deems not influential. Its house blogger has openly solicited votes ranking those same celebrities on their physical appearance. Alexander Russo's "Hot for Education" series clarified the purpose of contemporary American education journalism: It has nothing to do with truth, justice, or progress and everything to do with seeing and being seen, rubbing elbows with glitterati, and maintaining one's status on their invitation lists (see, e.g., Russo, 2005). The ironic end result is that the most "influential" newspaper in education helps the vested interests to suppress information.

The dissolution of education knowledge is unfortunate for our society, but it is no small task to convince those outside the field that the problem even exists. Some skeptics simply refuse to believe that censorship and suppression on such a scale is possible in the Internet age, inadvertently reinforcing it. Others inside the education business benefit profoundly, personally, and professionally and would not be keen to relinquish their advantage.

REFERENCES

American Federation of Teachers. (1995). *Defining world class standards*. Washington, DC: Author.

Association for Supervision and Curriculum Development. (2005). *ASCD 1984–2004: Defining moments, future prospects.* Alexandria, VA: Author.

Association for Supervision and Curriculum Development. (2008, January 22). *ASCD SmartBrief.* Alexandria, VA: Author.

Barth, P. (2006, April 9). *High stakes testing and instruction: What the research says.* Washington, DC: National School Boards Association, Center for Public Education. Retrieved January 15, 2007, from http://www.centerforpubliceducation .org/atf/cf/%7B13A13846-1CA6-4F8A-B52E-2A88576B84EF%7D/HIGH-STAKES_TESTING_04092006.pdf

Bazerman, M. H., & Malhotra, D. (2006). Economics wins, psychology loses, and society pays. In D. de Cremer, M. Zeelenberg, & J. K. Murnighan (Eds.), *Social psychology and economics* (pp. 263–280). Mahwah, NJ: Erlbaum.

Becker, B. J. (1990, Fall). Coaching for the Scholastic Aptitude Test: Further synthesis and appraisal. *Review of Educational Research, 60,* 373–417.

Bourque, M. L. (2005). Leave no standardized test behind. In R. P. Phelps (Ed.), *Defending standardized testing* (pp. 227–253). Mahwah, NJ: Erlbaum.

Bridgeman, B. (1991, June). Essays and multiple-choice tests as predictors of college freshman GPA. *Research in Higher Education, 32,* 319–332.

Briggs, D. C. (2001, Winter). The effect of admissions test preparation. *Chance, 14*(1), 10–18.

Britton, E. D., Hawkins, S., & Gandal, M. (1996). Comparing examinations systems. In E. D. Britton & S. A. Raizen (Eds.), *Examining the examinations* (pp. 201–218). Boston: Kluwer Academic.

Brookhart, S. M. (1993, Summer). Teachers' grading practices: Meaning and values. *Journal of Educational Measurement, 30*(2), 123–142.

Cannell, J. J. (1987). *Nationally normed elementary achievement testing in America's public schools: How all fifty states are above the national average* (2nd ed.). Daniels, WV: Friends for Education.

Cannell, J. J. (1989). *How public educators cheat on standardized achievement tests.* Albuquerque, NM: Friends for Education.

Chandler, M. (Producer). (1999, Fall). Secrets of the SAT [Television series episode]. *Frontline.* Washington, DC: Public Broadcasting System.

Cizek, G. J. (2001). More unintended consequences of high-stakes testing? *Educational Measurement: Issues and Practice, 20*(4), 19–27.

Cole, N., & Willingham, W. (1997). *Gender and fair assessment.* Princeton, NJ: Educational Testing Service.

Corbett, H. D., & Wilson, B. (1991). *Testing, reform, and rebellion.* Norwood, NJ: Ablex.

Crocker, L. (2005). Teaching for the test. In R. P. Phelps (Ed.), *Defending standardized testing* (pp. 159–174). Mahwah, NJ: Erlbaum.

Dempster, F. N. (1991, April). Synthesis of research on reviews and tests. *Educational Leadership,* 71–76.

Dempster, F. N. (1997). Using tests to promote classroom learning. In R. F. Dillon (Ed.), *Handbook on testing* (pp. 332–346). Westport, CT: Greenwood Press.

de Tocqueville, A. (2003). *Democracy in America.* New York: Penguin Classics. (Original work published 1835 and 1840)

Domhoff, G. W. (2006). *Who rules America? Power, politics, and social change* (5th ed.). New York: McGraw-Hill.

Eckstein, M. A., & Noah, H. J. (1993). *Secondary school examinations: International perspectives on policies and practice.* New Haven, CT: Yale University Press.

Farkus, S., Johnson, J., & Duffet, A. (1997). *Different drummers: How teachers of teachers view public education.* New York: Public Agenda.

Farkus, S., Johnson, J., Immerwahr, J., & McHugh, J. (1998). *Time to move on.* New York: Public Agenda.

Feinberg, L. (1990, Fall). Multiple-choice and its critics: Are the "alternatives" any better? *The College Board Review, 157,* 13–17, 30–31.

Feuer, M. J., & Fulton, K. (1994). Educational testing abroad and lessons for the United States. *Educational Measurement: Issues and Practice, 13*(2), 31–39.

Geisinger, K. F. (2005). The testing industry, ethnic minorities, and individuals with disabilities. In R. P. Phelps (Ed.), *Defending standardized testing* (pp. 187–204). Mahwah, NJ: Erlbaum.

Goodman, D., & Hambleton, R. K. (2005). Some misconceptions about large-scale educational assessments. In R. P. Phelps, (Ed.), *Defending standardized testing* (pp. 91–110). Mahwah, NJ: Erlbaum.

Greene, H. A., & Jorgensen, A. N. (1929). *The use and interpretation of educational tests.* New York: Longmans, Green.

Guskey, T. R., & Gates, S. L. (1986). Synthesis of research on the effects of mastery learning in elementary and secondary classrooms. *Educational Leadership, 43,* 73–80.

Haney, W. M., Madaus, G. F., & Lyons, R. (1993). *The fractured marketplace for standardized testing.* Boston: Kluwer Academic.

Hanushek, E. A. (2006). *Policy analysis: Is it, or could it be, the Fifth Estate?* (2005 Spencer Foundation Distinguished Lecture in Education Policy and Management). Washington, DC: Association for Public Policy Analysis and Management.

Hanushek, E. A., & Raymond, M. E. (2002, June 9–11). *Lessons about the design of state accountability systems.* Paper presented at the conference "Taking Account of Accountability: Assessing Policy and Politics," Harvard University, Cambridge, MA.

Hanushek, E. A., & Raymond, M. E. (2003). Lessons about the design of state accountability systems. In P. E. Peterson & M. R. West (Eds.), *No child left behind? The politics and practice of accountability* (pp. 126–151). Washington, DC: Brookings Institution.

Hartigan, J. A., & Wigdor, A. K. (1989). *Fairness in employment testing: Validity generalization, minority issues, and the General Aptitude Test Battery.* Washington, DC: National Academies Press.

Haynie, W. J., III. (1994). Effects of multiple-choice and short-answer tests on delayed retention learning. *Journal of Technology Education, 6*(1), 32–44.

Haynie, W. J., III. (2007). Effects of test taking on retention learning in technology education: A meta-analysis. *Journal of Technology Education, 18*(2), 24–36.

Heubert, J. P., & Hauser, R. P. (Eds.). (1999). *High-stakes: Testing for tracking, promotion, and graduation.* Washington, DC: National Research Council.

Interview: Rod Paige. (2001, September). Boston: WGBH. Retrieved November 3, 2006, from http://www.pbs.org/wgbh/pages/frontline/shows/schools/interviews/paige.html

Jacob, B. A. (2001). Getting tough? *Educational Evaluation and Policy Analysis, 23,* 99–121.

Jacob, B. A. (2002). *Accountability, incentives and behavior: The impact of high-stakes testing in the Chicago Public Schools.* Unpublished manuscript.

Jacob, B. A. (2003). High stakes in Chicago. *Education Next, 1,* 66.

Jones, B. D., & Egley, R. J. (2003, April). *The carrot and the stick.* Paper presented at the Annual Meeting of the Eastern Educational Research Association, New Orleans, LA.

Jones, B. D., & Johnston, A. F. (2002, April). *The effects of high-stakes testing on instructional practices.* Paper presented at the Annual Meeting of the American Educational Research Association, New Orleans, LA.

Jones, E. H. (1923–1924). The effects of examination on the permanence of learning. *Archives of Psychology, 10,* 36–54.

Kellaghan, T., & Madaus, G. F. (1995). National curricula in European countries. In E. W. Eisner (Ed.), *The hidden consequences of a national curriculum* (pp. 79–118). Washington, DC: American Educational Research Association.

Kellaghan, T., Madaus, G. F., & Airasian, P. W. (1982). *The effects of standardized testing.* Boston: Kluwer-Nijhoff.

Kellaghan, T., Madaus, G. F., & Raczek, A. (1996). *The use of external examinations to improve student motivation.* Washington, DC: American Educational Research Association.

Kiplinger, V. L., & Linn, R. L. (1993). *Raising the stakes of test administration: The impact on student performance on NAEP* (CSE Technical Report 360). Los Angeles, CA: Center for Research on Education Standards and Student Testing.

Klein, S. P., Hamilton, L. S., McCaffrey, D. F., & Stecher, B. M. (2000). *What do test scores in Texas tell us?* Santa Monica, CA: RAND Education.

Kohn, A. (2000). Standardized testing and its victims. *Education Week, 20*(4), 60, 46–47.

Koretz, D. M. (1996). Using student assessments for educational accountability. In E. A. Hanushek & D. W. Jorgenson (Eds.), *Improving America's schools: The role of incentives* (pp. 171–195). Washington, DC: National Academies Press.

Koretz, D. M., & Hamilton, L. S. (2007). Testing for accountability in K–12. In R. L. Brennan (Ed.), *Educational measurement* (4th ed., pp. 531–578). Washington, DC: American Council on Education.

Koretz, D. M., Linn, R. L., Dunbar, S. B., & Shepard, L. A. (1991, April 5). *The effects of high-stakes testing on achievement: Preliminary findings about generalization across tests.* Paper presented at the Annual Meeting of the American Educational Research Association, Chicago.

Lieberman, M. (2007). *The educational morass: Overcoming the stalemate in American education.* Lanham, MD: Rowman & Littlefield.

Linn, R. L. (2000, March). Assessments and accountability. *Educational Researcher,* 4–16.

Lohman, D. F. (2006). Beliefs about differences between ability and accomplishment: From folk theories to cognitive science. *Roeper Review, 29,* 32–40.

Madaus, G. F. (1991a, June). *The effects of important tests on students.* Paper presented at the American Educational Research Association Conference on Accountability as a State Reform Instrument, Washington, DC.

Madaus, G. F. (1991b, November). The effects of important tests on students: Implications for a national examination system. *Phi Delta Kappan,* 226–231.

Madaus, G. F., & Kellaghan, T. (1991). *Student examination systems in the European Community: Lessons for the United States* (OTA Contractor PB92-127570). Washington, DC: Office of Technology Assessment, U.S. Congress. (ERIC Document Reproduction Service No. ED340781)

McMillan, J. H. (2001). Secondary teachers' classroom assessment and grading practices. *Educational Measurement: Issues and Practice, 20*(1), 20–32.

McNeil, L. M. (2000). *Contradictions of school reform.* New York: Routledge.

McNeil, L. M., & Valenzuela, A. (2000). *The harmful impact of the TAAS system of testing in Texas.* Cambridge, MA: Harvard University, Civil Rights Project.

Medina, N., & Neill, M. (1990). *Fallout from the testing explosion.* Cambridge, MA: FairTest.

Mehrens, W. A. (1998). Consequences of assessment: What is the evidence? *Education Policy Analysis Archives, 6*(13). Retrieved January 19, 2008, from http://epaa.asu.edu/epaa/v6n13.html

Merrow, J. (2002, March 29). *Testing our schools* [Transcript, Live Online discussion]. Retrieved September 26, 2008, from http://discuss.washingtonpost.com/zforum/02/tv_frontline032902.htm

Mitchell, R. (2006, March 30). *Key lessons: High-stakes testing and effects on instruction.* Washington, DC: National School Boards Association, Center for Public Education. Retrieved January 14, 2008, from http://www.centerforpubliceducation.org/site/c.kjJXJ5MP IwE/b. 1533781/k.B7BE/Key_lessons_Highstakes_testing_and_effects_on_instruction.htm

Moore, W. P. (1991). *Relationships among teacher test performance pressures, perceived testing benefits, test preparation strategies, and student test performance.* Unpublished doctoral dissertation, University of Kansas, Lawrence.

National Commission on Excellence in Education. (1983, April). *A nation at risk: The imperative for educational reform.* Washington, DC: U.S. Department of Education. Available at http://www.ed.gov/pubs/NatAtRisk/index.html

National Commission on Testing and Public Policy. (1990). *From gatekeeper to gateway: Transforming testing in America.* Chestnut Hill, MA: Author.

Neill, M. (1992). Correcting business leaders' assumptions about testing [Letter]. *Education Week, 11*(27), 46.

New Report Confirms Accountability Tests Are Powerful Tool in Ensuring Students Are Not Left Behind [Press release]. (2003, February 11). U.S. Congress, Committee on Education and the Workforce.

Office of Technology Assessment. (1992). *Testing in American schools: Asking the right questions* (OTA-SET-519). Washington, DC: U.S. Government Printing Office.

Olson, L. (2002, June 19). Accountability studies find mixed impact on achievement. *Education Week, 21*(41), 13.

Palmer, J. S. (2002). *Performance incentives, teachers, and students: Estimating the effects of rewards policies on classroom practices and student performance.* Unpublished doctoral dissertation, The Ohio State University, Columbus.

Phelps, R. P. (n.d.). Censorship has many fathers. Admonitions on tone, rigor, polemic, and other excuses for censoring information that one dislikes. *Third Education Group Review.* Retrieved July 7, 2008, from http://www.thirdeducationgroup.org/Foundation/CensorshipHasManyFathers

Phelps, R. P. (1994). The fractured marketplace for standardized testing [Book review]. *Economics of Education Review, 13,* 367–370.

Phelps, R. P. (1996, Fall). Are U.S. students the most heavily tested on Earth? *Educational Measurement: Issues and Practice, 15*(3), 19–27.

Phelps, R. P. (1997). The extent and character of system-wide student testing in the United States. *Educational Assessment, 4,* 89–121.

Phelps, R. P. (1998, Fall). The demand for standardized student testing. *Educational Measurement: Issues and Practice, 17*(3), 5–23.

Phelps, R. P. (1999, April). Education establishment bias? A look at the NRC's critique of test utility studies. *The Industrial–Organizational Psychologist, 36*(4), 37–49.

Phelps, R. P. (2000a, December). High stakes: Testing for tracking, promotion, and graduation [Book review]. *Educational and Psychological Measurement, 60*(6), 992–999.

Phelps, R. P. (2000b). Trends in large-scale, external testing outside the United States. *Educational Measurement: Issues and Practice, 19*(1), 11–21.

Phelps, R. P. (2001, August). Benchmarking to the world's best in mathematics. *Evaluation Review, 25,* 391–439.

Phelps, R. P. (2003). *Kill the messenger.* New Brunswick, NJ: Transaction.

Phelps, R. P. (Ed.). (2005a). *Defending standardized testing.* Mahwah, NJ: Erlbaum.

Phelps, R. P. (2005b). Persistently positive. In R. P. Phelps (Ed.), *Defending standardized testing* (pp. 1–22). Mahwah, NJ: Erlbaum.

Phelps, R. P. (2005c). The rich, robust research literature on testing's achievement benefits. In R. P. Phelps (Ed.), *Defending standardized testing* (pp. 55–90). Mahwah, NJ: Erlbaum.

Phelps, R. P. (2005d). The source of Lake Wobegon. *The Third Education Group Review, 1*(2). Retrieved July 7, 2008, from http://www.thirdeducationgroup.org/Review/Articles/v1n2.pdf

Phelps, R. P. (2007a, Summer). The dissolution of education knowledge. *Educational Horizons, 85,* 232–247.

Phelps, R. P. (2007b). *Standardized testing primer.* New York: Peter Lang.

Picus, L. O., & Tralli, A. (1998). *Alternative assessment programs: What are the true costs?* (CSE Technical Report 441). Los Angeles, CA: Center for Research on Education Standards and Student Testing.

Plake, B. S. (2005). Doesn't everyone know that 70% is passing? In R. P. Phelps (Ed.). *Defending standardized testing* (pp. 175–186). Mahwah, NJ: Erlbaum.

Posner, R. A. (2001). *Public intellectuals: A study of decline.* Cambridge, MA: Harvard University Press.

Powers, D. E., & Kaufman, J. C. (2002). *Do standardized multiple-choice tests penalize deep-thinking or creative students?* (Research Report RR-02-15). Princeton, NJ: Educational Testing Service.

Powers, D. E., & Rock, D. A. (1999). Effects of coaching on SAT: I. Reasoning test scores. *Journal of Educational Measurement, 36,* 93–118.

Roderick, M., Jacob, B., & Bryk, A. (2002). The impact of high-stakes testing in Chicago on student achievement in the promotional gate grades. *Educational Evaluation and Policy Analysis, 24,* 333–357.

Roediger, H. L., & Karpicke, J. D. (2006a). The power of testing memory: Basic research and implications for educational practice. *Perspectives on Psychological Science, 1,* 181–210.

Roediger, H. L., & Karpicke, J. D. (2006b). Test-enhanced learning: Taking memory tests improves long-term retention. *Psychological Science, 17,* 249–255.

Roediger, H. L., & Marsh, E. J. (2005). The positive and negative consequences of multiple-choice testing. *Journal of Experimental Psychology: Learning, Memory, and Cognition, 31,* 1155–1159.

Rogosa, D. (2005). A school accountability case study. In R. P. Phelps (Ed.), *Defending standardized testing* (pp. 205–226). Mahwah, NJ: Erlbaum.

Ross, C. C. (1941). *Measurement in today's schools.* New York: Prentice-Hall.

Rothman, R. (1995). *Measuring up.* New York: Wiley.

Rudman, H. C. (1992). Testing for learning [Book review]. *Educational Measurement: Issues and Practice, 11*(3), 31–32.

Russo, A. (2005, August 12–13). Hot for education: The top five best-looking school reformers in the nation. *This Week in Education.* Retrieved July 19, 2008, from http://thisweekineducation.blogspot.com/2005_08_01_archive.html

Sacks, P. (1999). *Standardized minds.* Cambridge, MA: Perseus.

Sandham, J. L. (1998). Ending SAT may hurt minorities. *Education Week, 17,* 5.

Shepard, L. A., Kreitzer, A. E., & Grau, M. E. (1987). *A case study of the Texas teacher test* (CSE Report No. 276). Los Angeles, CA: Center for Research on Education Standards and Student Testing.

Sireci, S. G. (2005). The most frequently unasked questions about testing. In R. P. Phelps (Ed.), *Defending standardized testing* (pp. 111–121). Mahwah, NJ: Erlbaum.

Smith, M. L. (1991a). *The role of testing in elementary schools* (CSE Technical Report 321). Los Angeles: Center for Research on Education Standards and Student Testing.

Smith, M. L. (1991b, June). Put to the test. *Educational Researcher, 20,* 8–11.

Smith, M. L. (1991c, Fall). Meanings of test preparation. *American Educational Research Journal, 28,* 521–542.

Smith, M. L., & Rottenberg, C. (1991). Unintended consequences of external testing in elementary schools. *Educational Measurement: Issues and Practice, 10,* 10–11.

Snowman, J. (2002). *Psychology applied to teaching.* Boston: Houghton-Mifflin.

Stiggins, R. J., & Conklin, N. F. (1992). *In teachers' hands: Investigating the practices of classroom assessment.* New York: SUNY Press.

Strauss, V. (2006, October 10). The rise of the testing culture. *Washington Post,* p. A09.

Teel, M. L. (Producer). (2001, April 1). *CBS Sunday Morning* [Television broadcast]. New York: CBS News.

Thomson, J. A. (2000, October 26). *Statement of Rand President and CEO James A. Thomson.* [Press release]. Santa Monica, CA: Rand.

Thompson, T. D. (1990). *When mastery testing pays off.* Unpublished doctoral dissertation, University of Oklahoma, Norman.

Traub, R. E. (1993). On the equivalence of the traits assessed by multiple choice and constructed-response tests. In R. E. Bennett & W. C. Ward (Eds.), *Construction versus choice in cognitive measurement* (pp. 29–44). Hillsdale, NJ: Erlbaum.

Tuckman, B. W. (1994, April). *Comparing incentive motivation to metacognitive strategy in its effect on achievement.* Paper presented at the Annual Meeting of the American Educational Research Association, New Orleans, LA. (ERIC Document Reproduction Service No. ED368790).

Tuckman, B. W., & Trimble, S. (1997, August). *Using tests as a performance incentive to motivate eighth-graders to study.* Paper presented at the 105th Annual Convention of the American Psychological Association, Chicago. (ERIC Document Reproduction Service No. ED418785)

U.S. General Accounting Office. (1993, January). *Student testing: Current extent and expenditure* (GAO/PEMD-93-8). Washington, DC: Author.

Viadero, D. (1994). National tests in other countries not as prevalent as thought. *Education Week, 13*(37), 10.

Wolk, R. A. (2002, April). Multiple measures. *Teacher Magazine, 13*(7), 3.

APPENDIX 3.1
SELECTED CITATIONS FROM 20TH-CENTURY
RESEARCH RELEVANT TO THE DESIGN OF
THE NO CHILD LEFT BEHIND ACT

Studies marked with an asterisk (*) are research reviews, research syntheses, or meta-analyses.
Studies that are listed more than once are given in shortened form after the first listing.

EFFECTS OF STANDARDS, ALIGNMENT, GOAL SETTING,
SETTING REACHABLE GOALS

Aguilera, R. V., & Hendricks, J. M. (1996, September). Increasing standardized achievement scores in a high risk school district. *Curriculum Report, 26*(1), 1–6.

Anderson, J. O., Muir, W., Bateson, D. J., Blackmore, D., & Rogers, W. T. (1990, March 30). *The impact of provincial examinations on education in British Columbia: General report.* Victoria, British Columbia, Canada: British Columbia Ministry of Education.

*Bamburg, J., & Medina, E. (1993). Analyzing student achievement: Using standardized tests as the first step. In J. Bamburg (Ed.), *Assessment: How do we know what they know?* (pp. 35–40). Dubuque, IA: Kendall-Hunt.

Banta, T. W., Lund, J. P., Black, K. E., & Oblander, F. W. (1996). *Assessment in practice: Putting principles to work on college campuses.* San Francisco: Jossey-Bass.

Bishop, J. H. (1993, December). *Impact of curriculum-based examinations on learning in Canadian secondary schools* (Working Paper 94-30). Ithaca, NY: Center for Advanced Human Resource Studies, New York State School of Industrial and Labor Relations, Cornell University.

Bottoms, G., & Mikos, P. (1995). *Seven most-improved "High Schools That Work" sites raise achievement in reading, mathematics, and science.* Atlanta, GA: Southern Regional Education Board.

Brooke, N., & Oxenham, J. (1984). The influence of certification and selection on teaching and learning. In J. Oxenham (Ed.), *Education versus qualifications? A study of relationships between education, selection for employment and the productivity of labor* (pp. 147–175). London: George Allen & Unwin.

Brown, D. F. (1992, April). *Altering curricula through state testing: Perceptions of teachers and principals.* Paper presented at the Annual Meeting of the American Educational Research Association, San Francisco.

Czikszentmihalyi, M. (1990). *Flow: The psychology of optimal experience.* New York: Harper Perennial.

Eckstein, M. A., & Noah, H. J. (1993). *Secondary school examinations: International perspectives on policies and practice.* New Haven, CT: Yale University Press.

Estes, G. D., Colvin, L. W., & Goodwin, C. (1976, April). *A criterion-referenced basic skills assessment program in a large city school system.* Paper presented at the Annual Meeting of the American Educational Research Association, San Francisco.

Heyneman, S. P., & Ransom, A. W. (1992). Using examinations and testing to improve educational quality. In M. A. Eckstein & H. J. Noah (Eds.), *Examinations: Comparative and international studies* (pp. 105–121). Oxford, England: Pergamon Press.

Hilloks, G., Jr. (1987). Synthesis of research on teaching writing. *Educational Leadership, 44*(8), 71–82.

LaRoque, L., & Coleman, P. (1989). Quality control: School accountability and district ethos. In M. Holmes, K. A. Leithwood, & D. F. Musella, (Eds.), *Educational policy for effective schools* (pp. 168–191). Toronto, Ontario, Canada: Ontario Institute for Studies in Education.

*Levine, D. U., & Lezotte, L. W. (1990). *Unusually effective schools: A review and analysis of research and practice.* Madison, WI: The National Center for Effective Schools Research and Development.

Mattsson, H. (1993, May–June). *Impact of assessment on educational practice and student behavior in the Swedish schools system, School-based and external assessments: Uses and issues.* Paper presented at the 19th Annual Conference of the International Association for Educational Assessment, Mauritius.

Miles, W., Bishop, J., Collins, J., Fink, J., Gardner, M., Grant, J., et al. (1997). *Ten case studies of "All Regents" high schools: Final report to the State Education Department.* Albany, NY: State Education Department.

Mitchell, F. M. (1999, April). *All students can learn: Effects of curriculum alignment on the mathematics achievement of third-grade students.* Paper presented at the Annual Meeting of the American Educational Research Association, Montréal, Québec, Canada.

Morgan, R., & Ramist, L. (1998, February). *Advanced placement students in college: An investigation of course grades at 21 colleges* (Rep. No. SR-98-13). Princeton, NJ: Educational Testing Service.

*Natriello, G., & Dornbusch, S. M. (1984). *Teacher evaluative standards and student effort.* New York: Longman.

Office of Program Policy Analysis and Government Accountability, the Florida Legislature. (1997, June). *Improving student performance in high-poverty schools.* Tallahassee, FL: Author.

Ogle, D., & Fritts, J. B. (1981). Criterion-referenced reading assessment valuable for process as well as for data. *Phi Delta Kappan, 62*(9), 640–641.

Panlasigui, I., & Knight, F. B. (1930). The effect of awareness of success or failure. In F. B. Knight (Ed.), *Twenty-ninth yearbook of the National Society for the Study of Education: Report of the society's committee on arithmetic* (pp. 611–619). Chicago: University of Chicago Press.

Pomplun, M. (1997). State assessment and instructional change: A path model analysis. *Applied Measurement in Education, 10*(3), 217–234.

Rentz, R. R. (1979). Testing and the college degree. In W. B. Schrader (Ed.), *Measurement and educational policy: New directions for testing and measurement* (pp. 71–78). San Francisco: Jossey-Bass.

Resnick, D. P., & Resnick, L. B. (1985). Standards, curriculum, and performance: A historical and comparative perspective. *Educational Researcher, 14*(4), 5–20.

*Rosswork, S. G. (1977). Goal setting: The effects of an academic task with varying magnitudes of incentive. *Journal of Educational Psychology, 69*, 710–715.

Schmoker, M. (1996). *Results: The key to continuous school improvement.* Alexandria, VA: Association for Supervision and Curriculum Development.

*Southern Regional Education Board. (1998). *High schools that work: Case studies.* Available at http://www.sreb.org

U.S. General Accounting Office. (1993, April). *Educational testing: The Canadian experience with standards, examinations, and assessments* (GAO/PEMD-93-11). Washington, DC: Author.

Wellisch, J. B., MacQueen, A. H., Carriere, R. A., & Duck, G. A. (1978). School management and organization in successful schools. *Sociology of Education, 51,* 211–226.

Whetton, C. (1992, April). *Advice to US systems contemplating performance assessment.* Paper presented at the Annual Meeting of the American Educational Research Association, San Francisco.

Willingham, W. W., & Morris, M. (1986). *Four years later: A longitudinal study of advanced placement students in college* (College Board Rep. 86-2). New York: College Entrance Examination Board.

EFFECTS OF TESTS, ACCOUNTABILITY PROGRAMS, OR BOTH ON MOTIVATION AND INSTRUCTIONAL PRACTICE

Brown, S. M., & Walberg, H. J. (1993). Motivational effects on test scores of elementary students. *Journal of Educational Research, 86*(3), 133–136.

Brunton, M. L. (1982, March). *Is competency testing accomplishing any breakthrough in achievement?* Paper presented at the Annual Meeting of the Association for Supervision and Curriculum Development, Anaheim, CA.

Chao-Qun, W., & Hui, Z. (1993). Educational assessment in mathematics teaching: Applied research in China. In M. Niss (Ed.), *Cases of assessment in mathematics education: An ICMI study* (pp. 183–192). Boston: Kluwer Academic.

Clarke, D., & Stephens, M. (1996). The ripple effect: The instructional impact of the systemic introduction of performance assessment in mathematics. In M. Birenbaum & F. J. R. C. Dochy (Eds.), *Alternatives in assessment of achievements, learning processes and prior knowledge* (pp. 63–92). Boston: Kluwer Academic.

Eckstein and Noah (1993)

Egeland, P. C. (1995). *The effect of authentic assessments on fifth-grade student science achievement and attitudes.* Unpublished doctoral dissertation, Northern Illinois University, Dekalb.

Foss, O. (1977, May). A new approach: Vocational foundation courses and examinations. In F. M. Ottobre (Ed.), *Criteria for awarding school leaving certificates: An international discussion* (pp. 191–209). Based on the Proceedings of the 1977 Conference of the International Association for Educational Assessment held at the Kenyatta Conference Center, Nairobi, Kenya. Cambridge, England: International Association for Educational Assessment.

Johnson, J. F., Jr. (1998). The influence of a state accountability system on student achievement in Texas. *Virginia Journal of Social Policy & the Law, 6*(1), 155–178.

Keys, N. (1934). The influence on learning and retention of weekly tests as opposed to monthly tests. *Journal of Educational Psychology, 25,* 427–436.

*Kirkland, M. C. (1971). The effects of tests on students and schools. *Review of Educational Research, 41,* 303–350.

*Levine and Lezotte (1990)

Marsh, R. (1984, November/December). A comparison of take-home versus in-class exams. *Journal of Educational Research, 78*(2), 111–113.

Miles et al. (1997)

O'Sullivan, R. G. (1989, February). *Teacher perceptions of the effects of testing on students.* Paper presented at the Annual Meeting of the National Council on Measurement in Education, San Francisco.

Pennycuick, D., & Murphy, R. (1988). *The impact of graded tests.* London: Falmer Press.

Plazak, T., & Mazur, Z. (1992). University entrance in Poland. In P. Black (Ed.), *Physics examinations for university entrance: An international study* (Science and Technology Education Document Series No. 45, pp. 135–149). Paris: UNESCO.

Prais, S. (1995). *Productivity, education and training* (Vol. 2). London: National Institute for Economic and Social Research.

Ritchie, D., & Thorkildsen, R. (1994). Effects of accountability on students' achievement in mastery learning. *Journal of Educational Research, 88*(2), 86–90.

Schafer, W. D., Hultgren, F. H., Hawley, W. D., Abrams, A. L., Seubert, C. C., & Mazzoni, S. (1997). *Study of higher-success and lower-success elementary schools.* College Park, MD: University of Maryland, School Improvement Program.

Singh, J. S., Marimutha, T., & Mukjerjee, H. (1990). Learning motivation and work: A Malaysian perspective. In P. Broadfoot, R. Murphy, & H. Torrance (Eds.), *Changing educational assessment: International perspectives and trends* (pp. 177–198). London: Routledge.

Solberg, W. (1977). School leaving examinations: Why or why not?: The case for school leaving examinations: The Netherlands. In F. M. Ottobre (Ed.), *Criteria for awarding school leaving certificates: An international discussion* (pp. 37–46). Based on the Proceedings of the 1977 Conference of the International Association for Educational Assessment held at the Kenyatta Conference Center, Nairobi, Kenya. Cambridge, England: International Association for Educational Assessment.

Somerset, A. (1968). *Examination reform: The Kenya experience* (Rep. No. EDT64). Washington, DC: The World Bank.

*Southern Regional Education Board (1998)

Steedman, H. (1992). *Mathematics in vocational youth training for the building trades in Britain, France and Germany* (Discussion Paper No. 9). London: National Institute for Economic and Social Research.

Stevens, F. I. (1984, December). *The effects of testing on teaching and curriculum in a large urban school district* (ERIC/TM Rep. 86). Washington, DC: ERIC Clearinghouse on Tests, Measurement, and Evaluation.

Stevenson, H. W., & Lee, S.-L. (1997). *International comparisons of entrance and exit examinations: Japan, United Kingdom, France, and Germany.* Washington, DC: U.S. Department of Education, Office of Educational Research and Improvement.

Stuit, D. B. (Ed.). (1947). *Personnel research and test development in the Bureau of Naval Personnel.* Princeton, NJ: Princeton University Press.

Tuckman, B. W. (1994, April). *Comparing incentive motivation to metacognitive strategy in its effect on achievement.* Paper presented at the Annual Meeting of the American Educational Research Association, New Orleans, LA.

Tuckman, B. W., & Trimble, S. (1997, August). *Using tests as a performance incentive to motivate eighth-graders to study.* Paper presented at the 105th Annual Convention of the American Psychological Association, Chicago, IL.

Wall, D., & Alderson, J. C. (1993). Examining washback: The Sri Lankan Impact Study. *Language Testing, 10,* 41–69.

Waters, T., Burger, D., & Burger, S. (1995, March). Moving up before moving on. *Educational Leadership, 52*(6), 35–40.

Wolf, A., & Rapiau, M. T. (1993). The academic achievement of craft apprentices in France and England: Contrasting systems and common dilemmas. *Comparative Education, 29*(1), 29–43.

Zigarelli, M. A. (1996). An empirical test of conclusions from effective schools research. *Journal of Educational Research, 90*(2), 103–110.

THE LEARNING EFFECTS OF TESTS THEMSELVES

Banta et al. (1996)

Dempster, F. N. (1991, April). Synthesis of research on reviews and tests. *Educational Leadership, 48,* 71–76.

Dempster, F. N. (1997). Using tests to promote classroom learning. In R. F. Dillon (Ed.), *Handbook on testing* (pp. 332–346). Westport, CT: Greenwood Press.

Kirkpatrick, J. E. (1934). The motivating effect of a specific type of testing program. *University of Iowa Studies in Education, 9,* 41–68.

Ross, C. C., & Henry, L. K. (1939). The relation between frequency of testing and learning in psychology. *Journal of Educational Psychology, 69,* 710–715.

Toppino, T. C., & Luipersbeck, S. M. (1993). Generality of the negative suggestion effect in objective tests. *Journal of Educational Research, 86*(6), 357–362.

EFFECTS OF VARYING TYPES OF INCENTIVES OR THE OPTIMAL STRUCTURE OF INCENTIVES

Abbott, R. D., & Falstrom, P. (1977). Frequent testing and personalized systems of instruction. *Contemporary Educational Psychology, 2,* 251–257.

Banta et al. (1996)

Brooke and Oxenham (1984)

Brookover, W. B., & Lezotte, L. W. (1979, May). *Changes in school characteristics coincident with changes in student achievement* (Occasional Paper No. 17). East Lansing, MI: Michigan State University, Institute for Research on Teaching.

Brooks-Cooper, C. (1993, August). *The effect of financial incentives on the standardized test performance of high school students.* Unpublished master's thesis, Cornell University, Ithaca, NY.

Corcoran, T. B., & Wilson, B. L. (1986, October). *The search for successful secondary schools: The first three years of the secondary school recognition program.* Philadelphia: Research for Better Schools.

Cronbach, L. J. (1960). *Essentials of psychological testing.* New York: Harper & Row.

*Crooks, T. J. (1988). The impact of classroom evaluation practices on students. *Review of Educational Research, 58*(4), 438–481.

Duran, R. P. (1989). Assessment and instruction of at-risk Hispanic students. *Exceptional Children, 56*(2), 154–158.

Eckstein and Noah (1993)

*Guskey, T. R., & Gates, S. L. (1986). Synthesis of research on the effects of mastery learning in elementary and secondary classrooms. *Educational Leadership, 43*(8), 73–80.

Heneman, H. G., III. (1998). Assessment of the motivational reactions of teachers to a school-based performance award program. *Journal of Personnel Evaluation in Education, 12,* 143–159.

Heyneman and Ransom (1992)

Hurlock, E. B. (1925, September). The effects of incentives on the constancy of the I.Q. *Pedagogical Seminary, 32,* 422–434.

Jacobson, J. E. (1992, October 29). *Mandatory testing requirements and pupil achievement.* Unpublished doctoral dissertation, Massachusetts Institute of Technology, Boston.

*Kazdin, A., & Bootzin, R. (1972). The token economy: An evaluative review. *Journal of Applied Behavior Analysis, 5,* 343–372.

Kelley, C. (1999). The motivational impact of school-based performance awards. *Journal of Personnel Evaluation in Education, 12*(4), 309–326.

*Kulik, C.-L., & Kulik, J. A. (1987). Mastery testing and student learning: A meta-analysis. *Journal of Educational Technology Systems, 15,* 325–345.

*Levine and Lezotte (1990)

McMillan, J. H. (1977). The effect of effort and feedback on the formation of student attitudes. *American Educational Research Journal, 14*(3), 317–330.

*O'Leary, K. D., & Drabman, R. (1971). Token reinforcement programs in the classroom: A review. *Psychological Bulletin, 75,* 379–398.

Oxenham, J. (1984). *Education versus qualifications?* London: Unwin Education.

Richards, C. E., & Shen, T. M. (1992, March). The South Carolina school incentive reward program: A policy analysis. *Economics of Education Review, 11*(1), 71–86.

*Southern Regional Education Board (1998)

*Staats, A. (1973). Behavior analysis and token reinforcement in educational behavior modification and curriculum research. In C. E. Thoreson (Ed.), *72nd yearbook of the NSSE: Behavior modification in education* (Part 1, pp. 195–229). Chicago: University of Chicago Press.

Trelfa, D. (1998, June). The development and implementation of education standards in Japan. *The educational system in Japan: Case study findings* (pp. 59–106). Washington, DC: U.S. Department of Education, Office of Educational Research and Improvement, National Institute on Student Achievement, Curriculum, and Assessment.

Venesky, R. L., & Winfield, L. F. (1979, August). *Schools that succeed beyond expectations in teaching* (University of Delaware Studies on Education Tech. Rep. No. 1). Newark: University of Delaware.

EFFECTS OF VARYING PATTERNS AND
FREQUENCIES OF TESTING

*Bangert-Drowns, R. L., Kulik, J. A., & Kulik, C.-L. C. (1991). Effects of frequent classroom testing. *Journal of Educational Research, 85*(2), 89–99.

Beardon, D. (1997). *An overview of the elementary mathematics program 1996–97* (Research Rep. REIS97-116-3). Dallas, TX: Dallas Public Schools.

Gaynor, J., & Millham, J. (1976). Student performance and evaluation under variant teaching and testing methods in a large college course. *Journal of Education Psychology, 68,* 312–317.

Khalaf, A. S. S., & Hanna, G. S. (1992). The impact of classroom testing frequency on high school students' achievement. *Contemporary Educational Psychology, 17*(1), 71–77.

Kika, F. M., McLaughlin, T. F., & Dixon, J. (1992). Effects of frequent testing of secondary algebra students. *Journal of Educational Research, 85*(3), 159–162.

*Kulik, J. A., & Kulik, C.-L. C. (1989). The concept of meta-analysis. *International Journal of Education Research, 13*(3), 227–340.

Mullis, I. V. S. (1997, April). *Benchmarking toward world-class standards: Some characteristics of the highest performing school systems in the TIMSS.* Paper presented at the Annual Meeting of the American Educational Research Association, Chicago.

Rohm, R. A., Sparzo, F. J., & Bennett, C. M. (1986). College student performance under repeated testing and cumulative testing conditions: Report on five studies. *Journal of Educational Research, 80*(2), 99–104.

Taylor, B., Pearson, P. D., Clark, K., & Walpole, S. (2000). Effective schools and accomplished teachers: Lessons about primary grade reading instruction in low-income schools. *The Elementary School Journal, 10,* 121–165.

*Thompson, T. D. (1990). *When mastery testing pays off: The cost benefits and psychometric properties of mastery tests as determined from item response theory.* Unpublished doctoral dissertation, University of Oklahoma, Norman.

EFFECTS OF MONITORING, FEEDBACK, AND
EVALUATION OF PERFORMANCE

Anderson et al. (1990)

Burrows, C. K., & Okey, J. R. (1975, April). *The effects of a mastery learning strategy.* Paper presented at the Annual Meeting of the American Educational Research Association, Washington, DC.

Corbett, H. D., & Wilson, B. (1989). *Raising the stakes in statewide mandatory minimum competency testing.* Philadelphia: Research for Better Schools.

*Crooks (1988)

Engel, G. S. (1977, March–April). One way it can be. *Today's Education, 66,* 50–52.

Friedman, H. (1987). Repeat examinations in introductory statistics. *Teaching of Psychology, 14,* 20–23.

Fuller, B. (1987). What school factors raise achievement in the Third World? *Review of Educational Research, 57*(3), 255–292.

Goodson, M. L., & Okey, J. R. (1978, November). The effects of diagnostic tests and help sessions on college science achievement. *Journal of College Science Teaching, 8,* 89–90.

Hess, A. C., & Lockwood, R. E. (1986, April). *The relationship of a basic competency education program to overall student achievement: A state perspective.* Paper presented at the Annual Meeting of the National Council on Measurement in Education, San Francisco.

*Heyneman, S. P. (1987). *Uses of examinations in developing countries: Selection, research, and education sector management* (Seminar Paper No. 36). Washington, DC: Economic Development Institute, The World Bank.

Heyneman and Ransom (1992)

Lerner, B. (1990, March). Good news about American education. *Commentary, 91*(3), 19–25.

Magruder, J., McManis, M. A., & Young, C. C. (1997). The right idea at the right time: Development of a transformational assessment culture. *New Directions for Higher Education, 100,* 17–29.

Moss, H. A., & Kagan, J. (1961). Stability of achievement in recognition setting behaviors from early childhood through adulthood. *Journal of Abnormal and Social Psychology, 62,* 504–513.

Rodgers, N., Paredes, V., & Mangino, E. (1991, April). *High stakes minimum skills tests: Is their use increasing achievement?* Paper presented at the Annual Meeting of the American Educational Research Association, Chicago.

Ross, J. A., Rolheiser, C., & Hoaboam-Gray, A. (1998). *Impact of self-evaluation training on mathematics achievement in a cooperative learning environment.* Ottawa, Ontario, Canada: Social Science and Humanities Research Council.

Swanson, D. H., & Denton, J. J. (1976). *A comparison of remediation systems affecting achievement and retention in mastery learning.* (ERIC Document Reproduction Service No. ED131037)

EFFECTS OF TESTING ON AT-RISK STUDENTS, COMPLETION, DROPPING OUT, AND CURRICULAR OFFERINGS

Boylan, H., Bonham, B., Abraham, A., Anderson, J., Morante, E., Ramirez, G., & Bliss, L. (1996). *An evaluation of the Texas Academic Skills Program.* Austin, TX: Texas Higher Education Coordinating Board.

Enochs, J. C. (1978, May). Modesto, California: A return to the four Rs. *Phi Delta Kappan, 59*(9), 609–610.

Grisay, A. (1991). Improving assessment in primary schools: "APER" research reduces educational failure rates. In P. Weston (Ed.), *Assessment of pupil achievement: Motivation and school success* (Report of the Educational Research Workshop held in Liège [Belgium] 12–15 September, Council of Europe; pp. 103–118). Amsterdam, the Netherlands: Swets & Zeitlinger.

Jacobson (1992)

Johnstone, W. (1990, January). *Local school district perspectives.* Paper presented at the Annual Meeting of the Southwest Educational Research Association, Austin, Texas.

Jones, J. B. (1993). *Effects of the use of an altered testing/grading method on the retention and success of students enrolled in college mathematics.* Unpublished doctoral dissertation, East Texas State University, Tyler.

Jones, J. (1996). Offer them a carrot: Linking assessment and motivation in developmental Mathematics. *Research and Teaching in Developmental Education, 13*(1), 85–91.

McWilliams, J. M., & Thomas, A. C. (1976). The measurement of students' learning: An approach to accountability. *Journal of Educational Research, 70*, 50–52.

Pronaratna, B. (1976). *Examination reforms in Sri Lanka* (Experiments and Innovations in Education, No. 24). Paris, France: UNESCO.

Schleisman, J. (1999, October). *An in-depth investigation of one school district's responses to an externally-mandated, high-stakes testing program in Minnesota.* Paper presented at the Annual Meeting of the University Council for Educational Administration, Minneapolis, MN. (ERIC Document Reproduction Service No. ED440465)

*Southern Regional Education Board (1998)

Task Force on Educational Assessment Programs. (1979). *Competency testing in Florida: Report to the Florida Cabinet, Part 1.* Tallahassee, FL: Author.

Webster, W. J., Mendro, R. L., Orsack, T., Weerasinghe, D., & Bembry, K. (1997a). The Dallas Value-Added Accountability System. In J. Millman (Ed.), *Grading teachers, grading schools: Is student achievement a valid evaluation measure?* (pp. 81–99). Thousand Oaks, CA: Corwin Press.

Webster, W. J., Mendro, R. L., Orsack, T., Weerasinghe, D., & Bembry, K. (1997b). Little practical difference and pie in the sky. In J. Millman (Ed.), *Grading teachers, grading schools: Is student achievement a valid evaluation measure?* (pp. 120–131). Thousand Oaks, CA: Corwin Press.

Wellisch et al. (1978)

EFFECTS OF MINIMUM-COMPETENCY TESTING AND THE
PROBLEMS WITH A SINGLE PASSING SCORE

Brunton (1982)

Findley, J. (1978, May). Westside's minimum competency graduation requirements: A program that works. *Phi Delta Kappan, 59*(9), 614–618.

Frederiksen, N. (1994). *The influence of minimum competency tests on teaching and learning.* Princeton, NJ: Educational Testing Service.

Ligon, G., Brightman, M., Davis, E., Hoover, H. D., Johnstone, W., Mangino, E., et al. (1990, January). *Statewide testing in Texas.* A symposium presented at the Annual Meeting of the Southwest Educational Research Association, Austin, TX.

Losack, J. (1987). *Mandated entry- and exit-level testing in the state of Florida: A brief history, review of current impact, and a look to the future.* Miami, FL: Miami-Dade Community College and Florida Office of Institutional Research.

Mangino, E., & Babcock, M. A. (1986, April). *Minimum competency testing: Helpful or harmful for high level skills?* Paper presented at the Annual Meeting of the American Educational Research Association, San Francisco.

Ogden, J. (1979, April). *High school competency graduation requirements: Do they result in better graduates?* Paper presented at the Annual Meeting of the American Educational Research Association, San Francisco.

Parramore, B. M. (1980, November). *Effects of mandated competency testing in North Carolina: The class of 1980.* Paper presented at the Annual Meeting of the Evaluation Research Society, Washington, DC.

Serow, R. C., Davies, J. J., & Parramore, B. M. (1982). Performance gains in a competency test program. *Educational Evaluation and Policy Analysis, 4*(4), 535–542.

Winfield, L. F. (1990, March). *School competency testing reforms and student achievement: Exploring a national perspective* (Research Rep.). Princeton, NJ: Educational Testing Service.

Note. For more information, see Phelps (2005c).

4

COLLEGE ADMISSION TESTING: MYTHS AND REALITIES IN AN AGE OF ADMISSIONS HYPE

WAYNE J. CAMARA

More than 3 million students were projected to graduate from high school in 2006, and nearly 50% of those students were projected to enroll immediately in a 4-year postsecondary institution (National Center for Educational Statistics, 2005). Four-year college matriculation rates among graduating high school students have remained remarkably consistent since the mid-1970s despite some shifts within ethnic and gender groups and increased enrollment among adult students. During this time, applications to colleges have surged; selective colleges have both admitted and turned away more qualified applicants, open-door institutions accommodated increased numbers of students, and several states instituted policies encouraging students to study at 2-year institutions before transferring to 4-year state institutions (Western Interstate Commission on Higher Education, 2003).

More than two thirds of higher education institutions have reported increases in the number of applicants during each year since 2000, and fewer than 20% have seen a decrease in applications over the same time (Hawkins & Clindinst, 2006). The Higher Education Research Institute reported that students are applying to an increasing number of colleges, with about 35% of students applying to five or more in 2001 compared with fewer than 20% in 1984 (Astin, Oseguera, Sax, & Korn, 2002). Media attention to selective college admissions has certainly focused greater attention on the most prestigious institutions, yet only 14% of 4-year colleges are considered "most selective" and accept fewer than 50% of applicants (mean selection rate for these colleges was 35%). These institutions accounted for 25% of all applications but only 13% of freshmen in 2002 (National Center for Educational Statistics, 2002). In addition, students appear increasingly to seek opportunities to distinguish themselves, as evidenced by increasing enrollments in advanced placement (AP) courses; increased participation on SAT Subject Tests, test preparation, or coaching programs; and use of early action or early decision programs.

There are many reasons for the increased energy focused on college admissions today. Since the late 1980s, Americans have seen a steep decline in high-wage manufacturing jobs, an increase in demand for entry-level occupations requiring high skills, and widespread recognition that the wage differential between college graduates and nongraduates has nearly doubled in the since 1990. Relative to high school graduates, the percentage change in real wages for college graduates has more than doubled, and the percentage change for adults with postcollege education has nearly tripled during the same time (Lerman, 1997). Because education is increasingly valued as the most direct route to higher wages and success, the college one attends has been perceived as increasingly important.

Admissions officers have adopted practices such as early decision and early action that appear partially to feed the stress and chaos in admissions reported in the media (Loftus, 2008). Fifty percent of the most selective colleges reported offering early decision, and about half of early decision colleges reported an increase in applications and admission rates for these students in 2004. On average, the acceptance rate of 66.6% for students applying under early decision is about 10% higher than the overall admission rate for these same colleges responding to the 2004 Admission Trends Survey from the National Association of College Admission Counselors (Hawkins & Clindinst, 2006). There is only a 4% advantage in admission rates in favor of early action applications among institutions offering this option. A review of several college handbooks illustrates that several selective institutions admit at least one quarter of their freshman class through early decision, which further persuades parents and students that their odds for admission are greatly enhanced if they move up their college search activities. However, comparisons of admission rates among applicants selecting early decision or early action with the larger applicant pool are imprecise because the qualifications of applicants applying under these programs may differ greatly at individual institutions. Both hard evidence and anecdotal reports indicate that students are applying to more colleges each year. Only 56 and 199 4-year colleges are considered "most difficult" and "very difficult," respectively, for admissions out of 2,214 institutions listed in *Peterson's Four-Year Colleges* (2005).

The importance placed on college rankings by colleges themselves and those who contribute to their endowments, the increased use of merit aid to lure the best and brightest to colleges, and runaway grade inflation[1] in high schools are also viewed as transforming admissions into more of a contest than a true effort to find the best institutional fit for each student, according to Don Bishop (2006). In 2001, one third of students said their college's offer of financial assistance was very important in their decision to attend. This represents nearly a 50% increase from 1984 and is the one factor that has shown the greatest change in the past 2 decades from among 22 separate reasons for college choice (Astin et al., 2002). Bishop (2006) has stated that

> the news media have served the public interest poorly on this topic. It seems that about 95% of the national coverage is obsessed with how hard it is to get into the top 20 to 30 colleges. The public has precious little usable, unbiased information. (Bishop, 2006, p. B21)

ADMISSIONS AND ADMISSION TESTS TODAY

In 2005, eight factors were identified as of considerable or moderate importance by at least one third of colleges responding to the Admission Trends Survey (Hawkins & Clindinst, 2006):

1. Grades in college prep courses (or all classes)—89.5%;
2. Standardized admission test scores—87.8%;
3. Class rank—64.5%;
4. Recommendations (counselor and teacher)—60.7%;
5. Essay or writing sample—58.1%;
6. Work/extracurricular activities—47.1%;
7. Interview—37.5%; and
8. Students' demonstrated interest—36.2%.

The National Association of College Admission Counselors has been collecting annual data on college admission practices since 1993. The most significant changes in ratings of practices of considerable importance occurred for grades in all courses (a low of 37% in 1994 and a high of 57% in 2004), admission tests (a low of 43% in 1994 and a high of 61% in 2003), and class rank (a low of 28% in 1993 and a high of 42% in 2004). Essays and students' demonstrated interest were of considerable importance in 2005 for 23% and 15% of institutions, respectively. Whereas 94% selective institutions with 3,000 or more students place some importance on admission test

---

[1]See Camara, Kimmel, Scheuneman, and Sawtell (2003) for a review of high school grades and grade inflation.

scores, two thirds of public colleges have reported that they are of considerable or moderate importance compared with just 57% of private colleges. In addition, a significantly lower percentage of New England colleges indicated admission tests were of considerable importance when compared with the rest of the nation (Hawkins & Clindinst, 2006). Zwick (2007) noted that colleges have consistently attributed considerable importance to grades and course rigor, but the percentage of institutions reporting considerable importance to admissions tests has increased since the mid-1990s.

Admission tests are used for college entrance throughout many of the developed nations, and specialized instruments have been developed for admission to graduate schools as well as programs in medicine, law, dentistry, and business. However, it is the use of admission tests for entrance into undergraduate college that has received the overwhelming amount of criticism and media scrutiny since the 1970s.

The ACT and SAT are taken by well over 2 million college-bound seniors who comprise about two thirds of all graduating high school students. The SAT as well as the Subject Tests, which are produced by the College Board and Educational Testing Service (ETS), and the ACT, developed by ACT, are among the most highly researched large-scale tests produced in the world. Of freshmen in 2003, 64.0% submitted SAT scores to 4-year colleges compared with 50.5% of students who submitted ACT scores. Hawkins and Clindinst (2006) stated that "students who enroll in private, 4-year colleges with high selectivity and low yield were the most likely to submit their SAT scores" (p. 40). The SAT, which was established several decades before the ACT, continues to be subjected to more scrutiny, probably because it is more popular among students and colleges on the East and West Coasts of the United States, where national media are concentrated, and because it is more often associated with students seeking admission to more selective colleges.

In 2005, the SAT added the Writing Test to the Critical Reading and Mathematics tests and made other changes in the format of questions and content of the test to better reflect the instructional practices in schools and skills required for success in college (Milewski, Johnsen, Glazer, & Kubota, 2005). Similarly, the ACT, which includes subtests in reading, English, science, and math, also introduced an optional essay in 2005 and conducts curriculum surveys to ensure that the test remains aligned to content in high schools. The correlation between total scores for students who take both the ACT and SAT has been .89 to .92 in three separate concordance studies, which is similar to the magnitude of test–retest reliabilities reported for both tests (Schneider & Dorans, 1999). Both testing organizations have published substantial amounts of research on their tests, provided detailed longitudinal data on subgroup performance, and conducted hundreds of validity studies that establish the effectiveness of the tests in predicting college success for all groups of students. Table 4.1 provides a general overview of the scores, timing, and questions contained on the ACT and SAT. Overall, the tests are

TABLE 4.1
SAT and ACT Scores and Overall Design

Design elements	SAT	ACT
Testing time	3 hours and 45 minutes	3 hours and 25 minutes (with essay); 2 hours and 55 minutes (without essay)
Separate scores	Critical Reading, Mathematics, and Writing (200–800 scale)	English, Reading, Math, and Science (1–36); Writing score (1–36);[a] Essay (2–12)[a]
Total no. of test items[b]	171 (Critical Reading = 67, Mathematics = 54, Writing = 50)	215 or 216
Price	$41.50	$43.00 ($29.00 without essay)
No. (%) of high school graduates in 2006 taking test	1,465,744 (48.2%)	1,206,455 (39.7%)
Total scores	None	Composite (English, Reading, Math, and Science), 1–36 (essay is not added to composite)

[a]Optional sections on ACT. [b]Not including essay.

similar in content, design, administrative features, and psychometric specifications.

Most of the criticism of admission tests is directed at their use in the selection process; however, admissions tests have other uses. Many colleges use SAT and ACT scores for placement in entry-level math or composition courses, or they establish a specific cut score on these tests that exempt students from taking a second placement test. In these instances, students are able to avoid taking additional placement tests. When students who have not taken an admission test enter many colleges, they may actually be required to take the SAT or ACT when enrolling for placement or for other institutional purposes.

Admission test scores can be beneficial to students and families in other ways. First, test scores are used by many colleges to identify students who may be eligible for an honors program or an academic scholarship. ACT, the College Board, and other organizations assist colleges and universities in identifying students who may "fit" their profile and meet their academic qualifications. Students' scores on the ACT and SAT or their respective practice tests, PLAN and PSAT/NMSQT, are an important factor used by many colleges in identifying and recruiting prospective students. Scores are also used by colleges and other organizations as one criterion in identifying prospective students who may be eligible for scholarships. Second, particularly low scores on admission tests can indicate a student may lack the preparation required for rigorous entry-level courses, and many colleges will use such indicators to identity students who may need remediation or additional academic monitoring or support (Allen & Sconing, 2005). Third, admission test scores can also provide students, families, and school counselors with some indication of a student's relative chances for admission to colleges with different levels of selectivity. Some may consider it inappropriate to use test scores to narrow the range of colleges to which a student may apply. However, if we assume that the nearly 1.5 million college applicants each year apply to 3 colleges each, then a total of nearly 5 million applications are being submitted to 200,000 colleges. This is a massive sorting and selection problem. Today 44% of college-bound students report having an A– average or higher in high school, and most of these students are taking rigorous courses (College Board, 2006). Admission test scores provide students with some sense of their individual qualifications vis-à-vis their competition for the college.

BENEFITS OF ADMISSION TESTS

A committee of the National Research Council (NRC) that examined college admission tests practices concluded "that the standardized tests available today offer important benefits that should not be overlooked in any discussion about changing the (admissions) system" (Greenwood & Linn, 1999, p. 21). The committee then proceeded to discuss many of the benefits admission tests provide to students, parents, colleges, and society, such as the following:

- Standardization—curricula, grading standards, and course content vary enormously across high schools, and admission tests offer an efficient source of comparative information for which there is currently no substitute.
- Efficiency—admission tests are provided at a relatively low cost to students and are efficient for institutions that must review thousands of applications.
- Opportunity—for students whose academic records are not particularly strong, who have not taken the most rigorous courses, or who attend less competitive high schools, standardized tests provide an opportunity to demonstrate talent. (Greenwood & Linn, 1999, p. 22)

Today the ACT and SAT are the only standardized measures colleges receive about applicants. High school courses differ not only in content but also in rigor. Increasingly, students who attend private and highly competitive suburban high schools have a greater opportunity to take more AP and honors courses and participate in an increased variety of activities and sports than their counterparts in many urban and rural schools. Grading standards are not comparable across courses, and there is considerable variation in grades that different teachers assign for the same papers and work (Willingham, Pollack, & Lewis, 2000). In 2006, 43% of college-bound students had an A average, up from 28% in 1987, and the mean high school grade point average (GPA) reported by these students increased to 3.33 from 3.04 (College Board, 2006). Camara, Kimmel, Scheuneman, and Sawtell (2003) reported that from 1981 to 2002, high school grades increased by one third of a point on a 4.0 GPA scale, whereas SAT Verbal scores remained flat, and SAT Mathematics scores increased marginally. Camara et al. examined changes in high school grades and test score by ethnicity, gender, and parental education and found increases in grades particularly benefited female students, Asian Americans, students at the top end of the distribution of grades, and students from more educated families. The effect size for changes in grades during this 21-year period was .50 for Asian American and White students whose parents had a bachelor's degree or higher. Effect sizes for changes in grades were nearly double those of changes in SAT scores for the same students.

Admission tests are also useful for teachers, counselors, and parents in assisting students in choosing a college major or exploring possible careers. They can help students identify and select colleges where they are likely to find an appropriate level of academic competition and to evaluate their competitiveness in admissions. The vast majority of students who take the PSAT/NMSQT, PLAN, SAT, and ACT approve the release of their names to colleges and scholarship competitions. These students are contacted and recruited by colleges, some of which they may have not considered without such outreach efforts. The SAT and ACT also assist colleges in recruitment, talent identification, course placement, and comparison of students who have different academic backgrounds.

THE CRITICS

Admission tests, like any test that is used in sorting and selection, have come under intense criticism for decades. There are two general schools of testing critics. One school is critical of tests such as the ACT or SAT because of specific concerns about group differences, reliance on multiple-choice questions, or a perceived lack of curricular relevance. These critics may advocate different types of tests that include more constructed response tasks, measure different constructs, or use state or local assessments for decision making. In the end, these comparatively responsible critics support the use of assessments for educational decision making and even recognize the utility and efficiency assessments offer, but they believe the current instruments can be greatly improved or replaced. The second school of critics focuses on negative sound bites that are attractive to a media that can only devote 60 seconds or 200 words to an educational issue. Often critics offer no alternatives to admissions tests and no substantive ideas on how to improve the massive sorting and selection processes in college admissions or educational accountability, other than relying exclusively on subjective judgments. When asked for a solution, they advocate using local teachers' grades or background information on applicants (e.g., overcoming adversity, demonstrating persistence), which are often not operationally defined or verified. Some critics are equally opposed to any external measures of school quality or student achievement and would rely solely on teacher grades and perceptions. They have a simple message—tests are bad—and they use every opportunity to criticize a specific test or a specific feature of a test, but in the end they offer no responsible alternatives for selection.

Perhaps the most notable of such critics is the National Center for Fair and Open Testing (FairTest) located in Cambridge, Massachusetts. FairTest has effectively used sound bites in staking out the antitesting position. FairTest will often change its criticisms of tests on the basis of media interest. For example, in the 1990s, it regularly criticized the Graduate Record Examination (GRE) for using a computer-adaptive format and now is equally critical of the linear format in the redesigned test (FairTest, 2006a). Moreover, a few years ago, FairTest (2001a) was highly critical of tests such as the ACT, SAT, and GRE for not measuring important skills such as writing and critical thinking and for omitting constructed response items that were present on more performance-based assessments. However, it is now critical of the writing tests and the additional essay on the same tests. Similarly, it was critical of analogies when they were on the SAT (FairTest, 2001b), and today it is equally critical of the Critical Reading test after the removal of analogies (FairTest, 2005). Such sound-bite criticism is not aimed at improving assessment but rather at eliminating assessment and any objective component of accountability systems or high-stakes decisions.

Because selective colleges can only admit a fraction of applicants, and highly attractive workplaces can only hire a fraction of applicants, selection decisions will not go away any time soon. Standardized tests and any metric used for selection or accountability cannot capture the total breadth of factors that will ultimately determine future success. Behavioral science—specifically, the prediction of human behavior—does not lend itself to the same level of certainty as the laws of physics for obvious reasons.[2] Selection will occur with or without tests. The most relevant question to ask is on what basis such decisions will be made. Alternative methods for decision making are discussed later in this chapter, but it is evident that the most vocal critics of standardized testing would prefer widespread use of nonequivalent and

---

[2]It is important to note that many "scientific tests" (e.g., medical tests) actually have comparable or lower levels of reliability and validity than educational and psychological tests and procedures but are perceived to be "hard science" with results and interpretations challenged much less frequently by nonexperts.

subjective processes that are based solely on teacher judgment and student choice. They have failed to understand that students from more affluent families are more likely to be advantaged in terms of the quality of schools they attend, supplemental educational support that is available (e.g., tutors, summer programs), opportunities to participate in school and community activities, and travel and service opportunities. The perennial criticisms of admission tests have centered on issues of misuse, fairness, bias in tests and test items, utility and validity, and claims about coaching.

MISUSE OF RESULTS FROM ADMISSION TESTS

Until recently, a primary concern with admission tests has been that minimum test scores would be used for admission. Following two widely publicized Supreme Court decisions in 2003, most institutions have removed any reference to minimum test scores for admission and adopted more holistic or comprehensive admission models that are based on an evaluation of a student's total application (including test scores; *Gratz et al. v. Bollinger et al.*, 2003; *Grutter v. Bollinger et al.*, 2003). The use of formulaic or mechanistic approaches for admission appears to have dissipated in light of these court decisions and more resources in admissions. The University of California (2005) is one of the few institutions that has retained both a minimum GPA and minimum test score policy for initial eligibility for admission to any of its campuses. Unlike the University of California, the National Collegiate Athletic Association's minimum test requirement is set at 400 for the combined Critical Reading and Mathematics scores (the lowest score possible on the 400–1600 scale) for students with a high GPA. The National Merit Scholarship Corporation also uses minimum PSAT/NMSQT scores based on percentiles across states to identify semifinalists, but final selection is based on many factors, including grades, academic rigor, and extracurricular activities (National Merit Scholarship Corporation, 2004).

The use of test scores as the sole indicator for educational decisions has been hotly debated, and officials at the University of California have been critical of the use of PSAT/NMSQT scores as an initial first step in identifying eligible semifinalists by the National Merit Scholarship Corporation even though the university's institutions have relied on minimum test scores to establish eligibility for admissions among students with high school grades at specific ranges. Many universities and colleges continue to use SAT and ACT scores as the only metric for placement into honors programs or receipt of merit scholarships (Louie, 2005). The *Standards for Educational and Psychological Testing* (American Educational Research Association, American Psychological Association, & National Council on Measurement in Education, 1999) and the College Board's (2002) *Guidelines on the Uses of College Board Test Scores and Related Data* offer some guidance on these issues but are largely silent on what constitutes a single test score and under what circumstances it is permitted. The College Board's *Guidelines* explicitly oppose reliance on a single test score for admission uses only. The *Standards* advise against the use of a single test score for decisions that will have a major impact on students. They sanction the use of minimum cut scores for placement, college credit, certification, and licensure if proper validation studies have been conducted, and it appears that they are most concerned when a single test score is used as the basis for selection (in college or other contexts), graduation, or promotion. The *Standards* do not address the types of additional information that should be included in these instances. States that require passing a graduation test apparently have been successful in arguing to the U.S. Department of Education that providing students multiple opportunities to pass a graduation test meets this professional requirement.

Second, concerns have been raised about treating specific scores as more precise than is justified. The NRC committee examining college admission tests recommended that colleges and universities avoid treating scores as more precise and accurate than they are and cautioned against relying on fine distinctions among test scores of applicants (Greenwood & Linn, 1999). The committee also urged test producers to intensify efforts to emphasize the standard error of measurement and the significance of score differences in materials and on score reports. Confidence intervals or the standard error of measurement are prominently displayed on student and institutional score reports across all college admission tests, and the College Board and ACT have led efforts to move colleges and college guidebooks to report the middle 50% of scores rather than score means of admitted students. However, on K through 12 reports, mean scores of states, districts, and schools are continually reported by the test publishers and state departments, often with no reference to confidence intervals or the standard error of measurement. This has been a legitimate criticism (Grissmer, 2000). Yet in an age of increased accountability, testing organizations, policymakers, educational officials, and the media continue to overuse aggregate scores to make inferences about the quality of education.

In 2006, there were a significant number of media stories and press releases by states in response to larger than average score changes on both the ACT and SAT. Many state and local educational officials went to great lengths to explain a .2 increase on the ACT Composite or a 7-point decrease on the SAT without any reference to the frequency and significance of such minor score changes. In fact, the 7-point decrease in mean SAT scores in 2006 generated significant media attention, and some state education officials attempted to associate the score decrease with changes to the test (Maryland Department of Education, 2006). A similar 6-point increase in scores 3 years earlier generated no such concern because state and local education officials were very willing to take credit for this minor score increase in student performance.

A third concern has been the recent use of admission tests for No Child Left Behind Act (2001) and state accountability. The ACT has been adopted for statewide accountability in Colorado, Illinois, Michigan, and West Virginia. Similarly, the SAT has been adopted for accountability in Maine, and the PSAT/NMSQT is used statewide in six states to prepare all students for college success. Two major criticisms against using admission tests for this dual role are that the tests were not designed and have not been validated for this purpose (R. Schaffer, personal communication, September 21, 2005).

Reckase (2004) defended such uses but acknowledged that because the high school curriculum varies substantially for individual students and among schools, test makers can write a wide variety of questions and still argue that the test matches the curriculum. He noted that admission tests probably cover a narrower range of topics than state-developed assessments, are more difficult, and are likely to be of higher quality and more consistent across years. Although the ACT and SAT were originally developed for admission and placement decisions, other uses are permissible if the publishers and users have developed validation evidence to support such additional uses. However, test developers must determine what additional validation evidence is required to support the use of such tests for accountability purposes and whether such evidence is available for existing state assessments. The primary type of evidence is likely to be studies that demonstrate alignment between the test framework and measurable content standards (Rothman, 2003). In some instances and with a moderate augmentation, standardized norm-referenced tests can have alignment similar to state-developed tests (Reckase, 2004).

WHAT'S IN A NAME?

Much of the criticism directed against the SAT today focuses on the history of the original test form. Carl Brigham, a psychologist at Princeton University who is associated with the first modern standardized test, the Army Alpha, created in response to the need for a rapid mobilization for World War I, is also associated with the creation of the SAT (then called the Scholastic Aptitude Test; Hanson, 1993). Many critics of the SAT have cited Brigham's racist beliefs concerning the superiority of immigrants from Nordic cultures but have ignored his recant of such earlier views. Conflicting impulses motivated the pioneers of college admission tests in the 1930s, with some hoping to open the nation's ivory towers to able students from diverse backgrounds and others seeking "scientific" means to exclude specific groups (Wigdor & Garner, 1982).[3] James Conant, the first chairman of the ETS

---

[3]For different interpretative histories of the SAT, see Donlon (1984), Fuess (1950), and Lehman (1999).

Board of Trustees, saw the SAT as a means of leveling the playing field and a vehicle for eliminating an artificial aristocracy in American higher education in which family wealth and heritage were the principal determinants of college entrance (Lehman, 1999). After four major revisions to the SAT, the legacy of association between the original standardized tests in the United States with the now-discredited theories about racial differences and racist policies of the early 20th century is still used to attack standardized tests—and the SAT (Wigdor & Garner, 1982, p. 87–93). Critics often have cited the fact that the SAT has changed its name three times since its introduction as evidence of bias or some sinister plot to obfuscate what the test measures. They also have pointed out that both the SAT and the ACT are no longer acronyms but rather the name of each test, which "stands for nothing" (Gardner, 2006, p. 26).

TEST BIAS

For decades, the most pervasive and unsubstantiated claim against standardized tests has been that they are biased and unfair to different groups.[4] Efforts to link standardized tests—and particularly the SAT—to xenophobia and racist policies in the early 20th century provide a subtle suggestion that today's tests must be similarly biased against minorities, female students, and individuals from families with lower socioeconomic status (SES). A summary statement in the NRC report (Greenwood & Linn, 1999) and substantial research it cited (e.g., Jencks, 1998), as well as other studies on this issue (Cooper, Kuncel, Sackett, Waters, & Arneson, 2006; Sackett, Borneman, & Connelly, 2008), should put this allegation to rest:

> Whatever the problems in the construction of the earlier instruments, a considerable body of research has explored the possibility of bias in the current admissions tests, and it has not substantiated the claim that the test bias accounts for score disparities among groups. (Greenwood & Linn, 1999, p. 21)

Large and persistent score gaps exist between the performance of African American and Hispanic students and that of Asian American and White students on national standardized tests in math, science, reading, and writing. Similar gaps between ethnic groups are found across undergraduate and graduate admission tests, national survey tests (e.g., National Assessment of Educational Progress, National Educational Longitudinal Survey), and performance assessments. These gaps do not suddenly emerge in high school or

---

[4]See, for example, FairTest (2007) statements about the ACT that claimed "race, class and gender biases give White, affluent and male test-takers an unfair advantage" (¶ 4) and about the SAT that claimed the speeded nature of the test imposes an unfair burden on students for whom English is not the first language (¶ 4).

on college entrance examinations but have been consistently reported on tests and other educational outcome measures in elementary school (Camara & Schmidt, 1999). Subgroup differences often have been reported out of context by the popular media and critics. Similar gaps in college grades, graduation rates, remediation, and persistence frequently have been ignored (Greenwood & Linn, 1999). The mere presence of large score gaps is not evidence of test bias or a lack of fairness in test use. For example, African Americans earn slightly lower grades throughout college than Whites and Asian Americans who have the same admissions test scores, and this gap is widest at the top of the score distribution (Jencks, 1998).

Young and Kobrin (2001) conducted a review of 49 published studies of differential validity and prediction of admission tests. They reached the following two conclusions:

1. Findings for differential prediction were consistent: The SAT and ACT overpredict college grades for minority groups. That is, the lower scores for minority groups still overestimate their eventual college grades. The greatest overprediction was observed for African Americans, followed by Hispanics.
2. Findings for differential validity were mixed: The correlation between admission tests and high school grades was generally lower for African Americans and Hispanics than for Whites and Asian Americans.

The lower correlations found between predictors and criteria for some minority groups are not evidence of bias in tests because the same relationship has been found for high school grades and other predictors. It simply means that other factors play a greater role in predicting the academic success in college for underrepresented minorities than for Whites and Asian Americans. Bridgeman, McCamley-Jenkins, and Ervin (2000) found that the SAT was slightly better than high school GPA in predicting freshman college grades for female, Asian American, and African American students, which is consistent with hundreds of other studies. The highest predictive accuracy for all gender and ethnic groups results from using the SAT and high school GPA in combination.

Hunter and Schmidt (2000) noted that since the late 1970s, civil rights lawyers, journalists, and others have alleged that cognitive ability and educational tests are biased against minorities. Thousands of test bias studies have been conducted, and these studies have disconfirmed that hypothesis. Hunter and Schmidt cited two studies by the National Academy of Sciences that reviewed research and concluded that such tests are not biased; the authors then argued that the issue of test bias is scientifically dead. Reynolds (2000) noted that "it is common to read literature in the lay press—unchallenged—that IQ or aptitude tests are biased against minorities" (p.145). He went on to explain that this cultural bias hypothesis has been dismissed but that when bias is found, it favors minorities in the predictive context.

BIAS IN THE QUESTIONS

In the face of consistent scientific evidence that dismisses the cultural bias hypothesis, test critics have shifted their arguments away from test bias and toward item bias. The argument is that perhaps the test is not biased, or the bias cannot be detected, but individual test questions certainly are biased. Most such arguments have asserted that item bias is not detected because the bias is in both directions—for example, some items favor Whites and other items favor minorities. Hunter and Schmidt (2000) stated that such arguments are logically inconsistent and not plausible.

Jay Rosner (2003) of the Princeton Review Foundation took this argument to the extreme and contended that the bias is all in favor of Whites and holds true on virtually every admissions test form. He based his claim on the fact that a higher percentage of White students correctly answered every question on an SAT form. He reasoned that test developers exclude any question that a higher proportion of African American students answered correctly from the SAT and cited this as evidence of bias. The argument was originally published in the *Santa Clara Law Review* (Kidder & Rosner, 2002) as well as in *The Nation* (Rosner, 2003). Rosner has presented the same false argument at conferences on college admissions and forums on civil rights (Rosner, 2007), and he has persuaded the media to include his findings in stories on admission testing (e.g., Sexton, 2001; Young, 2003). He has succeeded in circulating his argument despite the illogical and uninformed nature of his theory. This is a classic example of how a spurious argument with no scientific basis not only is published in the national media but has also been repeated by professionals with little knowledge or expertise in test development or psychometrics. Criticisms of tests that have no scientific merit are often appealing to the media and policymakers. There is apparently no effort to have such arguments reviewed by independent credentialed experts in testing and psychometrics. Rather, these arguments seem plausible to some in the lay audience and are repeated enough in the media that they become the new urban myths of testing.

Briefly, let us dissect Rosner's argument that a higher proportion of each minority group must correctly answer some test questions if a test is to be free of bias. How many more items must African American students answer correctly than White students? How many more items should White students answer more correctly than Asian American students? Should items be selected only on the basis of which groups are more likely to correctly answer an item? Of course, pretesting of items in educational testing is not done to ensure that a specific proportion of items favor each group but rather to examine the difficulty of items, their relationship to each other, and whether there is *differential item functioning* (DIF)—comparisons of students from two groups who are matched on overall test score or ability (e.g., male vs. female, African American vs. White), a well-accepted test development process.

African American and White students typically differ, on average, by about 100 points on the SAT Critical Reading, Mathematics, and Writing tests, with comparable differences found on other tests and educational outcomes (Camara & Schmidt, 1999). Given this difference, it is not unreasonable to expect that a higher percentage of White students will answer nearly every individual question on the test correctly compared with African American students. When assembling a final test form from items that have been pretested, test developers will normally exclude any item exhibiting DIF among African American and White students *who have similar total test scores*. DIF is one of several processes that are used in test development to ensure items are free from bias. If test takers from two groups have the same knowledge or ability (as measured by performance on the total test), then they should perform relatively similarly on each item regardless of gender, ethnicity, or race.

In the DIF procedure, students are matched according to their total test score (e.g., male test takers who score about 500 are compared with their female counterparts who score about 500). Next, the individual test items are examined across subgroups within each of the ability levels. An item exhibits DIF if students of equal knowledge or ability from different ethnic or gender groups have a different probability of answering that item correctly. Following the logic behind the DIF procedure, if one looks at students who scored 500 on the SAT, a higher percentage of Whites than African Americans correctly answered 40 of 78 verbal items and 30 of 60 mathematics items on an SAT form in 2004. Furthermore, a higher percentage of African Americans correctly answered 38 of the 78 verbal items and the remaining 30 of the 60 mathematics items.

An intellectually more interesting argument about item bias was leveled against the SAT by Roy Freedle, a psychologist who had worked at ETS. Like Rosner's, his views were picked up by national media outlets with little to no external review before publication. Freedle (2003) found that when African American and White students were matched on total SAT scores, the former group did slightly better on the difficult items and the latter group slightly better on easier items. His proposal was to use just hard items to construct SAT forms. Freedle's original research appeared in the *Harvard Educational Review*, but despite its prestigious name, the *Review* does not require an independent peer review from other academics with expertise in the field. Dorans (2004) identified several errors in the table Freedle constructed for his analyses. Dorans then replicated the analyses with the corrected table and found little to no effect for African American scores. Wainer and Skorupski (2005) conducted a simulation of a completely fair test and showed it had the same subgroup differences that Freedle had found. They reported that these findings are largely due to statistical artifacts and that after removing the artifact, opposite results were found using operational SAT data.

Jencks (1998) noted that the gap between Blacks and Whites (as well as Asian Americans) is similar across a wide range of achievement and skills tests and no greater on tasks that appear to measure content more familiar to White and middle-class culture. The subgroup differences "go far beyond such apparently trivial matters as knowing who wrote *Faust* or what a sonata is" (p. 83).

VALIDITY AND UTILITY

A common criticism of admission tests is that they add little additional information or incremental validity beyond high school grades and that admission decisions will change relatively infrequently based on the additional test information. Crouse and Trusheim (1988) conceded that the SAT was in fact a valid predictor of college grades, but the addition of SAT scores only resulted in a 3% increase in accurate admission decisions, which was meaningless. However, Bond (1990) found that about 70% of admission decisions would remain unchanged whether they were based solely on high school record or admission tests. Moreover, when the second predictor is used, about one third of the decisions would change, and there is intrinsic value in having confirming evidence for the majority of applicants for whom the admission decision would not change. The proportion of variance additional predictors account for is typically small after one or more predictors are used in regressions. Zwick (2007) provided a comprehensive explanation of issues as well as the distinction between a validity coefficient and the proportion of variance accounted for by a predictor.

Bridgeman et al. (2000) examined the predictive validity of the SAT using data from test takers who entered 23 colleges in 1995. They found the average correlation of SAT scores with 1st-year college grades is .52 (27% of the variance explained), and the correlation of high school grades with 1st-year college grades is .54 (29% of the variance explained). Although high school grades are often found to be a slightly better predictor than admission tests, there is only a trivial difference in the variance explained. More important, SAT scores and high school grades together provide the best prediction of college performance, as is indicated by the validity coefficients of .55 to .61 (explaining 30% to 37% of the variance). Because they are sources of different types of information about students, the two measures combined are better than one. Certainly, some critics may argue that .27%, .29%, or even .37% of variance in predicting college grades is not significant. The question, then, is what predictor(s) would they use that could do a better job of predicting college grades?

A large-scale meta-analysis of the SAT predictive validity (Hezlett et al., 2001) found a mean weighted validity coefficient of .62, corrected for range restriction and criterion unreliability, for predicting freshman GPA, and that "the SAT predicts criteria such as study habits, persistence, and degree attainment . . . [and] shows incremental validity over high school GPA . . . and a lack of predictive bias" (p. 123).[5] Occasionally, a local validation study finds a significantly lower correlation with admission test scores, and this is seized on by critics while the hundreds of other validation studies and results from meta-analysis are ignored. For example, in its discussion of the ACT's predictive accuracy, FairTest cited only a 14-year-old study of scores at Chicago State University that reported lower than average validity (FairTest, 2007). Likewise, an unpublished study from one selective liberal arts college that showed little difference in cumulative grades and graduation rates between students who submitted and did not submit SAT scores was the only study referenced by Gardner (2006) to conclude that the SAT lacked validity and utility.

A related criticism of admission tests is that they only predict freshman grades. Validity studies have been conducted primarily using freshman GPA as the outcome criterion because freshman courses and grades are most comparable across colleges and majors and because many students drop out of college before graduation, which further restricts the sample for validity studies beyond the restrictions imposed by admissions. It is often difficult to obtain grades beyond freshman year from colleges for a number of reasons. However, available studies show only a small decrease in the validity coefficient of SAT and high school grades when predicting cumulative GPA (Burton & Ramist, 2001; Hezlett et al., 2001). Studies have also found correlations of .60 or greater with grades in specific college courses (particularly those in math and science), and the relationship of SAT scores and college grades often exceeds correlations between high school GPA and course grades (Burton & Ramist, 2001; Hezlett et al., 2001; Ramist, Lewis, & McCamley-Jenkins, 1993). College persistence and graduation rates are influenced by a host of nonacademic factors (e.g., financial support, adaptation, family circumstances, psychological and medical health), and therefore the correlation with test scores and high school grades is lower than with college grades. However, among all information available to colleges before matriculation, SAT scores

[5]A statistical correction for restriction of range is often used in validity studies because the full range of predictor performance is not represented in the sample. In a validity study at a particular college, the full ranges of SAT or ACT scores are not normally represented because students with low scores may not be admitted. The validity coefficient represented in such college studies will underrepresent the true validity of the predictor. Because of restriction of range, these validity coefficients are smaller than what would be found if the entire population of college applicants were admitted and included in a study. To compensate for the restriction in the sample, a correction for restriction of range is used to estimate what the coefficient would have been (see Gulliksen, 1987, pp. 165–166; Zwick, 2007, p. 20). Grades serve as the criterion or outcome variable in validity studies, and they are often inconsistent or biased across students and courses. A statistical correction for criterion unreliability can similarly be used to adjust for such inconsistency and unreliability.

in combination with high school grades is still the best available predictor (Camara & Echternacht, 2000).

Demonstrating the utility of admission tests is often difficult because scores are highly correlated to high school grades. That is, when two predictors correlate around .50, most students will have a relatively similar rank on both measures. In the case of the SAT, about 68% of students have an SAT score and high school GPA that are within 1 standard deviation of each other (Baydar, 1990; Kobrin & Milewski, 2002). The remaining 32% of students are equally divided among those who have an SAT score at least 1 standard deviation above their GPA and those whose GPA is at least 1 standard deviation above their SAT score. As expected, the most accurate prediction of college success is made when using the SAT and grades for students who perform relatively similarly on the two predictors. What is surprising is that neither high school record nor SAT scores alone have been as useful in predicting college grades for the group of students who have a significantly higher high school GPA compared with their admission test scores (Kobrin & Milewski, 2002).

Burton and Ramist (2001) conducted a comprehensive review of studies examining college persistence and graduating, finding solid evidence that there is an academic component to both outcomes that is measured by the SAT. Adelman (1999) reported a strong relationship between a shortened version of the SAT and college graduation, with only 7% of students scoring in the bottom quintile attaining a bachelor's degree compared with 67% of those with scores in the top quintile. A study of 800,000 ACT test takers who enrolled in college found benchmarks set for all four subtests (English, math, reading, and science) had a higher retention rate than students who did not meet all four benchmarks (Noble, Maxey, Ritchie, & Habley, 2005).

Bridgeman, Pollack, and Burton (2004) took an unusual tack in illustrating the impact of small differences in SAT scores among students who have similar high school grades and academic rigor and attend colleges of similar academic intensity. For example, after controlling for high school grades, course rigor, and the academic intensity of their college, a 200-point increase (from 1,010–1,200 to 1,200–1,400) in SAT scores increased the probability of obtaining a cumulative college GPA of 3.5 from 30% to 51%. These same students, matched on other academic dimensions, more than doubled their probability of a GPA above 3.5 if their SAT score exceeded 1,400. One of the most popular attacks against admission tests is to cite small increases in correlations and variance accounted for when SAT scores are added to the high school GPA in prediction equations. Certainly, an increase of .05 to .10 in correlations is not likely to impress faculty, policymakers, the media, and the public at large. However, the utility of tests cannot be based solely on incremental validity. This dramatic increase in the probability of graduation, persistence, or academic success in college that is associated with a modest change in scores when grades are held constant provides a tangible and transparent illustration of utility. In addition, the cost of selection errors that result in more students taking remedial courses, requiring additional time to graduate, and transferring or dropping out of college entirely should be considered in any utility analysis. Institutions that choose not to use admission test scores face a reduction in information for those students who do not submit their scores. The financial and human costs of selection errors at these particular institutions, as well as the benefits that even a small increase in the overall validity can have on the same human and economic factors, should be weighted before changes are made to selection systems.

SOCIOECONOMIC STATUS

As criticism of ethnic and racial bias on standardized tests has subsided since the late 1980s, the debate has moved to SES and whether tests are a proxy for family wealth and education. Small to moderate correlations have been reported between test scores and SES as well as other educational predictors and outcomes. Critics of tests focus on the correlation between the SAT and family income. They generally ignore similar correlations between family income and the academic rigor of courses completed in high school, college GPA, and college graduation. Unadjusted Pearson correlations were reported for approximately 1.3 million college-bound students who took the SAT in 2002 as well as a sample of nearly 35,000 freshmen at 30 institutions participating in SAT validity studies (Camara, Kobrin, & Sathy, 2005). Table 4.2 illustrates the relationship of family income and parental education with SAT scores, high school grades, high school course rigor, and college grades. Moderate correlations between SES and SAT scores ($r = .10–.29$), college grades ($r = .11–.16$) and academic rigor are reported ($r = .13–.29$), whereas high school grades have smaller correlations with SES ($r = .03–.14$).

The correlations between the academic rigor of the curriculum and parental education are as large as or larger than any correlations between the SAT and SES. In addition, correlations between the SAT and high school grades, academic rigor, and college grades are double those between the SAT and SES. There is clearly a relationship between SAT and SES, but the magnitude of the relationship and variance accounted for is similar to that of other educational measures and SES and pales in comparison with the intercorrelations among the educational measures. Rothstein (2006) found that the odds ratio of receiving a bachelor's degree increased more for students coming from a family with a high income than when students' ethnicity, SAT scores, or various indices of high school academic rigor were taken into account. "We know that the gap in degree completion between the highest and lowest SES quintiles is far wider than any pair of race/ethnicity comparisons" (Adelman, 2004, p. 34). Only 6% of high school graduates from the

TABLE 4.2

Unadjusted Pearson Correlations for Socioeconomic Status and Educational Variables in College-Bound Seniors 2002 and Validity Study with 30 Colleges

Outcome	College-bound seniors 2002 (n = 1,309,990)[a]					Validity study (n = 34,638)[b]					
	HSGPA	SAT total score	Academic rigor	Parents' income	Parents' education	FGPA	HSGPA	SAT total score	Academic rigor	Parents' income	Parents' education
FGPA						—	.46	.40	.29	.11	.16
HSGPA	—	.53	.45	.06	.14		—	.48	.40	.03	.09
SAT V+M		—	.53	.10	.20			—	.55	.23	.29
Academic rigor			—	.16	.25				—	.13	.29
Parents' income				—	54					—	.46

Note. FGPA = freshman GPA; HSGPA = high school GPA; SAT V+M = SAT Verbal and Math test scores. From Camara et al. (2005).
[a]HSGPA (N = 1,066,875), parents' education and parents' income (N = 1,257,010). [b]HSGPA (N = 32,520).

lowest SES quintile group who attended a 4-year college at some time graduated. These students completed bachelor's degrees at a rate of 35.9%, compared with 55.4% for students in the middle (third) SES quintile, and 79.7% for students in the highest SES quintile (Adelman, 2006, p. 104). For example, 28% of students from families with a high school diploma had an A average in high school as opposed to 47% of students from families in which one or both parents had attended graduate school, and 39% of students from families with incomes below $35,000 were in the top 20% of their class versus 52% of students from families with incomes above $100,000 (Camara & Schmidt, 1999).

Geiser and Studley (2001) claimed that SAT scores add little incremental validity when the regression analysis controls for SES. Results from this study have been cited as evidence that the SAT does not predict college grades if SES status is controlled. Zwick, Brown, and Sklar (2003) reported methodological problems in the study that caused this aberrant finding. Johnson (2004) explained that the regression analyses had already included SAT II scores that are highly correlated to freshman GPA, and adding two variables measuring SES was interpreted as meaning the SAT contributed nothing to predicting GPA.

> The correct interpretation, however, is that the SAT I contributes nothing to the prediction of freshman GPA beyond what was predicted by the SAT II, regardless of whether or not SES was included . . . when two SES variables are added to the SAT I alone, the squared multiple correlation increases from .1333 to .1337. (Johnson, 2004, pp. 123–134)

Few empirical studies have directly investigated the influence of SES on test validity. A recent meta-analysis was conducted that included results from 30 studies and 37 independent samples in which the relationships among the SAT, SES, and college grades were studied (Arneson, Waters, Sackett, Kuncel, & Cooper, 2006). They found that the relationship between SAT scores and college grades was unaffected after removing the influence of SES. Arneson et al. (2006) concluded that although a small SES–test relationship was found, there is strong evidence that admission tests are not merely "wealth tests." The same authors then examined the relationships among SES, test scores, and college grades using five longitudinal databases (Cooper et al., 2006). Results showed that the correlation between test scores and grades changed by only .01 to .02 across the five studies when SES was removed. Often the presence of a moderate correlation between test scores and SES is taken as evidence that tests primarily measure wealth; however, such correlations do not explore or explain whether SES has any impact on the validity and utility of admission tests in predicting performance. In both studies just described, the authors found small to moderate correlations between SES and test scores but no evidence that SES moderated the validity of test scores in predicting grades.

COACHING

The issue of coaching may be the most often-cited reason for eliminating admission tests today. There is no single area in which folklore about admission tests has spread more and has been based exclusively on claims of commercial test preparation firms and anecdotal information. Respected educators who would demand evidence to support claims about charter schools or class size are willing to accept and repeat the mantra of commercial coaching firms without reference to any published research (Gardner, 2006).

Approximately 30 published studies include original research, reviews, or meta-analytic studies on coaching (Sathy, 2005). Several of these studies were conducted by ETS staff, and coaching firms have been quick to dismiss such studies as "not credible," yet their methodologies are supplied, the data have been available for reanalysis, and results have often appeared in peer-reviewed journals. There are even more studies published by academic researchers with no affiliation to testing organizations. Results across these studies are remarkably consistent: "A typical student enrolling in a (commercial) test preparation program can expect a total score gain of between 25 to 32 points on the verbal and math sections beyond what they could expect to gain without attending such programs" (Powers & Camara, 1999, p. 9). Briggs (2001) conducted the most recent comprehensive study of coaching on the SAT and ACT using external data from the National Education Longitudinal Survey (NELS) of 1988. His findings were consistent with those reported by ETS and independent researchers.

> After controlling for group differences, the average coaching boost on the math section of the SAT is 14 to 15 points. The boost is smaller on the verbal section of the test, just 6 to 8 points. The combined effect of coaching on the SAT for the NELS sample is about 20 points. . . . The effect of coaching is similar on comparable sections of the ACT. . . . This analysis suggests unequivocally that the average effect of coaching is nowhere near the levels previously suggested by commercial test preparation companies. (Briggs, 2002, pp. 17–18)

Students who attend commercial coaching programs differ in important ways from other test takers. They are more often from high-income families, Asian American, have private tutors helping them with their coursework, use other methods to prepare for admission tests (e.g., books, software), and apply to more selective colleges (Briggs, 2001; Powers, 1998).

One national coaching company has long "guaranteed" a score increase on the SAT and ACT, citing internal surveys of former customers who reported that their scores have increased as evidence of the efficacy of its program. That coaching company does not guarantee a refund if scores do not increase; rather, students are allowed to retake the same course a second time. There are other deceptive practices that permit some commercial coaching firms to associate large score gains with their programs, such as (a) not clarifying that the 100-point gain claimed for coaching on the SAT is based on the combined Verbal and Math scores; (b) computing a score increase based on the coaching firms' own pretest, which may be more difficult and is certainly not equivalent to an actual SAT or ACT test form; and (c) not adjusting score gains for the restricted population of students attending their programs or using a control group to subtract the average score gain by students not attending coaching These practices are deceiving for several reasons. First, the practice of using a 100-point combined score increase across two or more SAT tests is deceiving because there is no composite or total score across tests on the SAT. Students, schools, and colleges receive separate scores on the Critical Reading, Math, and Writing scales that each range from 200 to 800 points. Second, students who take the SAT twice typically increase their score by 30 points; the average increase for students taking the SAT three times is 53 points. The only published studies reporting larger score increases attributable to coaching lack control groups for comparison.

The importance of employing a control group is widely accepted across all scientific areas, yet it is often ignored when evaluating claims about the efficacy of coaching. Testing critics routinely cite findings from small sample studies with no control groups as the primary basis to counter the peer-reviewed published studies discussed earlier. For example, an unpublished study at Deerfield Academy (Franker, 1986–1987) that has frequently been cited found 19 students who completed a commercial test preparation course increased their SAT score by an average of 80 points. Often ignored is the fact that 119 uncoached students at Deerfield also increased their SAT score by the exact same amount. FairTest (2006b) has promoted results from a study by a professor at Quinnipiac College who was able to raise SAT mathematics scores for 21 of 34 students with whom he worked over six summers by more than 80 points. Again, there was no control group or attention to whether these 21 students attending a summer program were representative of national test takers.

Murray (2007) stated that "on average, coaching raises scores by no more than a few dozen points, enough to sway college admissions in exceedingly few cases" (¶ 39). He continued,

> I am not reporting a scholarly literature with a two-sided debate. No study published in a peer-reviewed journal shows average gains approaching the fabled 100-point and 200-point jumps you hear about in anecdotes. . . . I asked Kaplan and Princeton Review for such evidence. Kaplan replied that it chooses not to release data for proprietary reasons. Princeton Review did not respond at all. (¶ 40)

The popular media often perpetuates these myths because they focus almost exclusively on individual success stories that may be referred by tutors or commercial coaching firms. In his cover story in the *New York Times Maga-*

zine, Schwartz (1999) devoted a significant amount of attention to the successes of a private tutor who charged $415 per hour and worked with his students twice a week for at least a year. This private tutor claimed that 91% of students had increases of at least 100 points on the SAT. Further in the article, one discovers that the tutor "isn't so much teaching the test as simply teaching—in this case intensive tutorials in math or reading" (p. 56). It is not surprising to see that students who receive more than 100 hours of individualized instruction by highly qualified and compensated teachers can increase their reasoning skills, school grades, and SAT scores.

The SES advantage that is associated with admission tests applies to all areas of education. Children who grow up in more affluent and educated families enjoy the advantages of attending higher quality schools, greater parental engagement in learning, more cultural opportunities and broader travel, a culture of high expectations and achievement, private tutoring that will raise their school grades, private college counseling, and greater financial resources (Rothstein, 2004; Schwartz, 1999). Inequality exists throughout educational opportunities. Affluent students with savvy parents will always have an advantage over less affluent students and will press that advantage relentlessly (Oakes, as cited in Laird, 2001, p. L2).

SAT OPTIONAL SCHOOLS

Over the past few years, there has been an undeniable increase in test-optional policies among strong private liberal arts colleges. Many of these colleges cite their interest in recruiting a broader and more diverse group of students, many of whom may not have applied because of relatively poor admission test scores. They also cite the importance of high school grades and other factors in predicting success and a concern about students' increased obsession with test scores.

FairTest (2006c) reported that 733 institutions currently have a test-optional policy. Although the number of institutions that are test optional has almost doubled since 2002, this does not appear to have had an impact on the number or proportion of students who take admission tests, which has also continued to increase during this time. Test-optional policies do not appear to have affected the number of students who take the SAT or ACT, either, because the tests are required for one or more institutions to which students will apply or, more likely, because students will take a test and the vast majority of them will report their scores even to test-optional institutions.

Competitive liberal arts colleges with such policies in place have generally reported that approximately 65% to 85% of applicants typically submit SAT or ACT scores. Only one third of the institutions on the current test-optional list (289 institutions of the 733 listed) have a comprehensive test-optional policy for all applicants. It is much more common to find institutions listed that will exempt some applicants from submitting admission test scores but require additional academic documentation or testing. For example, 22% of the institutions will only permit applicants with a specific high school GPA or high school rank to omit submission of test scores (e.g., California State Universities, University of Texas), and often this applies only to in-state applicants. An additional 17% of institutions require the SAT or ACT for placement or advising but do not use scores in admission (e.g., University of Northern Iowa), and approximately 7% of institutions accept SAT Subject Tests or other tests in lieu of the SAT and ACT (e.g., Art Institute of Boston at Lesley University). Among the remaining institutions are a large number of religiously affiliated institutions, art and music institutes, open admission institutions, and distance education schools. About 4% exempt in-state applicants only or applicants to specific programs.

Hiss and Neupane (2004) reported that after 20 years, the test-optional policy at Bates College has been largely responsible for increases in total applications and applicant diversity while the quality of the admitted class has been maintained. They also noted that there have been only small differences in the graduation rates, GPAs, and academic ratings of submitters and nonsubmitters. Shaw and Milewski (2004) examined the first set of claims for three highly selective liberal arts colleges with test-optional policies in place for several years and compared changes in applications (number of applications, acceptance rate, enrollment rate), the student body (percentage minority, percentage international, percentage of students with need-based aid, percentage in the top 10% of their class, freshmen retention rate, and percentage of freshman graduating in 6 years), and test score ranges with comparable institutions in terms of size, location, and selectivity. They also sought institutions for the control group that had high rates of crossover applications with the test-optional institutions. There were no systematic differences among the three selective colleges with long-standing test-optional policies and comparable colleges in terms of applications, the composition of the student body, or academic qualifications of students. This is not to say that the colleges with test-optional policies have not nearly doubled the number of applications, increased the diversity of their student body, or admitted classes with higher grades and GPAs over time. However, comparable colleges that require test scores have seen the same increases in these outcome measures during the same period of time. For example, the percentage of minorities enrolled at the three SAT optional colleges changed by 3%, 14%, and −1% from the year before the test-optional policy was implemented to the 2003 freshman class. The percentage of minorities enrolled at comparison institutions during those same years also increased by comparable proportions and actually exceeded the percentage at two of the three institutions. Each institution in the study, irrespective of its testing policy, has had a small increase in the percentage of the freshman class with need-based aid and more than doubled the percentage of international students in its freshman class since the mid-1990s.

In evaluating any intervention, changes within an institution are only a partial indicator of its effectiveness. Comparisons of changes with comparable institutions that have not had the intervention or, in this case, comparison with institutions that have not adopted a test optional policy, are essential to determine whether changes can be attributed to the policy or other environmental factors. In this small study, it appears that the increase in applications, enrollment rates, diversity of enrolled students, and SAT scores of applicants has occurred at selective liberal arts colleges in the Northeast irrespective of their testing policies. Single institutional studies that lack a comparison or control group often provide biased estimates of change over time in any discipline but particularly in dynamic environments such as college admissions.

Today the majority of colleges and universities have adopted comprehensive admission policies that evaluate all the information available on applicants. Admission test scores and high school grades are certainly important factors in admission for many selective institutions, but comprehensive admission policies use a compensatory model. Low grades in foreign-language courses may be overlooked if a student's academic record is strong. Similarly, lower test scores can similarly be compensated for by a strong and rigorous high school record and other accomplishments. Given the resources available at most private liberal arts colleges to review each individual application in detail and use compensatory strategies to consider the entire student application, test-score-optional policies appear to serve primarily as a recruitment tool. Having more information on all applicants cannot be bad, especially when experienced admission officers can conduct a detailed review and either deemphasize or dismiss any one indicator (e.g., low test score, poor grades in a subject) that is not consistent with the entire record. Eliminating mechanistic formulas for admission is highly preferable to eliminating a source of valuable information, and unlike test-optional policies, it will not lead to more strategizing by applicants who are deciding whether it is in their benefit to submit scores and, if so, to which institutions.

In 2001, the University of California at Berkeley had 36,000 applications for 8,800 admission places (Laird, 2001). Admission officers read each folder and carefully evaluated test scores and other factors against an applicant's circumstances and history. A score of 1,200 may be an outstanding score for a student from a low-performing high school whose parents did not attend college but an undistinguished score for another student coming from a much more affluent and enriched environment. Some of the test-optional schools have cited "faults with admissions tests" as their rationale, yet every indicator of academic ability is imperfect. The president of Reed College noted that "if standardized tests are so imperfect, we should scrap them altogether. It's illogical to count a test score if it is high but ignore it if it is low" (Diver, 2006, p. 27). He further argued that by placing less weight and emphasis on test scores, institutions can admit more disadvantaged students without adopting practices and rationalizations that are aimed at climbing the pecking order in college rankings.

When test scores are not available, colleges will place greater emphasis on other factors, and the other primary academic factors that are available include high school grades, the academic intensity and rigor of the curriculum, and the quality of the school attended. A large majority of students applying to the three selective liberal arts colleges with test-optional policies discussed earlier had a high school GPA of 3.8 or higher. Grades have minimal impact, especially at highly selective schools where there is often little variance among the majority of applicants. For example, Pope (2006) reported that at the University of California at Los Angeles (UCLA), 21,000 of the 47,319 applicants in 2006 had a high school GPA of 4.0 or higher. UCLA admitted 11,360 students, which is approximately 50% of the number of applicants with a 4.0 GPA. With such little variation in grades, factors such as the quality of school attended and the opportunity to take many AP and honors courses must certainly have determinative importance for most decisions. Students who do not attend high quality schools where many AP, international baccalaureate, or honors courses are offered would seem to have little chance of admission if test scores were ignored. Admission policies that give more weight to these factors may not necessarily be more egalitarian than policies that use tests in a compensatory manner. Students attending private high schools and wealthy suburban public schools may ultimately be more advantaged in access to more rigorous curricula, leadership opportunities, and other experiences that distinguish more among students when tests are not present and grades do not vary among applicants.

CONCLUSION

A simple observation of the number of books published on college admissions and the increased media attention on selective college admissions reveals that there is an overemphasis on the admissions process as a contest. Small differences in admission test scores have been misused and misinterpreted, with the result that many parents, students, and educators have overemphasized the importance of test scores in ways that colleges do not. The current frenzy about college admissions is not limited to test scores. In the hope of bolstering their applications and hence their chances for admission, many students overwhelm themselves with extracurricular activities, community service, or cultural experiences they perceive as likely to impress admission officers. Many students also get help with their admission essays and take as many honors or AP courses as they can to obtain a higher weighted GPA. A more rational approach to college admissions will not evolve with the elimination of test scores, as is evident by the number of selective liberal arts colleges with test-optional policies today.

Admission tests are an easy target because the objective data they provide are often troubling and discomforting. The large and persistent group differences in performance are not as easily ignored as similar differences in college success and academic intensity in high school that are not systematically reported nationally or regionally. There is a mystery about how admission decisions are made and the role of test scores in those decisions for different groups of students. This chapter has attempted to address myths and misunderstandings about admission tests within the broader context of college admissions.

Too often, educators, academics, and the media are willing to accept assumptions, advertised claims from commercial firms, and statements from so-called experts above and beyond data and results based on published scientific studies. In education, particularly as it relates to testing, the media and the educational establishment readily accept the opinions of an economist or sociologist as equally credible to the findings of psychometricians, educational psychologists, and educational measurement professionals. It is not uncommon for distinguished academics with no unique expertise or credentials in measurement, psychometrics, or testing to comment on the validity or fairness of educational tests on the basis of their perceptions and beliefs. Often, these same scientists base their opinions of tests on single-institution studies, with small samples and inadequate designs that they would reject if conducted in their own field of expertise. The media is unable to distinguish among academics with qualifications in testing and measurement and those with opinions about testing and measurement. It is highly unlikely that the media or policymakers will seek the views of psychologists about supply-side economics or global warming, yet we commonly see academics and other professionals cited as experts in educational testing.

The harmful, antiscientific practice of characterizing anecdote as fact and ignoring existing research that contradicts beliefs is increasingly prevalent in the media and even among some educational leaders and policymakers (Camara, 2006). Some of the strongest criticism against admission testing continues to emanate from individuals and organizations that offer no serious alternative. Often tests are considered much more precise than their developers or uses have ever stipulated and are relied on too heavily. In education, tests are increasingly used as the sole means for measuring accountability of schools and states with little concern for professional standards and cautions issued by measurement experts. Educational testing has become increasingly polarized, with strong proponents and even stronger critics unwilling and unable to appreciate the complexities and nuances involved in understanding student achievement and learning. Each side wants simple answers, slogans, and talking points.

Admission tests are neither good nor bad in and of themselves. They are neither fair nor unfair, valid nor invalid. To understand the validity, utility, and appropriate uses of admission tests requires a more in-depth analysis of research and the complexities associated with their use in college admission decisions. This chapter has attempted to take on the myths and undocumented criticisms leveled against admission testing and present a more complex and contextualized explanation of their appropriate role in admissions today.

REFERENCES

Adelman, C. (1999). *Answers in the tool box: Academic intensity, attendance patterns, and bachelor's degree attainment.* Washington, DC: U.S. Department of Education.

Adelman, C. (2004). *Principal indicators of student academic histories in postsecondary education, 1972–2000.* Washington, DC: U.S. Department of Education.

Adelman, C. (2006). *The tool box revisited: Paths to degree completion from high school through college.* Washington, DC: U.S. Department of Education.

Allen, J., & Sconing, J. (2005). *Using ACT assessment scores to set benchmarks for college readiness* (ACT Research Report 2005-3). Iowa City, IA: ACT.

American Educational Research Association, American Psychological Association, & National Council on Measurement in Education. (1999). *Standards for educational and psychological testing.* Washington, DC: American Educational Research Association.

Arneson, J., Waters, S. D., Sackett, P. R., Kuncel, N. R., & Cooper, S. R. (2006, April). *A meta-analytic investigation of the role of SES in ability test-grade relationships.* Paper presented at the 21st Annual Conference of the Society for Industrial and Organizational Psychology, Dallas, TX.

Astin, S. W., Oseguera, L., Sax, L. J., & Korn, W. S. (2002). *The American freshmen: Thirty-five year trends.* Los Angeles: Higher Education Research Institute, University of California at Los Angeles.

Baydar, N. (1990). *Profiles of the students who have discrepant high school GPA and SAT scores.* (Available from Educational Testing Service, Corporate Headquarters, Rosedale Road, Princeton, NJ 08541)

Bishop, D. (2006, July 7). Admissions officers speak out on private counselors. *Chronicle of Higher Education: Admissions & Student Aid, 44*(71), 52.

Bond, L. (1990). Analyzing the predictive value of the SAT. *Contemporary Psychology, 35,* 354–355.

Bridgeman, B., McCamley-Jenkins, L., & Ervin, N. (2000). *Predictions of freshmen grade-point average from the revised and recentered SAT I: Reasoning Test* (College Board Research Report 2000-1). New York: College Board.

Bridgeman, B., Pollack, J., & Burton, N. (2004). *Understanding what SAT reasoning test scores add to high school grades: A straightforward approach* (College Board Research Report 2004-4). New York: College Board.

Briggs, D. C. (2001). The effect of admissions test preparation: Evidence from NELS:88. *Chance, 14,* 10–18.

Burton, N. W., & Ramist, L. (2001). *Predicting success in college: SAT studies of classes graduating since 1980* (College Board Research Report 2001-2). New York: College Board.

Camara, W. J. (2006). Critic of SAT favors anecdotes over facts. *Education Week, 25,* 47.

Camara, W. J., & Echternacht, G. (2000). *The SAT I and high school grades: Utility in predicting success in college* (College Board Research Note RN-10). New York: College Board.

Camara, W. J., Kimmel, E., Scheuneman, J., & Sawtell, E. A. (2003). *Whose grades are inflated?* (College Board Research Report 2003-4). New York: College Board.

Camara, W. J., Kobrin, J., & Sathy, V. (2005, April). *Is there an SES advantage for the SAT and college success?* Paper presented at the Annual Meeting of the National Council on Measurement in Education, Montréal, Canada.

Camara, W. J., & Schmidt, A. E. (1999). *Group differences in standardized testing and social stratification* (College Board Research Report 1999–5). New York: College Board.

College Board. (2002). *The College Board's guidelines on the uses of College Board test scores and related data.* New York: Author.

College Board. (2006, August 29). *College-bound seniors 2006.* New York: Author.

Cooper, S. R., Kuncel, N. R., Sackett, P. R., Waters, S., & Arneson, J. (2006, April). *The role of SES in the SAT-performance relationship: Results from national longitudinal studies.* Paper presented at the 21st Annual Conference of the Society for Industrial and Organizational Psychology, Dallas, TX.

Crouse, J., & Trusheim, D. (1988). *The case against the SAT.* Chicago: University of Chicago Press.

Diver, C. S. (2006, September 18). Skip the test, betray the cause. *New York Times,* p. A27.

Donlon, T. F. (1984). *The College Board technical handbook for the scholastic aptitude test and achievement tests.* New York: College Board.

Dorans, N. J. (2004). Freedle's Table 2: Fact or fiction? *Harvard Educational Review, 74,* 62–72.

FairTest. (2001a, October 18). *Examining the GRE: Myths, misuses, and alternatives.* Retrieved August 14, 2006, from http://www.fairtest.org/facts/gre.htm

FairTest. (2001b, August 21). *The SAT: Questions and answers.* Retrieved December 7, 2006, from http://www.fairtest.org/facts/satfact.htm

FairTest. (2005, June). *The "New" SAT: A better test or just a marketing ploy?* Retrieved December 7, 2006, from http://www.fairtest.org/univ/newsatfact.htm

FairTest. (2006a, August). *Not ready for "prime time"—New GRE postponed.* Retrieved July 8, 2008, from http://www.fairtest.org/not-ready-prime-time-new-gre-postponed

FairTest. (2006b, August). *Redux: Test coaching works.* Retrieved July 8, 2008, from http://www.fairtest.org/redux-test-coaching-works

FairTest. (2006c, September). *Schools that do not use SAT I or ACT scores for admitting substantial numbers of students into bachelor degree programs as of September 2006.* Retrieved September 17, 2006, from http://www.fairtest.org/optstate.html

FairTest. (2007). *The ACT: Biased, inaccurate, coachable and misused.* Retrieved July 18, 2008, from http://fairtest.org/facts/act.html

Franker, L. (1986–1987, Winter). The Princeton Review reviewed. *The Newsletter,* 3–4. (Available from Deerfield Academy, 1 Albany Road, Deerfield, MA 01342)

Freedle, R. O. (2003). Correcting the SAT's ethnic and social-class bias: A method for reestimating SAT scores. *Harvard Educational Review, 73,* 1–43.

Fuess, C. (1950). *The College Board: Its first 50 years.* New York: The College Entrance Examination Board.

Gardner, W. (2006). UnSATisfactory: Why education's most famous test fails the test. *Education Week, 25,* 26–27.

Geiser, S., & Studley, R. (2001). *UC and the SAT: Predictive validity and differential impact of the SAT I and SAT II at the University of California.* Retrieved November 13, 2004, from http://www.ucop.edu/sas/readearch/researchandplanning/pdf/sat_study.pdf

Greenwood, M. R. C., & Linn, R. L. (Eds.). (1999). *Myths and tradeoffs: The role of tests in undergraduate admissions.* Washington, DC: National Academies Press.

Gratz et al. v. Bollinger et al. certiorari to the U.S. Court of Appeals for the Sixth Circuit No. 02-516. Argued April 1, 2003; decided June 23, 2003.

Grutter v. Bollinger et al. certiorari to the U.S. Court of Appeals for the Sixth Circuit No. 02-241. Argued April 1, 2003; decided June 23, 2003.

Grissmer, D. W. (2000). The continuing use and misuse of SAT scores. *Psychology, Public Policy, and Law, 6,* 223–232.

Gulliksen, H. (1987). *Theory of mental tests.* Hillsdale, NJ: Erlbaum.

Hanson, F. A. (1993). *Testing testing: Social consequences of the examined life.* Berkeley: University of California Press.

Hawkins, D., & Clindinst, M. (2006). *The state of college admissions.* Alexandria, VA: National Association for College Admission Counseling.

Hezlett S. A., Kuncel, N. R., Vey, M., Ahart, A., Ones, D. S., Campbell, J. P., & Camara, W. J. (2001). The predictive validity of the SAT: A comprehensive meta-analysis. In D. S. Ones & S. A. Hazlett (Chairs), *Predicting performance: The interface of I-O psychology and educational research.* Symposium conducted at the 16th Annual Conference of the Society for Industrial and Organizational Psychology, San Diego, CA.

Hiss, W. C., & Neupane, P. R. (2004, October). *Twenty years of optional SATs at Bates.* Paper presented at the Annual Meeting of the National Association for College Admission Counseling, Milwaukee, WI.

Hunter, J. E., & Schmidt, F. L. (2000). Racial and gender bias in ability and achievement tests: Resolving the apparent paradox. *Psychology, Public Policy, and Law, 6,* 151–158.

Jencks, C. (1998). Racial bias in testing. In C. Jencks & M. Phillips (Eds.). *The Black–White test score gap* (pp. 55–85). Washington, DC: Brookings Institution Press.

Johnson, J. W. (2004). Not all affirmative action rewards merit. *American Psychologist, 59,* 123–124.

Kidder, W. C., & Rosner, J. (2002). How the SAT creates "Built-in headwinds": An educational and legal analysis of disparate impact. *Santa Clara Law Review, 43,* 131–211.

Kobrin, J. L., & Milewski, G. B. (2002). *Students with discrepant high school GPA and SAT I scores* (College Board Research Note RN-15). New York: College Board.

Laird, R. (2001, July 8). The case for not scrapping the SAT. *The Sacramento Bee,* p. L2.

Lehman, N. (1999). *The big test: The secret history of the American meritocracy.* New York: Farrar, Straus & Giroux.

Lerman, R. I. (1997). *Meritocracy without rising inequality: Wage rate differences are widening by education and narrowing by gender and race.* Washington, DC: Urban Institute Press.

Loftus, M. (2008). The early-bird dilemma. In *America's best colleges 2008* (p. 52). Washington, DC: U.S. News & World Report.

Louie, V. (2005, July 18). UC ends support for merit scholarship. *The Daily Californian.* Retrieved October 10, 2007, from http://dailycal.org/printable.php?id=19016

Maryland Department of Education. (2006, August 29). *Maryland students continue strong performance on AP, PSAT and ACT assessments; Baseline scores on the broadly revised SAT also released.* Retrieved September 20, 2006, from http://www.marylandpublicschools.org/msde/pressrelease_details/2006_08_29.htm

Milewski, G. B., Johnsen, D., Glazer, N., & Kubota, M. (2005). *A survey to evaluate the alignment of the new SAT Writing and Critical Reading sections to curriculum and instructional practices* (College Board Research Report 2005-1). New York: College Board.

Murray, C. (2007, July/August). Abolish the SAT. *The American.* Retrieved October 5, 2007, from http://american.com/archive/2007/july-august-magazine-contents/abolish-the-sat

National Center for Educational Statistics. (2002). *The integrated postsecondary education data system* [Searchable database]. Available at http://nces.ed.gov/ipeds

National Center for Educational Statistics. (2005). *Digest of education statistics* [Data tables]. Retrieved August 1, 2006, from http://nces.ed.gov/programs/digest/d05/tables/dt05_179.asp and http://nces.ed.gov/programs/digest/d02/dt383.asp

National Merit Scholarship Corporation. (2004, October 31). *Annual Report 2003–2004.* Evanston, IL: Author.

Noble, J., Maxey, J., Ritchie, J., & Habley, W. (2005, October). *Enhancing college student retention: Identification and intervention.* Paper presented at the National Symposium on Student Retention, Dallas, TX.

No Child Left Behind Act of 2001, Pub. L. No. 107-110, 107th Congress, January 8, 2002.

Peterson's four-year colleges. (2005). Lawrenceville, NJ: Thomson Peterson's.

Pope, J. (2006, November 19). Admissions boards face grade inflation. *Trenton Times,* p. B1.

Powers, D. (1998). *Preparing for the SAT I Reasoning test—An update* (College Board Research Report 98-5). New York: College Board.

Powers, D., & Camara, W. (1999). *Coaching and the SAT I* (College Board Research Note 06). New York: College Board.

Ramist, C., Lewis, C., & McCamley-Jenkins, L. (1993). *Student group differences in predicting college grades: Sex, language and ethnic groups* (College Board Research Report 1993-1). New York: College Board.

Reckase, M. (2004, May 26). ACT vs. MEAP: Schools search for right test standard. *Detroit Free Press.* Retrieved September 19, 2005, from http://www.detnews.com/2004/editorial/0405/26/a11-163917.htm

Reynolds, C. R. (2000). Why is psychometric research on bias in mental testing so often ignored? *Psychology, Public Policy, and Law, 6,* 144–150.

Rosner, J. (2003, April 14). On White preferences. *The Nation,* p. 24.

Rosner, J. (2007, October 15). *University admissions tests: Are minority outcomes disparate by design?* Presentation at the TRPI Educational Conference. Retrieved July 19, 2008, from http://www.trpi.org/PDFs/Jay%20Rosner.pdf

Rothman, R. (2003, March). *Imperfect matches: The alignment of standards and tests.* Unpublished manuscript prepared for the Committee on Test Design for K–12 Science Achievement Center for Education, National Research Council, Washington, DC.

Rothstein, R. (2004). *Class and schools: Using social, economic and educational reform to close the Black–White achievement gap.* Washington, DC: Economic Policy Institute.

Rothstein, R. (2006). [Odds ratio from logistic regression on bachelor's degree completion for the 1999 graduating seniors cohort]. Unpublished raw data.

Sackett, P. R., Borneman, M. J., & Connelly, B. S. (2008). High-stakes testing in higher education and employment: Appraising the evidence for validity and fairness. *American Psychologist, 63*(4), 215–227.

Sathy, V. (2005, September). *Coaching studies on the SAT conducted by external researchers.* Retrieved September 11, 2006, from http://search.collegeboard.com/research/pdf/06-0487_CoachingStudies_9-21.pdf

Schneider, D., & Dorans, N. (1999). *Concordance between SAT I and ACT scores for individual students* (College Board Research Note RN-07). New York: College Board.

Schwartz, T. (1999, January 10). The test under stress. *New York Times Magazine,* pp. 30–35, 51, 56, 63.

Sexton, S. (2001, February 21). Experts contest whether SAT is racially biased. *The Daily Californian.* Retrieved July 19, 2008, from http://www.dailycal.org/printable.php?id=4649#

Shaw, E. J., & Milewski, G. B. (2004). *Characteristics of admissions test optional colleges compared to matched control groups*. (Available from College Board Research & Development, wcamara@collegeboard.org)

University of California. (2005). *Freshman admission*. Retrieved August 18, 2006, from http://www.universityofcalifornia.edu/admissions/undergrad_adm/paths_to_adm/freshman.html

Wainer, H., & Skorupski, W. P. (2005). Was it ethnic and social-class bias or statistical artifact? Logical and empirical evidence against Freedle's method for reestimating SAT scores. *Chance, 18*(2), 17–24.

Western Interstate Commission on Higher Education. (2003). *Knocking at the door: Projections of high school graduates by state, income, and race/ethnicity 1988 to 2018*. Boulder, CO: Author.

Wigdor, A., & Garner, W. R. (Eds.). (1982). *Ability testing: Uses, consequences, and controversies. Part 1 of the report of the committee* (Report of the Committee on Ability Testing, Commission on Behavioral and Social Sciences and Education, National Research Council). Washington, DC: National Academies Press.

Willingham, W., Pollack, J. M., & Lewis, C. (2000). *Grades and test scores: Accounting for observed differences* (ETS Research Report RR-00-14). Princeton, NJ: Educational Testing Service.

Young, J. (2003, October 10). Researchers charge racial bias on the SAT. *Chronicle of Higher Education, 50*, A34–35.

Young, J. W., & Kobrin, J. L. (2001). *Differential validity, differential prediction, and college admission testing: A comprehensive review and analysis* (College Board Research Report 2001-6). New York: College Board.

Zwick, R. (2007). *College admissions testing*. Retrieved October 10, 2007, from http://www.nacacnet.org/NR/rdonlyres/21062AE7-F087-4CF8-A5BA-E5C3474F07C4/0/Standardized_Testing.pdf

Zwick, R., Brown, T., & Sklar, J. C. (2003). *California and the SAT: A reanalysis of University of California admissions data*. Berkeley, CA: Center for Studies in Higher Education.

5

CRITICISMS OF EMPLOYMENT TESTING: A COMMENTARY

ERNEST H. O'BOYLE JR. AND MICHAEL A. McDANIEL

When people think of employment testing, they typically consider only written tests of cognitive ability and personality. However, applicants are screened for jobs with a variety of measures, including reviews of resumes and applications, cognitive ability tests, personality assessments, integrity testing, employment interviews, drug testing, and reference checks. The U.S. federal guidelines on employee selection (Equal Employment Opportunity Commission [EEOC], Civil Service Commission, Department of Labor, & Department of Justice, 1978) consider any method used to screen job applicants to be an employment test. Our use of the word *test* in this chapter is consistent with these federal guidelines. Employment testing is one example of high-stakes testing (Sackett, Schmitt, Ellingson, & Kabin, 2001), in which those who perform well on the test are considered for employment and those who perform less well are not considered for employment.

The purpose of this chapter is to review commonly offered criticisms of employment testing. We then evaluate these critiques in light of research findings. In selecting the criticisms to address, we relied on our experience with employment testing and solicited common criticisms from others who have substantial experience with employment testing. We identified 11 such criticisms. Although one can classify criticisms of employment testing in several ways, for this chapter we organized the criticisms into three categories: fairness, accuracy, and administrative efficiency.

Concerning fairness, employment tests are said to be

- unfair to ethnic and racial minorities,
- illegal when ethnic and minority groups obtain lower scores on average,
- unfair because they have not been validated for every type of job and across every type of context, and
- an invasion of privacy.

Concerning accuracy, employment tests are said to

- result in some bad hiring decisions,
- tell one nothing one would not learn by talking with the applicant,
- be useful but often assess the wrong content, and
- be easily faked.

Concerning administrative efficiency, the employment tests are said to

- be unnecessary because one can train anyone to do any job,
- take too long, and
- be too expensive.

We address each of these criticisms in turn.

CRITICISMS RELATED TO FAIRNESS

Employment Testing Is Unfair to Ethnic and Racial Minorities

Many criticisms of employment testing are based on concerns regarding the lower performance, on average, of Blacks and Hispanics on employment tests relative to the performance of Whites and Asians. Some criticisms are based on the assumption that there are no job-related ability differences among the various racial and ethnic groups, and so if employment tests show such differences, something must be wrong with the tests. The critics are correct in their observation that Blacks and Hispanics on average obtain substantially lower scores than Whites and Asians on most employment tests, particularly on tests of cognitive ability (Murray, 2005; Sackett et al., 2001). Such differences are also common when educational credentials (degrees, grade point average) are used as a test or when job-related knowledge or skills are assessed. Roth, BeVier, Bobko, Switzer, and Tyler (2001) documented that after correcting for range restriction, there was a difference of roughly 1 standard deviation between the means of Blacks and Whites in general cognitive ability and a substantial but somewhat smaller difference in mean scores between Whites and Hispanics. Because many employment tests are designed to assess cognitive ability, or are at least moderately correlated with cognitive ability, it is more common than not for employment tests to show substantial mean differences between Blacks and Whites and between Hispanics and Whites. These differences are not restricted to employment tests. Large mean ethnic–racial differences are found in educational assessments as well.

Research on changes in the magnitude of mean ethnic–racial differences in cognitive ability is controversial, with some arguing the differences are narrowing in recent decades (Dickens & Flynn, 2006), whereas the bulk of the research indicates that these mean differences have been relatively intractable (Murray, 2005; Rushton & Jensen, 2006). Even if one accepts the position that mean racial differences are shrinking over time, they are still large enough to cause substantial disparities in hiring decisions.

The large mean ethnic–racial differences in employment test scores prompted much research, occurring primarily in the 1970s, examining whether employment tests are biased against Blacks and Hispanics. It was argued that employment tests might be biased through either differential validity or differential prediction (Boehm, 1972; Bray & Moses, 1972; Kirkpatrick, Ewen, Barrett, & Katzell, 1968).

Differential validity studies addressed the hypothesis that a test may have validity for Whites but not for Blacks or that the test may have a larger validity for one group than another. By *validity*, we refer to the extent to which an employment test correlates with a measure of job performance (e.g., a supervisor rating of one performance, the amount of product sold, the number of customers served). Thus, a hypothesis about differential validity might hold that a test predicts performance of Whites but not Blacks. In the 1980s, after substantial research examined this issue, it was shown that differential validity is uncommon (Schmidt, 1988; Schmidt & Hunter, 1981; Wigdor & Garner, 1982).

It became apparent that it would be more appropriate to look for differential prediction than differential validity because even if a test has the same validity for all ethnic–racial subgroups, the best regression lines to predict job performance might be different.[1] Differential prediction can occur if the regression lines for ethnic–racial subgroups yield either different slopes or

---

[1]A correlation is useful for estimating the relationship between an employment test and a measure of job performance. However, it does not give the one the information needed to predict a job performance score from an employment test score. For this, one needs to run a regression analysis. A regression equation for the prediction of job performance is of this form: job performance = $a + b$ (employment test score). This regression formula describes a straight line that summarizes the relationship between the employment test and the job performance measure. The a value is called the *intercept*. When the variables have been standardized, the b value (the *regression weight*) equals the correlation coefficient and describes the slope of the regression line.

different intercepts. The research indicated that different slopes for different racial–ethnic subgroups occur at no higher than chance levels (Bartlett, Bobko, Mosier, & Hannan, 1978).

Different intercepts are more common, but the error in prediction tends to favor minority groups. Specifically, when the prediction of job performance for Black or Hispanic groups and Whites is based on a common regression line, performance of Blacks and Hispanics is overpredicted on average (Hartigan & Wigdor, 1989; Schmidt, Pearlman, & Hunter, 1980). Thus, to the extent that differential prediction occurs in employment tests, it is to the disadvantage of White applicants but not Black or Hispanic applicants.

Employment Testing Is Illegal When Ethnic and Minority Groups Score More Poorly on Average Than Whites

Some critics of employment testing assert that under U.S. federal law, it is illegal to use employment tests when ethnic–racial groups score lower than Whites, on average. This criticism is not factual. The *Uniform Guidelines on Employee Selection Procedures* (EEOC et al., 1978) are the executive agency guidelines that are given deference by U.S. courts. The *Uniform Guidelines* do not address ethnic–racial mean score differences but do address adverse impact. *Adverse impact* as defined by the EEOC is a "selection rate for any race, sex, or ethnic group which is less than four-fifths (or eighty percent) of the rate for the group with the highest rate" (EEOC et al., 1978, p. 60-3.4 D). If an organization's screening instruments show adverse impact and someone challenges the employment test, the employer must demonstrate its job relatedness.

Unfortunately, the *Uniform Guidelines* are more than 30 years old and inconsistent with current scientific findings and professional guidelines (McDaniel, 2007). Specifically, they are biased in favor of local validation studies, differential validity and differential prediction studies, and a preference for costly and detailed job analysis data. As such, the procedures advocated by the *Uniform Guidelines* are often inappropriate and needlessly cumbersome. Thus, critics who argue that employment testing is illegal when mean ethnic–racial differences exist are incorrect. However, federal guidelines place an expensive burden on employers when adverse impact is present.

McDaniel (2007) raised the question, "Why have the *Uniform Guidelines* not been revised to be consistent with professional standards?" (p. 168). He speculated that the

> primary use of the *Uniform Guidelines* is to pressure employers into using suboptimal selection methods in order to hire minorities and Whites at approximately the same rates. If employers do not hire minorities at about the same rates as Whites, the *Uniform Guidelines* are invoked by enforce-

ment agencies and plaintiffs to require the employer to prepare substantial validity documentation. (pp. 168–169)

It is unfortunate that the *Uniform Guidelines*, which are inconsistent with professional principles (American Educational Research Association, American Psychological Association, & National Council on Measurement in Education, 1999; Society of Industrial and Organizational Psychology, 2003) and scientific findings, are used to promote race-conscious hiring in violation of the U.S. Civil Rights Act of 1991, the very legislation that they are intended to enforce.

Employment Tests Are Unfair Because They Have Not Been Validated for Every Type of Job and Across Every Type of Context

This criticism is based on the belief that each job in a field is unique in terms of duties, environment, and personnel needed. Therefore, any attempt to generalize the validity findings of an employment test from one job to another or one location to another is flawed. This argument is known as the *situational specificity hypothesis* (Schmidt & Hunter, 1977, 1998). This hypothesis was developed in response to the frequent observation that an employment test used in one setting did not yield the same or nearly the same validity coefficient when used in another similar setting for the same or similar job. This caused some to speculate that there were yet-to-be-discovered characteristics of situations or jobs that caused the differing validity coefficients. It was the prevalence of the situational judgment theory in the mid-1970s that influenced the authors of the *Uniform Guidelines* to emphasize the need for detailed job analysis information and local validation studies. The seminal work of Schmidt and Hunter in the 1970s and 1980s showed that the situational specificity hypothesis was incorrect (Pearlman, Schmidt, & Hunter, 1980; Schmidt, Gast-Rosenberg, & Hunter, 1980; Schmidt & Hunter, 1977; Schmidt, Hunter, & Pearlman, 1981). Specifically, they found that the validities varied from study to study primarily because of simple random sampling error. Thus there is no scientific basis to support the position that employment tests need to be validated for each situation in which they are used. There is, however, a pragmatic reason for employers to continue to validate employment tests. This reason is legal defensibility under EEOC guidelines. As discussed in this chapter, job-specific test validation is the federal government's preferred (although misguided) method of demonstrating test validity, and many employers would rather waste thousands of dollars on test validation than millions of dollars in litigation. Employers must weigh heavily the need for local validation and ensure that their decision is based on several contingencies that go beyond the thinking that "this test worked for someone else; therefore, it should work for me."

Employment Tests Are Invasions of Privacy

The content of some employment tests causes critics to argue that the tests are an invasion of privacy. Typically this criticism is directed toward clinically oriented personality tests designed to identify severe psychological disorders. Such clinically oriented personality tests are often used for police applicant screening and may contain questions that applicants may find intrusive (e.g., questions concerning one's private bodily functions). Other types of tests, known as *biodata* tests, ask questions about one's background and interests in areas that are not viewed as relevant to the job (e.g., recreational interests, experiences in high school). Criticisms related to invasions of privacy are primarily limited to items that have little explicit relation to the job. Employers should evaluate whether the information obtained through clinically oriented personality tests and biodata tests is sufficiently valuable as a predictor to justify their inclusion in an employment test.

CRITICISMS CONCERNING THE ACCURACY OF EMPLOYMENT TESTS

Employment Tests Result in Some Bad Hiring Decisions

Some critics argue that using employment tests sometimes results in bad hiring decisions. For example, an applicant who scored well on an employment test was an unproductive employee. Alternatively, a person who would have been an excellent employee was not hired because of a low test score. This criticism has some merit. Predictions from employment test scores are not perfect. Figure 5.1 shows an illustrative scattergram for a sample of data in which an employment test score correlates .50 with a measure of job performance. In the upper left section of the graph, an arrow identifies a person who scored relatively low (about 3) on the employment test but scored relatively high (about 7) on the job performance measure. Had the employer not hired anyone with scores as low 3, this productive employee would not have been hired. The arrow in the right section shows another employee who scored very high (almost 9) on the employment test but performed poorly on the job (about 3.5). Thus, even though an employer uses an employment test, some hires prove to be less than productive employees.

Employers can take several actions to minimize hiring errors. Abandoning the employment test and hiring people randomly will result in substantially greater hiring errors. Replacing one employment test with another is a useful solution if the new employment test has better validity (fewer hiring errors) than the original test. Another solution is to supplement the original test with additional information to reduce selection errors. For example, one could supplement a cognitive ability test with an interview in hopes of reducing hiring errors. These decisions are best made by evaluating

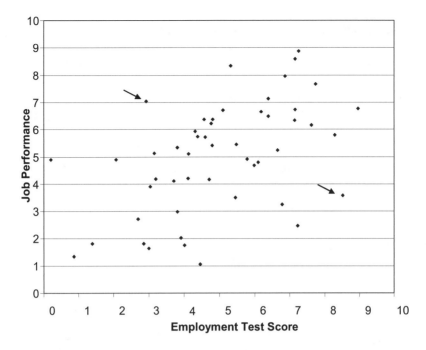

Figure 5.1. A scattergram of the relationship between an employment test and job performance (simulated data). In the upper left section, an arrow identifies a person who scored relatively low (about 3) on the employment test but scored relatively high (about 7) on the job performance measure. The arrow in the right section shows another employee who scored very high (almost 9) on the employment test but performed poorly on the job (about 3.5).

cumulative evidence concerning the effectiveness of various tests. Schmidt and Hunter (1998) summarized 80 years of employment test validity information to identify which employment tests work best and which should not be used. These cumulative research results should guide employers regarding which tests to use.

Some employers evaluate the validity of a test by trying it out on a few incumbents, for example, five employees. If the test scores match their perception of the employees, the test is judged a good measure, otherwise the test is judged a bad measure. Although intuitively appealing, this approach yields near random results. The five employees are a small sample of a population of employees, and small sample estimates of correlations have large amounts of sampling error.

By way of example, consider an employment test that correlates about .20 with a measure of job performance. If you collect data on 5 individuals, the correlation that you estimate based on the five individuals can range from −.61 to .80.[2] Even evaluating the test with 50 incumbents, the correla-

---

[2]The range of values in this example are the 80% confidence interval (10th percentile to 90th percentile) for a population correlation for the varying sample sizes listed in the example.

tion could range from .02 to .37. Only with large numbers of incumbents—say, 500—will the correlation likely be sufficiently free from sampling error that one can be confident of the precision of the validity coefficient (for sample size of 500, the correlations could range from .14 to .25). Therefore, relying on a limited sample of incumbent data does not tell one much about the validity of the test. To evaluate the validity of a test, one would be best served by relying on cumulative research evidence for the test.

Employment Tests Do Not Tell One Anything That Would Not Be Learned by Talking With the Applicant

We have often heard hiring managers argue that employment tests do not provide any information additional to what one would get by talking with applicants or by examining their resumes or educational transcripts. This belief is not specific to employment testing and is often referred to as the *actuarial versus clinical debate*. The belief that "gut feelings" or past experiences are more accurate predictors than diagnostic tests is not a new argument. This debate was most vehemently argued in the field of clinical psychology, and it took nearly a century and dozens of empirical studies (for a review, see Marchese, 1992) to overcome the belief that a "good" clinician does not need tests to make a diagnosis (Dawes, Faust, & Meehl, 1989).

Talking with applicants (e.g., an interview) is a method of screening applicants. These types of employment screenings are known in the literature as *unstructured employment interviews*—"unstructured" in the sense that the manager is not bound to a specific set of questions. To evaluate the suggestion that the unstructured interview outperforms other employment screening tools and methods, one needs to compare the validities of the various employment tests. The argument is now a proposition that can be empirically evaluated. Schmidt and Hunter (1998) tested this argument by means of a meta-analysis using more than 85 years of employment data. They examined how much incremental validity (added predictive capability) a variety of employment tests have after taking into account an intelligence measure. The incremental validity for unstructured employment interviews was .04—one of the lowest incremental predictors and only marginally better than a handwriting analysis (Schmidt & Hunter, 1998).

Those who offer this criticism likely lack evidence to support the assertion that their employment test is better than the employment test they criticize. In part, this criticism reflects a tendency among many to discount scientific findings when the findings are counter to their own beliefs.

Employment Tests Can Be Useful, but Many Assess the Wrong Content

Some critics argue that employment tests often do not measure the most useful content for employment decisions. This criticism contains two arguments. The first is that employment tests do not measure content that is relevant for predicting job performance. The second is that there is other content that could be assessed in employment tests, but it is generally not assessed. These two arguments are addressed in turn.

The argument that employment tests do not measure job-relevant content is related to the face validity of the test. An employment test that is face valid contains content that is clearly relevant to the job and might even have an applicant perform a sample job activity. For example, a test of typing or word processing has clear face validity for jobs that demand fast and accurate typing. Other tests, such as measures of general cognitive ability, may have substantially less face validity. The value of an employment test is best evaluated on the cumulative evidence of its ability to predict job performance, and tests of general cognitive ability have been proved to be good predictors of job performance (Schmidt & Hunter, 1998). Thus, employment tests do not need to be face valid to be useful for evaluating job applicants. However, face-valid tests are more acceptable to applicants than tests that have no apparent relevance to the job.

The second argument holds that there is other content that could be assessed in employment tests but generally is not. The search for different content in employment testing is an active area of research in personnel selection (Frei & McDaniel, 1998; Hunter & Hunter, 1984; McDaniel, Morgeson, Finnegan, Campion, & Braverman, 2001; Reilly, 1996, Rynes & Connerley, 1993; Taylor, Keelty, & McDonnell, 2002; Verive & McDaniel, 1996). Much of the research on employment tests focuses on efforts to reduce mean racial differences in test scores (Outtz, 2002; Potosky, Bobko, & Roth, 2005; Reilly, 1996; Sackett et al., 2001). Recently, Sackett et al. (2001) reviewed some alternative employment tests and found that the tests provided no easy method for improving validity. Likewise, Potosky et al. (2005) found little evidence to support the contention that alternative selection methods automatically result in increased predictive accuracy coupled with smaller race differences.

Some researchers have postulated new constructs to be assessed in employment tests. These concepts include practical intelligence (Sternberg et al., 2000), successful intelligence (Sternberg et al., 2000), and emotional intelligence (Bar-On, 2000, 2002; Goleman, 1995; Mayer, Salovey, & Caruso, 2000). Although research on new constructs is encouraged, the value of such constructs needs to be evaluated. For example, assertions about the structure and correlates of practical intelligence as espoused by Sternberg et al. (2000) are not supported on the basis of reviews of research (Gottfredson, 2002; McDaniel & Whetzel, 2005). Likewise, a mixed-model measure of emotional intelligence has been demonstrated to be primarily an assessment of longstanding personality constructs (the Big Five: Agreeableness, Conscientiousness, Extraversion, Emotional Stability, and Openness) and is not recommended for use as an employment test because of the ease with which respondents can raise their score by faking (Grubb & McDaniel, 2007). Ability-based emotional intelligence models have been offered as a better alternative to the more personality-loaded mixed-model emotional intelligence tests. However, even with an ability-based emotional judgment test, Schulte, Ree, and Carretta (2004) concluded that the test was primarily saturated with cognitive ability and personality constructs. The substantial overlap of newly offered constructs with existing traditional constructs limits their ability to improve substantially the predictive accuracy of employment tests. Although research into new constructs is an important research goal for employment testing, research to date on alternative predictors is not encouraging.

Employment Tests Can Be Easily Faked

Some critics of employment tests argue that employment tests can be easily faked. This criticism is primarily directed at tests of personality, mixed-model emotional intelligence, or integrity. It is also sometimes directed at employment interviews. The criticism is based on the idea that the answers judged desirable by the organization are apparent to the applicant. Consider these items illustrative of those on personality tests purporting to measure conscientiousness:

- I am always prepared.
- I pay close attention to details of assignments.
- I seldom make errors at work.
- I complete my work successfully.

It would be clear to most applicants that the employer is seeking to hire someone who is dependable, and it would not be difficult for undependable applicants to assert that they are dependable.

The research literature supports the contention that such self-report measures are easily faked such that less suitable applicants can appear suitable. Viswesvaran and Ones (1999) conducted a meta-analysis to evaluate the extent to which one could improve one's scores on measures of the Big Five personality factors. They found that individuals could raise their scores on average by about 0.5 standard deviation. If an applicant has an average level (50th percentile) of conscientiousness, the applicant can respond so as to score at the 70th percentile. Thus applicants who choose to misrepresent themselves can respond so that they appear more suitable than those who truly are (Douglas, McDaniel, & Snell, 1996). Efforts to reduce faking on these measures is a topic of substantial research (Griffith, 2006). To date, however, no highly effective strategies to identify fakers or prevent faking on self-report measures have been developed.

Employers should recognize the limitations of such measures. When respondents are instructed to fake, the validity of employment tests sharply decline (Douglas et al., 1996). Nonetheless, personality tests have nonzero validities in applicant samples in which one would expect at least some of the respondents to be faking (Hough, 1998). Some employers use these instruments as pass–fail screens with low cutoffs to screen out those applicants who are both ill suited for the position and willing to admit it. These employers then use other employment tests to differentiate among those who passed the highly "fakable" test. Other employers shun personality tests and instead rely on nonfakable measures such as cognitive ability, job knowledge, or situational judgment with instructions to identify the best response (McDaniel, Hartman, Whetzel, & Grubb, 2007). These are maximal performance measures (Cronbach, 1984) in that applicants know they should answer to the best of their ability. In such situations, faking is not possible because the instructions are to provide the best answers and not descriptions of typical performance (Nguyen, Biderman, & McDaniel, 2005).

CRITICISMS CONCERNING ADMINISTRATIVE EFFICIENCY

Employment Tests Are Not Needed Because One Can Train Anyone to Do Any Job

The authors have sometimes heard from practitioners that testing is not needed because one can train anyone to do any job. Ultimately, this is an argument that all people are roughly equal in most regards in terms of traits and abilities. Although this is a socially desirable position to take, it is not grounded in reality. This criticism ignores a large literature indicating that cognitive ability is a strong predictor of training performance (Brown, Le, & Schmidt, 2006; Nijenhuis & van der Flier, 2000; Pearlman et al., 1980). Cognitive ability places limits on the amount and complexity of material that one can learn. The U.S. military established minimum cutoff scores for cognitive skills of individuals whom it is willing to accept because its research showed that individuals below these scores could not readily be trained.

This criticism of testing may sometimes reflect the idea that certain jobs are so simplistic or remedial, and such large swaths of the population could be trained to do them with ease, that employment testing is unnecessary. A counterpoint to this criticism would be that in any job in which differences in performance are possible, it is in the interest of the employer to select the applicant who can achieve peak performance in the shortest period of time. More goes into making a good worker than the ability to perform specific job duties. Even in the case of the most simplistic work, the employer would still likely desire employees to possess certain personality traits such as conscientiousness (showing up to work on time), agreeableness (getting along with managers and coworkers), and integrity (not engaging in counterproductive work behaviors). Employers would be better served by having at least some idea of where an applicant ranks on these traits regardless of how fast he or she can be trained to perform the job.

Employment Testing Takes Too Long

Some criticisms of employment testing do not concern the testing itself but the time it takes to develop and administer employment tests. Employment testing does take some time. Often job applicants apply for jobs in many organizations at the same time, and any delays associated with screening applicants may result in the best applicants being hired by the employer with the fastest screening procedure. Time needed to screen applicants increases when customized employment tests are developed. Likewise, at least for U.S. employers, the *Uniform Guidelines* encourages the use of time-consuming content validation procedures that typically entail the collection of detailed job analysis information. To minimize their legal liability in the face of adverse impact, many employers will not administer an employment test until a content validity study has been completed. Employment screening of public-sector employers is often particularly slow because of civil service regulations and other bureaucratic obstacles (Thompson, 2006).

Some of the time lag that critics attribute to employment testing is actually the result of other requirements of the larger recruitment and hiring effort. Vacant positions often need to be advertised. Applicants need time to apply. They also need time to consider offers and give notice to their current employers. The time associated with these activities would be spent regardless of whether employment testing was used.

Some technology has been applied to reduce employment testing time. Online applications have become common (Blyth, 2004), and employers are increasingly incorporating online employment testing into their application process.

Employment Testing Costs Too Much

Some employers shun employment testing because of its costs. The professional development of an employment test does require resources. However, many commercially available tests are inexpensive (less than $10 per administration). When compared with other costs associated with the hiring process (e.g., vacancy advertising, recruitment expenses), employment test costs are relatively insignificant.

More important, this criticism ignores the substantial productivity gains associated with employment testing. Good employees are much more productive than poor employees. Excellent employees are much more productive than good employees. Employment testing results in increased work output and improved learning of job skills (Hunter, Schmidt, & Judiesch, 1990). The dollar value of the increased productivity associated with using employment tests is substantial (Schmidt & Hunter, 1998) and makes the cost of testing trivial in comparison.

SUMMARY AND CONCLUSION

This chapter has reviewed 11 criticisms of employment testing. The criticisms fall into three categories: fairness, accuracy, and administrative efficiency. Two fairness criticisms arise from concerns about ethnic–racial differences in employment test results and the subsequent disparities in hiring rates. One concern over fairness arises from a belief in the discredited situational specificity hypothesis. A final fairness concern involves perceptions of invasion of privacy. Criticisms concerning the accuracy of employment testing center on the inability of employment tests to yield perfect predictions. Two of these criticisms concern some measures or test content being better than other content. A final criticism concerns the ease with which some employment tests, particularly personality and integrity tests, can be faked. Three criticisms are associated with the administrative efficiency of employment tests. One criticism falsely asserts that anyone can be trained for any job. Another concerns the time it takes to conduct employment testing, and the final administrative efficiency criticism concerns the cost of testing.

Human resources personnel must be aware of the importance testing plays in selection and the common pitfalls to avoid when improper selection procedures are used. Employers must invest some time and effort into deciding what characteristics they seek and should select measures that will help them best identify the applicants possessing those traits. There is no perfect measure, and employers should be wary of anyone (academic, consultant, or test publisher) purporting to possess one. In all likelihood, whichever testing method an employer uses will result in the rejection of qualified applicants on occasion and the acceptance of unqualified applicants on other occasions, but employers must not lose sight of the fact that formalized testing with valid measures will provide the best odds for avoiding these costly mistakes.

REFERENCES

American Educational Research Association, American Psychological Association, & National Council on Measurement in Education. (1999). *Standards for educational and psychological testing*. Washington, DC: American Educational Research Association.

Bar-On, R. (2000). Emotional and social intelligence: Insights from the Emotional Quotient Inventory. In J. D. A. Parker (Ed.), *The handbook of emotional intelligence* (pp. 363–390). San Francisco: Jossey-Bass.

Bar-On, R. (2002). *Bar-On Emotional Quotient Inventory: Short technical manual.* Toronto, Ontario, Canada: Multi-Health Systems.

Bartlett, C. J., Bobko, P., Mosier, S. B., & Hannan, R. (1978). Testing for fairness with a moderated multiple regression strategy: An alternative to differential analysis. *Personnel Psychology, 31,* 233–241.

Blyth, A. (2004, November 16). Winning recruitment race. *Personnel Today,* p. 26.

Boehm, V. R. (1972). Differential prediction: A methodological artifact? *Journal of Applied Psychology, 62,* 146–154.

Bray, D. W., & Moses, J. L. (1972). Personnel selection. *Annual Review of Psychology, 23,* 545–576.

Brown, K. G., Le, H., & Schmidt, F. L. (2006). Specific aptitude theory revisited: Is there incremental validity for training performance? *International Journal of Selection and Assessment, 14,* 87–100.

Cronbach, L. J. (1984). *Essentials of psychological testing* (4th ed.). New York: Harper & Row.

Dawes, R. M., Faust, D., & Meehl, P. E. (1989, March 31). Clinical versus actuarial judgment. *Science, 243,* 1668–1674.

Dickens, W. T., & Flynn, J. R. (2006). Black Americans reduce the racial IQ gap: Evidence from standardization samples. *Psychological Science, 17,* 913–920.

Douglas, E. F., McDaniel, M. A., & Snell, E. F. (1996, August). *The validity of non-cognitive measures decays when applicants fake.* Paper presented at the Proceedings of the Academy of Management, Cincinnati, OH.

Equal Employment Opportunity Commission, Civil Service Commission, Department of Labor, & Department of Justice. (1978). *Uniform guidelines on employee selection procedures. Federal Register, 43*(166), 38290–39315.

Frei, R., & McDaniel, M. A. (1998). The validity of customer service orientation measures in employee selection: A comprehensive review and meta-analysis. *Human Performance, 11,* 1–27.

Goleman, D. (1995). *Emotional intelligence.* New York: Bantam.

Gottfredson, L. S. (2003). Dissecting practical intelligence theory: Its claims and evidence. *Intelligence, 31,* 343–397.

Griffith, R. L. (2006). *A closer examination of applicant faking behavior.* Greenwich, CT: Information Age.

Grubb, W. L., III, & McDaniel, M. A. (2007). The fakability of Bar-On's Emotional Quotient Inventory Short Form: Catch me if you can. *Human Performance, 20,* 43–59.

Hartigan, J. A., & Wigdor, A. K. (Eds.). (1989). *Fairness in employment testing: Validity generalization, minority issues, and the General Aptitude Test Battery.* Washington, DC: National Academy Press.

Hough, L. M. (1998). Effects of intentional distortion in personality measurement and evaluation of suggested palliatives. *Human Performance, 11,* 209–244.

Hunter, J. E., & Hunter, R. F. (1984). Validity and utility of alternative predictors of job performance. *Psychological Bulletin, 96,* 72–98.

Hunter, J. E., Schmidt, F. L., & Judiesch, M. K. (1990). Individual differences in output variability as a function of job complexity. *Journal of Applied Psychology, 75,* 28–42.

Kirkpatrick, J. J., Ewen, R. B., Barrett, R. S., & Katzell, R. A. (1968). *Testing and fair employment.* New York: New York University Press.

Marchese, M. C. (1992). Clinical versus actuarial prediction: A review of the literature. *Perceptual and Motor Skills, 75,* 583–594.

Mayer, J. D., Salovey, P., & Caruso, D. (2000). Models of emotional intelligence. In R. J. Sternberg (Ed.), *Handbook of intelligence* (pp. 396–420). New York: Cambridge University Press.

McDaniel, M. A. (2007). Validity generalization as a test validation approach. In S. M. McPhail (Ed.), *Alternative validation strategies* (pp. 159–180). San Francisco: Jossey Bass.

McDaniel, M. A., Hartman, N. S., Whetzel, D. L., & Grubb, W. L., III. (2007). Situational judgment tests, response instructions and validity: A meta-analysis. *Personnel Psychology, 60,* 63–91.

McDaniel, M. A., Morgeson, F. P., Finnegan, E. B., Campion, M. A., & Braverman, E. P. (2001). Use of situational judgment tests to predict job performance: A clarification of the literature. *Journal of Applied Psychology, 86,* 730–740.

McDaniel, M. A., & Whetzel, D. L. (2005). Situational judgment test research: Informing the debate on practical intelligence theory. *Intelligence, 33,* 515–525.

Murray, C. (2005, September). The inequality taboo. *Commentary, 120,* 13–22.

Nguyen, N. T., Biderman, M. D., & McDaniel, M. A. (2005). Effects of response instruction on faking a situational judgment test. *International Journal of Selection and Assessment, 13,* 250–260.

Nijenhuis, J. T., & van der Flier, H. (2000). Differential prediction of immigrant versus majority group training performance using cognitive ability and personality measures. *International Journal of Selection and Assessment, 8,* 54–60.

Outtz, J. L. (2002). The role of cognitive ability tests in employment selection. *Human Performance, 15,* 161–172.

Pearlman, K., Schmidt, F. L., & Hunter, J. E. (1980). Validity generalization results for tests used to predict job proficiency and training success in clerical occupations. *Journal of Applied Psychology, 65,* 373–406.

Potosky, D., Bobko, P., & Roth, P. L. (2005). Forming composites of cognitive ability and alternative measures to predict job performance and reduce adverse impact: Corrected estimates and realistic expectations. *International Journal of Selection and Assessment, 13,* 304–315.

Reilly, R. R. (1996). Alternative selection procedures. In R. S. Barrett (Ed.), *Fair employment strategies in human resource management* (pp. 208–221). Westport, CT: Quorum Books/Greenwood.

Roth, P. L., BeVier, C. A., Bobko, P., Switzer, F. S., III, & Tyler, P. (2001). Ethnic group differences in cognitive ability in employment and educational settings: A meta-analysis. *Personnel Psychology, 54,* 297–330.

Rushton, J. P., & Jensen, A. R. (2006). The totality of available evidence shows the race IQ gap still remains. *Psychological Science, 17,* 921–922.

Rynes, S. L., & Connerley, M. L. (1993). Applicant reactions to alternative selection procedures. *Journal of Business and Psychology, 7,* 261–277.

Sackett, P. R., Schmitt, N., Ellingson, J., & Kabin, M. B. (2001). High stakes testing in employment, credentialing, and higher education: Prospects in a post-affirmative-action world. *American Psychologist, 56,* 302–318.

Schmidt, F. L. (1988). The problem of group differences in ability test scores in employment selection. *Journal of Vocational Behavior, 33,* 272–292.

Schmidt, F. L., Gast-Rosenberg, I. F., & Hunter, J. E. (1980). Validity generalization results for computer programmers. *Journal of Applied Psychology, 65,* 643–661.

Schmidt, F. L., & Hunter, J. E. (1977). Development of a general solution to the problem of validity generalization. *Journal of Applied Psychology, 62,* 529–540.

Schmidt, F. L., & Hunter, J. E. (1981). Employment testing: Old theories and new research. *American Psychologist, 36,* 1128–1137.

Schmidt, F. L., & Hunter, J. E. (1998). The validity and utility of selection methods in personnel psychology: Practical and theoretical implications of 85 years of research findings. *Psychological Bulletin, 124,* 262–274.

Schmidt, F. L., Hunter, J. E., & Pearlman, K. (1981). Task differences as moderators of aptitude test validity in selection: A red herring. *Journal of Applied Psychology, 66,* 166–185.

Schmidt, F. L., Pearlman, K., & Hunter, J. E. (1980). The validity and fairness of employment and educational tests for Hispanic Americans: A review and analysis. *Personnel Psychology, 33,* 705–724.

Schulte, M., Ree, M. J., & Carretta, T. R. (2004). Emotional intelligence: Not much more than g and personality. *Personality and Individual Differences, 37,* 1059–1068.

Society of Industrial and Organizational Psychology. (2003). *Principles for the validation and use of personnel selection procedures* (4th ed.). Bowling Green, OH: Author.

Sternberg, R. J., Forsythe, G. B., Hedlund, J., Horvath, J. A., Wagner, R. K., Williams, W. M., et al. (2000). *Practical intelligence in everyday life.* New York: Cambridge University Press.

Taylor, P., Keelty, Y., & McDonnell, B. (2002) Evolving personnel selection practices in New Zealand organisations and recruitment firms. *New Zealand Journal of Psychology, 31,* 8–18.

Thompson, J. R. (2006). The Federal Civil Service: The demise of an institution. *Public Administration Review, 66,* 496–503.

U.S. Civil Rights Act of 1991, Pub. L. No. 102-166, 105 Stat. 1071 (codified in various sections of 42 U.S.C.) (Suppl. III 1992).

Verive, J. M., & McDaniel, M. A. (1996). Short-term memory tests in personnel selection: Low adverse impact and high validity. *Intelligence, 23*, 15–32.

Viswesvaran, C., & Ones, D. S. (1999). Meta-analyses of fakability estimates: Implications for personality measurement. *Educational and Psychological Measurement, 59*, 197–210.

Wigdor, A. K., & Garner, W. R. (Eds.). (1982). *Ability testing: Use, consequences, and controversies*. Washington, DC: National Academy Press.

6

MISSION—PROTECT THE PUBLIC: LICENSURE AND CERTIFICATION TESTING IN THE 21ST CENTURY

STEPHEN G. SIRECI AND RONALD K. HAMBLETON

Licensure tests play a critical role in ensuring competence in numerous professional fields throughout the world. In the United States, examples of licensure tests include tests used to credential medical professionals (e.g., doctors, nurses, physical therapists, speech pathologists), lawyers, psychologists, accountants, architects, and stockbrokers, to name only a few. These tests are used by national or state regulatory boards to award licenses to professionals who serve the public. Thus, licensure tests serve a noble purpose—ensuring competence in professional practice, particularly in fields in which incompetence would have a direct impact on the well-being (physical, emotional, or financial) of the consumer.

Although licensure tests are designed to fulfill this need, they are sometimes criticized as preventing access to a profession. Like most tests, licensure tests are easy targets for criticism because it is extremely difficult to measure the intangible knowledge, skills, and abilities that exist within people but are difficult to see or measure directly. Licensure testing involves measurement of professional competence and the use of test scores to distinguish between candidates who are ready for professional practice and those who are not. These decisions are extremely important but are difficult to make. Licensure tests must balance the goals of providing access to the profession and protecting the public. The last goal—protection of the public—is a serious one. For example, who would like to be operated on by a doctor who has not demonstrated sufficient skill in surgery? Or who would like to be defended by a lawyer who has not demonstrated sufficient knowledge of case law and legal proceedings? The answer is no one, and licensure tests help prevent such frightening scenarios.

In this chapter, we describe current practices in licensure and certification testing to demonstrate how they fulfill their purposes. We also highlight changes that have recently occurred or will soon occur in this field because of increased public scrutiny and emerging technologies in computer-based testing. It would be a mistake or fallacy to think that these tests are only capable of assessing low-level factual knowledge, that they do not measure the key skills and knowledge in a profession, or that they cannot be of high technical quality. We demonstrate that all three of these fallacies and others are incorrect.

We include certification testing in this chapter because the issues are similar to those in licensure testing.[1] The difference between certification and licensure testing is that certification tests do not prohibit practice within a profession. Rather, they are used to certify excellence in a profession. For example, medical doctors are licensed for general practice, but they can also be certified by a credentialing board for work in a particular discipline (e.g., internal medicine, fertility). Similarly, elementary, middle, and high school teachers may or may not be licensed to teach in a particular state, but teachers can be certified as "Master Teachers" by the National Board of Professional Teaching Standards. One of the largest areas of certification is in the information technology profession. For example, there is no licensure program for troubleshooting software or hardware problems or for configuring a network, but Microsoft, Cisco, Hewlett-Packard, Novell, and other information technology companies have several certification programs and administer millions of certification tests worldwide. Employers appreciate such certification and look for it when they hire employees and consultants.

The *Standards for Educational and Psychological Testing* (American Educational Research Association, American Psychological Association, & National Council on Measurement in Education [AERA, APA, & NCME], 1999) provides authoritative guidelines for best practices in testing and in evaluating the utility and appropriateness of a test for particular purposes. The *Standards* describes the importance of credentialing tests in the following way:

---

[1]The term *credentialing tests* is often used as a general way to describe both licensure and certification tests.

Tests used in credentialing are intended to provide the public, including employers and government agencies, with a dependable mechanism for identifying practitioners who have met particular standards. The standards are strict, but not so stringent as to unduly restrain the right of qualified individuals to offer their services to the public. (p. 156)

We have stressed the importance of licensure and certification testing. To meet the important goal of ensuring sufficient competence for entry-level practice within a profession, great care is usually taken to develop and validate these tests. In this chapter, we describe contemporary practices in licensure and certification testing. An understanding of these practices exposes common criticisms of these tests as fallacies. Examples of fallacies associated with licensure and certification tests include the following: (a) these tests do not measure important skills for success in a profession, (b) these tests are predominantly "multiple-guess" and basically measure test-taking skills, (c) the passing scores on these tests are designed to limit access to the profession, and (d) these tests are used mainly in the United States and not in other countries.

In the sections that follow, we explain how such tests are developed to fulfill their purposes of providing access to a profession and protecting the public, and we illustrate why the aforementioned fallacies are inaccurate statements. Before doing so, however, we acknowledge the extreme changes that have occurred in licensure and certification testing over the past 2 decades. These changes are exciting and stem from the explosion of activity in testing as a result of increased scrutiny of tests in general, advances in testing methodology, and the opportunities provided by computer technology. An overview of some of these important changes is presented in Table 6.1. We elaborate on some of these developments in separate sections of this chapter. They are presented here at the beginning to give an appreciation of the complexity and comprehensiveness of contemporary practices in licensure and certification testing.

PROFESSIONAL STANDARDS FOR DEVELOPING AND EVALUATING LICENSURE TESTS

There are several steps in developing quality licensure and certification tests. The major steps include (a) defining the test purpose, (b) defining practice within the profession, (c) identifying the knowledge and skills to be assessed, (d) developing test specifications, (e) developing test items and scoring rubrics, (f) gathering data on these items (pilot testing), (g) statistical review of item performance, (h) qualitative (i.e., content, technical, and sensitivity) review of items, (i) assembling test forms or item banks, (j) administering the tests, (k) monitoring the functioning of the items and the

TABLE 6.1
A Comparison of 20th-Century and Contemporary Practices in Credentialing Tests

Feature	Typical 20th-century practice	Practice today
Item formats	Multiple-choice, essays	Multiple choice, multiple-selection, essays, drag and drop, highlighting text, simulations, specifying relationships, sequential problem solving, portfolios
Administration	Paper and pencil	Paper and pencil, computer
Design	Linear (everyone receives the same test or a strict parallel form)	Linear, linear on the fly, item-level adaptive, multistage adaptive
Standard setting	Norm referenced, criterion referenced	Criterion referenced
Measurement theory	Classical test theory	Both classical test theory and item response theory
Test security	Secure test booklets	Secure test booklets, secure item banks, monitoring of item exposure, video cameras, photo identification, and much more
Scoring	Scanners, human scoring	Scanners, human scoring, automated computer scoring
Score reporting	Pass–fail	Pass–fail, diagnostic
Population	National	National, international
Language	Single	Single, multiple

test itself, and (l) gathering validity evidence to evaluate the degree to which the test fulfills its intended purposes. In this section of the chapter, we describe three of the most crucial steps for understanding and evaluating contemporary licensure and certification tests: defining the purpose, conducting practice analyses, and preparing test specifications.

Defining the Purpose of a Licensure or Certification Test

The first step in the development of any test is an articulation of the testing purpose. The general purposes of licensure and certification tests were described earlier, but a few specific examples are provided here. The first comes from the American Institute of Certified Public Accountants, which develops and administers the Uniform CPA Examination. All public accountants in the United States must pass this test to be licensed for public practice. The purpose statement for the Uniform CPA Exam is as follows: "To admit individuals into the accounting profession only after they have demonstrated the entry-level knowledge and skills necessary to protect the public interest in a rapidly changing business and financial environment" (American Institute of Certified Public Accountants, 2005, ¶ 4). As can be seen from this definition, the states in which candidates seek licensure are the official licensing authorities, but all states and jurisdictions in the country require passing the Uniform CPA Exam as a requirement for licensure to practice in the state or jurisdiction.

The second purpose statement comes from the National Board of Medical Examiners. This board develops and administers several tests for the medical professions, the largest of which is the U.S. Medical Licensure Exam (USMLE), which is a series of three tests that must be passed to be a licensed medical doctor in the United States. The purpose statement for the USMLE begins with a statement explaining the licensing authority of the individual jurisdictions that use the test. It then describes the knowledge and skills measured on the test.

> In the United States and its territories the individual medical licensing authorities ("state medical boards") of the various jurisdictions grant a license to practice medicine. Each medical licensing authority sets its own rules and regulations and requires passing an examination that demonstrates qualification for licensure. Results of the USMLE are reported to these authorities for use in granting the initial license to practice medicine. The USMLE provides them with a common evaluation system for applicants for initial medical licensure. . . .
>
> The USMLE assesses a physician's ability to apply knowledge, concepts, and principles, and to demonstrate fundamental patient-centered skills that are important in health and disease and that constitute the basis of safe and effective patient care. Each of the three Steps of the USMLE complements the others; no Step can stand alone in the assessment of readiness for medical licensure. (USMLE, 1996–2008, ¶ 1, ¶ 3)

The purpose statements from these two professional licensing tests illustrate the great care that goes into clearly defining the testing purpose. A clear test purpose is essential for both guiding the test development process and providing a basis for evaluating any tests that are constructed. A clear statement of purpose also is an effective way to communicate with candidates and help them to prepare properly. But how do licensure testing agencies decide on the knowledge and skills to be tested? That is the next key step in developing a licensure test.

Practice Analysis and Test Specification Development

Practice analysis is a comprehensive study of what licensed or certified professionals do in performing their jobs. Practice analysis is more comprehensive than job analysis because licensed workers within a profession may have very different jobs. For example, some accountants focus on personal taxes, whereas others audit the financial statements of nonprofit corporations. The goal of a practice analysis is to identify the tasks performed by incumbents within a profession and the key knowledge, skills, and abilities needed for safe, effective, and competent practice. The results from a practice analysis are then used to identify the most important knowledge, skills, and abilities (KSAs) that will be measured on a test. As explained by Raymond (2005),

> A practice analysis . . . is the systematic study of a profession undertaken to identify and describe the job responsibilities of those employed in the profession. Once the professional responsibilities have been identified, it is possible to determine KSAs required to effectively carry out those responsibilities. These KSAs then serve as the basis for test specifications or test plans. (p. 29)

Raymond (2002) identified six models for practice analysis, the most common of which is the *task inventory*. The task inventory involves large-scale surveys of incumbent professionals to discover tasks that are performed on the job. Given that licensure tests focus on entry-level knowledge and skills, supervisors of entry-level professionals and those who were recently licensed are usually targeted as respondents to task inventory surveys. These surveys list tasks associated with professional practice and ask respondents to indicate the degree of importance or criticality of each task, as well as the frequency with which each task is typically performed.

The results of a task inventory practice analysis include lists of tasks and (a) their perceived criticality for safe and effective practice and (b) the frequency with which they are conducted on the job. Tasks that are viewed as highly critical, frequent, or both are likely to be well represented in the test specifications and on the test itself. Other practice analysis models, such as the professional practice model that is popular in the medical professions (LaDuca, 1994), have the same goal—identification of high-priority tasks encountered within different contexts of a profession. Regardless of the particular model used for describing job responsibilities within a profession, the data from practice analyses are used to derive test specifications that stipulate exactly what is covered on the test and the degree of coverage of different knowledge and skill areas associated with professional practice.

The test specifications for a licensure or certification test specify the knowledge and skill areas to be measured as well as the item formats to be used. The item formats found on contemporary licensure tests include multiple-choice items, written responses such as essays, and a variety of computerized innovative formats that we discuss in a subsequent section. Test specifications for licensure tests may take many forms. Some use two dimensions to represent the domain of practice measured by the test. One dimension is based on content area, and it is into this dimension that the tasks identified in the practice analysis as important for testing are placed. The other dimension is typically a skill dimension that describes the actions or cognitive skills that are used on the job. Other forms of test specifications include lists of KSAs stratified by content areas or contexts of professional practice.

Practice analysis and the test specifications derived from them provide important evidence that what is measured on a licensure or certification test is relevant to and representative of the job requirements for safe and effective practice. These test development steps are seen as providing important evidence for the validity of using these tests for licensure and certification decisions.

TEST DESIGNS AND ITEM FORMATS FOR LICENSURE AND CERTIFICATION TESTS

After test specifications are developed, the next step is the development of quality items to measure the specified KSAs in a manner that is relevant to real-world practice. Credentialing tests have traditionally used multiple-choice items because this item format can be objectively scored and can assess many KSAs in a short amount of testing time. Despite what some critics say, the multiple-choice item format remains a powerful way to assess many relevant skills on credentialing tests (see, e.g., Hambleton & Murphy, 1992). Also, the essay question has long been a popular format for credentialing tests.

Many changes are taking place regarding the choice of item formats because of the availability of the computer for test administration (Bartram & Hambleton, 2006), which can further enhance the validity and fidelity of credentialing tests. The computer has affected credentialing tests in two important ways. The first is the opportunity to use new innovative item formats to measure complex skills not amenable to tests using multiple-choice items but that can still be objectively scored (by the computer; see, e.g., Drasgow & Mattern, 2006). The second is in the area of test delivery. In addition to making testing programs more efficient from both item usage and measurement precision perspectives, computer technology has also made adaptive testing possible, which has significant advantages for credentialing tests (Wainer, 2000). Criticisms of credentialing tests because of the limited choice of item formats and linear and inflexible structure therefore have become even less valid. We elaborate on these developments in the following sections.

Innovative Item Formats

Several innovative item formats that use computer technology are currently in use on licensure and certification exams. These new formats range from the relatively simple multiple-response items that allow examinees to "check all that apply" to real-time, case-based vignettes that change as the examinee attempts to solve the problem. Zenisky and Sireci (2002; Sireci & Zenisky, 2006) reviewed the research and practice in innovative item formats and concluded that licensure and certification testing represented the most active use of these formats. In their review, they identified 20 innovative item formats that were in use or being researched at that time. An abbreviated summary of these item types is presented in Table 6.2. As can be seen in this table, the computer has made many new item formats available. However, Huff and Sireci (2001) cautioned that these item formats are most beneficial when they measure authentic skills that are not measurable using more traditional item formats.

One particular innovative item format used in licensure testing is the problem-solving vignette used on the USMLE. The vignette involves simulating a patient in a medical practice setting who needs treatment. Candidates work through the vignette from initial diagnosis to case management as the clock ticks down in real time. The consequences of medical decisions made by the examinee can be negative as well as positive, and they can be scored accordingly.

The National Council of Architectural Registration Boards also uses innovative problem-solving vignettes on the Architectural Registration Examination. On this exam, candidates are asked to complete several design tasks (such as designing a building or laying out a parking lot) using a variety of onscreen drawing tools (Bejar, 1991). Another example of problem-solving vignettes is the newly computerized version of the Uniform CPA Exam that presents realistic accounting scenarios to candidates and requires them to access onscreen resources to solve a problem (Breithaupt, Mills, & Melican, 2006; Devore, 2002). These item types illustrate the possibilities for more authentic assessment of professional practice in licensure and certification testing, and more agencies are starting to use these new item formats with considerable success.

Computer-Based Test Designs

One of the most exciting developments in contemporary licensure testing is *computerized adaptive testing* (CAT). CAT is a test administration system that uses the computer to select and deliver test items to examinees (Bartram & Hambleton, 2006; Wainer, 2000). These tests are called *adaptive* because the computer selects the items to be administered to a candidate based on the proficiency demonstrated on previously administered test items. Unlike many traditional tests in which all candidates take a single form of a test, the computer adapts or tailors the test to each candidate. This tailoring is done by keeping track of an examinee's performance on each test item and then using this information to select the next item to be administered. The criteria for selecting the next item to be administered can be complex and based on item response theory principles. However, the primary criterion is a desire to match the difficulty of the item to the examinee's current estimated proficiency. Currently, there are numerous examples of CAT programs in

TABLE 6.2

Brief Descriptions of Several Innovative Item Formats

Item format	Brief description
Drag and drop (select and place)	Given scenario or problem, examinees click and drag an object to the center of the appropriate answer field.
Graphical modeling	Examinees use line and curve tools to sketch a given situation on a grid.
Move figure or symbols in or into pictographs	Examinees manipulate elements of chart or graph to represent certain situations or adjust or complete image as necessary (e.g., extending bars in a bar chart).
Drag and connect, specifying relationships	Given presented objects, examinees identify the relationship(s) that exist between pairs of objects.
Sorting task	Given prototypes, examinees look for surface or deep structural similarities between presented items and prototypes and match items with prototype categories.
Ordering information (create a tree)	Examinees sequence events as required by the item stem (largest to smallest, most to least probable cause of event, if–then, etc.).
Inserting text	Examinees drag and drop text into passage as directed by the item stem (e.g., where it makes sense, serves as example of observation).
Passage editing	Examinees edit a short onscreen passage by moving the cursor to various points in a passage and selecting sentence rewrites from a list of alternatives on a drop-down menu.
Highlighting text	Examinees read a passage and select specific sentence(s) in the passage (main idea, particular piece of information, etc.).
Capturing or selecting frames and shading	Given directions or parameters, examinees use mouse to select portion of picture, map, or graph.
Mathematical expressions	Examinees generate and type in unique expression to represent mathematical relationship.
Numerical equations	Examinees complete numerical sentences by entering numbers and mathematical symbols in text box.
Multiple numerical response	Examinees type in more than one numerical answer (complete tax form, insert numbers into a spreadsheet, etc.).
Multiple selection	Examinees are presented with a stimulus (visual, audio, text) and select answer(s) from list (answers may be used more than once in series of questions).
Analyzing situations	Examinees are provided with visual and audio clips and short informational text and are asked to make diagnosis or decision; response can be free-text entry or extended matching.
Problem-solving vignettes	Problem-solving situations (vignettes) are presented to examinees, who are graded on features of a product.
Sequential problem solving and role-playing	Examinees provide a series of responses as dynamic situation unfolds; scoring attends to process and product.

Note. Adapted from "Technological Innovations in Large-Scale Assessment," by A. L. Zenisky & S. G. Sireci, 2002, *Applied Measurement in Education, 15*, pp. 340–341. Copyright 2002 by Taylor & Francis. Adapted with permission.

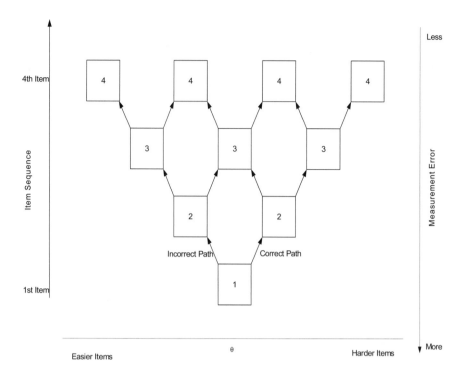

Figure 6.1. Example of computerized adaptive testing algorithm. The horizontal axis in this figure represents the item difficulty–examinee proficiency scale, which is typically denoted using the Greek letter theta (θ). The vertical axis represents the sequence of test items administered. As one moves from left to right, the items become more difficult. From *Measuring Up: Assessment Issues for Teachers, Counselors, and Administrators* (p. 687), by J. Wall & G. Walz (Eds.), Greensboro, NC: CAPS Press. Copyright 2004 by CAPS Press. Reprinted with permission.

the credentialing arena, including the licensure exams for nurses (e.g., National Council Licensure Examination) and the exam for Novell systems engineers.

A simplified example of how a traditional (item-level) CAT works is presented in Figure 6.1. As is evident from the figure, answering an item correctly results in the administration of a more difficult item, and answering an item incorrectly results in the administration of an easier item.

In addition to matching item difficulty to examinee proficiency and determining when a test ends, a CAT item selection algorithm may also control several other factors, including content representation and item exposure. *Content representation* refers to the ability of the algorithm to ensure that the content specifications of the test are adhered to for each examinee. For example, if the content specifications for a medical licensure exam require that 20% of the test measures tasks associated with emergency medicine, 35% measure tasks associated with outpatient care, 25% measure pediatrics, and 20% measure pharmacology, the algorithm can keep track of the content designations of each item to ensure these content specifications are met for all candidates. The algorithm can also keep track of how often an item is administered to make sure that item exposure levels do not get too high. If the same items were administered too often to examinees, knowledge of specific items may be relayed to future test takers, which would inflate their scores and reduce the overall level of test validity. Thus the item selection algorithm is critically important for ensuring testing efficiency, content validity, and item security (Sireci, 2004).

A variation of the CAT test design is computerized multistage adaptive testing. *Multistage testing* refers to the administration of several sets of items in an adaptive, sequential fashion. At the first stage, candidates are administered a routing test that determines the difficulty level of the test they will take at the second stage. Their performance on the second stage of the test determines the test they will take at the third stage, and so on. Multistage tests offer a compromise between the traditional, nonadaptive format and CAT. Content experts and sensitivity reviewers can review the sets of items (called *modules*) to evaluate content quality; candidates can skip, review, and change answers to questions within a module or stage, and their responses are used to tailor the remaining portions of the test to their specific proficiency level (see, e.g., Jodoin, Zenisky, & Hambleton, 2006).

SETTING PASSING SCORES ON LICENSURE AND CERTIFICATION TESTS

Regardless of the item formats or tests designs used, licensure and certification tests must fulfill their purpose of protecting the public from incompetent practitioners. To distinguish between candidates who are sufficiently competent for entry-level practice in a profession and those who are not yet competent, passing scores must be set on credentialing tests. Candidates who obtain a score above the passing score are deemed qualified to perform a professional function, and those who obtain a score below the cutoff point are deemed not qualified.

One fallacy associated with licensure and certification testing is that passing scores are set haphazardly or in a way that is designed to restrict access to the profession through the establishment of quotas. The truth is contrary to this fallacy. Research and practices on how to set passing scores on credentialing tests are some of the busiest activities in credentialing over the past few decades, and normative approaches to setting passing scores (i.e., choosing passing scores to fail specified percentages of candidates) have essentially disappeared from practice.

As described by the *Standards for Educational and Psychological Testing* (AERA, APA, & NCME, 1999), "Defining the minimum level of knowledge and skill required for licensure or certification is one of the most important and difficult tasks facing those responsible for credentialing" (p. 157). This importance is easily understood, given the goal of protection of the public. Thus, establishing a specified cut point on a score scale, at or above which candidates pass or are accepted, below which candidates fail or are rejected, is one of the most critical and controversial aspects of the credentialing examination process. This process is critical because pass–fail decisions have tremendous consequences for examinees. It is controversial because there is no perfect way to set a passing score (Meara, Hambleton, & Sireci, 2001). As we describe in the following paragraph, passing scores on credentialing tests are typically established by committees of individuals who use their expert judgment to determine where the passing standard should be set.

Given that appropriate standard setting is critical to the validity of credentialing examinations, it is not surprising that the psychometric literature contains numerous sets of guidelines and advice for setting standards on such tests (e.g., Cizek, 1996, 2001; Hambleton, 1998; Kane, 1994; Meara et al., 2001). Numerous methods also have been developed to set passing scores on these tests. Most of these methods are described as *test-centered methods* because they focus on the amount of test material that must be answered correctly to signify "minimal competence" for entry-level practice (reference). Thus, the methods used to set passing scores on licensure and certification tests are not *norm referenced* (i.e., passing or failing is determined by how well candidates perform relative to others who take the same test) but *criterion referenced* (i.e., passing is determined by sufficient performance on the well-defined domain of knowledge and skills measured by the test).

Contemporary methods to set passing scores on credentialing tests use experienced professionals in the field to review test items and consider the knowledge and skills that are required for safe and effective entry-level practice. These professionals are recruited to participate on a standard-setting panel. Standard-setting panelists are asked to review test items carefully (and scoring rubrics if constructed response items are present in the test) and provide judgments regarding expected levels of performance on each item by *minimally competent candidates* (MCCs)—those who possess "just enough" knowledge, skill, or ability to be worthy of licensure or certification.[2] The task required of panelists is to provide ratings regarding how well MCCs are likely to do on each item.

The most common method used to set passing scores on licensure tests is the *Angoff method* (Angoff, 1971), in which panelists discuss the characteristics of the MCC and are taught about the KSAs measured by the test. Next, they review each test item and provide a probability judgment regarding the

---

[2]In this chapter, we use the term *minimally competent candidate* (see Hambleton & Pitoniak, 2006). However, several other terms may be found in the literature including *minimally acceptable person* (Angoff, 1971), *borderline test taker* (Livingston & Zieky, 1982), and *just barely certifiable candidate* (Hambleton & Plake, 1995).

likelihood that an MCC would answer the item correctly. For example, if a panelist thinks someone who is minimally competent has a high probability of answering the item correctly, he or she might provide an Angoff rating of .90 for the item. The passing score for the test is calculated by first computing the passing score for each panelist by summing his or her item ratings, and then calculating the average of the panelists' passing scores. Newer variations on this method use the term *modified Angoff* to reflect the addition of one or more features not present in the original formulation. These newer features include providing empirical item data to panelists, encouraging discussions among panelists, and conducting several rounds of ratings to enable panelists to revise their estimates if they think it is appropriate to do so (Cizek, 1996; Hambleton & Pitoniak, 2006).

A recent variation of the Angoff method that has been proposed for use on licensure and certification tests is the *direct consensus* (DC) method (Sireci, Hambleton, & Pitoniak, 2004). We include a description here to provide readers with an idea for how the standard-setting process is carried out—the process used by many professional groups is extensive, thoughtful, well planned, and consistent with professional standards. The DC method contains many elements of the Angoff method, but it differs in that it allows the entire group of panelists to recommend the passing scores by consensus. Like other test-centered methods, the DC method involves comprehensive discussion of the MCC and review of the content specifications and test items. Items on the test are grouped together in some reasonable way, such as by major content area or item format. Panelists, usually 10 to 15, are then asked to review the items within the first group (content area) and mark the items they believe the MCC would answer correctly. This process is repeated for the remaining areas. This step provides a number-correct score associated with the MCC for each content area for each panelist. Summing across the areas yields the initial passing score for each panelist. Next, the summary data for each panelist are projected onto a screen. The panelists discuss their ratings sequentially by area. They can see the effect any changes they make have on their individual passing score as well as on the average passing score. Finally, the panelists are encouraged to arrive at a consensus about the desired passing score. They are first asked whether the average passing score would suffice as a consensus passing score. Panelists who believe the passing score should be higher or lower than the group average are asked to present their rationale for raising or lowering it. The group considers these arguments and may make adjustments to the consensus passing score. This process is repeated until all panelists are comfortable with the final result. If consensus cannot be reached, then the average score across panelists is used. Panelists often want to have control over the final result, and so this last fact is often helpful in getting the panelists to reach consensus.

Further information about the process of setting passing scores in credentialing tests can be found in more extensive treatments of this topic, including those by Cizek (2001), Hambleton and Pitoniak (2006), and Livingston and Zieky (1982). From the brief review presented here, it should be clear that the establishment of a passing score on a credentialing test is one of the most carefully executed processes in the testing enterprise. In fact, standard setting is one of the most scrutinized aspects of licensure and certification testing whenever such tests are challenged in court (Sireci & Green, 2000; Sireci & Parker, 2006). Every aspect of the process can be and will be challenged, including (a) the policy regarding the composition of the panel who will recommend the passing score; (b) the panel size; (c) the selection of panel members; (d) the choice of standard-setting method; (e) the training of panelists; (f) the actual standard-setting process itself, including the role of the facilitator; and (g) the validity associated with the process and results, including panelists' evaluation of the process, and internal validity evidence such as the level of agreement of passing scores among panelists.

TESTING ACROSS LANGUAGES AND CULTURES

Another fallacy associated with licensure and certification testing is that such testing is primarily limited to the United States because, as some critics argue, Americans are obsessed with testing. Once again, reality differs greatly from the fallacy. People all over the world strive to earn credentials that will help them enter a profession, secure a job, or increase their marketability. Yet the need to protect the public remains the same. Thus licensure and certification tests are used worldwide, and where they do not exist to control for entry into professions such as medicine and accounting, countries are striving to change the situation and introduce credentialing tests to protect the public and raise professional standards.

Given the rapid increase in the global marketplace, candidates from around the world often also seek a common credential. For example, the Microsoft Corporation administers more than 1 million tests a year in 72 countries as part of their Microsoft Certified Professional program (Sireci, Hambleton, Huff, & Jodoin, 2000). More moderately sized certification programs, such as the Information Systems Audit and Control Association, also administer their tests in several countries. The international use of credentialing tests is exciting and important but raises an additional challenge for testing agencies—assessing candidates who operate using different languages.

Because assessing the knowledge and skills of candidates around the world means assessing candidates who communicate using different languages, many credentialing agencies are offering their tests today in multiple languages (see Hambleton, Merenda, & Spielberger, 2005). Administering credentialing tests in multiple languages typically involves adapting a test from one language to other languages (e.g., some of Microsoft's tests are now available in more than 15 languages). This process has previously been called *test translation*, but the term *test adaptation* more accurately describes the complex processes required to ensure that the knowledge and skills measured by a credentialing test are consistent across language versions of a test.

There are at least three reasons for adapting credentialing tests for use in multiple languages (see Hambleton, 1994; Hambleton & Patsula, 1998). First, because the KSAs assessed are often the same across language groups, adapting a test rather than attempting to develop a parallel test in a second language by different test developers helps ensure that the content and structure of the test is consistent across languages. Second, adapting an existing test is more efficient than developing a unique test in each language—item writing, item review, field testing, test composition, and so on are often time-consuming and labor-intensive activities. Third, many credentialing programs originate in a single language, and the original test sets the standard for all subsequent versions. Test adaptation will often be an easier approach for ensuring test equivalence than initiating new test development procedures in multiple languages.

A key factor underlying reasons for adapting credentialing tests is fairness. Many credentialing organizations do not want facility with a particular language to interfere with measurement of the proficiencies represented by the credential. Thus, adapting a test for use in multiple languages is seen as an effective means for achieving comparability of candidates who operate in different languages.

As many credentialing organizations begin to adapt their tests for use in multiple languages, they discover how difficult it is to establish the equivalence of multiple language versions of a test. Unfortunately, popular approaches such as the use of a backward translation design or the use of bilingual candidates have serious flaws (see, e.g., Hambleton & Patsula, 1998). To do the job right requires several layers of quality control that involve both statistical and judgmental analyses. The *Guidelines for Adapting Educational and Psychological Tests* (Hambleton, 1994; van de Vijver & Hambleton, 1996) developed by the International Test Commission present 22 guidelines for adapting tests. These guidelines stress careful adaptation procedures that involve several quality control checks, as well as empirical analyses to evaluate the comparability of tests, items, and score interpretations across languages.

SUMMARY AND FUTURE DIRECTIONS

Licensure and certification tests fulfill a noble purpose and are used throughout the world to help ensure that professionals who serve the public in various ways are sufficiently competent to perform their duties. Contemporary practices in licensure and certification testing involve careful test development techniques; innovative item formats; computer-based test delivery and CAT designs; and, in many cases, assessment across multiple languages and cultures. We believe that these tests are of considerably higher quality than earlier tests, and perpetuation of many of the fallacies about these tests does a great injustice to the field of credentialing tests. At the same time, we are not so naive as to suggest that all credentialing tests are perfect, and certainly we recognize the need for many testing agencies to improve. In the main, however, the credentialing field itself has set high standards for the quality of credentialing tests, and many credentialing agencies are in compliance with these high standards.

The increased demands of licensure and certification tests also bring increased challenges. Threats to the security of these tests appear to be on the rise. Coaching courses, Web site chat rooms, and other outlets often try to replicate test items to help candidates pass a test. Thus, credentialing agencies must monitor these activities as well as their item statistics to evaluate whether compromises to test security occur. Increases in international testing also raise questions about the equality of passing scores across different language versions of a test, which requires evidence of score comparability. Recent progress in this area has been made (e.g., Sireci, Patsula, & Hambleton, 2005), but clearly more research is needed.

The *Standards for Educational and Psychological Testing* (AERA, APA, & NCME, 1999) lists five sources of evidence that should be used to support the use of a test for a particular purpose. These sources are evidence based on (a) test content, (b) response processes, (c) internal structure, (d) relations with other variables, and (e) consequences of testing. A full discussion of these sources of evidence is beyond the scope of this chapter (for more complete discussions of test validation, see AERA, APA, & NCME, 1999; Kane, 2006; Messick, 1989, or Sireci, 2005). However, validity evidence that licensure and certification tests are appropriate for their intended purposes is typically based on test content (e.g., practice analyses, content validity review, careful test construction procedures, standard setting) and internal structure (e.g., Pitoniak, Sireci, & Luecht, 2002), and this evidence has been consistently accepted as sufficient by the courts (Sireci & Green, 2000; Sireci & Parker, 2006). Nevertheless, we encourage credentialing agencies to gather further validity evidence whenever possible.

Contemporary licensure and certification testing illustrates how standardized assessments can facilitate fairness in decision making by providing a level playing field for candidates seeking a credential. In the future, we expect developments in this area to include use of the computer to administer and score more real-world tasks to candidates and greater use tests adapted for use across multiple languages. These developments present credentialing agencies with busy research agendas for the foreseeable future.

REFERENCES

American Educational Research Association, American Psychological Association, & National Council on Measurement in Education. (1999). *Standards for educational and psychological testing.* Washington, DC: American Educational Research Association.

American Institute of Certified Public Accountants. (2005). *CPA computer-based examination FAQs.* Retrieved May 12, 2007, from http://www.cpa-exam.org/cpa/computer_faqs_1.html

Angoff, W. H. (1971). Scales, norms, and equivalent scores. In R. L. Thorndike (Ed.), *Educational measurement* (2nd ed., pp. 508–600). Washington, DC: American Council on Education.

Bartram, D., & Hambleton, R. K. (2006). *Computer-based testing and the Internet: Issues and advances.* Chichester, England: Wiley.

Bejar, I. (1991). A methodology for scoring open-ended architectural design problems. *Journal of Applied Psychology, 76,* 522–532.

Breithaupt, K. J., Mills, C. N., & Melican, G. J. (2006). Facing the opportunities of the future. In D. Bartram & R. K. Hambleton (Eds.), *Computer-based testing and the Internet: Issues and advances* (pp. 219–251). Chichester, England: Wiley.

Cizek, G. J. (1996). Standard-setting guidelines. *Educational Measurement: Issues and Practice, 15*(1), 13–21, 12.

Cizek, G. J. (Ed.). (2001). *Setting performance standards: Concepts, methods, and perspectives.* Hillsdale, NJ: Erlbaum.

Devore, R. (2002, April). *Considerations in the development of accounting simulations.* Paper presented at the Annual Meeting of the National Council on Measurement in Education, New Orleans, LA.

Drasgow, F., & Mattern, K. (2006). New tests and new items: Opportunities and issues. In D. Bartram & R. K. Hambleton (Eds.), *Computer-based testing and the Internet: Issues and advances* (pp. 59–76). Chichester, England: Wiley.

Hambleton, R. K. (1994). Guidelines for adapting educational and psychological tests: A progress report. *European Journal of Psychological Assessment, 10,* 229–244.

Hambleton, R. K. (1998). Setting performance standards on achievement tests: Meeting the requirements of Title I. In L. Hansche (Ed.), *Handbook for the development of performance standards: Meeting the requirements of Title I* (pp. 87–114). Washington, DC: Council of Chief State School Officers.

Hambleton, R. K., Merenda, P., & Spielberger, C. (Eds.). (2005). *Adapting educational and psychological tests for cross-cultural assessment.* Hillsdale, NJ: Erlbaum.

Hambleton, R. K., & Murphy, E. (1992). A psychometric perspective on authentic measurement. *Applied Measurement in Education, 5,* 1–16.

Hambleton, R. K., & Patsula, L. (1998). Adapting tests for use in multiple languages and cultures. *Social Indicators Research, 45,* 153–171.

Hambleton, R. K., & Pitoniak, M. J. (2006). Setting performance standards. In R. L. Brennan (Ed.), *Educational measurement* (4th ed., pp. 433–471). Washington, DC: American Council on Education/Praeger.

Hambleton, R. K., & Plake, B. S. (1995). Using an extended Angoff procedure to set standards on complex performance assessments. *Applied Measurement in Education, 8,* 41–56.

Huff, K. L., & Sireci, S. G. (2001). Validity issues in computer-based testing. *Educational Measurement: Issues and Practice, 20*(3), 16–25.

Jodoin, M., Zenisky, A., & Hambleton, R. K. (2006). Comparison of the psychometric properties of several computer-based test designs for credentialing exams with multiple purposes. *Applied Measurement in Education, 19,* 203–220.

Kane, M. T. (1994). Validating the performance standards associated with passing scores. *Review of Educational Research, 64,* 425–461.

Kane, M. T. (2006). Validation. In R. L. Brennan (Ed.), *Educational measurement* (4th ed., pp. 17–64). Washington, DC: American Council on Education/Praeger.

LaDuca, A. (1994). Validation of professional licensure examinations: Professions theory, test design, and construct validity. *Evaluation and the Health Professions, 17,* 178–197.

Livingston, S. A., & Zieky, M. J. (1982). *Passing scores: A manual for setting standards of performance on educational and occupational tests.* Princeton, NJ: Educational Testing Service.

Meara, K. P., Hambleton, R. K., & Sireci, S. G. (2001). Setting and validating standards on professional licensure and certification exams: A survey of current practices. *CLEAR Exam Review, 12,* 17–23.

Messick, S. (1989). Validity. In R. Linn (Ed.), *Educational measurement* (3rd ed., pp. 13–100). Washington, DC: American Council on Education.

Pitoniak, M. J., Sireci, S. G., & Luecht, R. M. (2002). A multitrait–multimethod validity investigation of scores from a professional licensure exam. *Educational and Psychological Measurement, 62,* 498–516.

Raymond, M. R. (2002). A practical guide to practice analysis for credentialing examinations. *Educational Measurement: Issues and Practice, 21*(3), 25–37.

Raymond, M. R. (2005). Developing and administering practice analysis questionnaires. *Educational Measurement: Issues and Practice, 24*(2), 29–42.

Sireci, S. G. (2004). Computerized-adaptive testing: An introduction. In J. Wall & G. Walz (Eds.), *Measuring up: Assessment issues for teachers, counselors, and administrators* (pp. 685–694). Greensboro, NC: CAPS Press.

Sireci, S. G. (2005). Validity theory and applications. In B. Everitt & D. Howell (Eds.), *Encyclopedia of statistics in the behavioral sciences* (Vol. 4, pp. 2103–2107). West Sussex, England: Wiley.

Sireci, S. G., & Green, P. C. (2000). Legal and psychometric criteria for evaluating teacher certification tests. *Educational Measurement: Issues and Practice, 19*(1), 22–31, 34.

Sireci, S. G., Hambleton, R. K., Huff, K. L., & Jodoin, M. G. (2000). *Setting standards on licensure exams using direct consensus* (Laboratory of Psychometric and Evaluative Methods Research Rep. No. 395). Amherst: University of Massachusetts, School of Education.

Sireci, S. G., Hambleton, R. K., & Pitoniak, M. J. (2004). Setting passing scores on licensure exams using direct consensus. *CLEAR Exam Review, 15*(1), 21–25.

Sireci, S. G., & Parker, P. (2006). Validity on trial: Psychometric and legal conceptualizations of validity. *Educational Measurement: Issues and Practice, 25*(3), 27–34.

Sireci, S. G., Patsula, L., & Hambleton, R. K. (2005). Statistical methods for identifying flawed items in the test adaptations process. In R. K. Hambleton, P. Merenda, & C. Spielberger (Eds.), *Adapting educational and psychological tests for cross-cultural assessment* (pp. 93–115). Hillsdale, NJ: Erlbaum.

Sireci, S. G., & Zenisky, A. L. (2006). Innovative item formats in computer-based testing: In pursuit of improved construct representation. In S. M. Downing & T. M. Haladyna (Eds.), *Handbook of testing* (pp. 329–347). Hillsdale, NJ: Erlbaum.

U.S. Medical Licensing Examination. (1996–2008). *About USMLE.* Retrieved July 11, 2008, from http://www.usmle.org/General_Information/general_information_about.html

van de Vijver, F. J. R., & Hambleton, R. K. (1996). Translating tests: Some practical guidelines. *European Psychologist, 1,* 89–99.

Wainer, H. (Ed.). (2000). *Computerized adaptive testing: A primer* (2nd ed.). Hillsdale, NJ: Erlbaum.

Wall, J., & Walz, G. (Eds.). (2004). *Measuring up: Assessment issues for teachers, counselors, and administrators.* Greensboro, NC: CAPS Press.

Zenisky, A. L., & Sireci, S. G. (2002). Technological innovations in large-scale assessment. *Applied Measurement in Education, 15,* 337–362.

7

MISTAKEN IMPRESSIONS OF LARGE-SCALE COGNITIVE DIAGNOSTIC TESTING

JACQUELINE P. LEIGHTON

There are many types of diagnostic tests. People's experiences with diagnostic tests often take place when they visit the doctor's office. Some of the diagnostic tests used in medicine include electrocardiographs to evaluate the electrical activity of the heart, ultrasounds to create graphic images of internal structures using high-frequency sound waves, and blood sugar tests to indicate insulin resistance and diabetes mellitus. Diagnostic tests also flourish within psychology and education. As early as 1838, Jean Esquirol (1772–1840) was one of the first scientists to propose a distinction between mental illness and mental incapacity. Esquirol attempted to develop methods to distinguish between those individuals he called "mentally deranged" and those he labeled "idiots." The former he considered those who had once enjoyed intellectual capacity and then somehow lost it, and the latter those who never actually developed it in the first place (Sattler, 2001). Aside from Esquirol, other prominent scientists and educators were instrumental in pioneering diagnostic tests in psychology and education, such as Sir Francis Galton (1822–1911), Karl Pearson (1857–1936), James McKeen Cattell (1860–1944), and Alfred Binet (1857–1911).

The use of tests often inspires fallacies about their usefulness and integrity as measurement tools. The fallacies associated with diagnostic tests are many; too many perhaps to be covered fully in a single chapter or even in a single book. Given the sheer volume of information on this topic, its coverage has been distributed across chapters in this volume. In particular, chapters 1 and 2 focus on the fallacies associated with intelligence and psychological tests. The focus of the present chapter is on the emerging fallacies associated with *large-scale cognitive diagnostic testing* (LS-CDT). LS-CDT represents a new hybrid, encompassing aspects of traditional diagnostic tests used for screening students for special education programs and also encompassing aspects of well-known large-scale assessments (e.g., SAT). LS-CDT is emerging powerfully within educational measurement because of the rich information it can provide about the standards achieved by a large number of students. LS-CDT is used to identify what Jean Esquirol at one point in history unfortunately called *mental incapacity* but to what we now refer to as *cognitive strengths and weaknesses* in academic achievement—that is, the knowledge and skills with which students are struggling and the potential causes of these academic struggles. Before examining a series of mistaken impressions associated with LS-CDT, traditional educational diagnostic tests are described in the next section to distinguish these latter tests from the former.

TRADITIONAL DIAGNOSTIC TESTS IN EDUCATION

For many years diagnostic testing has played a pivotal role in helping educators identify students in need of special education initiatives (Pierangelo & Giuliani, 2006). According to the National Dissemination Center for Children with Disabilities (1999), diagnostic testing is one of many assessment tools used to create individualized education programs (IEPs) for students experiencing substantial difficulties in learning. Under the Individuals With Disabilities Education Improvement Act (2004), disabling learning conditions such as autism, deafness, deafness–blindness, emotional disturbances, hearing impairment, mental retardation, the presence of multiple disabilities, orthopedic injuries, and other health-related conditions can seriously impede a child's learning. Disabling learning conditions can also include the presence of specific and entrenched learning problems.

A multidisciplinary team consisting of parents, teachers, school psychologists, and representatives of service agencies uses a wide array of diagnostic tests to evaluate the needs of children with suspected learning disabilities. A teacher or parent may notice a consistent problem in the child's academic performance and request an evaluation. Team evaluations are comprehensive and include assessment of the child's vision, hearing, social and emotional status, general intelligence, communicative status, motor abilities, and academic performance. In particular, diagnostic tests of a child's academic performance often include measures of reading, mathematics, and written language, which are targeted to specific age groups. For example, to diagnose reading deficits, tests such as the Diagnostic Screening Test—Reading (3rd ed.; targeted to Grades 1–12) or the Gates–McKillop–Horowitz Reading Diagnostic Tests (targeted to Grades 1–6) are used (for a full list of tests, target grades, purposes, and publishers, the reader is referred to Pierangelo & Giuliani, 2006). To diagnose mathematical difficulties, tests such as the Comprehensive Mathematical Abilities Test (targeted to Grades 0–11) or the Stanford Diagnostic Mathematical Test—4 (targeted to Grades 1–12) are used. For written language, tests used might include the Mather–Woodcock Group Writing Tests (targeted to ages 6–18) or the Test of Early Written Language (2nd ed.; targeted to ages 3–10). There are also diagnostic tests that measure a comprehensive range of academic skills in reading, mathematics, and language use and production such as the Diagnostic Achievement Test for Adolescents (2nd ed.; targeted to Grades 7–12) and the Wide Range Achievement Test (4th ed.; targeted to ages 5–95). For more information, all tests mentioned here can be found in Pierangelo and Guiliani (2006). The value of these diagnostic tests is in providing rich, instructionally relevant information about learning-disabled students to improve their chances of success in school. It seems reasonable to expect that rich, instructionally relevant information about other, non–learning-disabled students is also a worthwhile goal. This is the aim of LS-CDT.

LARGE-SCALE COGNITIVE DIAGNOSTIC TESTING

Unlike traditional diagnostic tests in education, which are often administered individually and used to identify students' learning disabilities and develop IEPs, LS-CDT is designed to be administered to groups of students at the same time and used to identify transitory learning misconceptions or weaknesses that are not so serious as to be labeled disabilities. It is possible, of course, for these transitory misconceptions to become serious impediments to learning if left unchecked.

At this time, LS-CDT is often implemented by revisiting an existing, traditional large-scale achievement test (e.g., SAT), identifying the knowledge and processing skills assumed to be measured by the items, and applying diagnostic measurement models to response data to generate information about the knowledge and skills underlying students' total test scores. Ideally, an empirically based cognitive model of learning (which I refer to here as *cognitive model*; see National Research Council, 2001) should guide the extraction of knowledge and processing skills from the items. The expectation is that future LS-CDT will be designed, at the outset, from cognitive models so that every item included in the test can be cataloged to a unique part of the cognitive model in a way that meets not only reliability but also validity standards. LS-CDT will then be used to provide empirically defensible information about how examinees think about and use knowledge in the process of generating an answer or solution within a subject content domain such as reading, math, or science (Leighton & Gierl, 2007a; Marshall, 1990; Nichols, 1994; Nichols, Chipman, & Brennan, 1995). Because the goal of LS-CDT is to provide information that is instructionally relevant, the results of such testing must be able to provide useable information to parents and teachers about students' skills generally and about cognitive weaknesses, misconceptions, or learning impasses in particular. This is not meant to suggest that there will be a wholesale replacement of traditional large-scale tests, but for those stakeholders interested in having greater instructionally relevant information about examinees' test performance, LS-CDT is intended to be an option.

There are numerous examples of LS-CDT, such as Sheehan and Mislevy's (1990) application of a generalization of the linear logistic test model to the Survey of Young Adult Literacy (see also Kirsch & Jungeblut, 1986); Birenbaum and Tatsuoka's (1993) rule-space method applied to a test in multiplication and division of exponents; Tatsuoka, Corter, and Tatsuoka's (2004) rule-space method applied to the Third International Mathematics and Science Study—Repeat (TIMSS–R; see also Mullis et al., 2001); Gierl, Tan, and Wang's (2005) cognitive analysis of the SAT; and Jang's (2005) application of the fusion model system (see Roussos et al., 2007) to the Educational Testing Service LanguEdge English Language Learning assessment (see also Birenbaum, Tatsuoka, & Gutvirtz, 1992; Birenbaum, Tatsuoka, & Xin, 2005; Cui, Leighton, Gierl, & Hunka, 2006; Embretson & Gorin, 2001; N. Frederiksen, Glaser, Lesgold, & Shafto, 1990; Henson & Douglas, 2005; Irvine & Kyllonen, 2002; Junker & Sijtsma, 2001; Leighton & Gierl, 2007a; Nichols et al., 1995; Sheehan, 1997; Stout, 2002; Williams & Ryan, 2000). Many of these LS-CDT applications reflect the revisiting and mining of an existing large-scale achievement test, originally not intended to be diagnostic, for cognitive diagnostic purposes. Many applications are still in their experimental stage, testing the viability of diagnostic measurement models for whether the student information retrieved is sufficiently useful to invest in bona fide diagnostic tests developed directly from cognitive models. To provide a flavor of a LS-CDT application, Tatsuoka et al.'s (2004) rule-space method as applied to the TIMSS–R is now briefly described.

The *rule-space method* is used to analyze an unobservable (latent) variable, such as mathematical achievement, according to the component attributes (knowledge or skills) required to perform successfully on a test designed to measure the latent variable. After the attributes of the latent variable are identified, students' performance on the test is transformed into observable attribute mastery patterns. In effect, the rule-space method is used to "explode" students' item scores into attribute mastery patterns showing a profile of strengths and weaknesses. When Tatsuoka et al. (2004) applied the rule-space to the TIMSS–R eighth-grade math items, they first identified the attributes associated with successful test performance. Toward this end, they arranged for domain experts to solve the items; they also discussed the content of the items with teachers and reviewed verbal protocols of students solving the items—that is, they collected empirical evidence of students' problem solving on the items of interest. Three categories of attributes were ultimately identified (see Tatsuoka et al., 2004, Table 1): content-based attributes (e.g., basic concepts and operations in whole numbers and integers), process-based attributes (e.g., applying rules in algebra), and skill-based attributes (e.g., using propositional reasoning).

Using the identified attributes, Tatsuoka et al. (2004) coded the test items for the particular sequence of attributes required to answer each item successfully. Then a series of matrices were calculated and derived (e.g., adjacency, reachability, reduced-Q) to compute the attribute mastery patterns for examinees of 20 countries. The detailed results from this LS-CDT application indicated that students from high-achieving countries had different ways of performing on the test. In particular, students from Singapore achieved top performance on the TIMSS–R primarily by excelling on items measuring reading and computational attributes. In contrast, students from Japan achieved excellence by successfully answering items measuring higher level thinking attributes, and students from Belgium attained high scores by performing well on items measuring knowledge of fractions and proportional reasoning attributes. Students from lower achieving countries tended to show weaker higher level thinking skills. From Tatsuoka et al.'s (2004) LS-CDT application, conclusions about the component attributes that were most likely to correlate with successful math performance could be drawn, as well as ways in which educators might modify curriculum accordingly. Large-scale testing programs such as TIMSS–R are able to afford the research and development costs of developing psychometrically sound diagnostics and are increasingly setting the tone for instructional practice in the United States, Canada, and other nations (see Tatsuoka et al., 2004). LS-CDT applications are now being considered and explored for many large-scale tests, including the high-stakes SAT (e.g., Birenbaum et al., 1992, 2005; Cui et al., 2006; Gierl et al., 2005).

Although there is active research and interest in LS-CDT, this form of testing is still relatively new. The research on LS-CDT is especially impressive and in demand as stakeholders clamor for more instructionally relevant information from traditional large-scale assessment programs (Huff & Goodman, 2007). Therefore, it seems useful and appropriate to include a chapter on LS-CDT in this volume on antitesting fallacies because (a) there is great interest in combining cognitive models with test development in the form of LS-CDT; (b) untruths associated with LS-CDT will undoubtedly emerge as this type of testing gains ground in testing programs; and (c) although these untruths have yet to emerge in systematic form within the literature (and so I hesitate to attribute any mistaken impression to any one researcher or group of researchers at this early stage), one can nonetheless anticipate some of the criticisms of LS-CDT. Thus, I have put on my critic's hat and anticipated some mistaken impressions that might be associated with LS-CDT. These mistaken impressions can and should be addressed before they take hold and become persistent fallacies. In this way, those of us in the field can attempt to clarify the aims of LS-CDT, encourage researchers to investigate concerns associated with this form of testing, and focus on substantive challenges facing the future of LS-CDT. If we have the opportunity to address mistaken impressions about LS-CDT at the outset, why not take it?

LS-CDT offers reasons for optimism in delivering high-quality information to teachers and parents about why students perform as they do within a content domain. However, mistaken impressions can easily emerge about what this form of testing is and is not because it represents a hybrid of two distinct types of assessment: large scale and diagnostic. Although critics might argue that these mistaken impressions are not real antitesting fallacies because the field of LS-CDT is still too new, I would only partially agree. The field of LS-CDT is new, and the mistaken impressions might be general at this stage and in some cases hypothetical, but they certainly are specific to LS-CDT. They are specific to LS-CDT because they function to misconstrue the cognitive foundation of LS-CDT or, alternatively, misconstrue how LS-CDT fundamentally differs from other assessment practices. In other words, the mistaken impressions target the soft underbelly of any hybrid approach that aims to meet multiple objectives.

There are at least eight mistaken impressions about LS-CDT. These eight impressions in most cases reflect unwarranted pessimism and in another case reflect extreme optimism.[1] As with most issues, the practical truth is found somewhere in the middle. The mistaken impressions include the following:

1. Large-scale tests cannot be cognitively diagnostic because they measure lower level, basic knowledge and skills.
2. LS-CDT will narrow the implemented curriculum because cognitive models focus on a narrower set of processing skills than traditional large-scale tests.
3. The cognitive models used to develop LS-CDT are used to inform common problem solving and not less well-known problem solving.
4. Verbal reports are untrustworthy in the development of cognitive models for LS-CDT.

---

[1]Some might wonder why a mistaken impression reflecting excessive optimism is included on a list of antitesting fallacies. Excessive optimism about any product can set the expectations unrealistically high and create the inevitability of disappointment. Such excessive optimism is problematic because it has the potential to embitter advocates of LS-CDT.

5. Abilities tend to be correlated, so LS-CDT will essentially produce uninformative profiles.
6. LS-CDT is simply a new name for formative assessment.
7. LS-CDT essentially involves the reporting of subscores.
8. LS-CDT is the cure for high-stakes testing.

The first five impressions undermine the cognitive basis of LS-CDT. Impressions 6 and 7 question how LS-CDT fundamentally differs from traditional assessments practices, and Impression 8 is excessively optimistic and therefore problematic. The remainder of the chapter is devoted to exploring these impressions, explaining their nature, and, it is hoped, informing a more realistic appraisal of LS-CDT.

IMPRESSION 1. LARGE-SCALE TESTS CANNOT BE COGNITIVELY DIAGNOSTIC BECAUSE THEY MEASURE LOWER LEVEL, BASIC KNOWLEDGE AND SKILLS

Many investigators and practitioners have advanced strong rationales for LS-CDT, not the least of which is the use of this form of testing to inform and tailor instruction to the specific learning needs of students (e.g., Embretson, 1990; Kieras, 1990; Lesgold, Lajoie, Logan, & Eggan, 1990; Nichols, 1994; Nichols et al., 1995). Lesgold et al. (1990) stated,

> Ideally, we would prefer to understand why particular [test] performances or performance scores predict broader aspects of competence, just as physicians prefer to go beyond mere statistical indications to also consider causal models of healthy function and particular patients' departures from healthy function. (pp. 325–326)

Research studies examining the feasibility or practicality of LS-CDT have focused on how large-scale achievement measures could be made more informative in this way (Birenbaum et al., 1992, 2005; Cui et al., 2006). However, some might wonder why large-scale achievement measures would even be considered vehicles for cognitive diagnosis. One answer to this question is that large-scale testing programs often have the financial and human resources to invest in the research and development of LS-CDT, which includes hiring experts with the psychological, content domain, and psychometric–technical knowledge to develop, pilot, and ensure that cognitive diagnostic measures meet acceptable standards of reliability and validity (American Educational Research Association, American Psychological Association, & National Council on Measurement in Education, 1999).

One basis for opposing the use of large-scale tests as vehicles for cognitive diagnosis rests with the criticism that they can often fall prey to measuring surface-level skills (see Collins, 1990; N. Fredericksen, 1990; Lane, 2004). This appraisal of some existing large-scale tests may be justified. Many of these assessments, both norm and criterion referenced, are not developed from cognitive models of learning and so may not measure higher level processing skills (J. R. Frederiksen & White, 1990; Leighton, 2004; National Research Council, 2001; Nichols, 1994). Many of these large-scale tests often include a disproportionate number of multiple-choice items, and these items may not elicit the expected problem-solving skills of interest (N. Frederiksen, 1990). However, although there is research evidence to suggest that some large-scale, multiple-choice test items may fall short in measuring expected higher level knowledge and skills (Lane, 2004; Leighton & Gokiert, 2005; Rogers & Yang, 1996), there is also reason to believe that multiple-choice items can be logically designed to measure deeper forms of cognitive processing (e.g., M. Wilson & Sloane, 2000).

That some large-scale assessments may have poor optics in terms of measuring higher level processing skills should not lead us to the conclusion that all large-scale tests or test items fare equally badly—or that future large-scale assessment cannot be designed to measure higher level skills with the efficiency and assumed objectivity that the multiple-choice format affords. There are research programs investigating how multiple-choice items can be designed from cognitive psychological principles so that items elicit circumscribed processing skills (e.g., Embretson, 1998; Gierl, Leighton, & Hunka, 2007; Irvine & Kyllonen, 2002; Leighton, Gierl, & Hunka, 2004; Yang & Embretson, 2007) and provide the necessary evidence to support inferences about students' cognitive skills (Mislevy, Steinberg, & Almond, 2003; Rupp & Mislevy, 2007).

Large-scale tests do not have a monopoly on measuring surface-level skills. Lower level knowledge and skill questions can be created for large-scale tests as well as for classroom-based assessments (Lukin, Bandalos, Eckhout, & Mickelson, 2004). Thus, it is a mistaken impression that large-scale tests cannot accommodate or be developed for cognitive diagnostic purposes. An assessment is classified as diagnostic not because it is large or small scale but rather because its items can reliably and validly measure knowledge structures and processing skills, which provide accurate and instructionally relevant student information.

IMPRESSION 2. LARGE-SCALE COGNITIVE DIAGNOSTIC TESTS WILL NARROW THE IMPLEMENTED CURRICULUM BECAUSE COGNITIVE MODELS FOCUS ON A NARROWER SET OF PROCESSING SKILLS THAN TRADITIONAL LARGE-SCALE TESTS

This is a difficult impression to repudiate because it is in large part true; that is, traditional large-scale tests are designed to measure a broad range of knowledge and skills, whereas cognitive models reflect the detailed workings of a small set of processing skills (see N. Fredericksen et al., 1990; Leighton

& Gierl, 2007b; Yang & Embretson, 2007). Collins (1990) envisioned this potential problem well: "If diagnosis becomes an objective in *nationwide tests*, then it would drive education to the lower-order skills for which we can do the kind of fine diagnosis possible for arithmetic. Such an outcome would be truly disastrous" (p. 76).

Narrowing the implemented curriculum is not an intended outcome of LS-CDT. Rather, its goal is to provide instructionally relevant information about higher level thinking skills. Toward this end, the cognitive models of learning underlying LS-CDT must be detailed and precise and outline component-processing skills (Yang & Embretson, 2007). This level of detail forces a certain narrowness in terms of the content and skills covered because the set of processing skills required to perform a task within a domain would need to be measured by a test deserving of the label *diagnostic*. Otherwise, not much can be said in detail about students' cognitive strengths and weaknesses. Investigators such as Yang and Embretson (2007) recognized this dilemma and described the cognitive diagnostic measure as having a "fine-grained measurement construct" (p. 141). It would seem, then, that for LS-CDT to be aligned with cognitive models of learning, a single test must measure only a few skills and could narrow the implemented curriculum.

The assumption behind this mistaken impression, however, is that LS-CDT will be administered in the same way as traditional large-scale assessments—namely, once at the end of the school year and for summative purposes alone. If LS-CDT were administered in this way, it is likely that the test could end up measuring a narrow set of skills and possibly even narrow the implemented curriculum. As Collins (1990) stated, this would be disastrous indeed. Administering LS-CDT once during the year would make it difficult to measure the full content and skills desired by many stakeholders and required by many testing programs. Furthermore, it would not befit the purpose of LS-CDT to be administered in this way for maximum usability and benefit.

To avoid fulfilling this mistaken impression, a new system of administration could be developed for the success of LS-CDT (see Anderson, 1990; Collins, 1990; Gierl & Leighton, 2007). These tests could be implemented in such a way that they deliver the psychometric rigor of large-scale tests without sacrificing the instructional and psychological relevance of what diagnosis entails—cognitive information. One scenario would be to administer LS-CDT multiple times a year so that the formative aspects of this form of testing could be made useful to parents and teachers during the school term (Roussos et al., 2007). Another scenario would be to administer LS-CDT using a computerized adaptive framework to tailor the processing skills measured according to students' achievement level (Gierl & Leighton, 2007). Using the latter approach, students would not have to complete an entire LS-CDT form if they have shown mastery on advanced processing skills that presuppose mastery of other basic skills. In this way, students could complete fewer LS-CDT items at one curriculum strand and have the time to complete items measuring other, more advanced curriculum strands. The point is that LS-CDT will need to be administered by a new method (Gierl & Leighton, 2007); thus, the belief that LS-CDT would necessarily narrow the curriculum is premature at this time.

IMPRESSION 3. THE COGNITIVE MODELS USED TO DEVELOP LS-CDT INFORM COMMON PROBLEM SOLVING AND NOT LESS WELL-KNOWN PROBLEM SOLVING

A critique that can be levied against the models of learning that may be used to develop LS-CDT is that these models represent only common problem-solving processes and not lesser known ones. For example, in John R. Anderson's LISt Processing Programming (LISP) tutor (Anderson, 1990), about 80% of the errors students made matched the "buggy" productions in the tutor, which permitted the appropriate feedback or diagnosis to be made of student responses. However, the other 20% of student errors could not be matched and were left undiagnosed. In these cases, the tutor resorted to a default response of "I don't understand that." Other cognitive models show similar findings (e.g., Leighton et al., 2004; Roussos et al., 2007; Tatsuoka, 1995). That is, the cognitive model is often useful in matching or diagnosing a proportion, but not all, of student responses, thus requiring a zeta index (Tatsuoka, 1983) or person-fit index (Cui et al., 2006) to reveal the amount of discrepancy between the instantiated cognitive model and the data.

That not all students will show similar problem-solving trajectories when solving tasks is well documented (Alderton & Larson, 1994; Kossowska & Nêcka, 1994; Kyllonen, Lohman, & Woltz, 1984; Lohman, 2000; Nêcka & Orzechowski, 2005). In fact, there is evidence that students often use different strategies when solving classes of tasks in both mathematical verbal domains (Kyllonen et al., 1984; Lohman, 2000). For example, Kyllonen et al. (1984) administered a spatial synthesis task to a group of participants with distinct profiles of competence in spatial and verbal ability. The mathematical model that best characterized participants who were highly proficient in spatial ability but less proficient in verbal ability was one involving the mental synthesis of the stimuli. In contrast, participants who were high in g (general intelligence) but had less extreme profiles of competence (i.e., were not as highly proficient) in spatial ability exhibited the most strategy shifting.

More recently, Kossowska and Nêcka (1994) found that high-IQ participants preferred an analytical strategy to a holistic one when solving analogical reasoning problems. Those who preferred the analytical strategy spent more time reviewing the initial information of the tasks, whereas those who preferred the holistic strategy reviewed all the information quickly. Nêcka and Orzechowski (2005) concluded, "There is a kind of compatibility between the preferences toward certain cognitive strategies and levels of development of cognitive abilities that may be necessary to use them" (p. 134). Strategy shifting is a serious dilemma for LS-CDT, which no doubt adds to the complexity of this form of assessment. The models of learning used to create cognitive diagnostic measures cannot solely represent one way of solving problems but need to incorporate the many alternative ways students might reach an answer. However, in principle, it should be possible to design cognitive diagnostic test items that measure different strategies for solving classes of problems.

To envision the methods by which LS-CDT will yield the information expected, it is useful to apply innovative thinking. LS-CDT, to be fruitful, will require more extensive research into the psychology of learning and test taking than traditional tests because a model of learning will need to be identified to design the test and interpret item responses. Assuming, as suggested for Impression 2, that LS-CDT may require multiple administrations, possibly with the aid of computerized adaptive frameworks, it is not unreasonable to expect that such a framework should incorporate test items designed to measure multiple information-processing pathways to solutions. Clearly this would require extensive work in terms of identifying the full set of strategies students apply to solve test items and how these strategies fit within the model of learning aligned with the test. In principle, however, it does not appear to be unworkable. In fact, this framework is already observed in preliminary form in *item generation* initiatives (Irvine & Kyllonen, 2002)—that is, using computer technology, items are generated "on the fly" to reflect cognitive variables of known difficulty to efficiently assess participants' knowledge and skills. Although much of this groundbreaking work has been done with training batteries unrelated to primary and secondary schooling, it is not difficult to foresee such frameworks providing the infrastructure for K–12 cognitive diagnostic tests (see Yang & Embretson, 2007). It will be necessary not only to identify models of general strategies for successful performance but also to identify models of lesser known strategies that ingenious students often use to solve complex tasks (see Barnett & Ceci, 2002, 2005). Therefore, the impression that LS-CDT will only provide information for common problem solving is mistaken because multiple models of learning could be used to design test items and therefore measure a range of knowledge and problem-solving skills.

IMPRESSION 4. VERBAL REPORTS ARE UNTRUSTWORTHY FOR THE DEVELOPMENT OF COGNITIVE MODELS FOR LARGE-SCALE COGNITIVE DIAGNOSTIC TESTING

There are many methods for developing cognitive models of learning. At the most basic end of the spectrum, students' response latencies and eye fixations are recorded to measure the length of different cognitive processing skills and the duration and location of students' attentive gaze, respectively (Lohman, 2000). At the other end of the spectrum, students' verbal reports are elicited to identify the processing skills and knowledge structures students are aware of using as they solve a problem-solving task, and extended essay responses are collected to identify the thinking structures involved in tasks demanding complex organization and planning (Lohman, 2000). Although all these methods could be used to investigate human information processing and thus develop models of learning, some researchers in educational measurement have been particularly drawn to the collection of verbal reports (e.g., Hamilton, Nussbaum, & Snow, 1997; Katz, Bennett, & Berger, 2000; Leighton, 2004; National Research Council, 2001).

Verbal reports represent one of the most direct methods researchers have to find out about the processing skills students are aware of using as they solve tasks. Verbal reports are collected from interviews of participants as they solve problem-solving tasks (Chi, 1997; Ericsson, 2006; Ericsson & Simon, 1980, 1993; Pressley & Afflerbach, 1995; K. L. Taylor & Dionne, 2000). During an interview, an investigator asks a participant to "think aloud" as he or she solves a task while an audio recorder or videotape is used to capture the contents of the session. An important requirement when collecting verbal reports, especially if protocol analysis is used (Ericsson & Simon, 1993; Leighton & Gierl, 2007a) is to use tasks that elicit controlled problem-solving activity—that is, problem solving that requires participants to think consciously about and reflect on their solutions. For example, many of the psychological tasks (e.g., in mathematics or logic) traditionally used to elicit verbal reports involve the sequential transformation of knowledge toward an exact solution. After the reports are collected, they can be used to develop models of information processing and learning (Chi, 1997) or validate existing models (Ericsson, 2006; Ericsson & Simon, 1993).

Although the collection of verbal reports has received positive attention in the educational measurement community (especially through the *cognitive lab*, a procedure for investigating the mental processes a participant uses when completing a task such as solving a math problem or interpreting a passage of written text),[2] the protocol-analysis methodology is not as frequently used to develop or even validate large-scale achievement tests as one might expect (Leighton, 2004). The lack of use might have a number of root causes such as expense, insufficient access to student populations, or ambivalence about the quality of information verbal reports might actually yield

---

[2]Although similar in terms of asking participants to think aloud, cognitive labs have a slightly different purpose from Ericsson and Simons's (1993) protocol-analysis methodology. In particular, cognitive labs are regularly used to explore a participant's interpretation of survey questions or tasks, whereas verbal reports collected for the purpose of protocol analysis are often used to confirm or validate a cognitive model of information processing. The reader is referred to Leighton and Gierl (2007a) for a fuller description of these differences.

about processing skills. The first two reasons do not seem compelling, especially because government agencies and testing companies, the two dominant producers of tests, already expend extensive financial resources to develop and administer their assessments. There seems to be another stumbling block getting in the way: an implicit mistrust about the content of verbal reports (Ericsson & Simon, 1993; Leighton, 2004).

The mistrust of verbal reports is not new, having had its origins in the same community of researchers—psychologists—that pioneered the use of verbal reports, came to grow suspicious of them, and ultimately promoted their use once again (Ericsson & Simon, 1993). The impression that students cannot be trusted to articulate the knowledge structures and processing skills they use to solve tasks is therefore not new (e.g., T. D. Wilson, 1994). In fact, it is true that under some conditions the contents of verbal reports may be weak—for example, when the tasks used to elicit the reports are (a) overly easy and call for automatic skills and therefore do not require conscious processing; (b) overly difficult and do not elicit any processing skills, and the student is stumped without knowing where to begin; or (c) designed to measure attitudes or beliefs developing over time without individual awareness and therefore failing to require problem-solving skills for their solution. In these cases, the content of the reports should raise suspicion because the conditions under which they were collected are expected to yield inaccurate results (Ericsson, 2006; Ericsson & Simon, 1993). Recently, Ericsson (2006) warned that "many of the problems with verbally reported information obtained by other methods can be explained as violations of [the] recommended protocol-analysis methodology" (p. 230).

As with any method, verbal reports can be misused, and if misuses are systematic then it might be prudent to investigate why this methodology is so prone to error. Researchers and practitioners must be vigilant of the circumstances under which they use this method so that accurate information about student information processing is obtained. According to Ericsson and Simon (1993), the basic conditions are straightforward. First, the task used to elicit the report needs to be of moderate difficulty for the population of students to which it is administered. If the task is overly easy or difficult, students will not have much to say because they will either solve it automatically or not be able to solve it all. Second, the task should lead to a strategy for solution that can be communicated through words; Ericsson and Simon (1980) explained that the tasks should involve "direct articulation of information stored in a language (verbal) code" or "articulation or verbal recoding of nonpropositional information without additional processing" (p. 227) to produce accurate reports. Again, in Ericsson and Simon's (1980) words,

> When the subjects articulate information directly that is already available to them, the model predicts that thinking aloud will not change the course and structure of the cognitive processes. When the *information*

being processed in order to perform the main task is not verbal or propositional
[italics added], the model predicts that the performance may be slowed
down, and the verbalization may be incomplete. (p. 227)

Third, it is important that interviewers not bias or probe the student in
such a way that the student begins to explain, and possibly formulate incorrectly, his or her problem solving. Interviewers should probe students only if
they are silent for an extended period of time (anywhere from 15–60 seconds; see Ericsson & Simon, 1993, p. 83) and with the simple prompt, "Please
keep talking." Moreover, students participating in think-aloud studies should
be familiar with the act of thinking aloud and should be made to feel at ease
articulating their thoughts. Students who have difficulty expressing their
thoughts are not the best candidates for producing verbal reports (Chi, 1997;
Lohman, 2000). As a result, it is true that verbal reports lead to untrustworthy models of learning only if particular procedures, such as those outlined by
Ericsson and Simon (1993), are not followed.

IMPRESSION 5. ABILITIES TEND TO BE CORRELATED, SO
LARGE-SCALE COGNITIVE DIAGNOSTIC TESTING WILL
ESSENTIALLY PRODUCE UNINFORMATIVE PROFILES

There may be some skepticism about the informational value of LS-
CDT because of what intelligence testing has revealed about the nature of
underlying abilities. In short, abilities tend to be correlated (Jensen, 1998). If
a student reads well, then she most likely calculates well, applies what she
has learned appropriately, and develops solutions to new problems effectively.
If abilities are correlated, then what could a profile derived from a cognitive
diagnostic test tell us that we do not already know from a single total score?
In essence, if we expect, on average, most of the item responses to be either
right or wrong, there is not much new.

Part of addressing this mistaken impression involves probing more deeply
into the nature of correlations among abilities. Research (e.g., Abad, Colom,
Juan-Espinosa, & Garcia, 2003; Deary et al., 1996; Detterman & Daniel,
1989) has revealed that strong, positive correlations do not always hold among
different measures of intelligence across populations. For instance, Detterman
and Daniel (1989) found that correlations among intelligence tests tapping
different abilities are stronger in populations of lower intellectual competence than in populations of higher intellectual competence. At lower levels
of ability, tests of intelligence load on a single, general factor, but at higher
levels of ability, tests of intelligence load differentially on two factors, crystallized intelligence (g_c) and fluid intelligence (g_f). It seems that at the higher
levels of ability, educational and life experiences differ and, depending on
the previously acquired knowledge a test is measuring, this variety of experi-

ence leads to distinctions in g_c. Consequently, it would appear that the nature of the correlations among abilities is not as uniform as has been assumed in the past, undermining the expectation that cognitive diagnostic profiles may be necessarily flat or uninformative.

Another reason this mistaken impression is interesting to explore has to do with the nature of the assumption that underlies it. The assumption is that a specific type of measurement model will be used to summarize student performance. Ability testing often assumes a latent trait measurement model in which the ability of interest is viewed as a single continuous dimension in which individuals are to be ordered or ranked (Borsboom & Mellenbergh, 2007; Borsboom, Mellenbergh, & Van Heerden, 2004; N. Frederiksen, 1990; Yang & Embretson, 2007). A total score is computed after an individual has completed the test, and this score reflects how much of the latent trait a person possesses. The measurement model, however, has little to say about the features of the ability—just that the ability can be viewed as a dimension on which individuals can be ranked. This perspective is largely atheoretical (Borsboom et al., 2004; C. H. Frederiksen & Breuleux, 1990), meaning that it is not based on a causal understanding of the mechanisms that underlie the ability of interest. C. H. Frederiksen and Breuleux (1990) stated it as follows: "Knowledge and abilities associated with comprehension, reasoning, and problem-solving have long figured importantly in ability and achievement testing. However, such tests generally have not been based on formal theories of the processes that underlie performance" (p. 355).

This is precisely what LS-CDT aims *not* to be. The purpose of cognitive diagnostic testing is to measure the components of information processing within a domain—in particular, the specific knowledge structures and skills. Without measuring these components, it may be frustrating, if not impossible, to try to produce results from LS-CDT that are instructionally relevant. There first must be an understanding of the mechanism of learning within the domain—the details of how it works—before it can be measured and then later diagnosed as weak or strong. As such, psychometricians are turning their focus to developing measurement models and methods that can be used to report on the cognitive attributes or components of learning and achievement (e.g., Embretson, 1998; Gierl et al., 2007; Irvine & Kyllonen, 2002; Leighton et al., 2004; Luecht, 2007; Roussos et al., 2007; Rupp & Mislevy, 2007; Tatsuoka, 1995). Some of these measurement models report achievement of cognitive attributes in terms of attribute mastery patterns or latent classes in addition to a total test score (e.g., Gierl et al., 2007; Tatsuoka, 1995). Students can obtain a traditional score but, more important, a window into the specific knowledge structures and processing skills producing that score—a profile of their cognition as measured by the composite attributes of the test items. As a consequence, the impression that LS-CDT will be necessarily uninformative because abilities tend to be correlated is not completely fair because the presence (or absence) of strong associations among abilities depends in part on who is being measured, and how, and possibly within what learning domain.

IMPRESSION 6. LARGE-SCALE COGNITIVE DIAGNOSTIC TESTING IS SIMPLY A NEW NAME FOR FORMATIVE ASSESSMENT

There is a saying about old wine in new bottles that captures the essence of this sixth impression. Existing products are often repackaged and sold as new ones. Hence, it is often wise to be a little skeptical about the originality of something that looks strangely similar to what already exists but has a different name. It is understandable why some might view LS-CDT to be equivalent to the formative assessments teachers have been administering in their classes for decades—in other words, new bottle, but old wine. However, in this case, the new form of testing really is new wine, at least in principle.

To appreciate the difference between LS-CDT and formative assessment, it is useful to consider first some characteristics of classroom-based, formative assessments. Teachers often develop and use these assessments to find out whether students are on the right track in learning content and skills. Curriculum and textbook developers also facilitate formative assessment when they develop products to assist teachers in their instruction. These assessments, which can include guidelines for structured question-and-answer sessions, worksheets, essays, performance-based tasks, or even formal tests, are designed to provide teachers with information about students' knowledge and skills within a subject-content domain. These assessments often provide teachers with interim information of whether their students have mastered a topic or whether they might require extra instruction in particular areas. Classroom-based, formative assessments are therefore critical and necessary aspects of good teaching practices.

However, classroom-based, formative assessments are different from LS-CDT principally in design. First, these types of assessments are not typically designed to be aligned with empirically based cognitive models of learning, meaning that although these assessments may be useful to teachers, they have not been designed from first principles in cognitive psychology (Leighton & Gierl, 2007a). One of the most important characteristics of LS-CDT is that it be developed from empirically based cognitive models (e.g., Mislevy et al., 2003) so that this form of testing can be defensibly used to diagnose students' processing skills. One example of such a cognitive model is reflected in Anderson's (1990) LISP programming tutor mentioned earlier. This cognitive model was underwritten by a number of assumptions about the architecture of cognition, including the nature and acquisition of complex skills. Although these are stated as assumptions of the model, this reticence is exaggerated given that most of these assumptions are supported by empirical studies of human information processing. For example, the LISP tutor responds to students' actions by assuming that a skill such as programming can be decomposed into production rules, that the number of skills underlying an activity such as programming is large, that the production rules are hierarchically organized, that all knowledge begins as declarative, that declarative knowledge is compiled into procedural knowledge, that errors must be consciously corrected, that working memory has limitations, and that practiced knowledge tends to become stronger over time. As the tutor and student interact, the tutor constantly scrutinizes the student's problem solving and provides direction when the student goes off task. The tutor provides this direction by consulting its set of assumptions every time a student makes a move; thus, every student behavior becomes an indicator of an underlying information process in need of direction. Consequently, model-based diagnostics are powerful because students' responses are evaluated against what is known empirically about human information processing.

Classroom-based formative assessments, as the term suggests, are exclusively formative. As such, they are often administered in the middle of the school year so that teachers can use the results to modify their instruction before the school term ends. However, LS-CDT could in principle be used more flexibly, potentially serving both formative and summative purposes. LS-CDT can serve a formative role because it is designed to deliver instructionally relevant information about students' information-processing skills within a given academic content domain. However, given the research and development associated with LS-CDT, these tests may also be envisioned as serving a summative role so that they provide defensible information about a student's final standing in a course of study and provide teachers with information about their instructional foci for subsequent years (Huff & Goodman, 2007).

Although classroom-based assessments may be designed with the hope of yielding information about an examinee's level of knowledge or processing skill, these assessments are often developed in the absence of what has been called "assessment literacy," including empirically based rationales for their design and underlying construct (see Lukin et al., 2004). LS-CDT, in contrast, is in principle designed and/or aligned with empirically based cognitive models of learning and well-established psychometric principles. Consequently, although LS-CDT aims to provide instructionally relevant information to teachers and other stakeholders about student learning, LS-CDT is also expected to have the psychometric rigor of traditional large-scale testing, thus yielding student results that could function as summative measures of performance.

IMPRESSION 7. LARGE-SCALE COGNITIVE DIAGNOSTIC TESTING ESSENTIALLY INVOLVES THE REPORTING OF SUBSCORES

Although it is true that LS-CDT may involve the reporting of subscores, latent classes, or attribute mastery patterns, it is not the case that any test that conveys its results in the form of subscores, latent classes, or attribute mastery patterns is necessarily a cognitive diagnostic test. Whether a test is categorized as diagnostic depends principally on the empirical evidence supporting the accuracy of the inferences made from the test about the processing skills a student has or has not mastered. Understanding the foundation of LS-CDT as envisioned by Nichols (1994) and others (e.g., N. Fredericksen et al., 1990; Nichols et al., 1995) is important in this regard. Nichols (1994) made a critical observation about LS-CDT:

> These new assessments [cognitive diagnostic assessments] make explicit the test developer's substantive assumptions regarding the processes and knowledge structures a performer in the test domain would use, how the processes and knowledge structures develop, and how more competent performers differ from less competent performers. (p. 578)

Nichols's observation is useful in understanding the difference between traditional large-scale tests—even those that report subscores—and LS-CDT. He argued that unlike traditional large-scale tests, LS-CDT does not rely solely on logical taxonomies and content specifications to describe learning objectives. This is because "efforts to represent content are only vaguely directed at revealing mechanisms test takers use in responding to items or tasks" (Nichols, 1994, p. 585). Instead, LS-CDT relies largely on, and is informed by, the psychology of learning, reasoning, and problem solving to describe learning objectives. Furthermore, in designing the test, developers must make a defensible case for selecting the processing skills and knowledge structures being measured as appropriately representative of the construct.

Following the logic of Nichols's observations leads to the conclusion that even if traditional large-scale tests do report student performance using subscores, this does not immediately qualify the test as cognitively diagnostic. This is because there may be little evidence for the cognition that underwrites the design of the test. A test that is not aligned with a cognitive model of learning may still provide parents and teachers with useful information about the educational standards or content strands on which students performed well and not so well, but the results cannot be classified as cognitively diagnostic (Hamilton et al., 1997; Hamilton, Nussbaum, Kupermintz, Kerkhoven, & Snow, 1995). The test can only reasonably be described as cognitively diagnostic if it is aligned with an empirically based model of learning (Leighton & Gierl, 2007a; Mislevy et al., 2003; Nichols, 1994) that delivers information about the mechanisms of learning, including students' processing skills (National Research Council, 2001). It is for this reason that LS-CDT is not simply about reporting subscores to students, teachers, and parents; this can be done with any test that measures categories of content knowledge and skills. LS-CDT is expected to be about more than just how test scores are reported to stakeholders. LS-CDT is expected to be uniquely informative about students' learning processes and uniquely defensible in its psychological basis.

IMPRESSION 8. LARGE-SCALE COGNITIVE DIAGNOSTIC TESTING IS THE CURE FOR HIGH-STAKES TESTING

A great deal is riding on the promise of integrating cognitive psychological principles with educational measurement (Glaser, 1981; Snow & Lohman, 1989; Sternberg, 1981). In fact, there is so much riding on the utility of cognitive principles in measurement that some may even expect that LS-CDT will resolve ills in testing such as the backlash against high-stakes testing. This is overly optimistic and a mistaken impression. LS-CDT will not eliminate the perceived disadvantages of high-stakes testing and could in fact have the opposite effect, appearing just as perilous to some stakeholders (Norris, Leighton, & Phillips, 2004).

High-stakes testing has been around for decades, and its mandate for accountability has serious consequences for many people. A few of these consequences include using results to decide college placement, pay differentials for teachers on the basis of student scores, cash rewards to schools, and closing or reconstitution of schools that do not show improvement. High-stakes tests are often criticized for not measuring higher level cognitive skills, the implemented curriculum, and other facets of authentic learning. The use of high-stakes tests originates in part from the desire to measure an important outcome—student learning—and to hold someone or something accountable for the result. There are ardent critics of the format and content of some high-stakes tests, including teachers, researchers, and policymakers (see N. Frederiksen, 1990), as well as those who simply question the benefit of high-stakes tests to satisfy accountability systems (e.g., C. Taylor, 1994). The question, then, is whether LS-CDT could make high-stakes testing more palatable.

As mentioned previously, LS-CDT is designed to yield empirically based and instructionally relevant information about students' knowledge and processing skills so that inferences can be made about their cognitive strengths and weaknesses within a particular content domain. On the one hand, it is possible that if LS-CDT were used for high-stakes testing, many teachers might not find it problematic to teach to the test or have the test drive instruction in the classroom. After all, if the test is designed to be instructionally relevant and is measuring something of value, then why not make this the focus of classroom activities (see Mehrens, Popham, & Ryan, 1998)? On the other hand, one needs to consider that even if LS-CDT were used for high-stakes measurement, some might still find it problematic to have any test carry such significant weight in deciding college placement and other important educational outcomes. It is possible that LS-CDT, used for high-stake decisions, might be deemed more perilous because of its apparent rigor and psychological accuracy. In fact, LS-CDT, designed from cognitive models of learning and targeted to measure specific knowledge structures and processing skills, may yield results that are uncomfortably precise (see Norris et al., 2004). Such tests might be viewed as prying too closely into the clever but flawed strategies some students have acquired for solving problems (Rogers & Harley, 1999; Rogers & Yang, 1996), potentially leading to poor and disappointing results for students who rely on testwise cues. Unlike the common perception that high-stakes tests are fraught with shortcomings in their measurement of higher level processing skills, LS-CDT may not carry such a burden. In fact, it might be just the opposite. These new and improved tests, viewed as exacting from a cognitive–psychological perspective, may be harder to disparage even though their results may lead to the same consequences as previously used, traditional tests. Thus, it is a mistaken impression that LS-CDT could become a cure for high-stakes testing. Measures that lead to potentially undesirable consequences for stakeholders may always be open to critique.

SUMMARY AND DISCUSSION

Eight mistaken impressions have been reviewed as they pertain to LS-CDT. LS-CDT is designed from empirically based cognitive models of learning to measure how students process information in traditional academic domains such as math, science, and language arts (reading) to provide instructionally relevant information to teachers and stakeholders. The selling feature of LS-CDT is its alignment with cognitive models of learning and the relevancy of its information for providing precise and accurate feedback to stakeholders about learning outcomes. It is hoped that teachers and parents will use this "student processing" information productively to remediate any weaknesses in students' learning. Given the anticipation associated with LS-CDT, mistaken impressions undoubtedly will surface. Although this form of testing is still too new to have entrenched fallacies associated with it, this chapter has attempted to envision the kind of mistaken impressions that could easily arise about LS-CDT. These mistaken impressions are useful to review because they can alert those who are interested and actively engaged with this form of testing about the types of criticisms they should anticipate and may encounter, as well as how to begin to think about possible ways to address them. These mistaken impressions are often rooted in erroneous assumptions that can be circumvented.

- The first mistaken impression associated with LS-CDT is that large-scale tests cannot be cognitively diagnostic because they measure lower level, basic knowledge and skills. This is a mistaken impression because an assessment functions diagnostically on the basis of what its items are designed to measure, and nothing so far suggests that large-scale tests could not be developed to probe systematically ever more sophisticated levels of knowledge structures and processing skills.

- The second mistaken impression is that compared with traditional large-scale tests, LS-CDT will narrow the implemented curriculum because cognitive models focus on a narrow set of processing skills. This is a mistaken impression because although LS-CDT may adopt a fine-grained cognitive model (and construct), these types of tests are unlikely to be administered only once a year. Instead, multiple tests based on an array of models of learning are likely to be administered several times a year to exploit their role for informing instruction; thus cognitive diagnostic tests should not constrict the implemented curriculum.

- The third mistaken impression is that the cognitive models used to develop LS-CDT are used to inform common problem solving and not less well-known problem solving. This is a mistaken impression because LS-CDT will likely involve the development of multiple models of learning, including models of less well-known problem-solving strategies.

- The fourth mistaken impression is that verbal reports are untrustworthy in the development of cognitive models for LS-CDT. This is a mistaken impression because verbal reports should not lead to untrustworthy models of learning if the procedures for collecting accurate verbal reports (e.g., Ericsson & Simon, 1993) are followed.

- The fifth mistaken impression is that abilities tend to be correlated so LS-CDT will essentially produce uninformative profiles. This is a mistaken impression because cognitive diagnostic tests are not necessarily expected to measure abilities as normally considered using latent trait models. Rather, cognitive diagnostic tests are expected to assess knowledge and processing skills with the help of innovative measurement models.

- The sixth mistaken impression is that LS-CDT is simply a new name for formative assessment. This is a mistaken impression because classroom-based formative assessments are not developed from empirically based cognitive models of learning (Leighton & Gierl, 2007a) and are often developed in the absence of what has been called "assessment literacy" (see Lukin et al., 2004).

- The seventh mistaken impression is that LS-CDT essentially involves the reporting of subscores. This is a mistaken impression because the use of subscores does not necessarily entail cognitive diagnosis. Cognitive diagnoses can only be made defensibly when the test from which the diagnoses are being derived is aligned with an empirically based cognitive model of learning (see National Research Council, 2001).
- Finally, the eighth mistaken impression is that LS-CDT is the cure for high-stakes testing. This is an erroneous impression because these new measures will not resolve the political use of tests for accountability purposes.

Many of these mistaken impressions are premised on older ideas about testing. As such, they represent uncertainties about what the future holds when new, "untested," ideas are brought to the fore. Given the unrelenting and unequivocal focus on measuring processing skills, LS-CDT offers a new method for envisioning assessment and guiding instruction. However, whether these mistaken impressions are shown to be half-truths will depend on how LS-CDT actually takes form in educational measurement. If financial reluctance or creative timidity conspires to have LS-CDT be designed from traditional methods and administered from technically inadequate tools, then many of these mistaken impression could eventually become entrenched as truths.

REFERENCES

Abad, F. J., Colom, R., Juan-Espinosa, M., & Garcia, L. F. (2003). Intelligence differentiation in adult samples. *Intelligence, 31,* 157–166.

Alderton, D. L., & Larson, G. E. (1994). Cross-task consistency in strategy use and the relationship with intelligence. *Intelligence, 18,* 47–76.

American Educational Research Association, American Psychological Association, & National Council on Measurement in Education. (1999). *Standards for educational and psychological testing.* Washington, DC: American Educational Research Association.

Anderson, J. R. (1990). Analysis of student performance with the LISP tutor. In N. Frederiksen, R. Glaser, A. Lesgold, & M. G. Shafto (Eds.), *Diagnostic monitoring of skill and knowledge acquisition* (pp. 27–50). Hillsdale, NJ: Erlbaum.

Barnett, S. M., & Ceci, S. J. (2002). When and where do we apply what we learn? A taxonomy for far transfer. *Psychological Bulletin, 128,* 612–637.

Barnett, S. M., & Ceci, S. J. (2005). The role of transferable knowledge. In R. J. Sternberg & J. E. Pretz (Eds.), *Cognition and intelligence* (pp. 208–224). Cambridge, England: Cambridge University Press.

Birenbaum, M., Tatsuoka, C., & Xin, T. (2005). Large-scale diagnostic assessment: Comparison of eight graders' mathematics performance in the United States,

Singapore, and Israel. *Assessment in Education: Principles, Policy, & Practice, 12,* 167–181.

Birenbaum, M., & Tatsuoka, K. K. (1993). Applying an IRT-based cognitive diagnostic model to diagnose students' knowledge states in multiplication and division with exponents. *Applied Measurement in Education, 6,* 255–268.

Birenbaum, M., Tatsuoka, K. K., & Gutvirtz, Y. (1992). Effects of response format on diagnostic assessment of scholastic achievement. *Applied Psychological Measurement, 16,* 353–363.

Borsboom, D., & Mellenbergh, G. J. (2007). Test validity in cognitive assessment. In J. P. Leighton & M. J. Gierl (Eds.), *Cognitive diagnostic assessment for education: Theory and applications* (pp. 85–115). Cambridge, England: Cambridge University Press.

Borsboom, D., Mellenbergh, G. J., & Van Heerden, J. (2004). The concept of validity. *Psychological Review, 111,* 1061–1071.

Chi, M. T. H. (1997). Quantifying qualitative analyses of verbal data: A practical guide. *The Journal of the Learning Sciences, 6,* 271–315.

Collins, A. (1990). Reformulating testing to measure learning and thinking. In N. Frederiksen, R. Glaser, A. Lesgold, & M. G. Shafto (Eds.), *Diagnostic monitoring of skill and knowledge acquisition* (pp. 75–88). Hillsdale, NJ: Erlbaum.

Cui, Y., Leighton, J. P., Gierl, M. J., & Hunka, S. (2006, April). *The hierarchical consistency index: A person-fit statistic for the attribute hierarchical model.* Paper presented at the Annual Meeting of the National Council on Measurement in Education, San Francisco.

Deary, I. J., Egan, V., Gibson, G. J., Austin, E. J., Brand, C. R., & Kellaghan, T. (1996). Intelligence and the differentiation hypothesis. *Intelligence, 23,* 105–132.

Detterman, D. K., & Daniel, M. H. (1989). Correlations of mental tests with each other and with cognitive variables are highest in low IQ groups. *Intelligence, 13,* 349–360.

Embretson, S. (1990). Diagnostic testing by measuring learning processes: Psychometric considerations for dynamic testing. In N. Frederiksen, R. Glaser, A. Lesgold, & M. G. Shafto (Eds.), *Diagnostic monitoring of skill and knowledge acquisition* (pp. 407–432). Hillsdale, NJ: Erlbaum.

Embretson, S. (1998). A cognitive design system approach to generating valid tests. Application to abstract reasoning. *Psychological Methods, 3,* 380–396.

Embretson, S., & Gorin, J. (2001). Improving construct validity with cognitive psychology principles. *Journal of Educational Measurement, 38,* 343–368.

Ericsson, K. A. (2006). Protocol analysis and expert thought: Concurrent verbalizations of thinking during experts' performance on representative tasks. In K. A. Ericsson, N. Charness, P. J. Feltovich, & R. R. Hoffman (Eds.), *The Cambridge handbook of expertise and expert performance* (pp. 223–241). New York: Cambridge University Press.

Ericsson, K. A., & Simon, H. A. (1980). Verbal reports as data. *Psychological Review, 87,* 215–251.

Ericsson, K. A., & Simon, H. A. (1993). *Protocol analysis*. Cambridge, MA: MIT Press.

Frederiksen, C. H., & Breuleux, A. (1990). Monitoring cognitive processing in semantically complex domains. In N. Frederiksen, R. Glaser, A. Lesgold, & M. G. Shafto (Eds.), *Diagnostic monitoring of skill and knowledge acquisition* (pp. 351–391). Hillsdale, NJ: Erlbaum.

Frederiksen, J. R., & White, B. Y. (1990). Intelligent tutors as intelligent testers. In N. Frederiksen, R. Glaser, A. Lesgold, & M. G. Shafto (Eds.), *Diagnostic monitoring of skill and knowledge acquisition* (pp. 1–26). Hillsdale, NJ: Erlbaum.

Frederiksen, N. (1990). Introduction. In N. Frederiksen, R. Glaser, A. Lesgold, & M. G. Shafto (Eds.), *Diagnostic monitoring of skill and knowledge acquisition* (pp. ix–xvii). Hillsdale, NJ: Erlbaum.

Frederiksen, N., Glaser, R., Lesgold, A., & Shafto, M. G. (Eds.). (1990). *Diagnostic monitoring of skill and knowledge acquisition*. Hillsdale, NJ: Erlbaum.

Gierl, M. J., & Leighton, J. P. (2007). Future directions in cognitive diagnostic assessment. In J. P. Leighton & M. J. Gierl (Eds.), *Cognitive diagnostic assessment for education: Theory and applications* (pp. 341–351). Cambridge, England: Cambridge University Press.

Gierl, M. J., Leighton, J. P., & Hunka, S. M. (2007). Using the attribute hierarchy method to make diagnostic inferences about examinees' cognitive skills. In J. P. Leighton & M. J. Gierl (Eds.), *Cognitive diagnostic assessment for education: Theory and applications* (pp. 242–274). Cambridge, England: Cambridge University Press.

Gierl, M. J., Tan, A., & Wang, C. (2005, April). *Identifying content and cognitive dimensions on the SAT* (Research Rep. No. 2005–11). New York: College Board.

Glaser, R. (1981). The future of testing—A research agenda for cognitive psychology and psychometrics. *American Psychologist, 36,* 923–936.

Hamilton, L. S., Nussbaum, E. M., Kupermintz, H., Kerkhoven, J. I. M., & Snow, R. E. (1995). Enhancing the validity and usefulness of large-scale educational assessments: II. NELS:88 Science Achievement. *American Educational Research Journal, 32,* 555–581.

Hamilton, L. S., Nussbaum, E. M., & Snow, R. E. (1997). Interview procedures for validating science assessments. *Applied Measurement in Education, 10,* 181–200.

Henson, R., & Douglas, J. (2005). Test construction for cognitive diagnosis. *Applied Psychological Measurement, 29,* 262–277.

Huff, K., & Goodman, D. P. (2007). The demand for cognitive diagnostic assessment. In J. P. Leighton & M. J. Gierl (Eds.), *Cognitive diagnostic assessment for education: Theory and applications* (pp. 19–60). Cambridge, England: Cambridge University Press.

Individuals With Disabilities Education Improvement Act of 2004, Pub. L. No. 108-446, 20 U.S.C. 1414 (b) (1)-(3)-1412 (a)(b)(B). (2004).

Irvine, S. H., & Kyllonen, P. C. (2002). *Item generation for test development*. Mahwah, NJ: Erlbaum.

Jang, E. E. (2005). *A validity narrative: Effects of reading skills diagnosis on teaching and learning in the context of NG TOEFL.* Unpublished doctoral dissertation, University of Illinois, Champaign.

Jensen, A. R. (1998). *The g factor: The science of mental ability.* Westport, CT: Praeger.

Junker, B. W., & Sijtsma, K. (2001). Cognitive assessment models with few assumptions, and connections with nonparametric item response theory. *Applied Psychological Measurement, 25,* 258–272.

Katz, I. R., Bennett, E., & Berger, A. E. (2000). Effects of response format on difficulty of SAT—Mathematics items: It's not the strategy. *Journal of Educational Measurement, 37,* 39–57.

Kieras, D. E. (1990). The role of cognitive simulation models in the development of advanced training and testing systems. In N. Frederiksen, R. Glaser, A. Lesgold, & M. G. Shafto (Eds.), *Diagnostic monitoring of skill and knowledge acquisition* (pp. 51–74). Hillsdale, NJ: Erlbaum.

Kirsch, I. S., & Jungeblut, A. (1986). *Literacy: Profiles of America's young adults* (Final Rep. No. 16-PL-01). Princeton, NJ: Educational Testing Service.

Kossowska, M., & Nêcka, E. (1994). Do it your own way: Cognitive strategies, intelligence, and personality. *Personality and Individual Differences, 16,* 33–46.

Kyllonen, P. C., Lohman, D. F., & Woltz, D. J. (1984). Componential modeling of alternative strategies for performing spatial tasks. *Journal of Educational Psychology, 76,* 1325–1345.

Lane, S. (2004). 2004 National Council on Measurement in Education presidential address. Validity of high-stakes assessment: Are students engaged in complex thinking? *Educational Measurement: Issues and Practice, 23,* 6–14.

Leighton, J. P. (2004). Avoiding misconceptions, misuse, and missed opportunities: The collection of verbal reports in educational achievement testing. *Educational Measurement: Issues and Practice, 23,* 6–15.

Leighton, J. P., & Gierl, M. J. (2007a). (Eds.). *Cognitive diagnostic assessment for education: Theory and applications.* Cambridge, England: Cambridge University Press.

Leighton, J. P., & Gierl, M. J. (2007b). Defining and evaluating models of cognition used in educational measurement to make inferences about examinees' thinking processes. *Educational Measurement: Issues and Practice, 26,* 3–16.

Leighton, J. P., Gierl, M. J., & Hunka, S. (2004). The attribute hierarchy model: An approach for integrating cognitive theory with assessment practice. *Journal of Educational Measurement, 41,* 205–236.

Leighton, J. P., & Gokiert, R. J. (2005, April). *The cognitive effects of test item features: Identifying construct irrelevant variance and informing item generation.* Paper presented at the Annual Meeting of the National Council on Measurement in Education, Montréal, Canada.

Lesgold, A., Lajoie, S., Logan, D., & Eggan, G. (1990). Applying cognitive task analysis and research methods to assessment. In N. Frederiksen, R. Glaser, A. Lesgold, & M. G. Shafto (Eds.), *Diagnostic monitoring of skill and knowledge acquisition* (pp. 325–350). Hillsdale, NJ: Erlbaum.

Lohman, D. F. (2000). Complex information processing and intelligence. In R. J. Sternberg (Ed.), *Handbook of intelligence* (pp. 285–340). Cambridge, England: Cambridge University Press.

Luecht, R. M. (2007). Using information from multiple-choice distractors to enhance cognitive–diagnostic score reporting. In J. P. Leighton & M. J. Gierl (Eds.), *Cognitive diagnostic assessment for education: Theory and applications* (pp. 319–340). Cambridge, England: Cambridge University Press.

Lukin, L. E., Bandalos, D. L., Eckhout, T. J., & Mickelson, K. (2004). Facilitating the development of assessment literacy. *Educational Measurement: Issues and Practice, 23,* 26–32.

Marshall, S. P. (1990). Generating good items for diagnostic tests. In N. Frederiksen, R. Glaser, A. Lesgold, & M. G. Shafto (Eds.), *Diagnostic monitoring of skill and knowledge acquisition* (pp. 433–452). Hillsdale, NJ: Erlbaum.

Mehrens, W. A., Popham, W. J., & Ryan, J. M. (1998). How to prepare students for performance assessments. *Educational Measurement: Issues and Practice, 17,* 18–22.

Mislevy, R. J., Steinberg, L. S., & Almond, R. G. (2003). On the structure of educational assessments. *Measurement: Interdisciplinary Research and Perspectives, 1,* 3–67.

Mullis, I. V. S., Martin, O., Gonzales, E. J., O'Connor, K. M., Chrostowski, S. J., Gregory, K. D., et al. (2001). *Mathematics benchmarking report—TIMSS 1999 eighth grade.* Chestnut Hill, MA: International Study Center, Boston College.

National Dissemination Center for Children with Disabilities. (1999). *Questions and answers about IDEA.* Retrieved March 3, 2006, from http://www.nichy.org/pubs/newsdig/nd21txt.htm

National Research Council. (2001). *Knowing what students know: The science and design of educational assessment.* Washington, DC: National Academies Press.

Nêcka, E., & Orzechowski, J. (2005). Higher-order cognition and intelligence. In R. J. Sternberg & J. E. Pretz (Eds.), *Cognition & intelligence* (pp. 122–141). Cambridge, England: Cambridge University Press.

Nichols, P. (1994). A framework of developing cognitively diagnostic assessments. *Review of Educational Research, 64,* 575–603.

Nichols, P. D., Chipman, S. F., & Brennan, R. L. (Eds.). (1995). *Cognitively diagnostic assessment.* Hillsdale, NJ: Erlbaum.

Norris, S. P., Leighton, J. P., & Phillips, L. M. (2004). What is at stake in knowing the content and capabilities of children's minds? A case for basing high stakes tests on cognitive models. *Theory and Research in Education, 2,* 283–308.

Pierangelo, R., & Giuliani, G. (2006). *The special educator's comprehensive guide to 301 diagnostic tests* (Rev. and expanded ed.). San Francisco: Jossey-Bass.

Pressley, M., & Afflerbach, P. (1995). *Verbal protocols of reading: The nature of constructively responsive reading.* Hillsdale, NJ: Erlbaum.

Rogers, W. T., & Harley, D. (1999). An empirical comparison of three- and four-choice items and tests: Susceptibility to testwiseness and internal consistency reliability. *Educational and Psychological Measurement, 59,* 234–247.

Rogers, W. T., & Yang, P. (1996). Test-wiseness: Its nature and application. *European Journal of Psychological Assessment, 12,* 247–259.

Roussos, L., DiBello, L. V., Stout, W., Hartz, S., Henson, R. A., & Templin, J. H. (2007). The fusion model skills diagnosis system. In J. P. Leighton & M. J. Gierl (Eds.), *Cognitive diagnostic assessment for education: Theory and applications* (pp. 275–318). Cambridge, England: Cambridge University Press.

Rupp, A. A., & Mislevy, R. J. (2007). Cognitive foundations of structured item response models. In J. P. Leighton & M. J. Gierl (Eds.), *Cognitive diagnostic assessment for education: Theory and applications* (pp. 205–241). Cambridge, England: Cambridge University Press.

Sattler, J. M. (2001). *Assessment of children: Cognitive applications* (4th ed.). San Diego, CA: Jerome M. Sattler.

Sheehan, K. M. (1997). A tree-based approach to proficiency scaling and diagnostic assessment. *Journal of Educational Measurement, 34,* 333–352.

Sheehan, K. M., & Mislevy, R. J. (1990). Integrating cognitive and psychometric models to measure document literacy. *Journal of Educational Measurement, 27,* 255–272.

Snow, R. E., & Lohman, D. F. (1989). Implications of cognitive psychology for educational measurement. In R. L. Linn (Ed.), *Educational measurement* (3rd ed., pp. 263–331). New York: American Council on Education & Macmillan.

Sternberg, R. J. (1981). Testing and cognitive psychology. *American Psychologist, 36,* 1181–1189.

Stout, W. (2002). Psychometrics: From practice to theory and back. *Psychometrika, 67,* 485–518.

Tatsuoka, K. K. (1983). Rule space: An approach for dealing with misconceptions based on item response theory. *Journal of Educational Measurement, 20,* 345–354.

Tatsuoka, K. K. (1995). Architecture of knowledge structures and cognitive diagnosis: A statistical pattern recognition and classification approach. In P. D. Nichols, S. F. Chipman, & R. L. Brennan (Eds.), *Cognitively diagnostic assessment* (pp. 327–360). Hillsdale, NJ: Erlbaum.

Tatsuoka, K. K., Corter, J. E., & Tatsuoka, C. (2004). Patterns of diagnosed mathematical content and process skills in TIMSS—R across a sample of 20 countries. *American Educational Research Journal, 41,* 901–926.

Taylor, C. (1994). Assessment for measurement or standards—the peril and promise of large-scale assessment reform. *American Educational Research Journal, 31,* 231–262.

Taylor, K. L., & Dionne, J.-P. (2000). Accessing problem-solving strategy knowledge: The complementary use of concurrent verbal protocols and retrospective debriefing. *Journal of Educational Psychology, 92,* 413–425.

Williams, J., & Ryan, J. (2000). National testing and the improvement of classroom teaching: Can they co-exist? *British Educational Research Journal, 26,* 49–73.

Wilson, M., & Sloane, K. (2000). From principles to practice: An embedded assessment system. *Applied Measurement in Education, 13,* 181–208.

Wilson, T. D. (1994). The proper protocol: Validity and completeness of verbal reports. *Psychological Science, 5,* 249–252.

Yang, X., & Embretson, S. E. (2007). Cognitive diagnostic assessment and construct validity. In J. P. Leighton & M. J. Gierl (Eds.), *Cognitive diagnostic assessment for education: Theory and applications* (pp. 119–145). Cambridge, England: Cambridge University Press.

8

SUMMARY AND DISCUSSION

RICHARD P. PHELPS AND LINDA S. GOTTFREDSON

There are so many criticisms of standardized testing that some of them must be true.

The foregoing statement is fallacious, but there is one truth within it: Criticisms of standardized testing are myriad. However, most are simply false, and many turn the truth upside down. The chapters in this book have not shied away from pointing to testing's limitations, but they document how most criticism today avoids the evidence on testing altogether and instead conjures inconsistent but mutually reinforcing falsehoods meant to discredit the entire enterprise, from intent to impact. Exhibit 8.1 lists the fallacious criticisms described in this book, by chapter.

When one surveys the seeming multitude of fallacies across the various types of test use, however, many begin to look alike. Indeed, some of the apparent differences may reflect only variations in terminology. For example, the idea that psychological diagnostic (chap. 2) and employment (chap. 5) tests are easily faked differs only slightly from the idea that college admissions tests (chap. 4) are easily gamed, say, through test-preparation coaching. In each case, the tests are accused of invalidity because they are allegedly subject to manipulation.

For convenience's sake, we classify the fallacious criticisms of standardized tests into three groups:

The views expressed here are the authors' own and not necessarily those of ACT, Inc.

EXHIBIT 8.1
Fallacious Criticisms of Testing, by Chapter

CHAPTER 1: INTELLIGENCE TESTS

Test-Design Illogic

1. Yardstick mirrors construct.
2. Intelligence is a marble collection.

Test-Score-Differences Illogic

3. Nonfixedness proves malleability.
4. Improvability proves equalizability.
5. Interactionism (gene–environment codependence) nullifies heritability.
6. Similarity (99.9%) negates differences.

Test-Validation Illogic

7. Contending definitions negate evidence.

Causality Illogic

8. *Phenotype* equals *genotype.*
9. *Biological* equals *genetic.*
10. *Environmental* equals *nongenetic.*

Standards-of-Evidence Illogic

11. Tests are useful only if perfect.
12. Reject so-called dangerous conclusions until proved beyond all possible doubt.
13. Accept happy speculation until conclusively disproved.

CHAPTER 2: PSYCHOLOGICAL DIAGNOSTIC TESTS

1. Tests are too expensive.
2. Tests are not valid.
3. Tests lack cultural generalizability.
4. Tests are peculiar and irrelevant.
5. Tests may be (easily) faked.

CHAPTER 3: EDUCATIONAL ACHIEVEMENT TESTS

1. You can't stop progress.
2. Tests cost too much.
3. High stakes induce artificial test score increases.
4. There is little evidence of the effects of testing and no evidence of its benefits.
5. Mischaracterized because tests are difficult to understand.

CHAPTER 4: COLLEGE ADMISSION TESTS

1. Results are misused.
2. Original history of the SAT discredits current use.

3. Test items are biased.
4. Tests are neither valid nor useful.
5. Tests are just a proxy for socioeconomic status.
6. Tests can be coached.
7. An increasing number of colleges are making admission tests optional.

CHAPTER 5: EMPLOYMENT TESTS

Fairness Issues

1. Tests are unfair to ethnic and racial minorities.
2. Tests are illegal when ethnic and minority groups obtain lower scores on average
3. Tests are unfair because they have not been validated for every type of job and context.
4. Tests invade privacy.

Accuracy Issues

5. Tests result in some bad hiring decisions.
6. Tests tell nothing one would not learn by talking with the applicant.
7. Tests often assess the wrong content.
8. Tests can be easily faked.

Administrative Efficiency Issues

9. Tests are unnecessary because one can train anyone to do any job.
10. Tests take too long.
11. Tests are too expensive.

CHAPTER 6: LICENSURE AND CERTIFICATION TESTS

1. Tests do not measure important skills for success in a profession.
2. Tests are predominantly "multiple guess" and basically measure test-taking skills.
3. Passing scores are designed to limit access to a profession.
4. Tests are used mainly in the United States.

CHAPTER 7: LARGE-SCALE COGNITIVE DIAGNOSTIC TESTS (LS-CDTs)

1. Tests cannot be cognitively diagnostic because they measure lower level, basic knowledge and skills.
2. LS-CDTs will narrow the curriculum because they focus on a narrow set of processing skills.
3. LS-CDTs inform common problem solving and not less well-known problem solving.
4. Verbal reports are untrustworthy.
5. Abilities tend to be correlated and so will essentially produce uninformative profiles.
6. *Large-scale cognitive diagnostic test* is simply a new name for *formative assessment*.
7. LS-CDTs essentially involve the reporting of subscores.
8. LS-CDTs are the cure for high-stakes testing.

- Tests are not valid (e.g., they are not "natural" or "authentic"; they only measure some simple and low-level mental processes; they narrow curricula; their scores do not represent anything real).
- Tests do not work well (e.g., they are too long and expensive; they can be easily gamed, faked, and coached; they produce inaccurate results; they are inferior to readily available alternatives; parameters such as passing scores are set arbitrarily).
- Tests are not fair (e.g., they are biased against certain groups of people; they have shady historical origins; they only measure socio economic status).

A cross-classification of fallacious criticisms is shown in Table 8.1. The numbers in the cells correspond to the fallacies listed in Exhibit 8.1.

Censorship and suppression of evidence, which abet the widespread promotion of these false notions by self-interested parties, complete the picture of the antitesting epidemic. Yet what allows this phenomenon to persist, year after year, seemingly unchecked by contrary evidence?

SCIENCE AND ADVOCACY

In his foreword to this volume, Thomas Oakland reminds readers that authors were selected to participate in this volume on the basis of their demonstrated commitment to scientific principles, procedures, and goals. One of those goals is to find probable causes and effects. Especially in the social sciences, the attainment of absolute certainty is rare, if not impossible. However, one can—through a systematic review of a research literature, careful observation and measurement, consideration of rival hypotheses, and honest analysis—sometimes determine the most probable cause of an outcome or effect of an action.

Advocacy is different from science, however—as different as advertising is from good journalism or aggressive politicking is from consensual governing. For the zealous advocate, cause and effect are predetermined to serve one's interests. An advocate need not even believe a cause or effect that she claims; her goal is to persuade others to believe it.

An advocate searches not for probable causes and effects but, rather, for merely plausible ones—ones that others are willing to believe. This is not as easy as it may sound, as any advertising executive can attest; successful market research can be tedious and time consuming. Regardless, the desired outcome is neither truth nor understanding, but conversion—getting others to view a situation in a manner that serves one's own interests.

One senses our chapter authors' frustration with the need to respond to the nonscientific nature of much testing criticism. However, that criticism may well have originated as advocacy and been expressed in advocacy fo-

TABLE 8.1
Cross-Classification of Fallacious Criticisms of Testing, by Chapter

	Chapter						
Criticism	1	2	3	4	5	6	7
Tests are not valid, they . . .							
are not natural or authentic and measure the wrong things.	2, 3	4			7	1	3
only measure simple and low-level mental processes.						2	1
narrow curricula.			3				2
produce artificial scores.	4		3		3		7
are not supported by research.	7		1, 4				
Tests are not useful, they . . .							
can be gamed, faked, coached.		5		6	8		
are too long and expensive.		1	2		10, 11		
produce inaccurate, unreliable results.	11		3		5		5
are inferior to the alternatives.	5, 13				6, 9		6
are constructed arbitrarily.	1						4
Tests are not fair, they . . .							
are biased against [fill in the blank].	9	3		3	1, 2		
have shady historical origins.	8, 12			2			
are misused; are arbitrary.	6			1	4	3	7
only measure socioeconomic status.	10			5			

Note. Numbers in cells refer to the numbered lists beneath the corresponding chapter in Exhibit 8.1, this volume, pp. 248–249.

rums (rather than in scientific journals or at scientific meetings). In this context, advocates, and those who believe them, can make any cause-and-effect claims they wish, their persuasion limited only by plausibility—by what audiences unfamiliar with the subject, and the already converted, are willing to believe.

Plausible arguments are then reinforced through repetition. From our observation, this repetition is supported not so much by other professionals or idealists as by self-interested groups, and chief among these may be education researchers and administrators opposed to the use of standardized tests. Research articles on testing can differ dramatically in their conclusions on the basis of their venue, with those in psychology and technical measurement journals more willing to acknowledge positive results in studies of test use than those in education journals and practitioner magazines. Indeed, articles in the latter venues can be unrestrained in their conviction and criticism. Furthermore, as shown in chapter 3 of this volume and Appendix D (see the accompanying Web site to this volume: http://www.apa.org/books/resources/Phelps/), some education researchers have ventured outside their own domain of expertise to condemn the use of testing in other contexts (in this case, employment testing). The allegiance of so many education professionals and, in particular, education professors to the antitesting cause socializes a multitude of new critics and provides numerous venues in which only those critical of testing are heard and read, and supportive evidence is either ignored or declared not to exist.

Often these critics invoke the welfare of the public, parents, students, teachers, or any group but their own when leveling their criticisms. However, hundreds of polls conducted over the past 4 decades in North America verify solid and unwavering public support for standardized testing in the schools, in the workplace, and for psychological diagnosis (Phelps, 2005). In the area of certification and licensure, pollsters sometimes have difficulty finding more than a negligible proportion of the public opposed. Student support for testing has likewise been solid and unwavering and, until recently, so has teachers'.[1]

EDUCATION'S CENTRAL ROLE IN ANTITESTING CRITIQUES

Why, then, is the education profession and its allied professoriate such a wellspring of antitesting hostility? One answer lies in the democratic dilemma arising from cognitive diversity (see chap. 1, this volume). In no public arena is the dilemma more conspicuous yet more hotly contested than in the public schools, so in no other arena is evidence of cognitive diversity so unwelcome. Anyone or anything that provides unambiguous evidence of this diversity invites passionate rebuttal.

Many social scientists and others have assumed that equal educational chances for children from different social backgrounds would yield equal educational outcomes as well, apparently on the mistaken belief that intellectual talent and academic efforts are equally distributed across all individuals. They therefore wrongly conclude that schools have failed to equalize opportunity when they observe that schools have failed to equalize achievement for all students. Schools are fated not only to fail this latter, social leveling mission but also to underscore the very differences in learning ability and effort that sustain achievement differences.

Specifically, public education puts all students through graduated series of cognitive tasks (in reading, math, science, etc.) that increase in complexity from Grades 1 through 12. This steady escalation of cognitive demands is akin to administering a lengthy and highly public aptitude test battery to each cohort of a nation's children. School performance is influenced by many factors, of course, but none more powerful overall than the combination of ability and effort. Differences in academic achievement track IQ differences between demographic groups, between families, and even between siblings growing up in the same home.

---

[1]The decline in the proportion of teachers who favor the use of standardized testing in the past several years may be related to the provision of the No Child Left Behind Act that holds schools, but not students, accountable for student performance.

Moreover, American schools are now expected to educate a great diversity of children within the same classrooms through at least middle school, despite some children learning multiple times faster than other children. Although inclusion practices are meant to reduce differences in achievement and the stigma of separation, they make differences in ability and effort all the more conspicuous in the classroom by having students of markedly different academic dispositions work side by side, hour after hour, day after day. Achievement differences can be narrowed in inclusive classrooms only by restricting opportunities for ability and effort to affect observed performance, for example, by restricting how much material is taught or assessed (as do some forms of cooperative learning) or by lowering performance standards or making them less academic (as is the trend in gifted education). Organizations can relax standards only so far, however, before they cross the "point of organizational embarrassment" (Gordon, 1988, p. 84) and trigger outcries for higher academic standards.

Nonetheless, the schooling-related professions generally hold that equality and quality—EQuality—could be achieved simultaneously if they were given sufficient resources. They capitalize on reports of low test scores to justify calls for greater funding but argue that testing otherwise imperils the quality and equality of education: quality, when instruction is distorted by teaching to the test, and equality, when children are labeled or sorted by ability. In fact, they continue, the very notion of an intellectual hierarchy threatens EQuality, and students are better served by a belief in multiple, coequal intelligences whereby they can all be smart in some way—as if reality would follow belief.

As noted in chapter 1 of this volume, it is perhaps ironic that the federal No Child Left Behind Act of 2001 now holds schools accountable for the EQuality that educationists have said it is within their power to produce. Yearly progress toward meeting the Act's mandate to raise all student populations to the same high level of academic proficiency is gauged with state-developed tests in specified subjects and grade levels. Schools that fail to level-up performance on schedule face escalating sanctions, including state takeover. Massive failure looms,[2] as would be predicted by the democratic dilemma, and has prompted some states to create the illusion of progress by lowering the threshold for what counts as "proficiency" on their tests. These illusions are periodically punctured by results from the National Assessment of Educational Progress (NAEP). The U.S. government has administered the NAEP to national samples of students since the 1970s to provide "report cards" on public education. Recent NAEP test results in different academic

---

[2]Knowledge levels can be raised without increasing g, to be sure, but rising averages are usually accompanied by wider gaps in achievement when there is no artificial ceiling on performance (Ceci & Papierno, 2005).

subjects for different grades and demographic groups suggest only scant, spotty, and inconsistent progress toward higher proficiency levels and smaller gaps (Fuller, Wright, Gesilci, & Kang, 2007).[3]

PUBLIC DEBATES ABOUND, BUT ONLY ONE SIDE IS INVITED

The democratic dilemma helps address the main theme of this chapter: Why are there so many criticisms of testing? Furthermore, how have fallacious claims come to rule policy debates about testing? The answer to the second question lies partly in the way that any advertising campaign might succeed. That is, we believe that many antitesting advocates will try any argument that works—any argument they can persuade others to believe. They keep trying until their efforts are successful. The result is as many criticisms as audiences informed by only one side of the debate will accept.

Why, however, do antitesting advocates seem to succeed more easily than advertisers who seek to capture the market for their products? We suggest this answer: The critics play by different rules than do their competitors. Specifically, debate tactics differ between scientists and advocates. Scientists seek the scrutiny of their peers to confirm (or deny) the value of their work. Advocates may wish to avoid scrutiny, especially when selling happy falsehoods. Scientists do not circumvent the research literature but engage it. They must respond to rival hypotheses with counterevidence, not innuendo. Scientists confront conflicting scientific results, whereas advocates may simply ignore them or, as described in some chapters, repackage advocacy to look like superior science.

Indeed, as several chapter authors in this volume confirm, it has become common for testing opponents to declare nonexistent an enormous research literature that contradicts their claims. Moreover, with the help of the Fourth Estate, they seem to be fairly successful in eradicating from collective memory thousands of studies conducted by earnest researchers over the course of a century.

The easiest way to win a debate is by not inviting the opponent. The critics rightly fear an open, fair scientific contest.

REFERENCES

Ceci, S. J., & Papierno, P. B. (2005). The rhetoric and reality of gap closing—When the "have-nots" gain but the "haves" gain even more. *American Psychologist, 60*(2), 149–160.

---

[3]Trends in NAEP scores provide an imperfect benchmark for trends in the scores on state tests because NAEP's content standards are not aligned with those in most states. Indeed, the degree of alignment can vary quite a lot from state to state, with some state tests far less aligned to NAEP than others. Comparisons between NAEP and state test scores become more valid when adjustments are made for differences in content standards. For more information, see Zenisky, Hambleton, and Sireci (2008a, 2008b).

Fuller, B., Wright, J., Gesilci, K., & Kang, E. (2007). Gauging growth: How to judge No Child Left Behind? *Educational Researcher, 36*(5), 268–278.

Gordon, R. A. (1988). Thunder from the left [Review of *Storm over biology: Essays on science, sentiment, and public policy*]. *Academic Questions, 1,* 74–92.

No Child Left Behind Act of 2001, Pub. L. No. 107-110, 107th Congress, January 8, 2002.

Phelps, R. P. (2005). Persistently positive: Forty years of public opinion on standardized testing. In R. P. Phelps (Ed.), *Defending standardized testing* (pp. 1–22). Mahwah, NJ: Erlbaum.

Zenisky, A. L., Hambleton, R. K., & Sireci, S. G. (2008a, July). *Communicating the utility of NAEP score reports.* Paper presented at the Sixth International Test Commission Conference, Liverpool, England.

Zenisky, A. L., Hambleton, R. K., & Sireci, S. G. (2008b, July). *Customizing the view: Evaluating the communication of national assessment results.* Paper presented at the Sixth International Test Commission Conference, Liverpool, England.

GLOSSARY

adverse impact: The result of a test or policy that although identically administered across all individuals nevertheless results in a demographic group being hired or promoted at a rate lower than a different (usually majority) group (e.g., a firefighter test of upper body strength is administered identically for both male and female applicants, but female applicants score lower on the test and consequently are hired at a rate lower than their male counterparts).

Angoff method: A procedure for setting passing scores on tests that involves experts reviewing test items and making judgments about the likelihood that minimally qualified candidates would answer the item correctly.

aptitude tests: Tests that typically eschew specific subject matter content in favor of measuring a wide breadth of knowledge and content-free mental abilities—the theory being that someone with more skills and a broader foundation of knowledge on which to use those skills can construct a larger edifice of knowledge and skill (i.e., can know and do more in the future).

attribute mastery patterns: A series of binary vectors representing knowledge and skills assumed to underlie expected or ideal examinee test performance. Used to categorize observed examinee test performance into a knowledge state.

authentic tests: Tests with administrative procedures and/or response formats that mirror those in real life. For example, an authentic test in science might have an examinee conduct a science experiment, and one in airplane flight might have an examinee fly an airplane. Absent the genuine activity, an examinee might be asked to perform a simulation of it.

cognitive model: A representation that details the knowledge structures and processing skills associated with performance within a testing domain.

computerized adaptive testing: A procedure for administering tests to examinees in which the computer selects each test item based in part on how well the examinee answered previous test items. The test is adapted to the proficiency level of the examinee by targeting the difficulty of each item to the range of proficiency most suitable to the particular examinee.

computerized multistage adaptive testing: A procedure for administering tests to examinees in which the computer selects an entire set of test items based in part on how well the examinee answered a previous set of test items. The test is adapted to the proficiency level of the examinee by targeting the difficulty of each set of items to the range of proficiency most suitable to the particular examinee. Multistage adaptive testing is differentiated from computerized adaptive testing by the use of item sets as opposed to single items.

confidence interval: An interval between two values for which, given a specific level of probability, a score or value lies. For example, a 95% confidence interval for an unknown parameter is an interval computed from the sample data having the property that in repeated sampling, 95% of the intervals would be expected to contain the true parameter value.

confirmatory factor analysis: A statistical method for testing hypotheses about the factor structure of a set of variables, including the similarity of factor structures in different demographic groups, by specifying a prior pattern of factor loadings and then determining statistically whether they reproduce the observed correlation matrices.

construct validity: The property of a set of test scores that denotes the extent to which the existence and nature of a given theoretical trait are captured by the test, using evidence of how test scores relate to the same or similar constructs or factors thought to be related to the construct. For example, scores on a test that purports to measure the construct of intelligence would be expected to show higher rates of performance with increasing age of examinees because such abilities are understood, in part, as developmental phenomena.

content representation: The degree to which the items on a test represent the construct (knowledge and skill domain) the test is designed to measure.

content validity: Property of a test that denotes the extent to which the items composing a test adequately sample the domain of interest. In employment testing, the extent to which a test represents the content of the job.

criterion-referenced test: A test that allows its users to interpret scores in relation to a functional performance level—for example, the degree of competence attained by a particular student—without reference to the performance of others.

crystallized intelligence (G_c): Individual differences in highly general but culturally specific cognitive skills and knowledge that are acquired during the course of development, for example, as measured by the Vocabulary and Information subtests of the Wechsler Adult Intelligence Scale. From Horn and Cattell's theory of intelligence (see chap. 1, this volume, p. 42), which distinguishes two highly correlated factors (G_c and G_f) derived from intelligence test batteries.

deviation IQ: A unit for expressing the results of an intelligence test in terms of how far an individual's test score deviates from the mean score obtained by individuals of the same age used to develop and norm the test.

differential item functioning (DIF): A statistical procedure used to detect item bias. This procedure assumes that test takers have approximately the same knowledge (as measured by total test scores) and should perform in similar (although not identical) ways on individual test items regardless of their gender, race or ethnicity, or any other group status. Items identified with DIF are carefully reviewed by content experts and may be omitted or not included in computing a test score.

differential prediction: Occurs when the two demographic groups have differing optimal prediction equations or standard errors. The performance of one group is more accurately predicted than the other.

differential validity: Occurs when the correlation between the test score and job performance is significantly different by demographic group (e.g., the correlation is higher for Blacks than for Whites).

direct consensus method: A method for setting passing scores on tests that involves requiring subject matter experts to (a) review test items, examinee performance data, and other information relevant to the test; (b) discuss these data; and (c) provide a consensus opinion regarding where the passing score should be set.

exploratory factor analysis: A statistical method for detecting structure (broader dimensions of relatedness) in a set of correlated variables.

face validity: A subjective, non-data-based judgment of the extent to which a measure appears to be related to the construct being measured. In employment testing, the degree to which a test appears to relate to the job for which it was designed to predict performance.

factor analysis: A family of statistical techniques for representing the correlations among a set of variables (measurements) in terms of a smaller number of dimensions. Choice of particular technique depends on the purpose of the analysis: (a) data reduction (to reduce the number of variables used in an analysis while still representing them all), (b) exploratory factor analysis (to look for the underlying dimensions of human difference, or latent traits, that best account for the systematic correlations among particular tests and measures), or (c) confirmatory factor analysis (to test statistically a theory about the latent traits influencing scores on tests or other directly measured variables).

fidelity: The extent to which a test resembles the job or duplicates the key processes performed on the job (e.g., a typing test has greater fidelity than a cognitive ability test for a clerical employee even though the cognitive test may be a better predictor of job performance).

fluid intelligence (G_f): Individual differences in a largely culture-free general proficiency in nonverbal learning and reasoning, for example, as measured by the Block Design and Similarities subtests of the Wechsler Adult Intelligence Scale. From Horn and Cattell's theory of intelligence (see chap. 1, this volume, p. 42), which distinguishes two highly correlated factors (G_c and G_f) derived from intelligence test batteries.

fusion model system: Reparameterized unified model for measuring skill-based item parameters and skills-based examinee parameters in educational tests for cognitive diagnosis.

***g* loading:** A rating of tasks and tests according to how strongly differences in performance on them correlate with differences in *g* level among the individuals performing them.

general intelligence factor (g): A construct representing the common factor (latent trait) tapped by all cognitive tests and the core component of all cognitive abilities; for many researchers, a working definition of "general intelligence" at the level of phenotypic behavior.

hierarchical factor analysis: A technique in which the correlated factors derived from factor analyzing a broad set of tests are themselves factor analyzed to extract yet broader latent ability factors, the aim being to reveal the hierarchical structure of latent traits along a continuum from narrow to highly general and also determine how many "general" factors exist at the top of the hierarchy.

incremental validity: The additional predictive capability a test has above and beyond existing measures in explaining or prediction outcomes. For instance, does a test provide a significantly better result than using high school grade point average alone?

intelligence quotient (IQ): A metric for expressing the overall scores of an intelligence test in an interpretable manner. IQ scores were originally reported as quotients: the individual's mental age (MA), as derived from the test, divided by their chronological age (CA): $IQ = MA/CA \times 100$. Today, IQs are calculated as deviation scores: the distance of the individual's score from the mean of their age group, in which (for convenience) the mean score is represented by $IQ = 100$, and distance from the mean is expressed in standard deviation units, a 1-standard-deviation difference in turn being represented by 15 (or sometimes 16) IQ points.

item bias: An item is deemed biased if it displays **differential item functioning** (*see*).

item discrimination: Refers to how effectively each item differentiates between examinees who know most about the content area being tested and those who know least.

item response theory: An approach to test development that is considered to provide a more comprehensive description of how an item functions. Also, a mathematical model of how examinees at different ability levels for the trait measured by a test should respond to a test item. The likelihood of success on an item is expressed as a monotonically increasing function for which the probability of a correct response increases as proficiency with respect to the construct measured increases. Using item response theory, test items and examinees are placed on the same score scale.

Lake Wobegon effect: Score inflation or artificial test score gains.

large-scale cognitive diagnostic test: A standardized achievement test that is administered to large populations of examinees that has been designed and validated with one or more cognitive models of learning.

latent classes: Unobservable subgroups or segments; the cases within the same subgroup are similar or homogeneous on certain criteria, whereas cases in different subgroups are dissimilar from each other in important ways.

linear logistic test model: A generalization of Rasch's simple logistic model for responses to dichotomously scored test items. It involves a linear constraint that describes the difficulty of a test item according to the cognitive operations required to solve it.

local validation study (or **local evidence**): Validity is the degree to which accumulated evidence and theory support specific interpretations of test scores entailed by proposed uses of a test (*see* **validity**). A local validation study is typically based on empirical data collected for a specific set of test takers in a single institution or a specific location.

mastery testing: When students are tested periodically for diagnosis as many times as necessary to prove mastery of the material. In mastery learning regimes, each student may progress at a different pace but ends up in the same place, mastering the material.

measurement error: In classical test theory, the component of an observed test score that deviates from the true score that would be observed if the quality could be measured without error. In generalizability theory, those component(s) of variance influencing a set of test scores that for the purpose at hand are considered sources of error.

mental age: The results of an intelligence test expressed in age equivalents, whereby a child's raw score (number of items answered correctly) is assigned the chronological age at which that raw score is the mean among children taking the test. As a technique, the age-equivalent method is analogous to the grade-equivalent method.

minimum competency test: A high-stakes test that requires performance at or above a single threshold test score before certain educational attainment will be recognized.

model-based diagnostics: Information about student test performance that is based on an understanding of the mechanisms of learning and of the particular processes associated with task performance to provide feedback about students' cognitive strengths and weaknesses.

No Child Left Behind Act: The No Child Left Behind (NCLB) Act of 2001 reauthorized the Elementary and Secondary Education Act—the main federal law affecting education from kindergarten through high school. Proposed by President Bush shortly after his inauguration, NCLB was signed into law on January 8th, 2002. The testing and accountability provisions of the NCLB Act require states to implement statewide accountability systems covering all public schools and students and aligned to state standards. They include annual testing in reading and mathematics for all students in Grades 3 through 8 and annual statewide progress targets aimed at all groups of students reaching proficiency within 12 years. Results and targets must be broken out by income, race, ethnicity, disability, and limited English proficiency. School districts and schools failing to make adequate yearly progress toward state targets are subject to restructuring measures. Schools that meet or exceed adequate yearly progress objectives or narrow achievement gaps are eligible for awards.

norm-referenced test: A measure developed in such a way that its derived scores denote relative standing. The meaning of a given test taker's score on a norm-referenced test is established by comparing the score to the distribution of scores obtained by the test taker's peers.

outcome (criterion): An outcome is defined as either a measurement (e.g., college GPA) or an event (e.g., graduation) that is potentially predicted by some other measure (e.g., SAT scores). *Criterion* is another term for outcome.

performance-based test: Performance-based tests require the respondent to construct a response, demonstrate a skill, or follow a procedure. Examples include answering open-ended questions, conversing in a language, solving a mathematics problem while showing all calculations, writing an essay, or conducting a science experiment.

person-fit index. *See* **zeta index.**

predictive bias: The systematic under- or overprediction of performance on a given criterion or outcome for people belonging to groups differentiated by characteristics not relevant to criterion performance.

predictive validity: Indicates how accurately test data can predict criterion scores (test scores, grade point averages, or some other measure) that are obtained at a later time. *See also* **validity.**

psychometrically unitary: A latent trait that is unidimensional when derived from psychometric tests and measurements.

psychometrics: The science of mental measurement. Experts in mental, or psychological, measurement are psychometricians.

race norming: The practice of adjusting test scores by race to obtain the same distribution of normed scores for all races despite large racial differences in test performance. Also called *within-group scoring* or *scoring on a racial curve.* In the United States, race norming has been illegal in employment testing since 1991.

range restriction: Reduction in the observed score variance of an examinee sample compared with the variance of the entire examinee population as a consequence of constraints on the process of sampling examinees. The result is that validity coefficients are attenuated. For example, students admitted to a particular college are not necessarily representative of all applicants to the college and may comprise a more restricted sample than applicants (e.g., lower grades and SAT scores). Likewise, students applying to that college are not necessarily representative of all college-going students. Often, statistical adjustments are used to address the impact of such restrictions in the range of a variable between the total population and sample population.

Example: Harvard University generally accepts only those with the highest SAT scores; therefore, there is little variability in SAT scores among the students selected to attend the university (most students are above 1400). Because most Harvard students scored about the same on the test, the test does not correlate with college success nearly as well as it does when schools have lower cutoffs and the incoming students have wider ranges of SAT scores.

ratio measurement: A ratio scale counts in equal-size units (or intervals) beginning from zero. Ratio-level measurement is not yet available for psychological traits, in which test scores gain meaning only by comparing an individual's score to the distribution of scores obtained by individuals in an appropriate and well-defined reference group.

raw score: The unadjusted score on a test, often simply the number of items answered correctly, with no accounting for factors required to render raw scores interpretable, such as the difficulty and discriminability of the test's items at different ages.

regression analysis: A statistical procedure used to develop a mathematical equation showing how two or more variables or measures are related and/or to determine the extent to which one variable changes with changes in another variable or a number of other variables.

reliability: Property of a test that denotes the degree to which test scores are consistent, and therefore generalizable, across time, observers, or comparable measurements. Test reliability is often assessed by evaluating the comparability of scores obtained when a test is (a) taken a second time, (b) scored by different raters, or (c) presented in multiple forms. Ordinarily, test reliability is expressed quantitatively as a correlation coefficient.

rule-space method: A method that categorizes a student's test performance into an attribute mastery pattern, which is associated with cognitive strengths and weaknesses and provides the best account for the student's item response vector.

score inflation: A rise in test scores over time that is not caused by a genuine increase in the quality being measured, such as academic achievement (*see also* **Lake Wobegon effect**).

situational judgment test: A simulation method requiring the test taker to exercise judgment when responding to hypothetical problem situations that occur in work settings

situational specificity hypothesis: The discredited hypothesis stating that aspects of the environment are so influential on test results and subsequent job performance that testing across situations is inappropriate and validity findings are not generalizable outside of a single location or job.

standard error of measurement: An index of the extent to which students' obtained scores vary from their true scores. It represents the average differences in scores that would be obtained if it were possible to give the same test over and over again to the same student (assuming that no learning or memory effects take place between repeated testing). Because such data cannot generally be collected, the standard error of measurement is usually estimated from group data. Intervals extending 1 standard error above and below the true score (i.e., long-term average) for a test taker will include 68% of that test taker's obtained scores, and intervals extending 2 standard errors above and below the true score will include 95% of the test taker's obtained scores.

standardized test: A test with any aspect—format, procedures, or administration—uniform across test takers.

structural equation modeling: A collection of statistical techniques for testing causal hypotheses involving latent variables that combines (a) **confirmatory factor analysis** (*see*) to test and estimate the measurement model, which models relations between latent constructs and their measured indicators, and (b) multiple regression to test and estimate the structural model, which models hypothesized causal pathways between exogenous (independent) and endogenous (dependent) variables. Structural equation modeling is also sometimes referred to as *latent variable analysis, covariance structure modeling,* or *LISREL analysis.*

subscore: Score derived from subsections of a test that are similar in content and skill. Subscores are often used to form the total test score.

test bias: A systematic error in a test score. *Bias* may refer to construct underrepresentation or construct-irrelevant components of test scores that differentially affect the performance of different groups of test takers.

test score banding: A set of procedures for grouping test scores into broad categories (bands) and then treating all scores within a category as equivalent, the width of the band depending on technique and purpose.

test sensitivity: One measure of the diagnostic validity of a test; the proportion of true positives. For example, what proportion of patients who have cancer does the test correctly identify as having it (without misleading them by falsely indicating that they are cancer free)?

test specificity: One measure of the diagnostic validity of a test; the proportion of true negatives. For example, what proportion of patients who do not have cancer does the test correctly identify as being cancer free (and not misleading them by falsely indicating that they have it)?

validity: The extent to which a test measures the quality it purports to measure; there are several kinds (e.g., content, construct, criterion, consequential, predictive). Unlike reliability, validity can sometimes be difficult to measure precisely.

validity coefficient: In the case of employment test validity, the correlation between performance on a test and performance on a job.

zeta index (person-fit index): A measure of how well an observed response vector approximates an expected or ideal response vector with the same total test score.

AUTHOR INDEX

Numbers in italics refer to listings in the references.

266   *AUTHOR INDEX*

SUBJECT INDEX

tests requiring, 125
tests with/without, 95
"Contending definitions negate evidence" (test-validation fallacy), 45–46
Content
     in employment testing, 188–190, 192
     in psychological testing, 81–83
Content domain, 91
Content representation, 208–209
Content standards, 91
Content validity, 29
Correlated abilities testing, 232–234
Cost
     of educational achievement testing, 97, 99–102
     of employment testing, 192–193
     of psychological diagnostic testing, 73–76
Court decisions, 5
CRESST. *See* Center for Research on Evaluation, Standards, and Student Testing
Criterion-referenced indicators, 12, 31, 91, 210
Crystallized intelligence (g_c), 232–233
Cultural bias hypothesis, 158–160
Culture(s)
     generalizability of psychological testing across, 78–81
     licensure/certification testing across, 212–213
Cummings, Nicholas, xi
Curriculum focus, narrowing, 226–228
Custody issues, 83
Cut scores, 95

"The dangerous-thoughts trigger" (standards-of-evidence fallacy), 54–56
DC (direct consensus) method, 211
Debra P. v. Turlington, 5
Decision making, standardized testing for, 154–155
Declaration of Independence, x
Deerfield Academy, 169
Defending Standardized Testing (Phelps), 89, 113
Democratic dilemma, 11–14, 37, 252
Denominator, 31
Design fallacies, 21, 27–30
Destructive Trends in Mental Health (Wright and Cummings), xi
Detroit Edison Co. v. National Labor Relations Board, 5

Deviation IQ, 31–32
Diagnosis deferred, 71, 76
Diagnostic Achievement Test for Adolescents, 221
Diagnostic and Statistical Manual of Mental Disorders (DSM), 71
Diagnostic certainty, 76
Diagnostic criteria, changes in, 71–72
Diagnostic Screening Test–Reading, 221
Diagnostic tests, in education, 220–221, 227, 233
"Dialogue with the data," 45
Differential item functioning (DIF), 161
Differential prediction, 183–184
Differential validity, 183
Dionne, E. J., Jr., 37
Direct consensus (DC) method, 211
Direct inquiry, of test taker, 75
Discrimination, test results related to, 12
District of Columbia, 110
Division, 222
DSM (*Diagnostic and Statistical Manual of Mental Disorders*), 71
Dustbowl empiricism, 77

Early action (college admission), 148
Early decision (college admission), 148
Economics Wins, Psychology Loses, and Society Pays (Bazerman & Malhotra), 116
Economists, 116, 117, 125
Education advocates, 117, 121
Educational achievement testing, 3, 9, 89–128
     from 1895 to 1985, 94–96
     from 1985 to present, 96–97
     and belief in progress, 92–99
     complexity of, 117–123
     cost of, 97, 99–102
     court decisions about, 5
     defined, 91
     effects/benefits of, 107–117
     effects-of-testing research/researchers on, 98–99
     fallacies/rebuttal sources about, 90
     GAO report on, 101–102
     lack of information dissemination about, 93–94
     Lake Wobegon effect case study, 103–107
     NCLB Act and ignorance of research on, 124–126

and test score inflation, 103–106
Hiring decisions, 186–188
Hispanics
    educational testing of, 158, 159
    employment testing of, 183–184
    test impacts on, 12
Historians' Fallacies (Fischer), 4
Hitler, Adolf, 56
Holistic admissions, 53
Holistic problem solving, 228
Honors programs, 151, 155
Horizontal processes, 46
Horn–Cattell model, 42
"Hot for Education" series, 128
Howe, M. J. A., 35
How Public Educators Cheat on Standardized Achievement Tests (Cannell), 103
Human variation, 11–14

IEPs (individualized education programs), 220
Illinois, 157
"Imperfect measurement pretext" (standards-of-evidence fallacy), 52–54
"Improvability proves equalizability" (test-score-differences fallacy), 35, 37
Income. *See* Socioeconomic status
Individualized education programs (IEPs), 220
Individuals With Disabilities Education Improvement Act of 2004, 220
"Influentials," 126, 128
Information dissemination, 93–94, 111, 121
Information-processing skills, 235
Information suppression, 92–93, 113, 124, 127, 128, 250
Information Systems Audit and Control Association, 212
Information technology, 200
Integrity, 191
Intelligence(s). *See also* g (general intelligence)
    ability-based emotional model of, 190
    academic, 29
    Bell Curve's conclusions about, 17–18
    Carroll's model of, 42
    changes in absolute vs. relative levels of, 34–36
    crystallized vs. fluid, 232–233
    differences in, 9
    emotional, 189–190
    Gardner's seven, 42

as important/controversial scientific topic, 11
    phenotypic, 15
    practical, 189
    successful, 189
"Intelligence is marble collection" (test-design fallacy), 30
Intelligence quotient (IQ). *See* IQ levels
Intelligence tests and testing, ix, 11–59
    arguments against, 9
    causal-network fallacies about, 46–51
    court decisions about, 5
    examples of, 28
    fallacious reasoning about, 18–26
    human variation and democratic dilemma with, 11–14
    measurement model of, 19, 21
    as measure of general intelligence, 15
    public perceptions vs. scientific debate on, 14–18
    scientific debate over, 16–17
    standards-of-evidence fallacies about, 51–56
    test-design fallacies about, 21, 27–30
    test-score-differences fallacies about, 30–40
    test-validation fallacies about, 40–46
Intelligence theory, 34
"Interactionism nullifies heritability" (test-score-differences fallacy), 37–39
Intercept, 183n1, 184
International Test Commission, 79, 80, 213
Interpersonal Relatedness, 80n1
Interval-level scales, 32–33
Interview screening, 188
Invasion of privacy, 185
IQ levels, 14
    deviation, 31–32
    racial–ethnic differences in, 15
    stability of, 35
    Stanford–Binet calculation of, 31
Israel, 120
Item bias, 160–162
Item formats, 204–207
Item generation models, 228
Item rotation, 105

Jacob, B. A., 112
Japan, 223
Jaschik, S., 53
Jefferson, Thomas, x
Job analysis information, 185

Job performance, 183–184
Job training, effectiveness of, 191–192
Johnson, J. W., 167
Jones, E. H., 107
Jorgensen, Albert, 107
Judgment, 27
Just barely certifiable candidate, 210n2
Just social order, 13–14

Kellaghan, Thomas, 118
Kentucky, 101, 102, 104, 110
Kill the Messenger (Phelps), 89
Knowledge, skills, and abilities (KSAs), 204, 205
Knowledge levels, 253n2
Kohn, Alfie, 118
Koretz, Dan, 113
KSAs. *See* Knowledge, skills, and abilities

Lake Wobegon effect, 102–107
Language(s)
    of licensure/certification tests, 212–213
    of psychological tests, 79–80
LanguEdge English Language Learning (ELL) assessment, 222
Large-scale cognitive diagnostic testing (LS-CDT), 219–240
    and correlated abilities, 232–234
    examples of, 222
    fallacies/mistaken impressions about, 223–225
    and formative assessment, 234–235
    and high-stakes testing, 237–238
    and narrowing curriculum focus, 226–228
    practicality of, 225–226
    and problem solving, 228–229
    purpose of, 221–222
    and reporting of subscores, 236–237
    rule-space method of, 222–223
    and traditional diagnostic tests, 220–221
    and verbal reports, 229–232
Larry P. v. Riles, 5
"Late-blooming study," xi
Latent classes, 233
Latent trait modeling, 41
Learning disabilities, 220
Learning misconceptions or weaknesses, 221, 222
Legal incentives, 12
Legality, of employment testing, 184–185

Lesgold, A., 225
Lesley University, 171
Lewontin, R. C., 56–57
Licensing, court decisions about, 5
Licensure and certification testing, 199–214
    comparison of 20th century/contemporary practices in, 202
    defining passing scores for, 209–212
    defining purpose of, 202–203
    developing/evaluating, 201–205
    fallacies about, 201
    future research directions for, 213–214
    importance of, 200–201
    and language/culture, 212–213
    practice analysis/test specification development of, 203–205
    test designs/item formats for, 205–209
Linear logistic test model, 222
LISt Processing Programming (LISP) tutor, 228, 234–235
Literacy, 222
Literacy test, 99–101
Local school district testing, 101, 102
Local validation studies, 185
Low-stakes testing, 104–106
LS-CDT. *See* Large-scale cognitive diagnostic testing

MA (mental age), 31
Madaus, George, 118, 121–122
Madaus–Kellaghan–Feuer study, 118–121
Maine, 157
Malingering, 83
Malleability, 34–36
Managed care, 72
Masling, J. M., 70
"Master Teachers," 200
Mathematical difficulties, 221
Mathematics testing, 110, 111, 120, 222–223
Mather–Woodcock Group Writing Tests, 221
MCCs. *See* Minimally competent candidates
McDaniel, M. A., 184–185
Measurement in Today's Schools (Ross), 94, 95
Measurement model, of testing, 19, 21
Media reports
    on coaching for college testing, 169–170
    on college admissions, 148, 149
    on educational testing, 153, 156, 159–161
Medical licensure, 203, 206, 208–209

court decisions about, 5
cultural generalizability of, 78–81
current controversial issues with, 72–73
customized process of, 68–69
faking on, 83–84
goals of, 69
history of controversial issues with, 70–72
multivariate assessment in, 69
regulation of, 12
validity of, 76–78
Psychology research, 109, 123
Psychometrics, 9, 11, 117
Public, the
high-stakes testing supported by, 94, 109
licensure for protecting the, 200
scientific debate vs. perceptions of, 14–18
Public education
and antitesting critiques, 252–254
as equalizer, 37
"Public intellectuals," 125
Public policy, democratic dilemma and, 13–14
Public-sector jobs, 192
Punishment, of schools vs. students/teachers, 126

Quality control monitoring programs, 8
Questions bias, 160–162

Race
and *biological*-equals-*genetic* fallacy, 49
and dangerous-thoughts trigger, 54–55
and *environmental*-equals-*nongenetic* fallacy, 50–51
and *phenotype*-equals-*genotype* fallacy, 47–48
test results related to, 12
Race norming, 54
Racial balance, in employment settings, 13
Racial minorities
and educational testing, 158–160
employment-testing differences for, 184–185
and fairness of employment testing, 182–185
Racism, 157, 158
Rand Corporation, 97, 110–112
Range, restriction of, 163n5
Ratio measurement, lack of, 33, 35
Raw score, 31, 36

Reading attributes, 223
Reading deficits, 221
Reading testing, 110, 111
Received wisdom, 15
Regents of the State of California v. Bakke, 5
Regier, D. A., 84
Regression analysis, 183n1
Regression weight, 183n1
Regressive research, 96–97, 126
Regulation, of standardized testing, 5–7
Relative growth, 34–36
Reliability, 5
Remediation, 152
Repetition, 251
Reporting, of subscores, 236–237
Republican policy advisors, 114–117, 125
Research
education/psychology, 109, 123–124
federally-funded, 96–97
intelligence tests used in, 12
regressive, 96–97, 126
on testing, 251
Response latencies, 229–230
Retarded development, 27
Rhetoric, 18
Rice, Joseph Mayer, 8
Rosner, Jay, 160
Ross, C. C., 94–96
Rule-space method, 222–223
Russo, Alexander, 128

SAT (formerly Scholastic Aptitude Test)
achievement vs. aptitude testing by, 8
average-score changes on, 156
changes in, 150, 158
coaching for the, 168–170
cognitive analysis of, 222
for college placement, 151
for college recruitment, 153
criticism of, 154
as GPA predictor, 159
as group-administered test, 12
name changes of, 157–158
number of annual tests administered by, 121–122
predictive validity of, 162–165
racial/ethnic differences in scores of, 161
and socioeconomic status, 165–167
statistics about, 150, 151
and test-optional schools, 170, 171
Scholarships, 151, 155
Scholastic Aptitude Test. *See* SAT

School accountability
    ACT/SAT used for, 157
    g-loaded tests for, 37
    and information suppression about research, 94
    and No Child Left Behind Act, 95n1, 252n1, 253–254
    TECAT for, 99–101
    test-based, 126
School psychologists, 12
Schools, standardized testing used in, ix
Schwartz, T., 170
Science
    advocacy vs., 250–252, 254
    research based on, 6, 8, 123
    testing abilities in, 120, 222
Scientific debate, of intelligence testing, 14–18
"Scientific tests," 154n2
Scores
    defining passing licensure/certification, 209–212
    inflation of test, 102–107
    z, 32
Scoring fallacies. *See* Test-score-differences fallacies
"Second law of individual differences," 35
Security, test, 103–106
Segregating genes, 40
Self-report inventories, 84
Sensitivity, test, 54
SES. *See* Socioeconomic status
"Similarity of 99.9% negates differences" (test-score-differences fallacy), 39–40
Simon, H. A., 231–232
Simon, Théophile, 8, 21, 27, 31
Singapore, 223
Singham, M., 45
Sireci, Stephen G., 3–4
Situational specificity hypothesis, 185
Skills
    lower order vs. higher order learning of, 226–228
    surface-level vs. higher level testing of, 225–226
Skull measurements, 55
SmartBrief newsletter, 93–94
Snowman, J., 122
Social equality, 13, 252
Socioeconomic status (SES)
    and coaching for college testing, 170

and college admissions testing, 165–167
Sophistry, 18, 58
Spatial ability, 228
Specialized scales, 82–83
Specification development, for tests, 203–205
Stability, of IQ rank, 35
Stakes, 4, 91. *See also* High-stakes testing; Low-stakes testing; No-stakes tests
Stalin, Joseph, 56
Standard error of measurement, 156
Standardized tests and testing, ix–xii
    allegations about, x–xii
    applications of, ix
    defined, 5
    effects of, 113
    inequalities revealed in, x
    in North American context, 4, 5
    number of annual, 121–122
    and political agendas, xii
    prevalence of, ix
    professional standards/guidelines for use of, 7
    public support of, 252
    ratio measurement lacking in, 33
    regulation of, 5–7
    reputation of, 3–4
    in schools, ix
    scientific study of, 6, 8
    sources of evidence for supporting, 214
    training/ethics required for, x
Standards-of-evidence fallacies, 51–56
    "the dangerous-thoughts trigger," 54–56
    "happy-thoughts leniency," 56–57
    "imperfect measurement pretext," 52–54
Standards and guidelines, for test use, 7
Standards-based achievement tests, 91
Standard-setting panels, 210–212
Standards for Educational and Psychological Testing (AERA, APA, & NCME), 81, 155, 200, 209–210, 214
Stanford–Binet test, 28
Stanford Diagnostic Mathematical Test–4, 221
States' school testing, 101, 102, 110–112
Statistical pooling, 111
Stratum II, 42
Stratum III, 42
Subject matter area, 91
Subscales, 74
Subscores, 236–237

U.S. Civil Rights Act of 1991, 185
U.S. Department of Education, 156
U.S. Department of Labor, 108
U.S. Medical Licensure Exam (USMLE), 203, 206
U.S. military, 191
U.S. Office of Technology Assessment (OTA), 118–121
U.S. Supreme Court, 155
The Use and Interpretation of Education Tests (Greene & Jorgensen), 107
USMLE. *See* U.S. Medical Licensure Exam
Utility, test
    in college admissions, 164–165
    NRC study of, 107–108

Validation fallacies. *See* Test-validation fallacies
Validity
    of college admissions testing, 162–164
    content, 29
    differential, 183
    of employment testing, 185
    of psychological diagnostic testing, 76–78
    of standardized tests, 5
Validity coefficient, 163n5
V-codes, 71
Verbal ability, 228
Verbal reports, 229–232

Vertical processes, 46
Vocational counselors, 12
Voluntary National Tests, 119

Wechsler Adult Intelligence Scale (WAIS), 28, 43–44
Wechsler Intelligence Scale for Children (4th ed.; WISC–IV), 28
Wechsler Preschool and Primary Scale of Intelligence, 29
West Virginia, 102, 104, 157
Whites
    educational testing of, 158, 159, 161
    employment testing of, 183–184
Wide Range of Achievement Test, 221
Wiggins, J. S., 77
WISC–IV (Wechsler Intelligence Scale for Children, 4th ed.), 29
Within-individual growth, 34
World News Tonight With Peter Jennings (TV show), 34
Wright, Rogers, xi
Written language, 221

"Yardstick mirrors construct" (test-design fallacy), 29–30

Zeta-index, 228
z scores, 32

ABOUT THE EDITOR

Richard P. Phelps, PhD, grew up in St. Louis, Missouri, a few blocks from Route 66 and the Frisco Route main line. He received degrees from Washington University, St. Louis, Missouri; University of Indiana, Bloomington; and Harvard University, Cambridge, Massachusetts, as well as a PhD from the Wharton School at the University of Pennsylvania, Philadelphia. He taught secondary school mathematics in Burkina Faso, West Africa; worked at the Organisation for Economic Co-operation and Development in Paris, France; the U.S. General Accounting Office, Washington, DC; Westat, Rockville, Maryland; and the Indiana Department of Education, Indianapolis. Dr. Phelps is author or editor of four books, several statistical compendia, and dozens of articles in scholarly journals.